ASSASSINATION CLASSROOM

YUSEI MATSUI

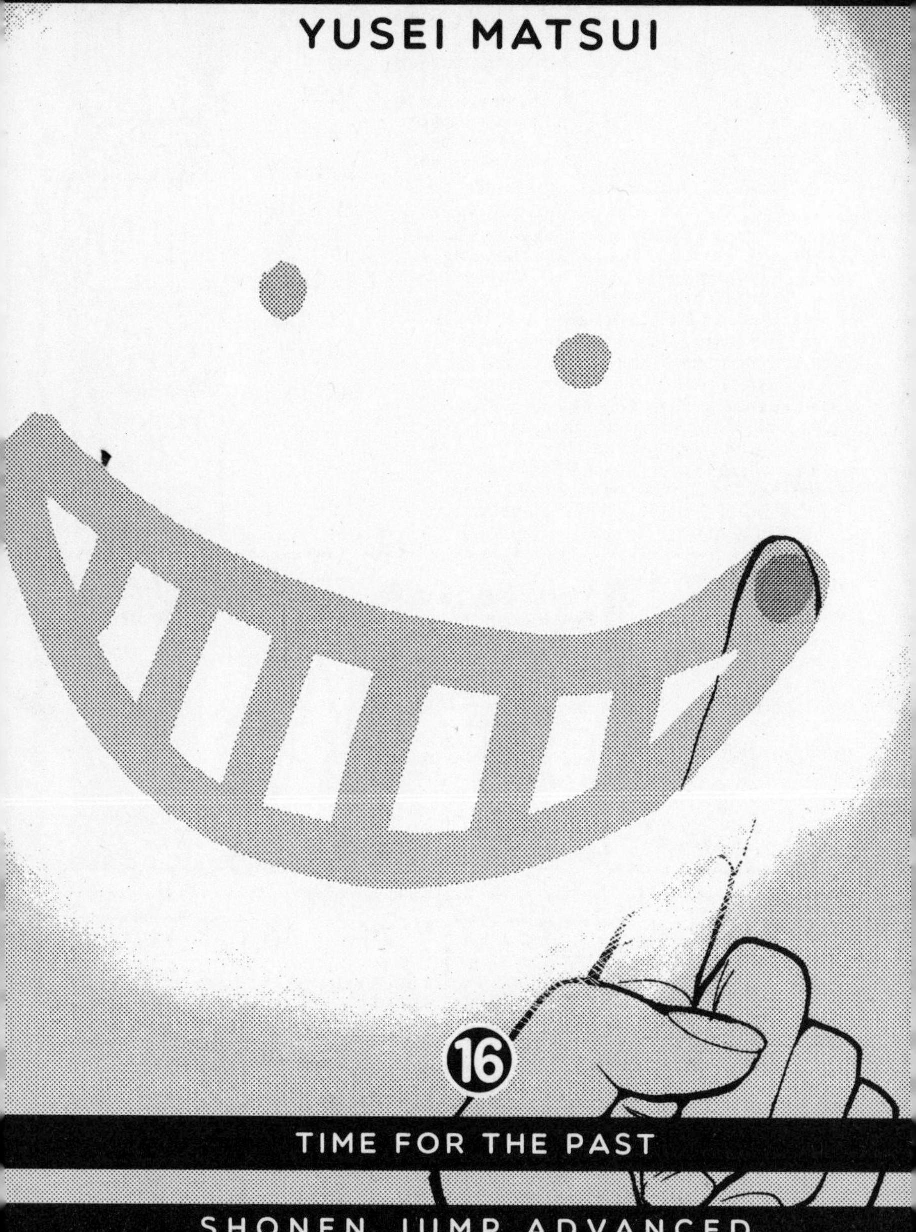

16

TIME FOR THE PAST

SHONEN JUMP ADVANCED

Koro Tribune

December Issue ②

Published by: Class 3-E Newspaper Staff

Although we have data on his weaknesses, we are still far from assassinating Koro Sensei...

Story Thus Far

MAKE THE MOST OUT OF YOUR KNOWLEDGE, INGENUITY AND HARD WORK.
I EXPECT TO SEE THE BEST ASSASSINATION YOU CAN POSSIBLY DO.
THAT IS WHAT I ENJOY SEEING MORE THAN ANYTHING IN THIS WORLD.

Kunugigaoka Junior High, Class 3-E is a class led by a monster who has disintegrated the moon and is planning to do the same thing to Earth next year in March.

Even the armies of the world, with the latest technology, can't kill the super creature Koro Sensei and collect the maximum thirty billion yen (300 million dollar) bounty! So it comes down to his students in 3-E, the so-called "End Class." Thanks to Koro Sensei's dedication to them, they grow to become fine students who can even outshine the top students in their school. Likewise, their martial skills rapidly improve with the help of Mr. Karasuma from the Ministry of Defense, molding them into a professional team of assassins. The first semester has gone by and the clock is ticking. Will they be able to successfully assassinate Koro Sensei?!

No one complained, but weren't the stars supposed to be Sugino and Kanzaki?

Koro Sensei

A mysterious, man-made, octopus-like creature whose name is a play on the words "koro senai," which means "can't kill." He is capable of flying at Mach 20 and his versatile tentacles protect him from attacks and aid him in everyday activities. Nobody knows who created him or why he wants to teach Class 3-E, but he has proven to be an extremely capable instructor.

Kayano has tentacles?! Was her identity as Kayano all a facade?!

Kaede Kayano

Class E student. She enrolled in Class E in order to kill Koro Sensei and avenge her sister.

Nagisa Shiota

Class E student. Skilled at information gathering, he has been taking notes on Koro Sensei's weaknesses. He has a hidden talent for assassinations and even the Assassin Broker Lovro sees his potential.

Taisei Yoshida

 **pick up!**

The most sensitive of the Team Terasaka menaces. He actually tries to wear fashionable socks, but no one notices because of his overall image and baggy pants.

Karma Akabane

Class E student. A quick thinker skilled at surprise attacks who managed to injure Koro Sensei a few times. His failure in the final exam of the first semester forced him to grow up and take things a bit more seriously.

Tadaomi Karasuma

Member of the Ministry of Defense and the Class E students' P.E. teacher. Though serious about his duties, he has successfully built good relationships with his students.

Rio Nakamura

Class E student. She was considered a prodigy back in elementary school, but she longed to be "ordinary," so she pretended to be a poor student. Now she has a dream she's aiming for, so she might get more serious.

Koro Sensei's past finally Revealed!!

Class E's theory was that Koro Sensei was originally an enhanced self-reproducing octopus designed to create octopus dumplings for military purposes. But let's find out the truth...

Irina Jelavich

A sexy assassin hired as an English teacher. She's known for using her "womanly charms" to get close to a target. She often flirts with Karasuma but hasn't had any success yet.

...solves this problem set...

The person who...

...will die...

DEATH TEXT

Coming to theaters this winter!!

Yanagisawa

Shiro's true identity. As a genius scientist, does he have something to do with the creation of Koro Sensei? And why does he want to kill him so badly...?!

Assassination Class Roster

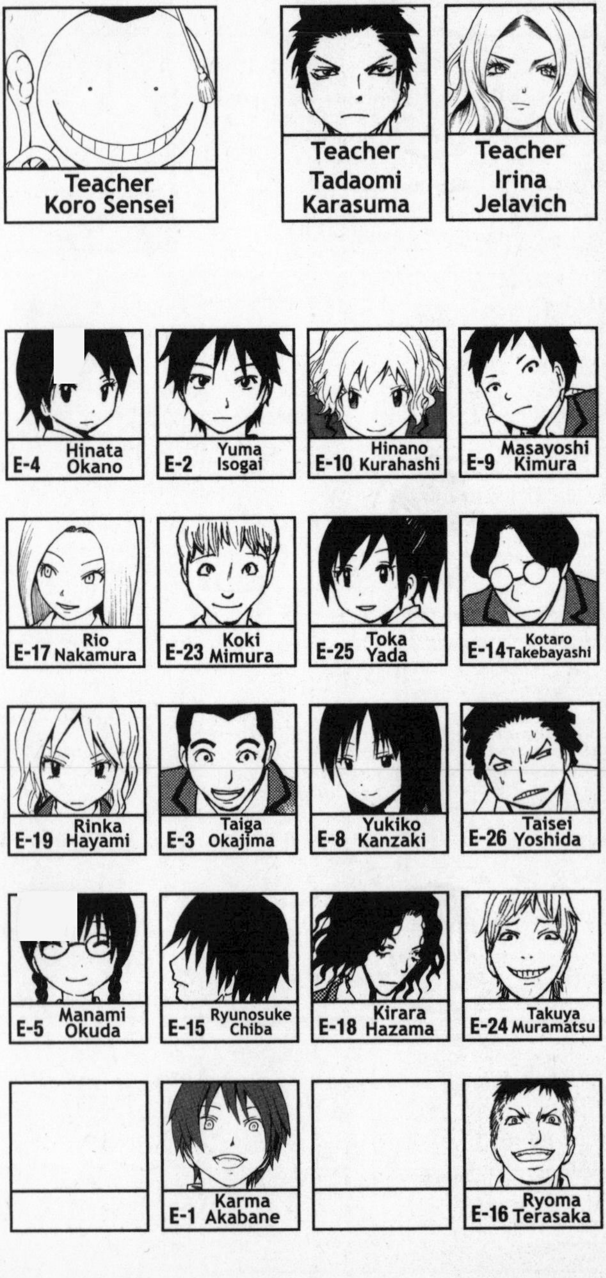

Teacher Irina Jelavich
Teacher Tadaomi Karasuma
Teacher Koro Sensei
E-9 Masayoshi Kimura
E-10 Hinano Kurahashi
E-2 Yuma Isogai
E-4 Hinata Okano
E-14 Kotaro Takebayashi
E-25 Toka Yada
E-23 Koki Mimura
E-17 Rio Nakamura
E-26 Taisei Yoshida
E-8 Yukiko Kanzaki
E-3 Taiga Okajima
E-19 Rinka Hayami
E-24 Takuya Muramatsu
E-18 Kirara Hazama
E-15 Ryunosuke Chiba
E-5 Manami Okuda
E-16 Ryoma Terasaka
E-1 Karma Akabane

Always assassinate your target using a method that brings a smile to your face.

I am open for assassinations at any time. But don't let them get in the way of your studying.

I won't harm students who try to assassinate me. But if your skills are rusty, expect a good scrubbing.

Individual Statistics

E-19 Rinka Hayami

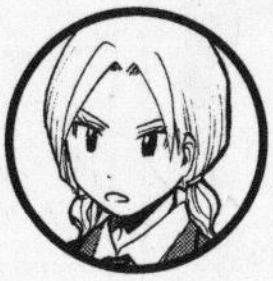

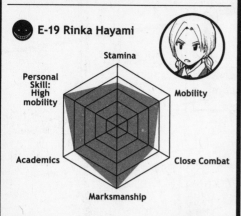

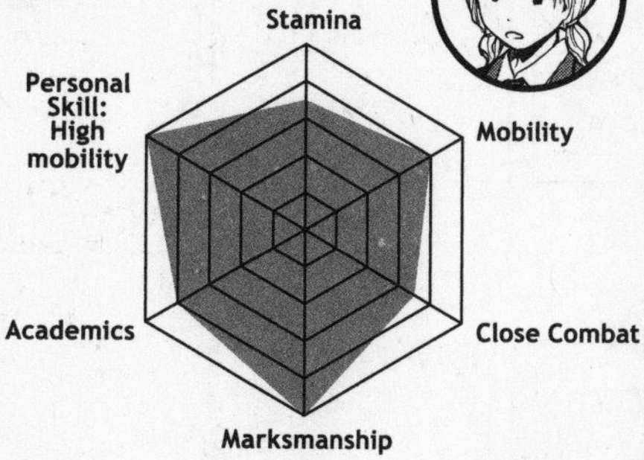
Stamina
Mobility
Close Combat
Marksmanship
Academics
Personal Skill: High mobility

E-20 Sumire Hara

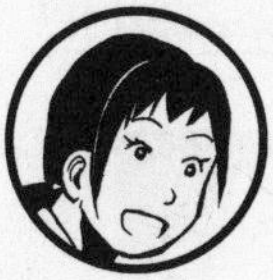

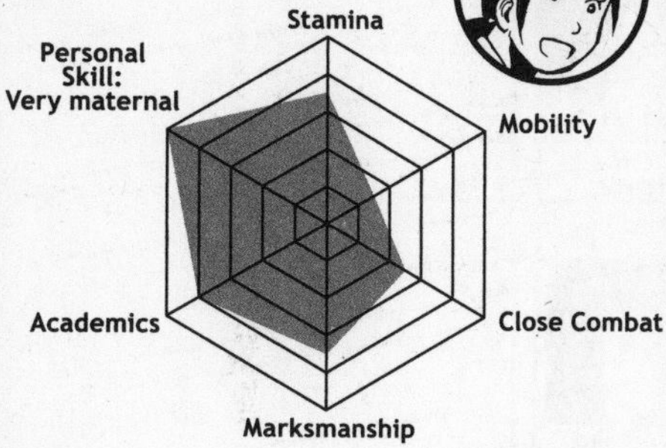
Stamina
Mobility
Close Combat
Marksmanship
Academics
Personal Skill: Very maternal

E-21 Yuzuki Fuwa

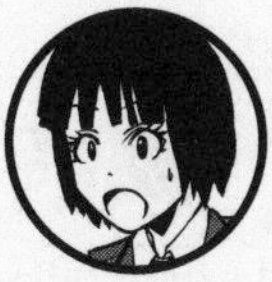

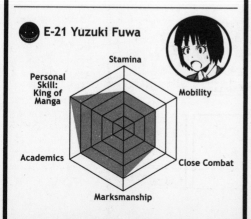

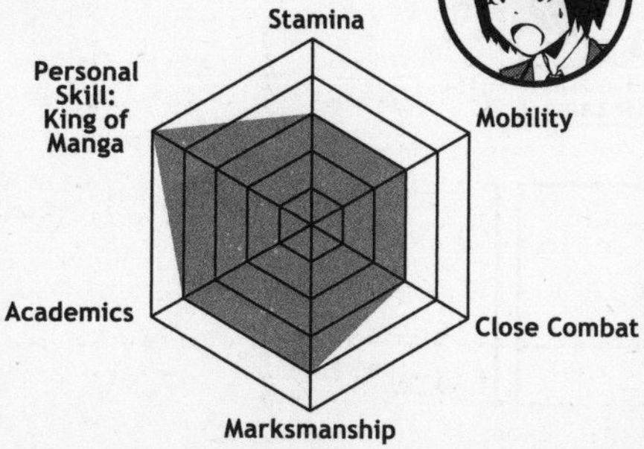
Stamina
Mobility
Close Combat
Marksmanship
Academics
Personal Skill: King of Manga

Kunugigaoka Junior High

3-E

Koro Sensei Class

Seating Arrangement

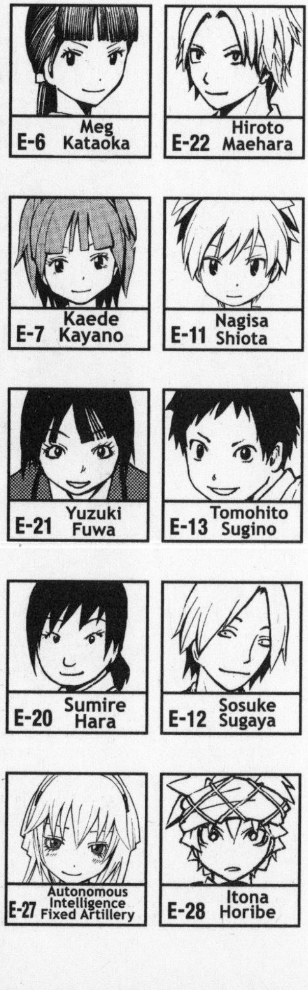
E-6 Meg Kataoka
E-22 Hiroto Maehara
E-7 Kaede Kayano
E-11 Nagisa Shiota
E-21 Yuzuki Fuwa
E-13 Tomohito Sugino
E-20 Sumire Hara
E-12 Sosuke Sugaya
E-27 Autonomous Intelligence Fixed Artillery
E-28 Itona Horibe

ASSASSINATION CLASSROOM 16 CONTENTS

(ANSWER SHEET)

Grade	3	Class	E	Name	CONTENTS	Score	

Math

Question 1): Solve the follow
uadratic inequalities:
1) $(x+4)(x-2)>0$
(2) $(2x-1)(3x+4)<0$
(3) $(2x+3)(3x-2)\leqq 0$
(4) $(3-4x)(x+2)\leqq 0$

(Question 2): With t
exception of Ritsu,
Class E has 14 stu
16 students for m
of which 11 stuc
qualified. If eac
of the 12 stude
qualified for

(Question
(1)

(2)

A
B
6
P
7
3
D
C

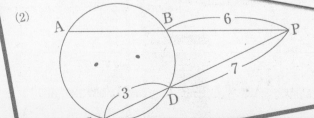

CLASS 134 TIME FOR THE PAST

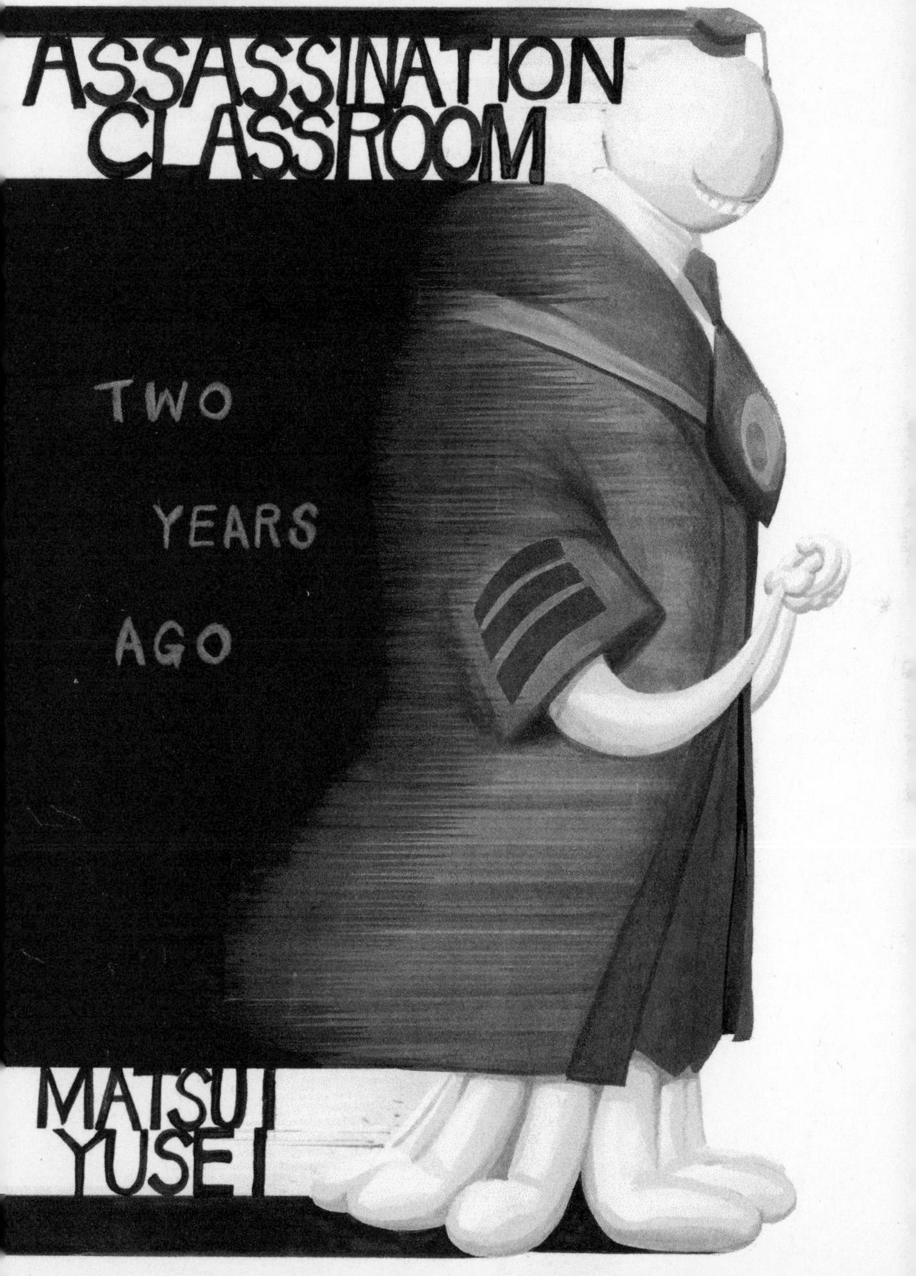
ASSASSINATION CLASSROOM
TWO YEARS AGO
MATSUI YUSEI

Overall Academics Class 3-E Top 5

Second semester final exam, the culmination of Class E's efforts, listed by subject

Japanese

Rank	Name	Score
1	Senioritis Akabane	100 Points
1	Yukiko Kanzaki	100 Points
3	Kirara Hazama	96 Points
4	Meg Kataoka	94 Points
5	Yuzuki Fuwa	91 Points

Overall

Rank	Name	Score
1	Damn Karma Akabane	500 Points
2	Rio Nakamura	461 Points
3	Yuma Isogai	457 Points
4	Kotaro Takebayashi	447 Points
5	Meg Kataoka	443 Points

English

Rank	Name	Score
1	Cool 'n' Aloof Akabane	Points
1	Rio Nakamura	100 Points
3	Meg Kataoka	92 Points
4	Nagisa Shiota	90 Points
5	Sumire Hara	88 Points

Math

Rank	Name	Score
1	Reddie Redhead Akabane	100 Points
2	Ryunosuke Chiba	90 Points
3	Kotaro Takebayashi	88 Points
4	Yuma Isogai	85 Points
4	Rio Nakamura	85 Points

Science

Rank	Name	Score
1	Mr. Humiliated Failure in the First Semester Akabane	100 Points
1	Manami Okuda	100 Points
3	Yuma Isogai	95 Points
4	Hinano Kurahashi	94 Points
5	Kotaro Takebayashi	92 Points

Social Studies

Rank	Name	Score
1	Twisted Twit Akabane	100 Points
1	Yuma Isogai	100 Points
3	Yukiko Kanzaki	98 Points
4	Rinka Hayami	95 Points
4	Koki Mimura	95 Points

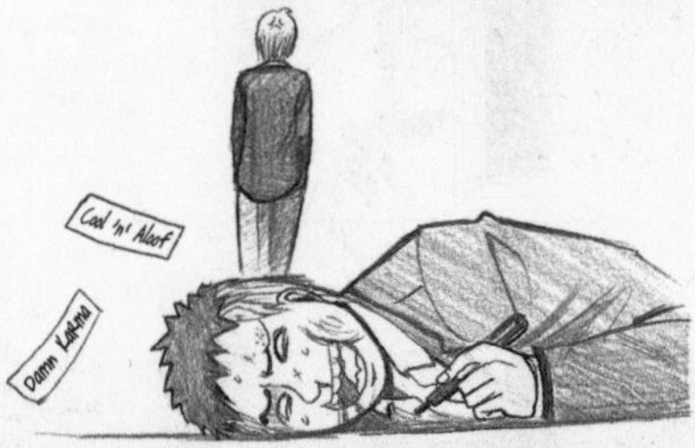
Cool 'n' Aloof
Damn Karma

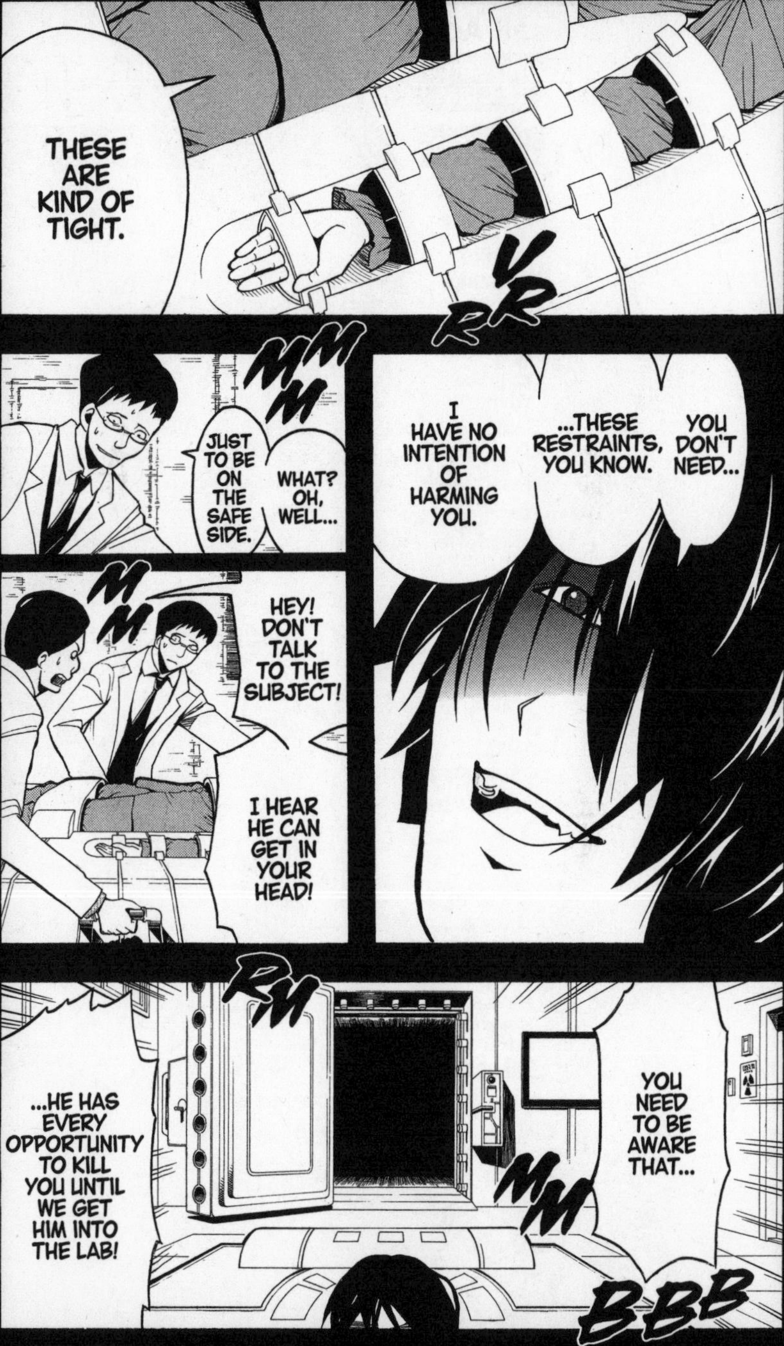
THESE ARE KIND OF TIGHT.
VRRR
YOU DON'T NEED...
...THESE RESTRAINTS, YOU KNOW.
I HAVE NO INTENTION OF HARMING YOU.
MMMM
WHAT? OH, WELL...
JUST TO BE ON THE SAFE SIDE.
MMM
HEY! DON'T TALK TO THE SUBJECT!
I HEAR HE CAN GET IN YOUR HEAD!
RM
YOU NEED TO BE AWARE THAT...
...HE HAS EVERY OPPORTUNITY TO KILL YOU UNTIL WE GET HIM INTO THE LAB!
MMM
BBB

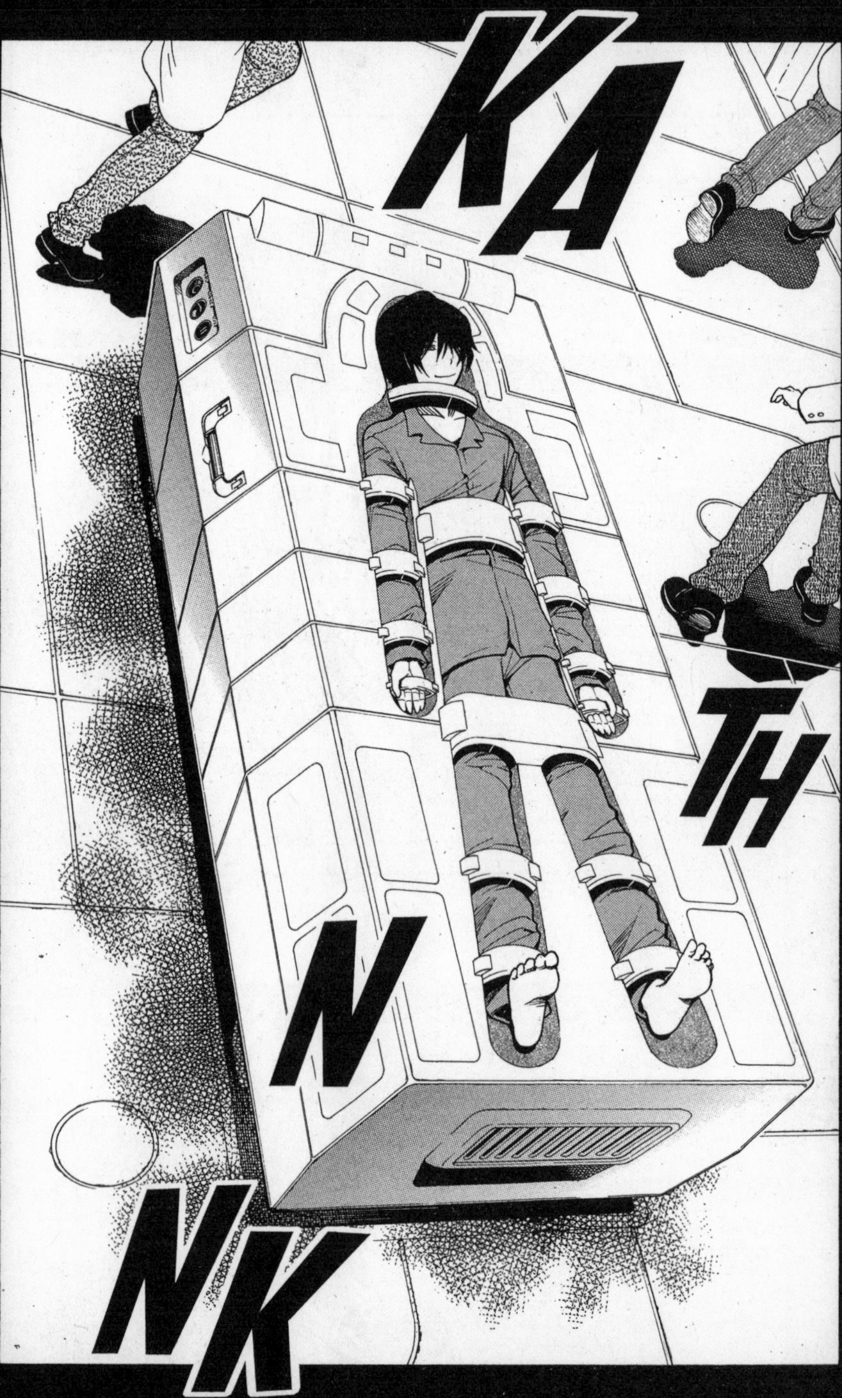
KA
TH
N
NK

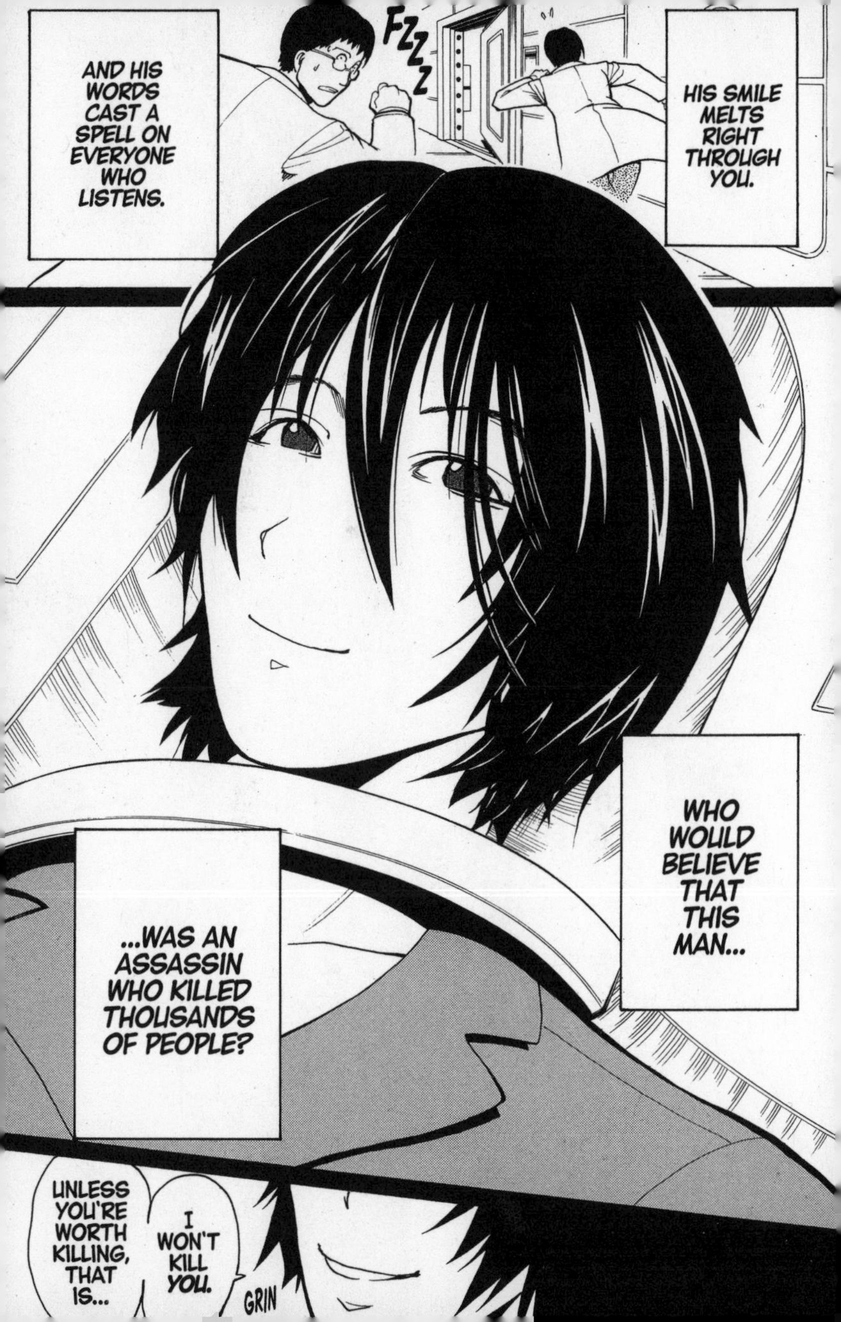
HIS SMILE MELTS RIGHT THROUGH YOU.
FZZZ
AND HIS WORDS CAST A SPELL ON EVERYONE WHO LISTENS.
WHO WOULD BELIEVE THAT THIS MAN...
...WAS AN ASSASSIN WHO KILLED THOUSANDS OF PEOPLE?
GRIN
I WON'T KILL YOU.
UNLESS YOU'RE WORTH KILLING, THAT IS...

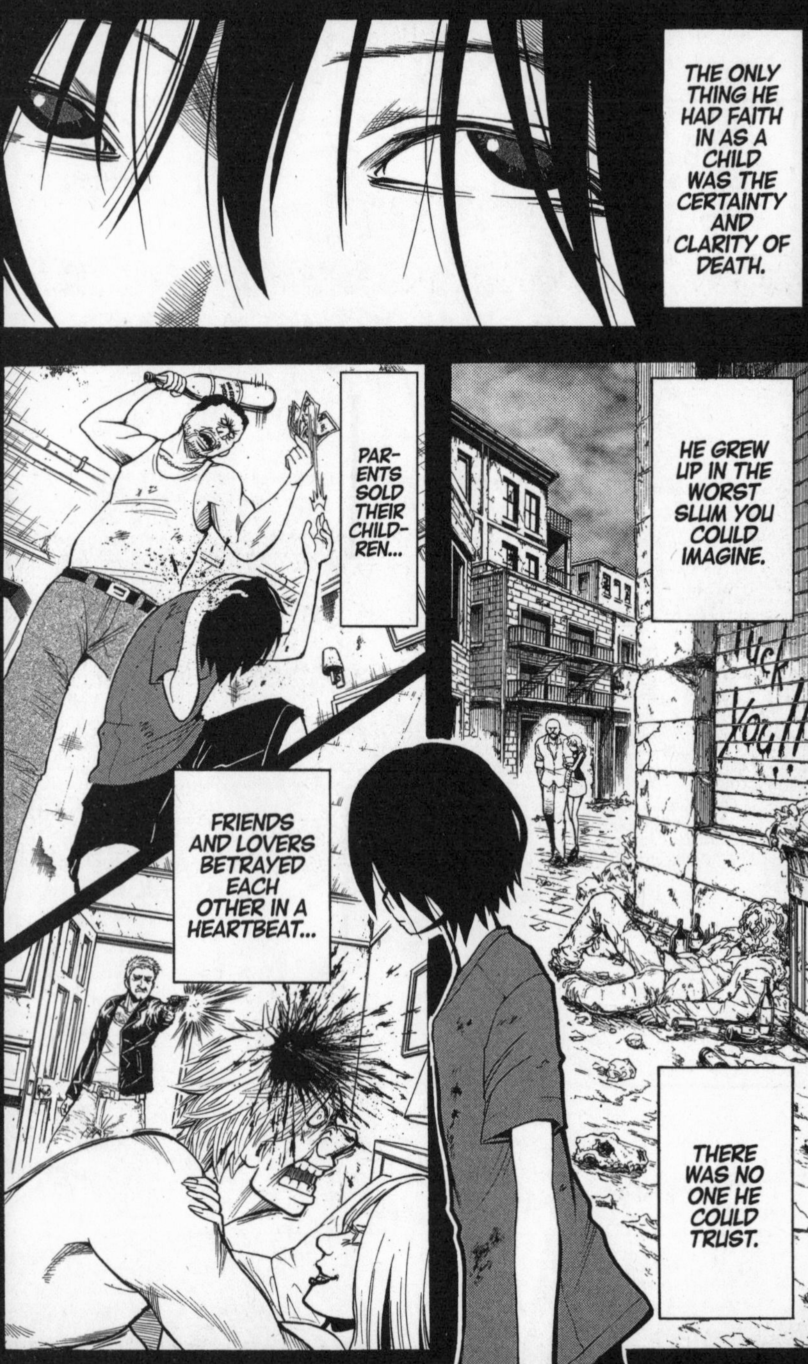
THE ONLY THING HE HAD FAITH IN AS A CHILD WAS THE CERTAINTY AND CLARITY OF DEATH.
HE GREW UP IN THE WORST SLUM YOU COULD IMAGINE.
THERE WAS NO ONE HE COULD TRUST.
PAR-ENTS SOLD THEIR CHILD-REN...
FRIENDS AND LOVERS BETRAYED EACH OTHER IN A HEARTBEAT...

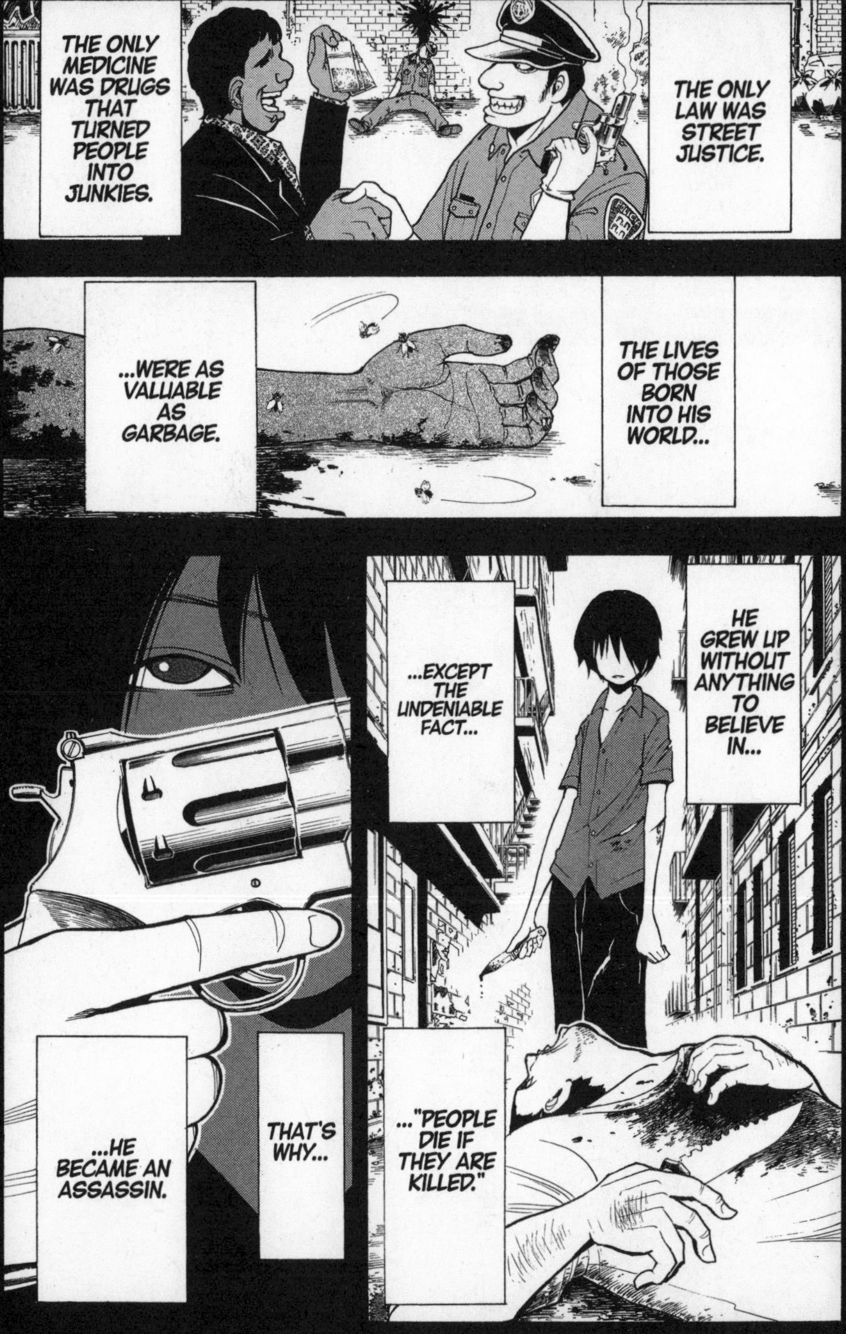

THE ONLY LAW WAS STREET JUSTICE.
THE ONLY MEDICINE WAS DRUGS THAT TURNED PEOPLE INTO JUNKIES.
THE LIVES OF THOSE BORN INTO HIS WORLD...
...WERE AS VALUABLE AS GARBAGE.
HE GREW UP WITHOUT ANYTHING TO BELIEVE IN...
...EXCEPT THE UNDENIABLE FACT...
..."PEOPLE DIE IF THEY ARE KILLED."
THAT'S WHY...
...HE BECAME AN ASSASSIN.

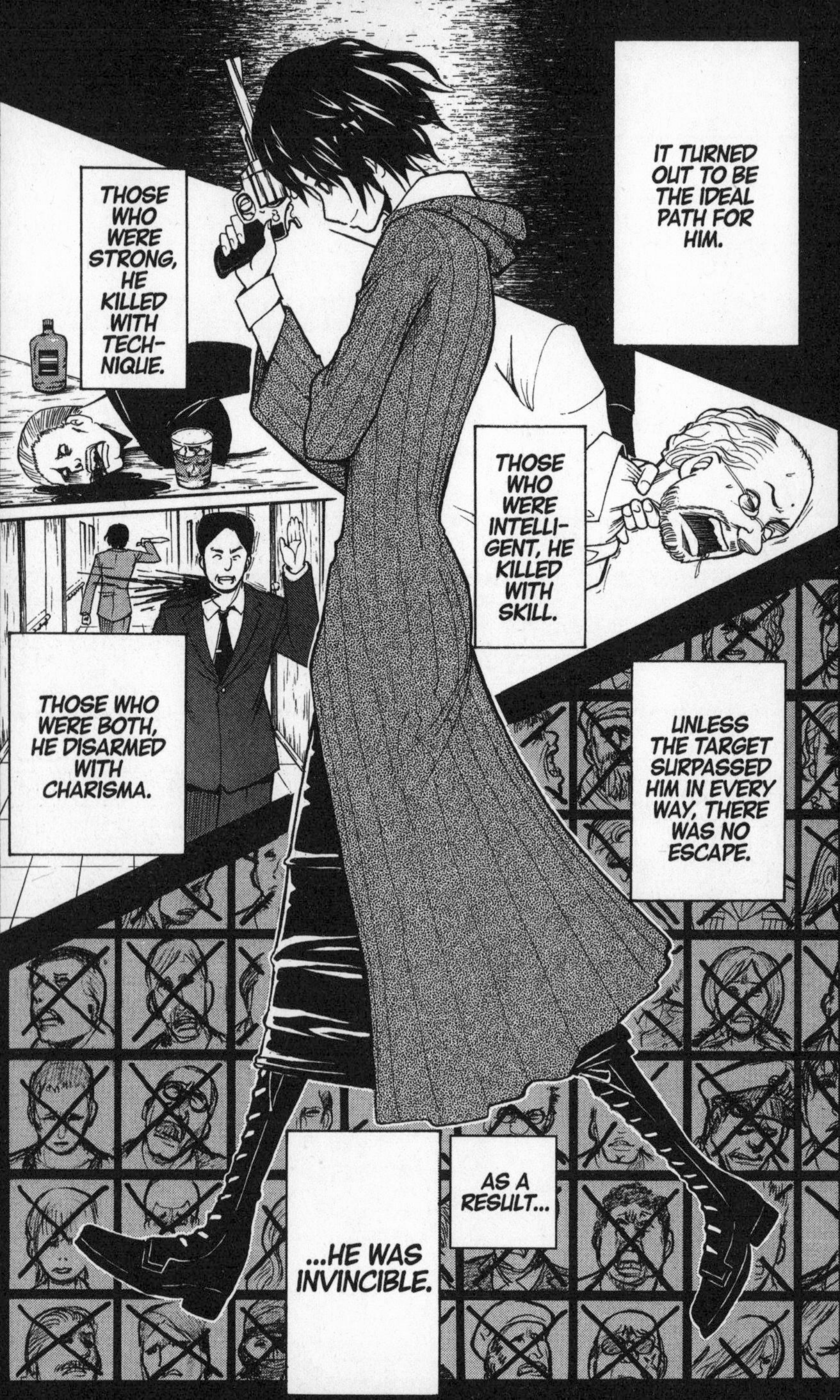

IT TURNED OUT TO BE THE IDEAL PATH FOR HIM.
THOSE WHO WERE STRONG, HE KILLED WITH TECH-NIQUE.
THOSE WHO WERE INTELLI-GENT, HE KILLED WITH SKILL.
THOSE WHO WERE BOTH, HE DISARMED WITH CHARISMA.
UNLESS THE TARGET SURPASSED HIM IN EVERY WAY, THERE WAS NO ESCAPE.
AS A RESULT...
...HE WAS INVINCIBLE.

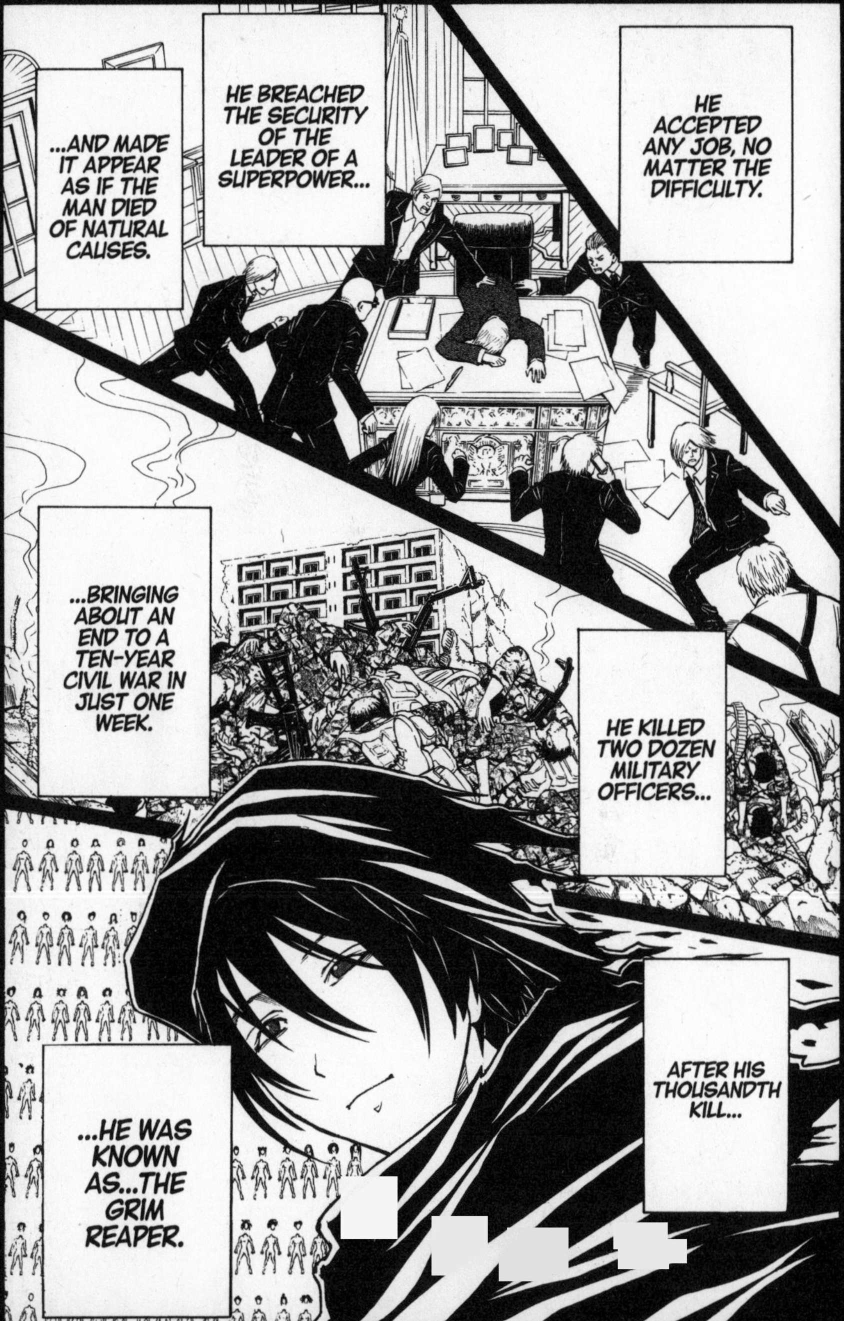
HE ACCEPTED ANY JOB, NO MATTER THE DIFFICULTY.
HE BREACHED THE SECURITY OF THE LEADER OF A SUPERPOWER...
...AND MADE IT APPEAR AS IF THE MAN DIED OF NATURAL CAUSES.
HE KILLED TWO DOZEN MILITARY OFFICERS...
...BRINGING ABOUT AN END TO A TEN-YEAR CIVIL WAR IN JUST ONE WEEK.
AFTER HIS THOUSANDTH KILL...
...HE WAS KNOWN AS...THE GRIM REAPER.

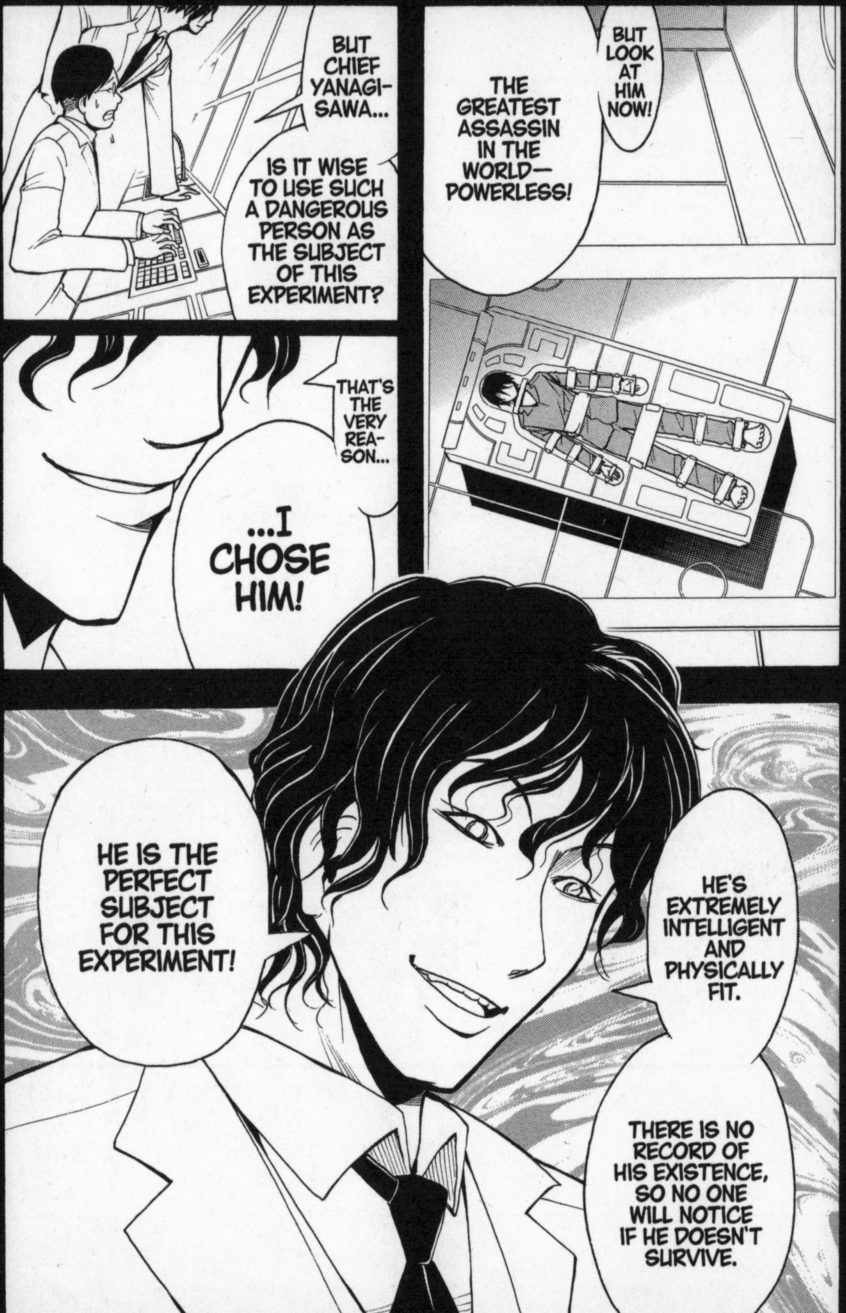
BUT LOOK AT HIM NOW!
THE GREATEST ASSASSIN IN THE WORLD— POWERLESS!
BUT CHIEF YANAGI-SAWA...
IS IT WISE TO USE SUCH A DANGEROUS PERSON AS THE SUBJECT OF THIS EXPERIMENT?
THAT'S THE VERY REA-SON...
...I CHOSE HIM!
HE'S EXTREMELY INTELLIGENT AND PHYSICALLY FIT.
THERE IS NO RECORD OF HIS EXISTENCE, SO NO ONE WILL NOTICE IF HE DOESN'T SURVIVE.
HE IS THE PERFECT SUBJECT FOR THIS EXPERIMENT!

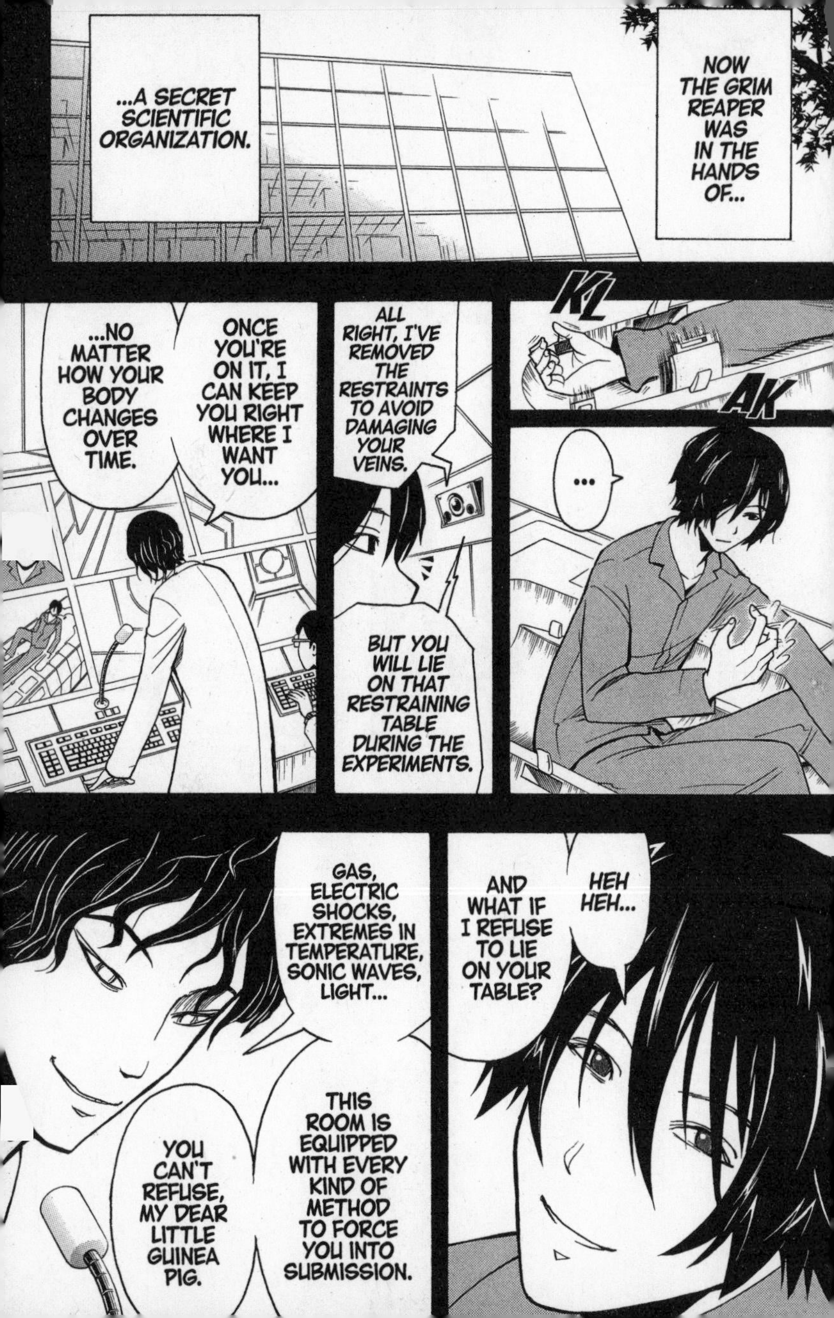
NOW THE GRIM REAPER WAS IN THE HANDS OF...
...A SECRET SCIENTIFIC ORGANIZATION.
KLAK
...
ALL RIGHT, I'VE REMOVED THE RESTRAINTS TO AVOID DAMAGING YOUR VEINS.
BUT YOU WILL LIE ON THAT RESTRAINING TABLE DURING THE EXPERIMENTS.
ONCE YOU'RE ON IT, I CAN KEEP YOU RIGHT WHERE I WANT YOU...
...NO MATTER HOW YOUR BODY CHANGES OVER TIME.
HEH HEH...
AND WHAT IF I REFUSE TO LIE ON YOUR TABLE?
GAS, ELECTRIC SHOCKS, EXTREMES IN TEMPERATURE, SONIC WAVES, LIGHT...
THIS ROOM IS EQUIPPED WITH EVERY KIND OF METHOD TO FORCE YOU INTO SUBMISSION.
YOU CAN'T REFUSE, MY DEAR LITTLE GUINEA PIG.

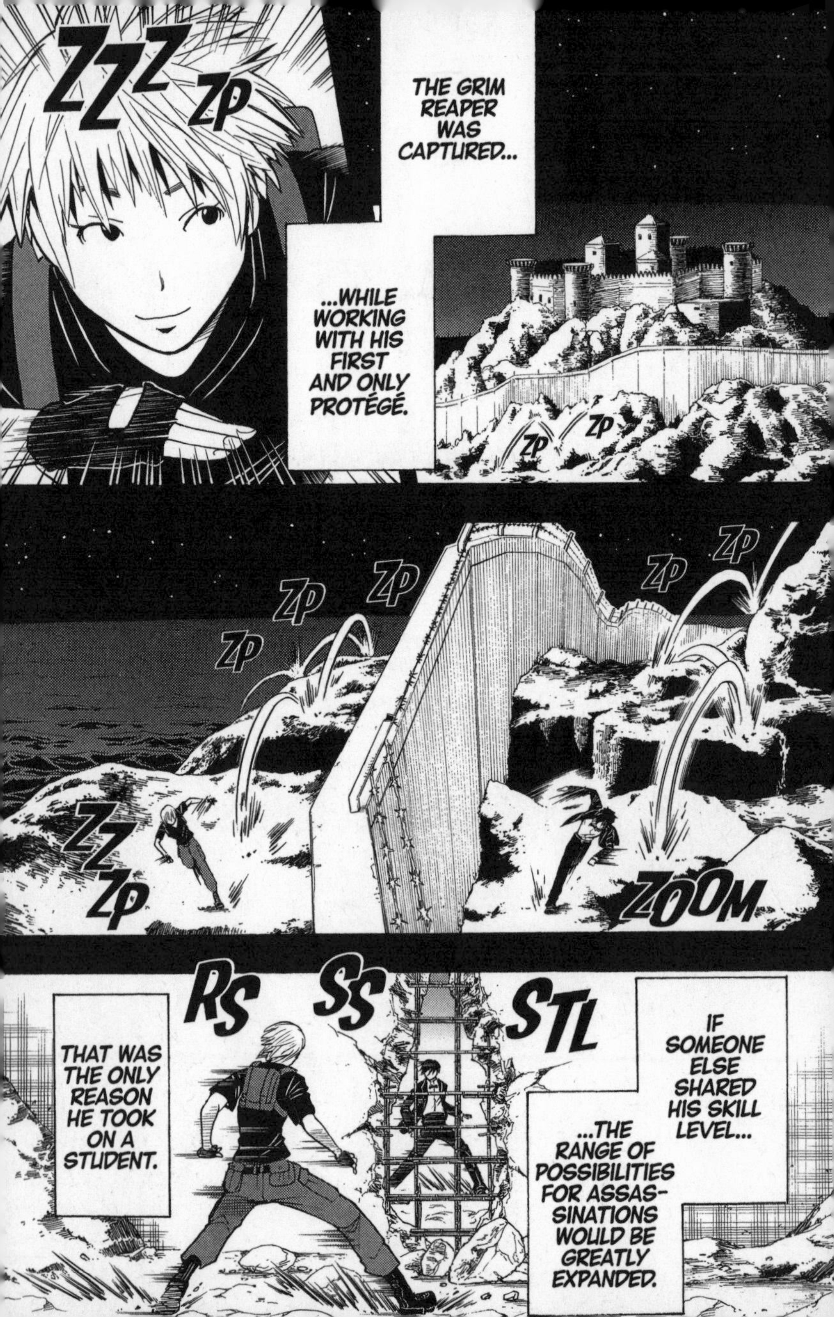
THE GRIM REAPER WAS CAPTURED...
...WHILE WORKING WITH HIS FIRST AND ONLY PROTÉGÉ.
ZP
ZP
ZZZZP
ZP
ZP
ZP
ZP
ZP
ZOOM
ZZZP
IF SOMEONE ELSE SHARED HIS SKILL LEVEL...
...THE RANGE OF POSSIBILITIES FOR ASSAS-SINATIONS WOULD BE GREATLY EXPANDED.
STL
SS
RS
THAT WAS THE ONLY REASON HE TOOK ON A STUDENT.

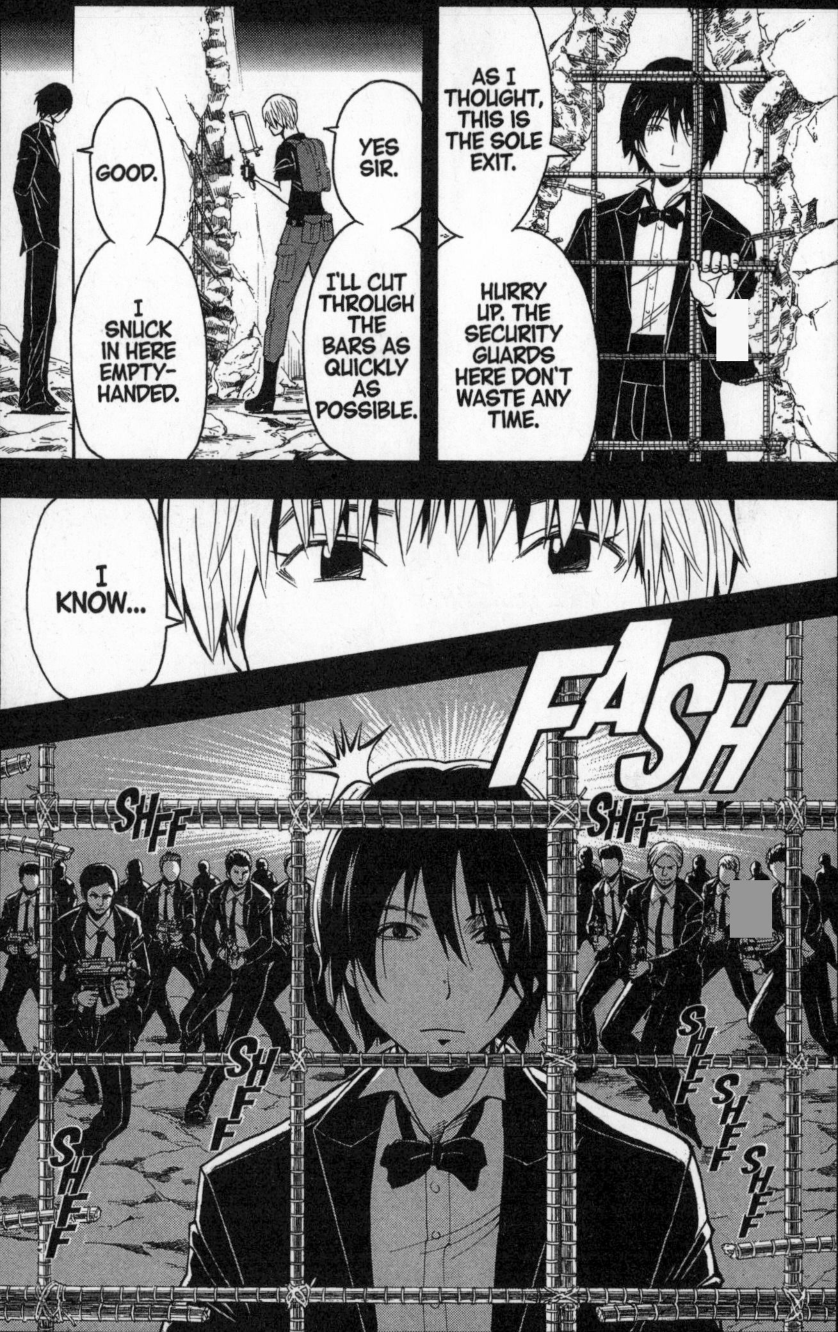
AS I THOUGHT, THIS IS THE SOLE EXIT.
HURRY UP. THE SECURITY GUARDS HERE DON'T WASTE ANY TIME.
YES SIR.
I'LL CUT THROUGH THE BARS AS QUICKLY AS POSSIBLE.
GOOD.
I SNUCK IN HERE EMPTY-HANDED.
I KNOW...
FASH
SHFF
SHFF
SHFF
SHFF
SHFF
SHFF
SHFF

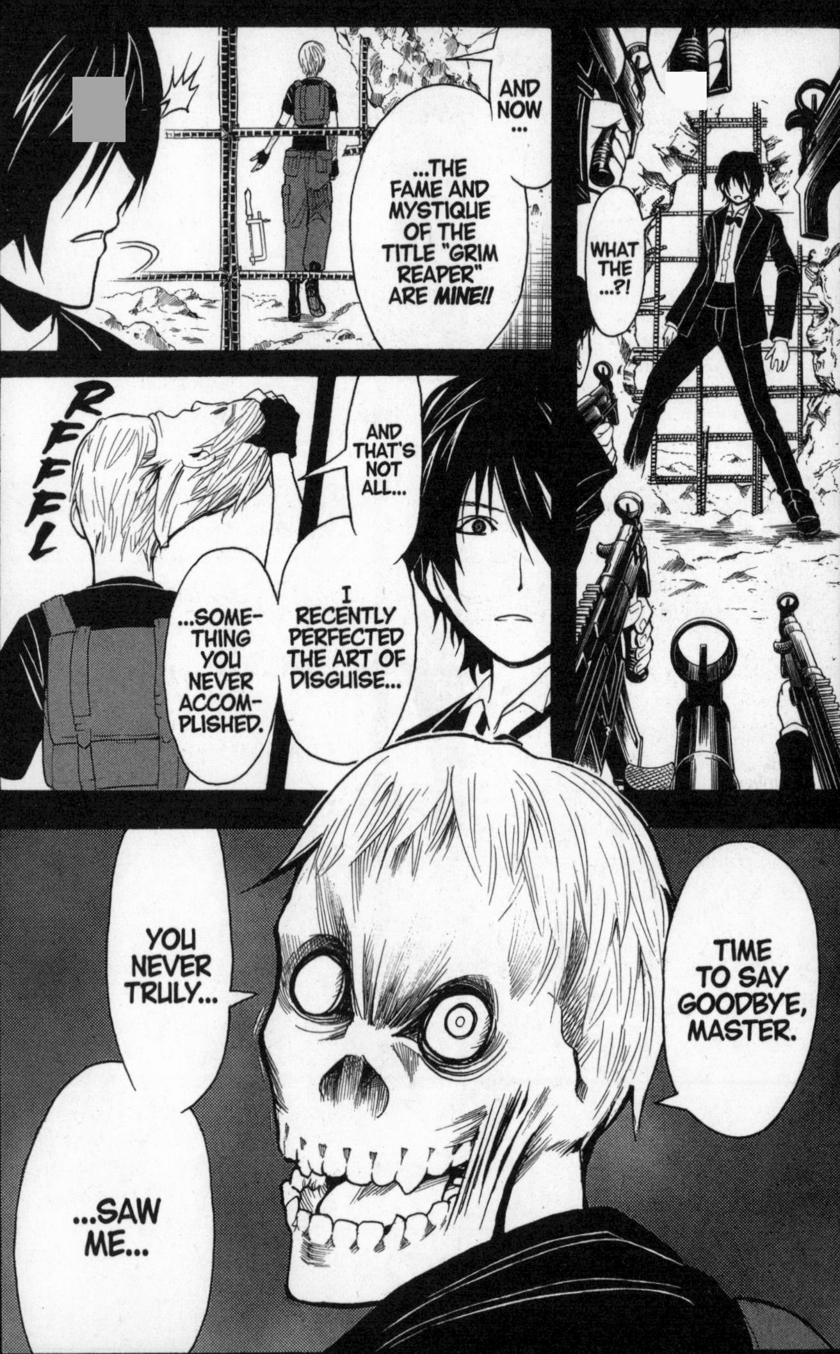
WHAT THE ...?!
AND NOW ...
...THE FAME AND MYSTIQUE OF THE TITLE "GRIM REAPER" ARE MINE!!
AND THAT'S NOT ALL...
RFFFL
I RECENTLY PERFECTED THE ART OF DISGUISE...
...SOME-THING YOU NEVER ACCOM-PLISHED.
TIME TO SAY GOODBYE, MASTER.
YOU NEVER TRULY...
...SAW ME...

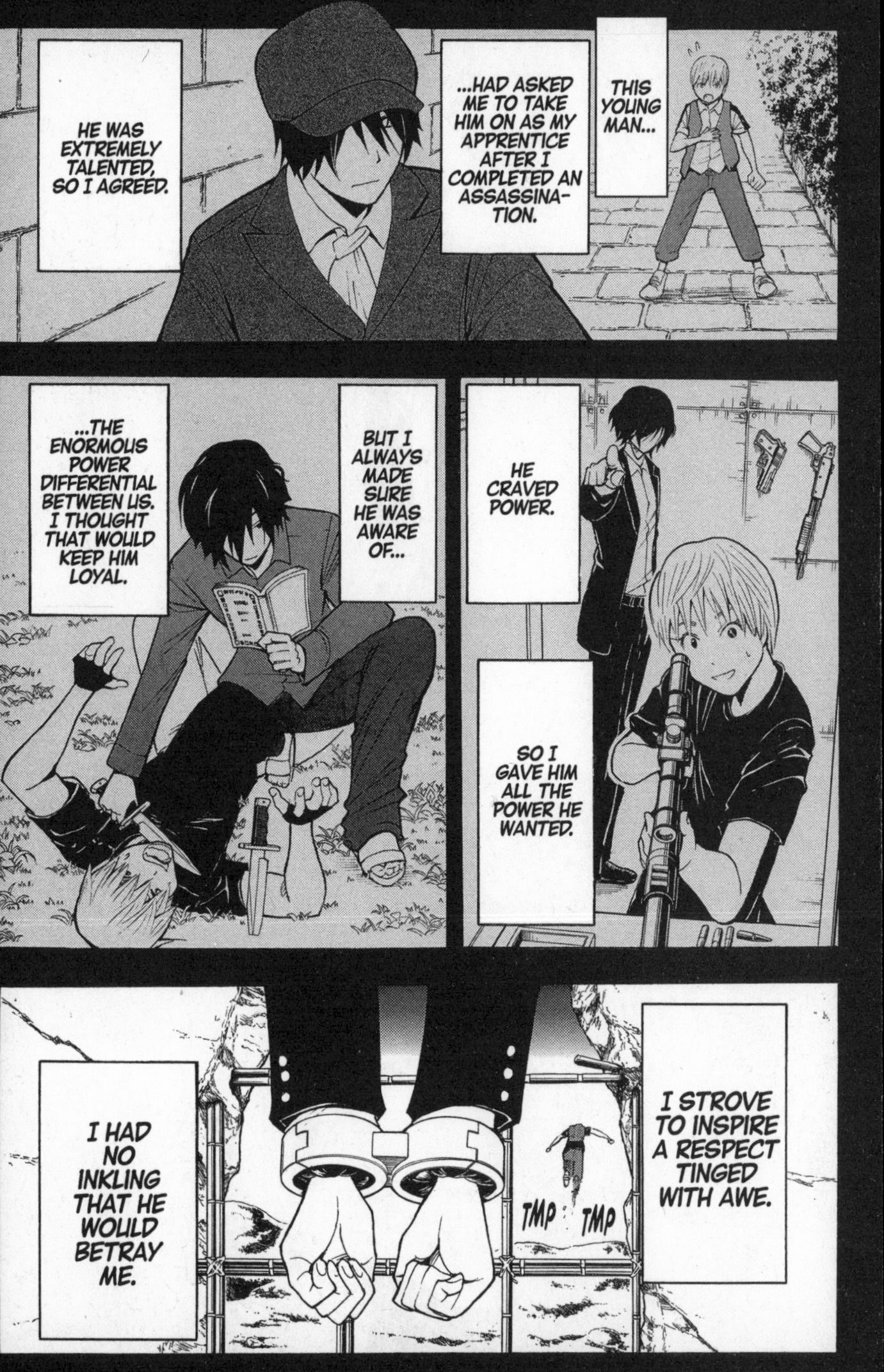
THIS YOUNG MAN...
...HAD ASKED ME TO TAKE HIM ON AS MY APPRENTICE AFTER I COMPLETED AN ASSASSINATION.
HE WAS EXTREMELY TALENTED, SO I AGREED.
HE CRAVED POWER.
SO I GAVE HIM ALL THE POWER HE WANTED.
BUT I ALWAYS MADE SURE HE WAS AWARE OF...
...THE ENORMOUS POWER DIFFERENTIAL BETWEEN US. I THOUGHT THAT WOULD KEEP HIM LOYAL.
I STROVE TO INSPIRE A RESPECT TINGED WITH AWE.
TMP TMP
I HAD NO INKLING THAT HE WOULD BETRAY ME.

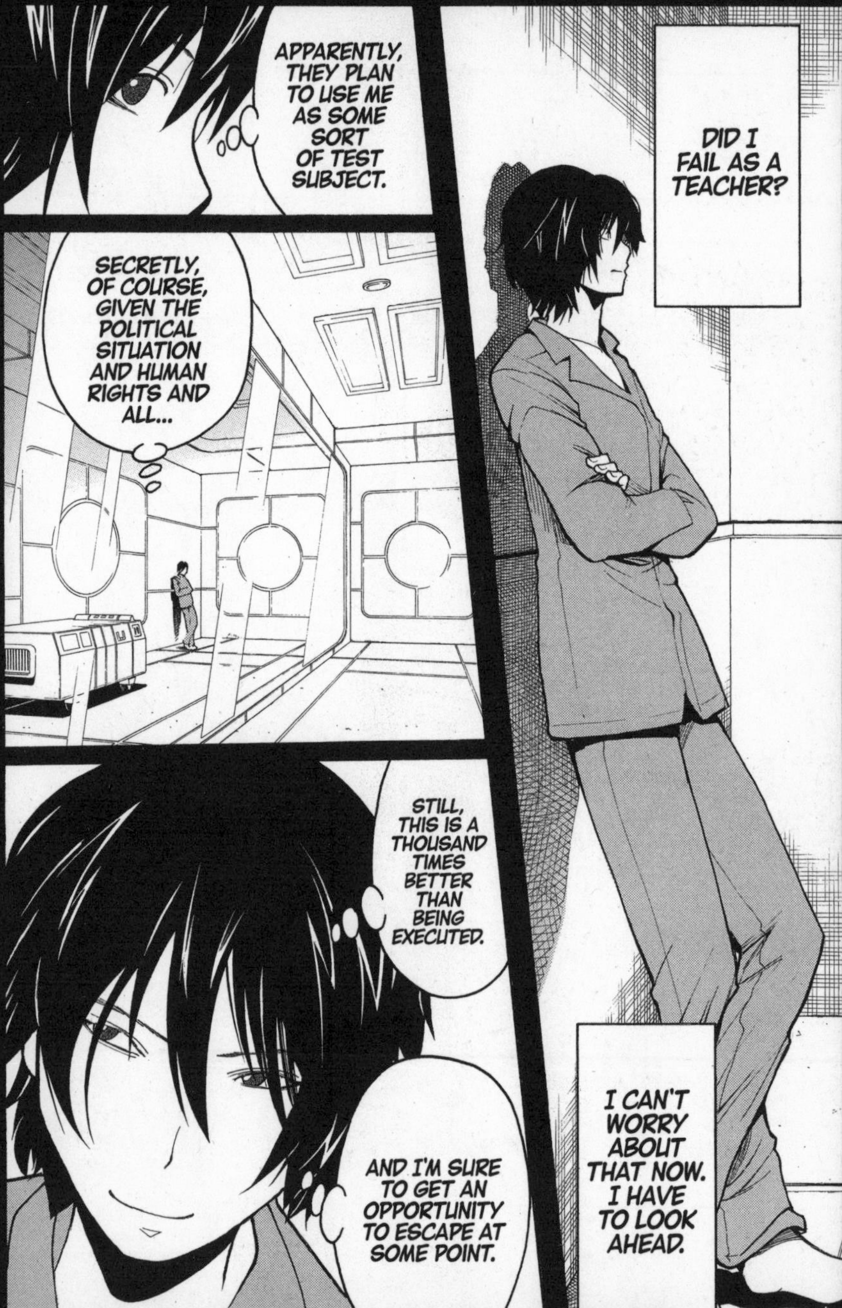
DID I FAIL AS A TEACHER?
I CAN'T WORRY ABOUT THAT NOW. I HAVE TO LOOK AHEAD.
APPARENTLY, THEY PLAN TO USE ME AS SOME SORT OF TEST SUBJECT.
SECRETLY, OF COURSE, GIVEN THE POLITICAL SITUATION AND HUMAN RIGHTS AND ALL...
STILL, THIS IS A THOUSAND TIMES BETTER THAN BEING EXECUTED.
AND I'M SURE TO GET AN OPPORTUNITY TO ESCAPE AT SOME POINT.

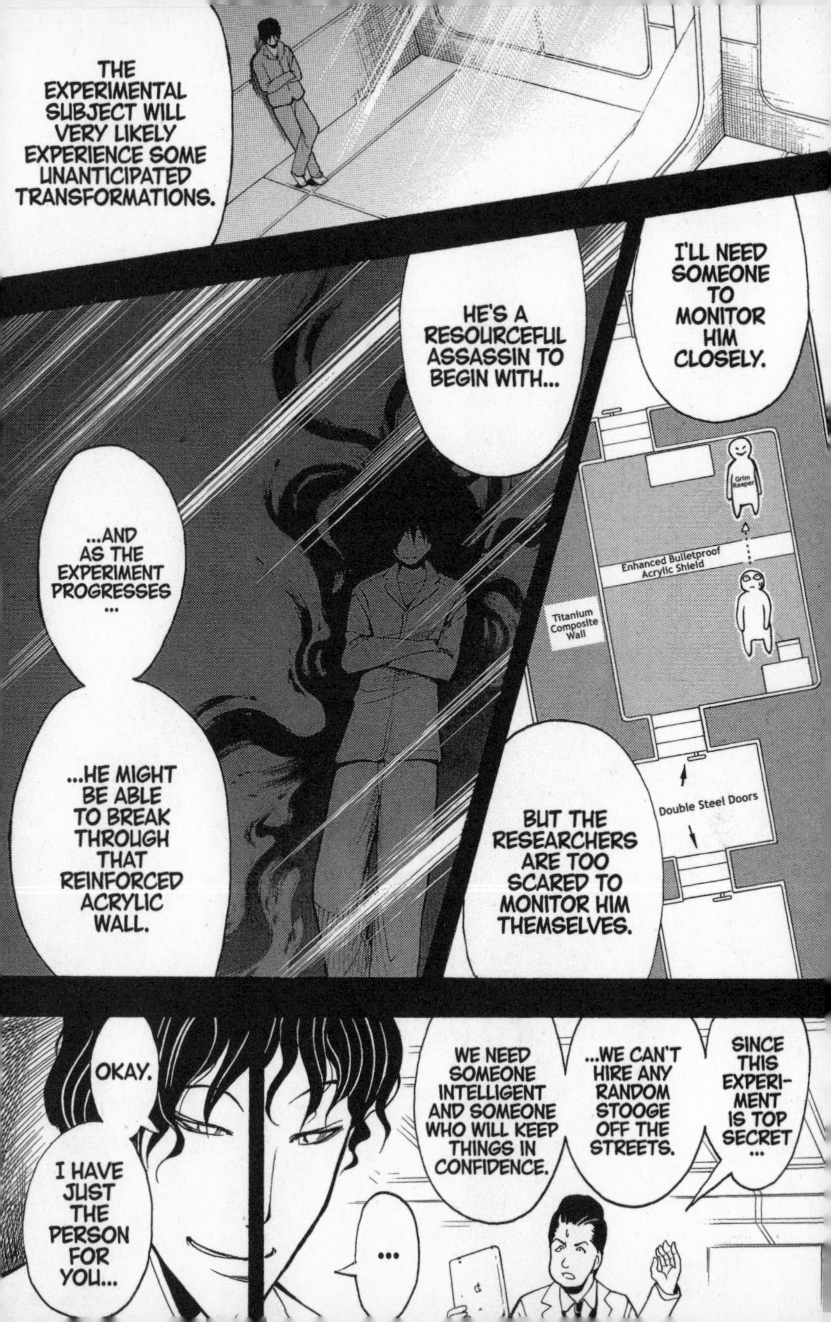
THE EXPERIMENTAL SUBJECT WILL VERY LIKELY EXPERIENCE SOME UNANTICIPATED TRANSFORMATIONS.
I'LL NEED SOMEONE TO MONITOR HIM CLOSELY.
Grim Reaper
Enhanced Bulletproof Acrylic Shield
Titanium Composite Wall
Double Steel Doors
BUT THE RESEARCHERS ARE TOO SCARED TO MONITOR HIM THEMSELVES.
HE'S A RESOURCEFUL ASSASSIN TO BEGIN WITH...
...AND AS THE EXPERIMENT PROGRESSES...
...HE MIGHT BE ABLE TO BREAK THROUGH THAT REINFORCED ACRYLIC WALL.
SINCE THIS EXPERIMENT IS TOP SECRET...
...WE CAN'T HIRE ANY RANDOM STOOGE OFF THE STREETS.
WE NEED SOMEONE INTELLIGENT AND SOMEONE WHO WILL KEEP THINGS IN CONFIDENCE.
...
OKAY.
I HAVE JUST THE PERSON FOR YOU...

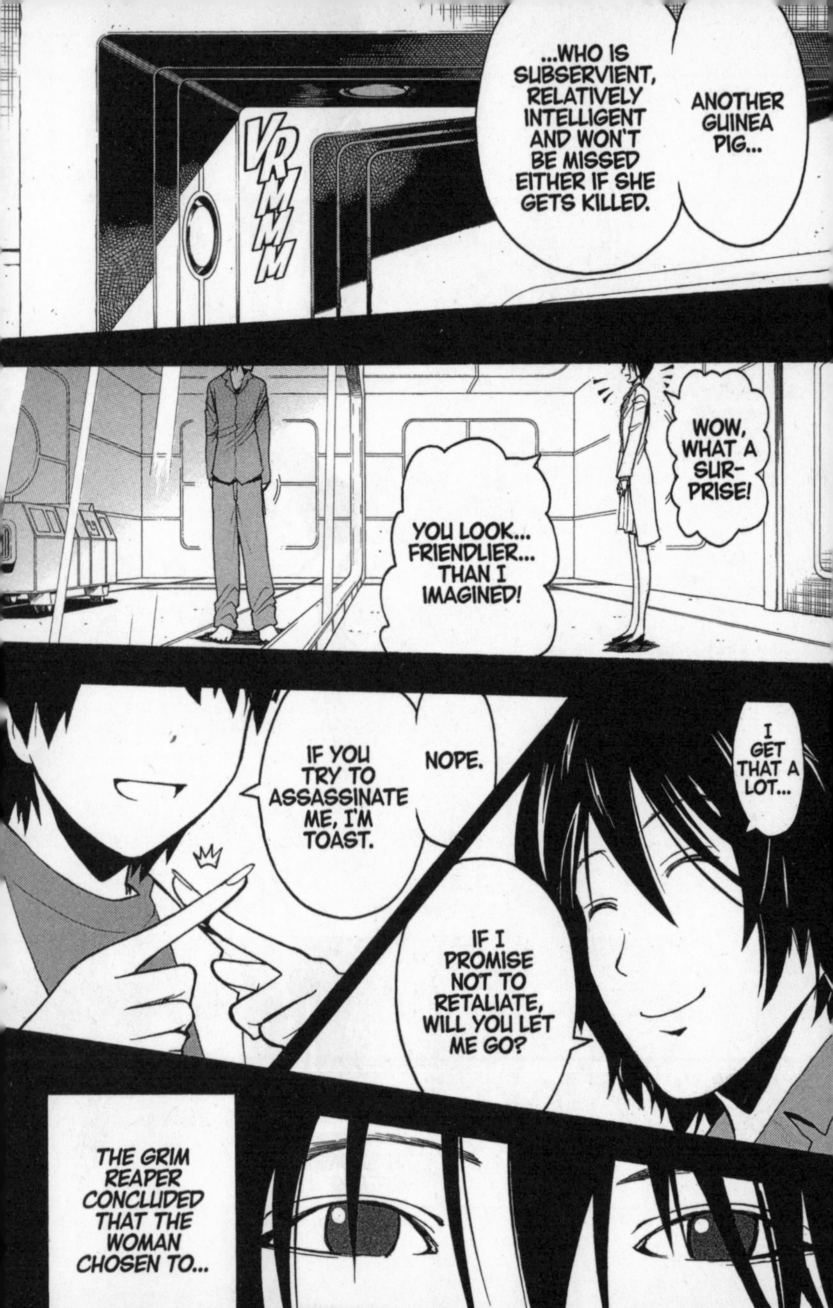
ANOTHER GUINEA PIG...
...WHO IS SUBSERVIENT, RELATIVELY INTELLIGENT AND WON'T BE MISSED EITHER IF SHE GETS KILLED.
VRMMM
WOW, WHAT A SUR-PRISE!
YOU LOOK... FRIENDLIER... THAN I IMAGINED!
I GET THAT A LOT...
IF I PROMISE NOT TO RETALIATE, WILL YOU LET ME GO?
NOPE.
IF YOU TRY TO ASSASSINATE ME, I'M TOAST.
THE GRIM REAPER CONCLUDED THAT THE WOMAN CHOSEN TO...

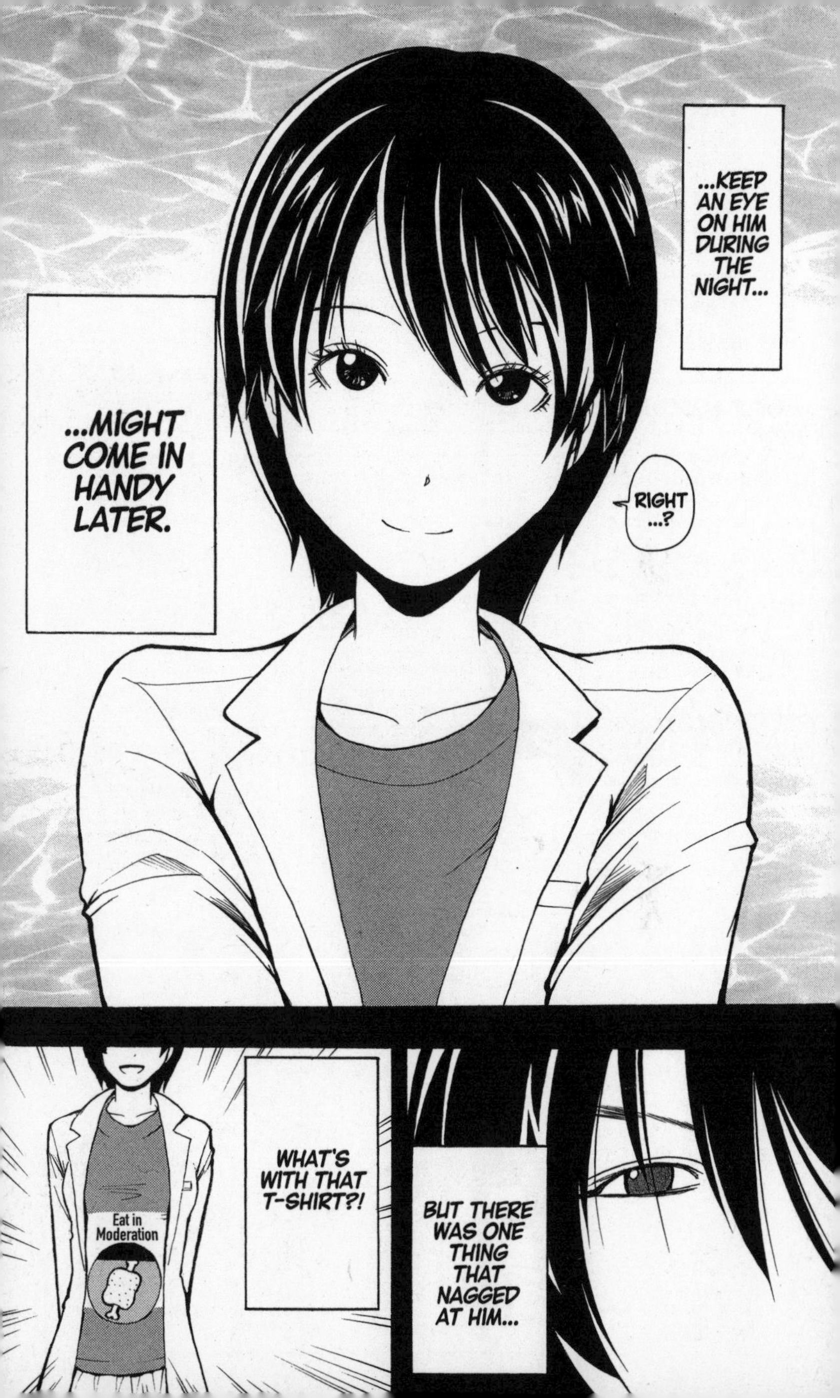
...KEEP AN EYE ON HIM DURING THE NIGHT...
RIGHT ...?
...MIGHT COME IN HANDY LATER.
BUT THERE WAS ONE THING THAT NAGGED AT HIM...
WHAT'S WITH THAT T-SHIRT?!
Eat in Moderation

Mr. Karasuma's Report Card ①

Training in basic and applied techniques was completed by the end of the second semester.

With the exception of some super-advanced training, the third semester is to be used for practical application of the training.

Therefore, in the final report, I have recorded the top-scoring students regarding each of the assassination techniques.

Long Distance Assassination
(Scores from the sharpshooting test in December—Total of 200 points)

Ambush Shooting			Moving & Shooting			Shooting from a Standstill		
1st Place	Ryunosuke Chiba	188 Points	1st Place	Rinka Hayami	182 Points	1st Place	Ryunosuke Chiba	198 Points
2nd Place	Nagisa Shiota	173 Points	2nd Place	Ryunosuke Chiba	158 Points	2nd Place	Rinka Hayami	173 Points
3rd Place	Rinka Hayami	168 Points	3rd Place	Yuma Isogai	118 Points	3rd Place	Yuma Isogai	160 Points
4th Place	Kirara Hazama	144 Points	4th Place	Yukiko Kanzaki	104 Points	4th Place	Takuya Muramatsu	135 Points
5th Place	Sosuke Sugaya	123 Points	5th Place	Masayoshi Kimura	96 Points	5th Place	Ryunosuke Chiba	122 Points

Highlight **Nagisa Shiota**	Highlight **Rinka Hayami**	Highlight **Ryunosuke Chiba**
Imperfect marksmanship skills, but compensated for by his ability to wait until the target is close enough for him to make the shot. Excels at camouflaging himself and waiting patiently for an opening.	Able to shoot while moving or despite unstable footing. The possibilities of sniper shots when she teams up with Chiba are countless.	Successfully targets sniper shots from twice as far as the student in second place. Given ideal conditions, no one can surpass him in hitting an unguarded target.

Rapid Fire			Night Sniping		
1st Place	Taisei Yoshida	164 Points	1st Place	Ryunosuke Chiba	171 Points
2nd Place	Rinka Hayami	164 Points	2nd Place	Rinka Hayami	157 Points
3rd Place	Itona Horibe	140 Points	3rd Place	Hinata Okano	139 Points
4th Place	Yuzuki Fuwa	122 Points	4th Place	Rio Nakamura	133 Points
5th Place	Yuma Isogai	121 Points	5th Place	Itona Horibe	120 Points

Highlight **Taisei Yoshida**	Highlight **Hinata Okano**
Skilled in stopping his target by delivering a wide barrage without too much concern about his aim. His dexterity enables him to quickly reload his weapon with a specially crafted magazine so as to continue shooting without pausing.	I was surprised when she removed her night-vision goggles during training, complaining that they annoyed her, and began shooting using only her naked eye. She can see clearly in the dark and also relies heavily on her sense of smell. She becomes a completely different person at night.

CLASS 135 TIME FOR THE PAST—2ND PERIOD

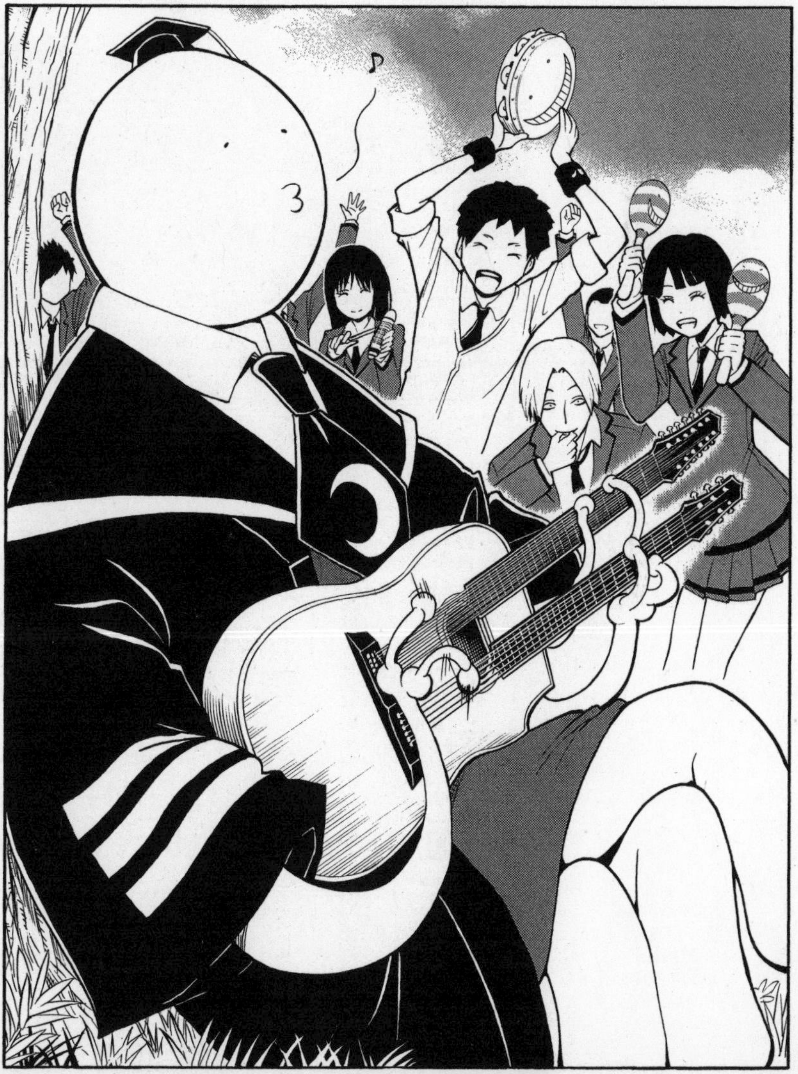
♪

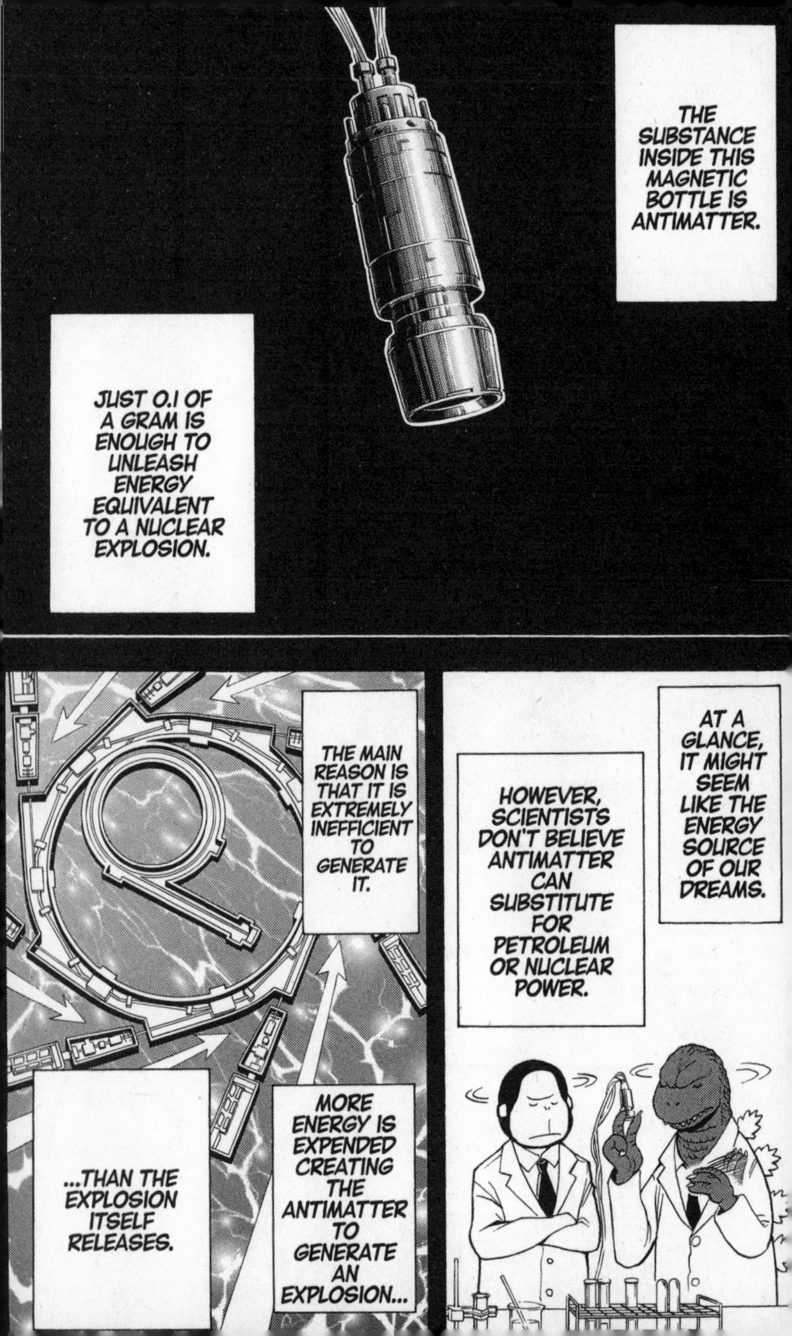
THE SUBSTANCE INSIDE THIS MAGNETIC BOTTLE IS ANTIMATTER.
JUST 0.1 OF A GRAM IS ENOUGH TO UNLEASH ENERGY EQUIVALENT TO A NUCLEAR EXPLOSION.
AT A GLANCE, IT MIGHT SEEM LIKE THE ENERGY SOURCE OF OUR DREAMS.
HOWEVER, SCIENTISTS DON'T BELIEVE ANTIMATTER CAN SUBSTITUTE FOR PETROLEUM OR NUCLEAR POWER.
THE MAIN REASON IS THAT IT IS EXTREMELY INEFFICIENT TO GENERATE IT.
MORE ENERGY IS EXPENDED CREATING THE ANTIMATTER TO GENERATE AN EXPLOSION...
...THAN THE EXPLOSION ITSELF RELEASES.

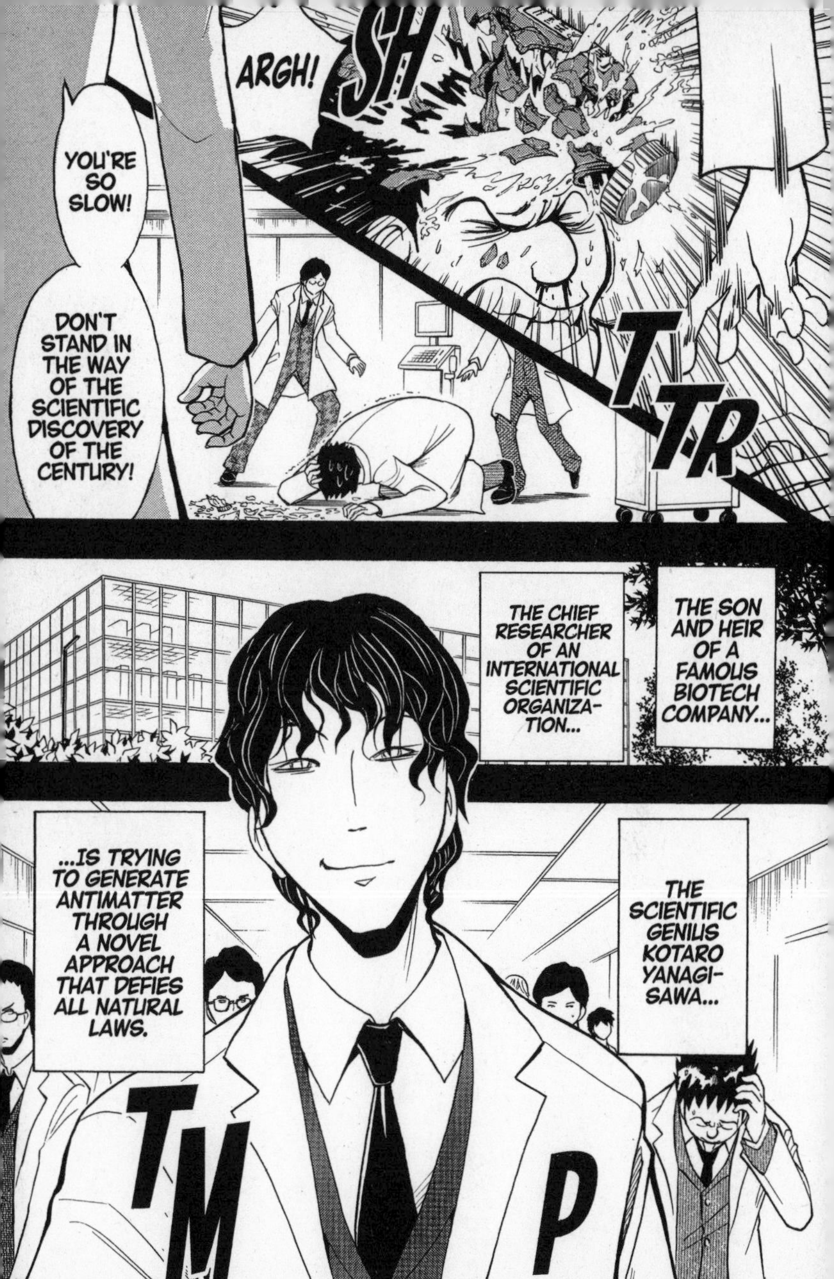
SH
ARGH!
T T·R
YOU'RE SO SLOW!
DON'T STAND IN THE WAY OF THE SCIENTIFIC DISCOVERY OF THE CENTURY!
THE SON AND HEIR OF A FAMOUS BIOTECH COMPANY...
THE CHIEF RESEARCHER OF AN INTERNATIONAL SCIENTIFIC ORGANIZATION...
THE SCIENTIFIC GENIUS KOTARO YANAGISAWA...
...IS TRYING TO GENERATE ANTIMATTER THROUGH A NOVEL APPROACH THAT DEFIES ALL NATURAL LAWS.
TMP

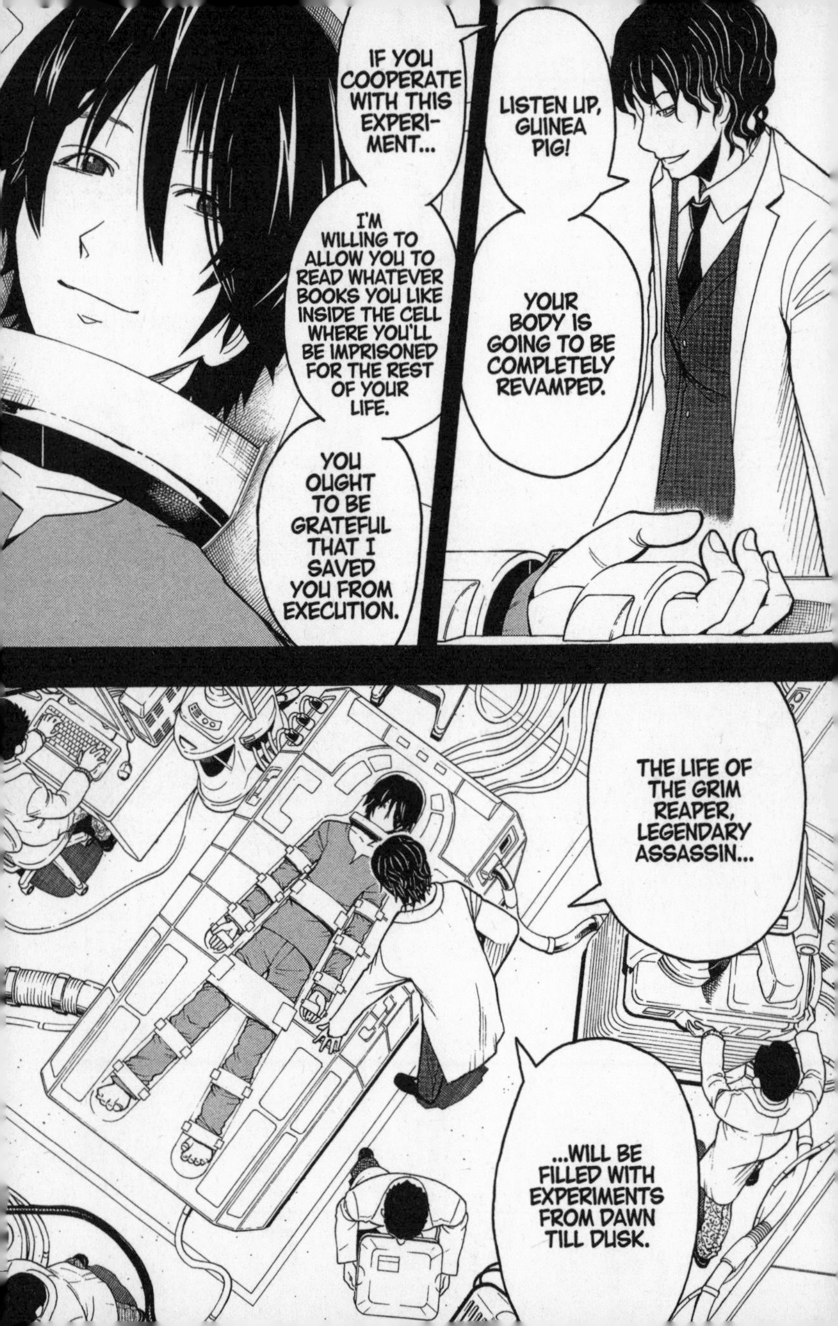
LISTEN UP, GUINEA PIG!
YOUR BODY IS GOING TO BE COMPLETELY REVAMPED.
IF YOU COOPERATE WITH THIS EXPERI- MENT...
I'M WILLING TO ALLOW YOU TO READ WHATEVER BOOKS YOU LIKE INSIDE THE CELL WHERE YOU'LL BE IMPRISONED FOR THE REST OF YOUR LIFE.
YOU OUGHT TO BE GRATEFUL THAT I SAVED YOU FROM EXECUTION.
THE LIFE OF THE GRIM REAPER, LEGENDARY ASSASSIN...
...WILL BE FILLED WITH EXPERIMENTS FROM DAWN TILL DUSK.

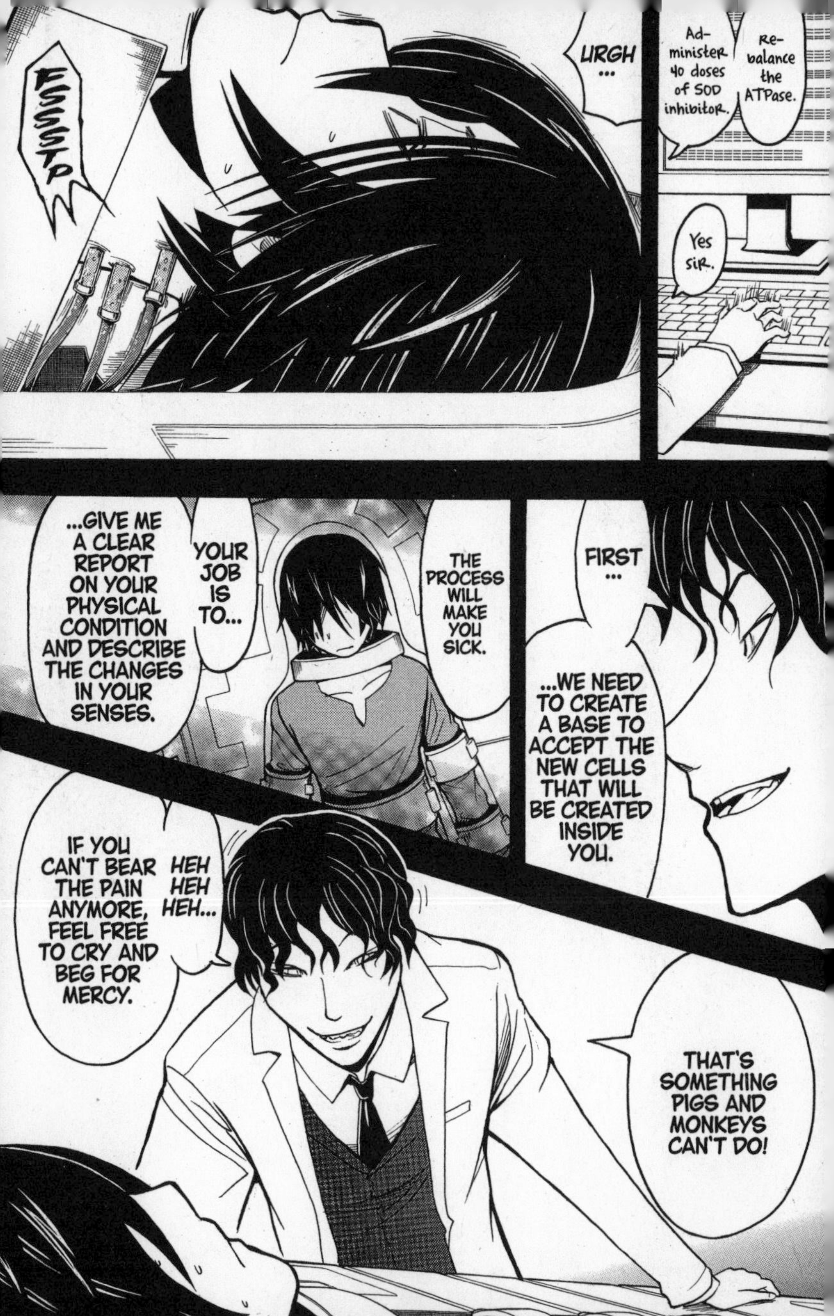
Re-balance the ATPase.
Ad-minister 40 doses of SOD inhibitor.
Yes sir.
URGH...
FSSSTP
FIRST...
...WE NEED TO CREATE A BASE TO ACCEPT THE NEW CELLS THAT WILL BE CREATED INSIDE YOU.
THE PROCESS WILL MAKE YOU SICK.
YOUR JOB IS TO...
...GIVE ME A CLEAR REPORT ON YOUR PHYSICAL CONDITION AND DESCRIBE THE CHANGES IN YOUR SENSES.
THAT'S SOMETHING PIGS AND MONKEYS CAN'T DO!
IF YOU CAN'T BEAR THE PAIN ANYMORE, FEEL FREE TO CRY AND BEG FOR MERCY.
HEH HEH HEH...

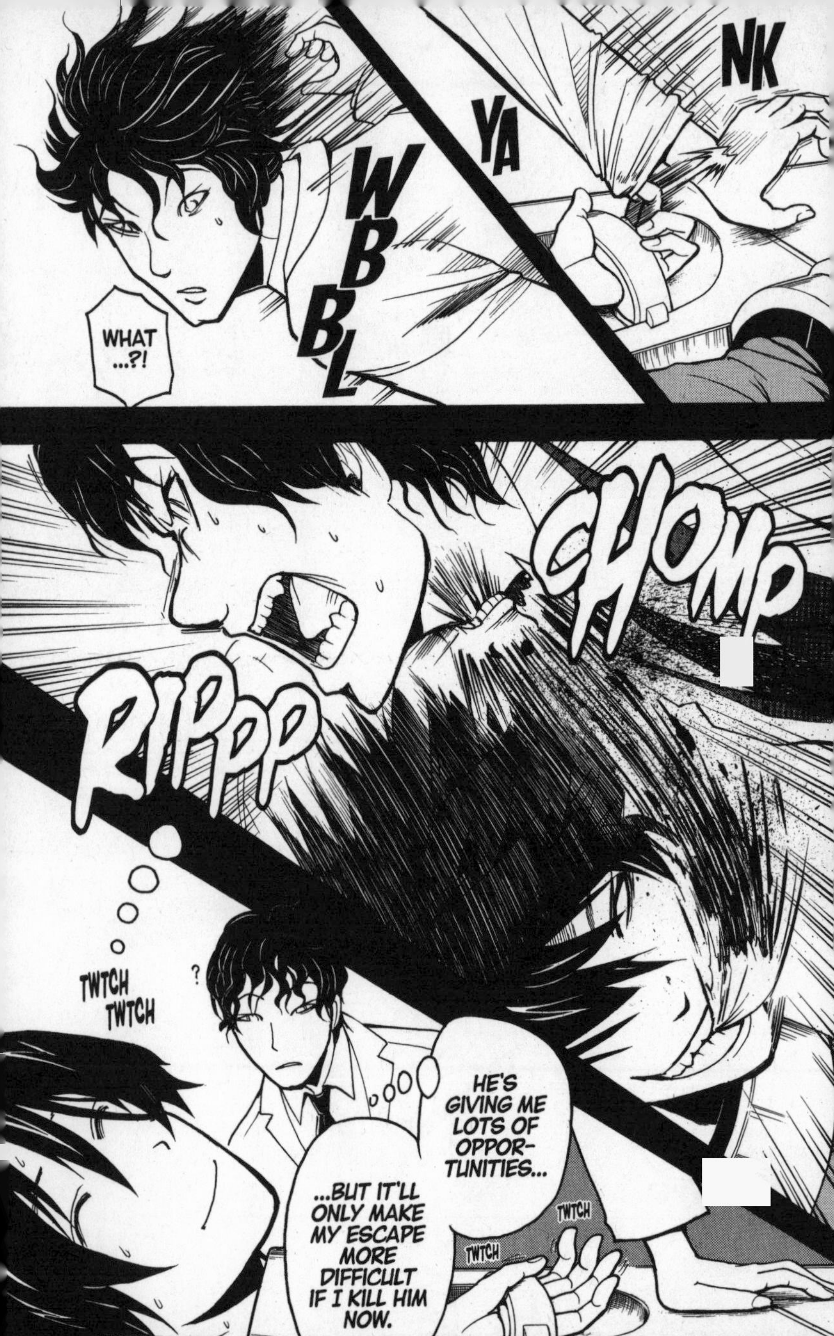
YA
NK
WBBL
WHAT ...?!
CHOMP
RIPPP
HE'S GIVING ME LOTS OF OPPOR-TUNITIES...
...BUT IT'LL ONLY MAKE MY ESCAPE MORE DIFFICULT IF I KILL HIM NOW.
TWTCH
TWTCH
?
TWTCH TWTCH

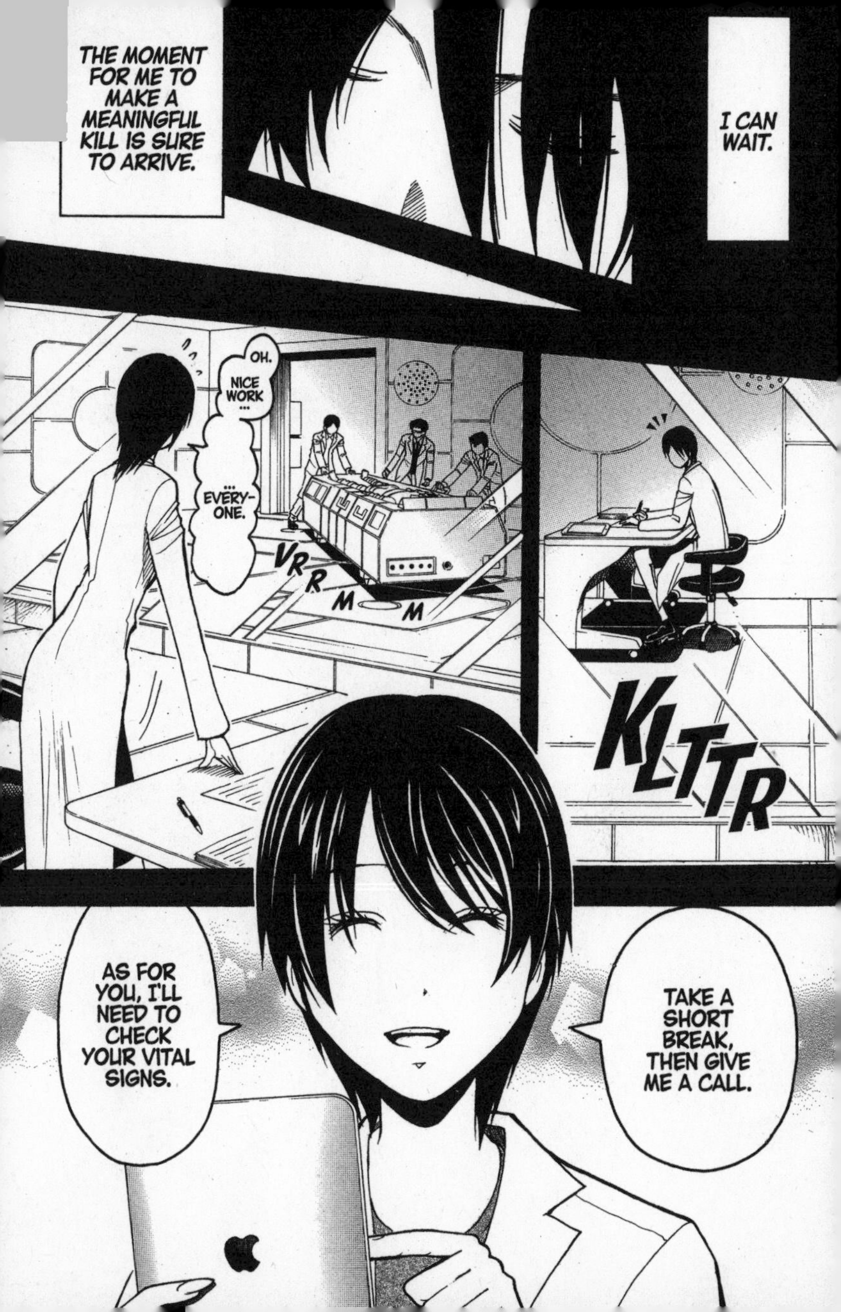

I CAN WAIT.
THE MOMENT FOR ME TO MAKE A MEANINGFUL KILL IS SURE TO ARRIVE.
OH. NICE WORK... ...EVERYONE.
KLTTR
VRRMMM
TAKE A SHORT BREAK, THEN GIVE ME A CALL.
AS FOR YOU, I'LL NEED TO CHECK YOUR VITAL SIGNS.

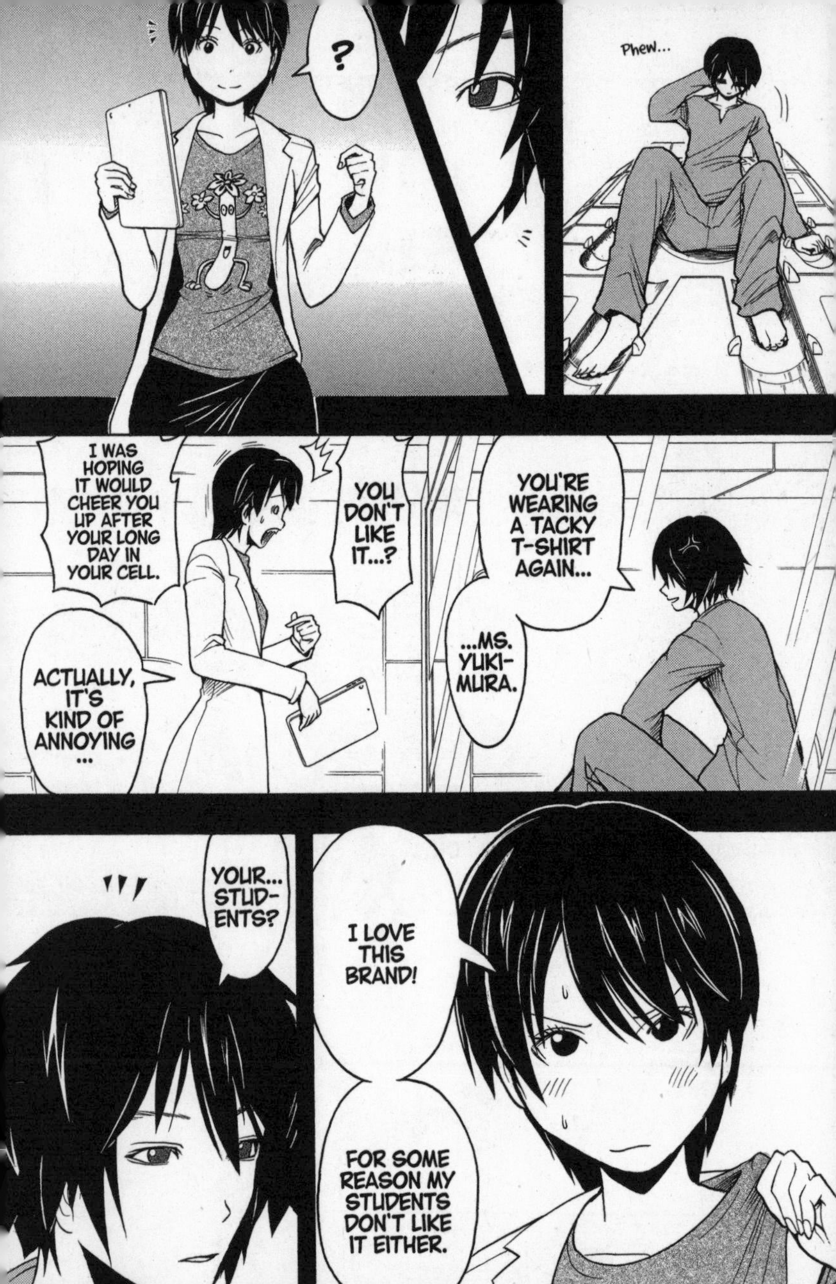
Phew...
?
YOU'RE WEARING A TACKY T-SHIRT AGAIN...
...MS. YUKI-MURA.
YOU DON'T LIKE IT...?
I WAS HOPING IT WOULD CHEER YOU UP AFTER YOUR LONG DAY IN YOUR CELL.
ACTUALLY, IT'S KIND OF ANNOYING...
I LOVE THIS BRAND!
FOR SOME REASON MY STUDENTS DON'T LIKE IT EITHER.
YOUR... STUD-ENTS?

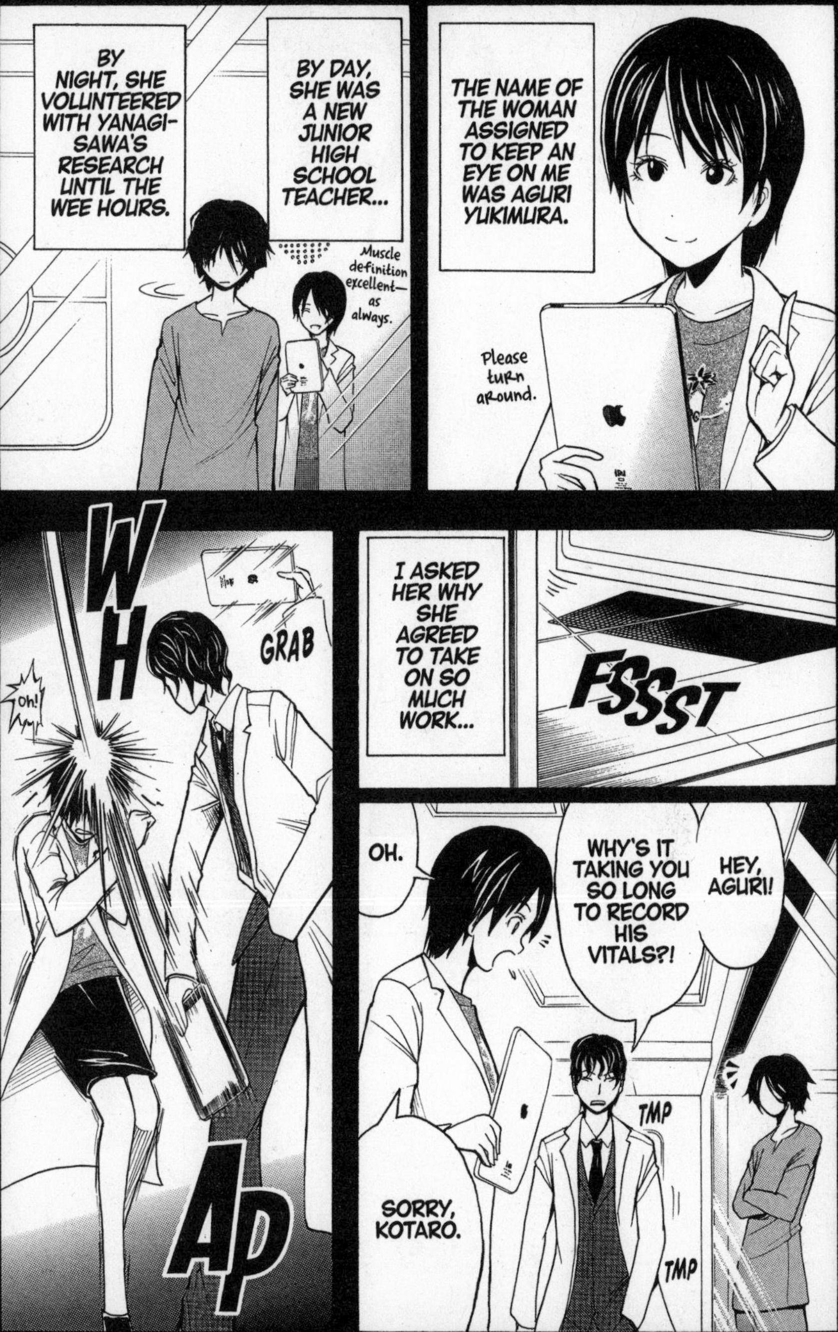

THE NAME OF THE WOMAN ASSIGNED TO KEEP AN EYE ON ME WAS AGURI YUKIMURA.
Please turn around.
BY DAY, SHE WAS A NEW JUNIOR HIGH SCHOOL TEACHER...
BY NIGHT, SHE VOLUNTEERED WITH YANAGI-SAWA'S RESEARCH UNTIL THE WEE HOURS.
Muscle definition excellent—as always.
I ASKED HER WHY SHE AGREED TO TAKE ON SO MUCH WORK...
FSSST
HEY, AGURI!
WHY'S IT TAKING YOU SO LONG TO RECORD HIS VITALS?!
OH.
TMP
TMP
SORRY, KOTARO.
GRAB
WH
Oh!
AP

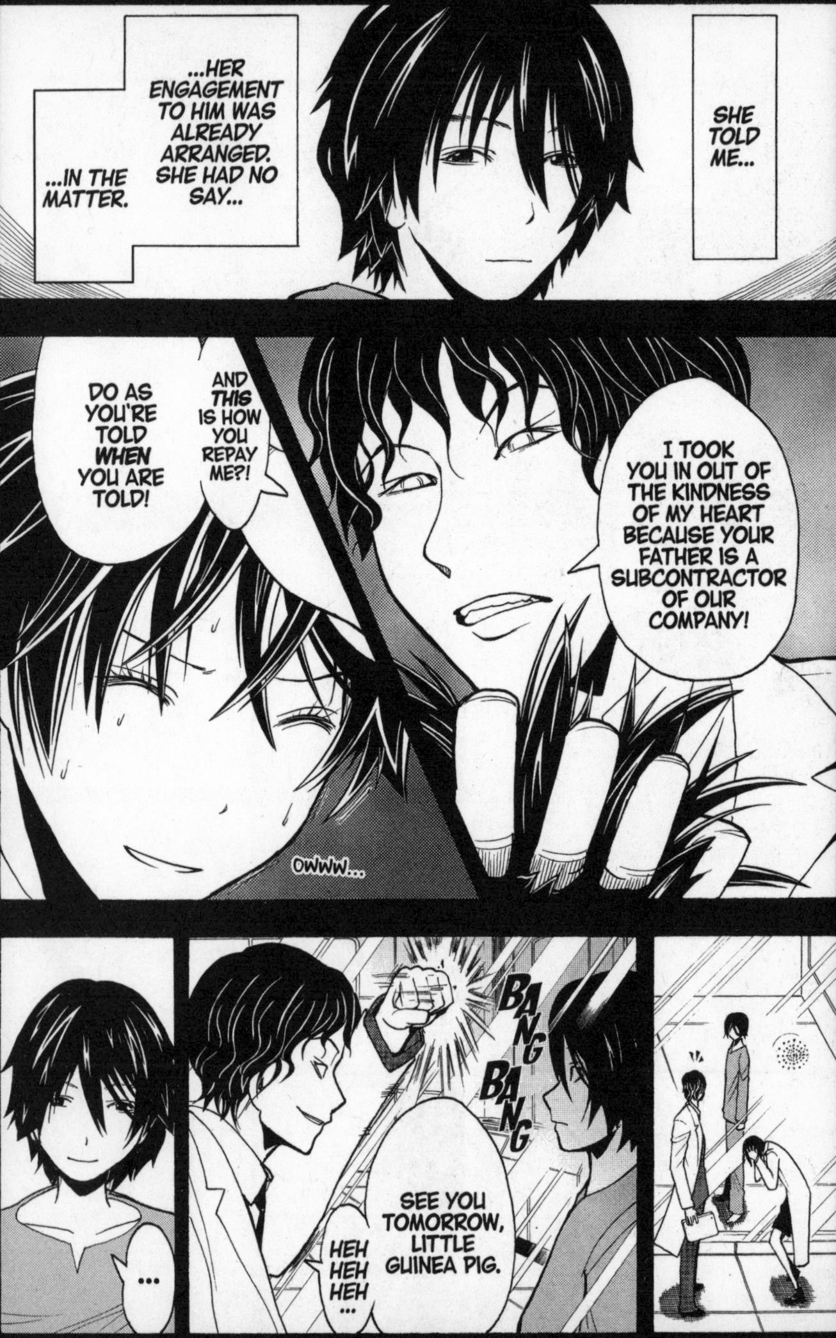
SHE TOLD ME...
...HER ENGAGEMENT TO HIM WAS ALREADY ARRANGED. SHE HAD NO SAY...
...IN THE MATTER.
I TOOK YOU IN OUT OF THE KINDNESS OF MY HEART BECAUSE YOUR FATHER IS A SUBCONTRACTOR OF OUR COMPANY!
AND THIS IS HOW YOU REPAY ME?!
DO AS YOU'RE TOLD WHEN YOU ARE TOLD!
OWWW...
BANG
BANG
BANG
SEE YOU TOMORROW, LITTLE GUINEA PIG.
HEH HEH HEH ...
...

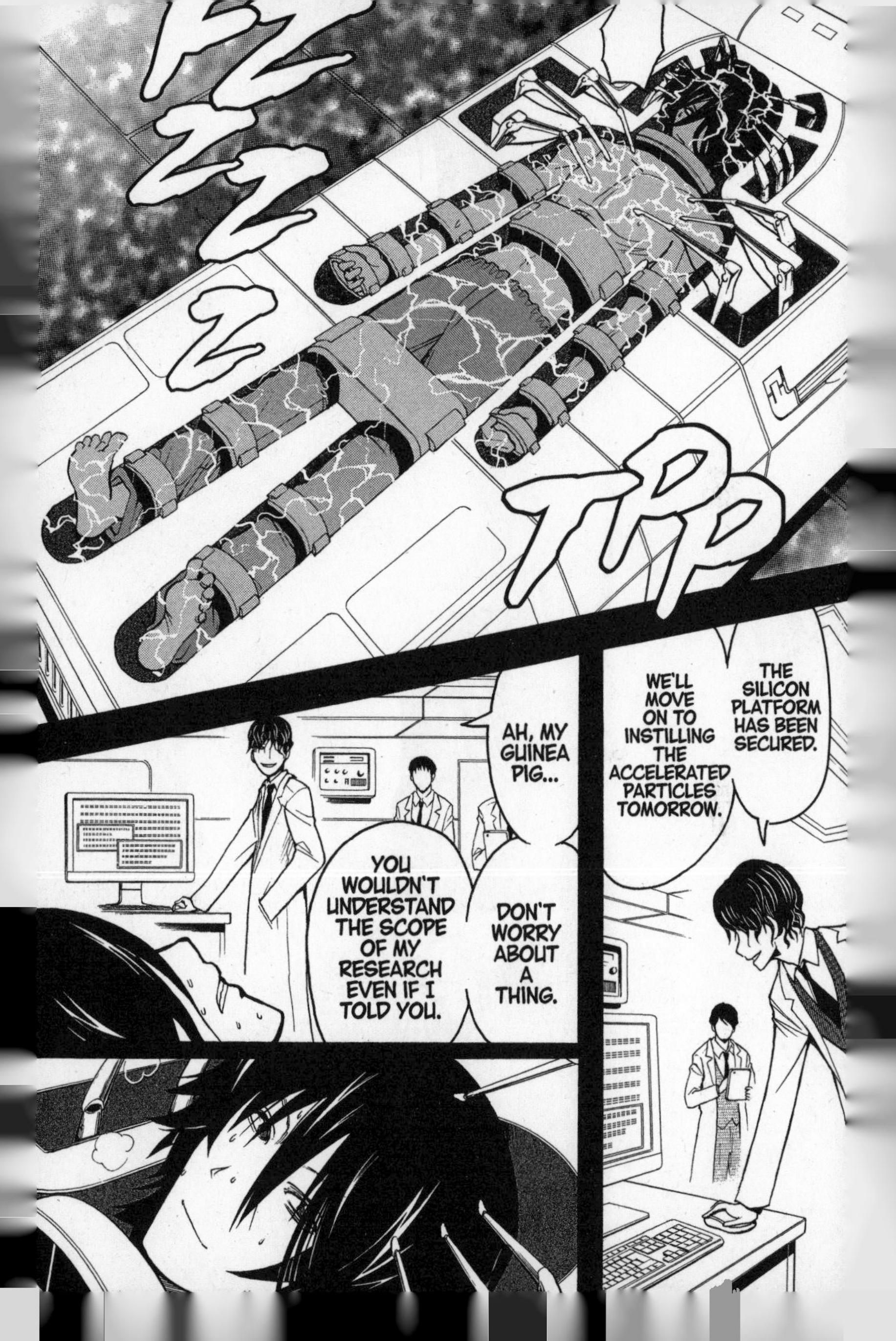
TPP
THE SILICON PLATFORM HAS BEEN SECURED.
WE'LL MOVE ON TO INSTILLING THE ACCELERATED PARTICLES TOMORROW.
AH, MY GUINEA PIG...
DON'T WORRY ABOUT A THING.
YOU WOULDN'T UNDERSTAND THE SCOPE OF MY RESEARCH EVEN IF I TOLD YOU.

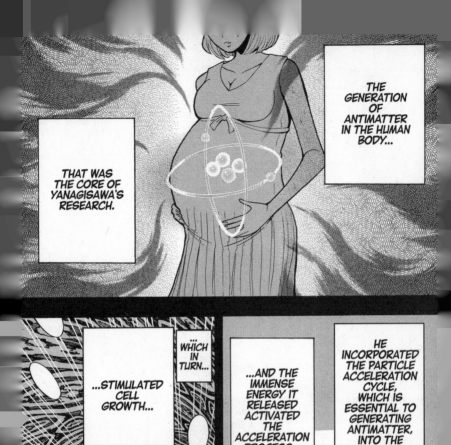

THE GENERATION OF ANTIMATTER IN THE HUMAN BODY...
THAT WAS THE CORE OF YANAGISAWA'S RESEARCH.
HE INCORPORATED THE PARTICLE ACCELERATION CYCLE, WHICH IS ESSENTIAL TO GENERATING ANTIMATTER, INTO THE NATURAL HUMAN LIFE CYCLE...
...AND THE IMMENSE ENERGY IT RELEASED ACTIVATED THE ACCELERATION PROCESS...
...WHICH IN TURN...
...STIMULATED CELL GROWTH...
...WHICH IN TURN GENERATED MORE ANTIMATTER— AS LONG AS THAT PERSON REMAINED ALIVE.

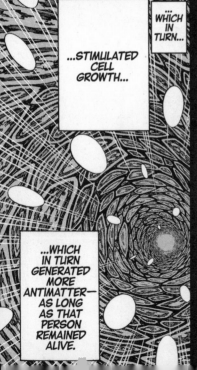

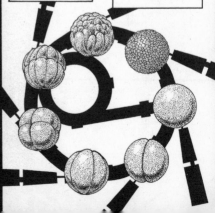

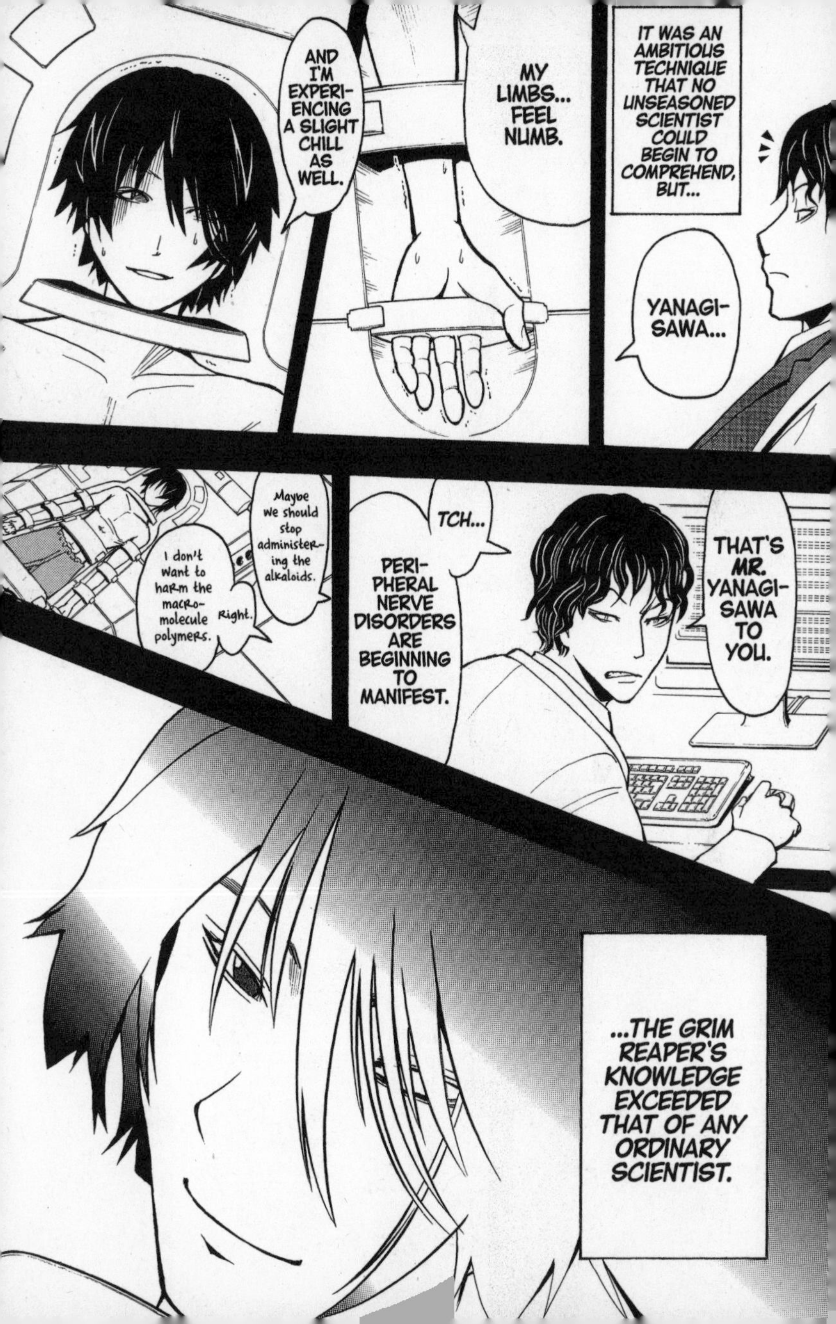
IT WAS AN AMBITIOUS TECHNIQUE THAT NO UNSEASONED SCIENTIST COULD BEGIN TO COMPREHEND, BUT...
YANAGI-SAWA...
MY LIMBS... FEEL NUMB.
AND I'M EXPERI-ENCING A SLIGHT CHILL AS WELL.
THAT'S MR. YANAGI-SAWA TO YOU.
TCH...
PERI-PHERAL NERVE DISORDERS ARE BEGINNING TO MANIFEST.
Maybe we should stop administer-ing the alkaloids.
I don't want to harm the macro-molecule polymers.
Right.
...THE GRIM REAPER'S KNOWLEDGE EXCEEDED THAT OF ANY ORDINARY SCIENTIST.

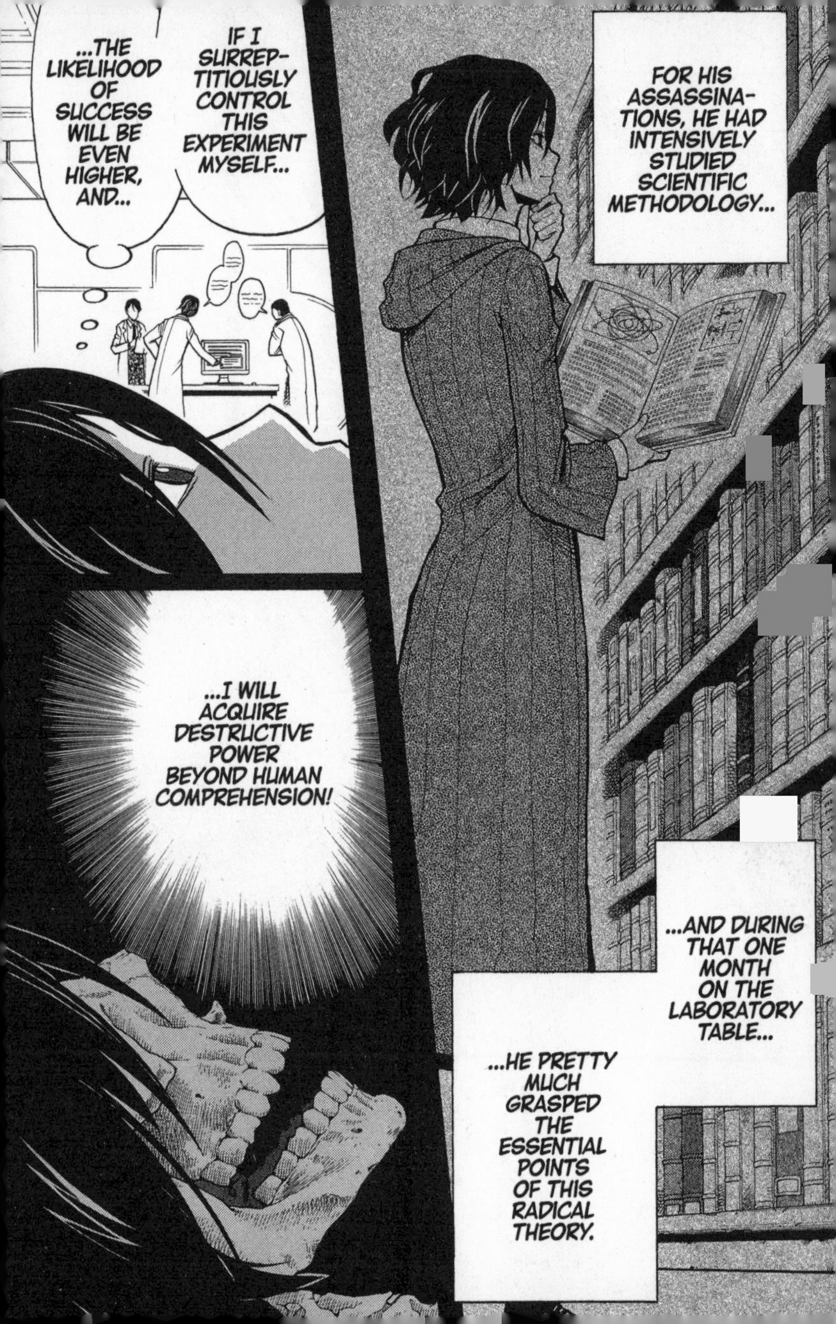
FOR HIS ASSASSINA-TIONS, HE HAD INTENSIVELY STUDIED SCIENTIFIC METHODOLOGY...
...AND DURING THAT ONE MONTH ON THE LABORATORY TABLE...
...HE PRETTY MUCH GRASPED THE ESSENTIAL POINTS OF THIS RADICAL THEORY.
IF I SURREP-TITIOUSLY CONTROL THIS EXPERIMENT MYSELF...
...THE LIKELIHOOD OF SUCCESS WILL BE EVEN HIGHER, AND...
...I WILL ACQUIRE DESTRUCTIVE POWER BEYOND HUMAN COMPREHENSION!

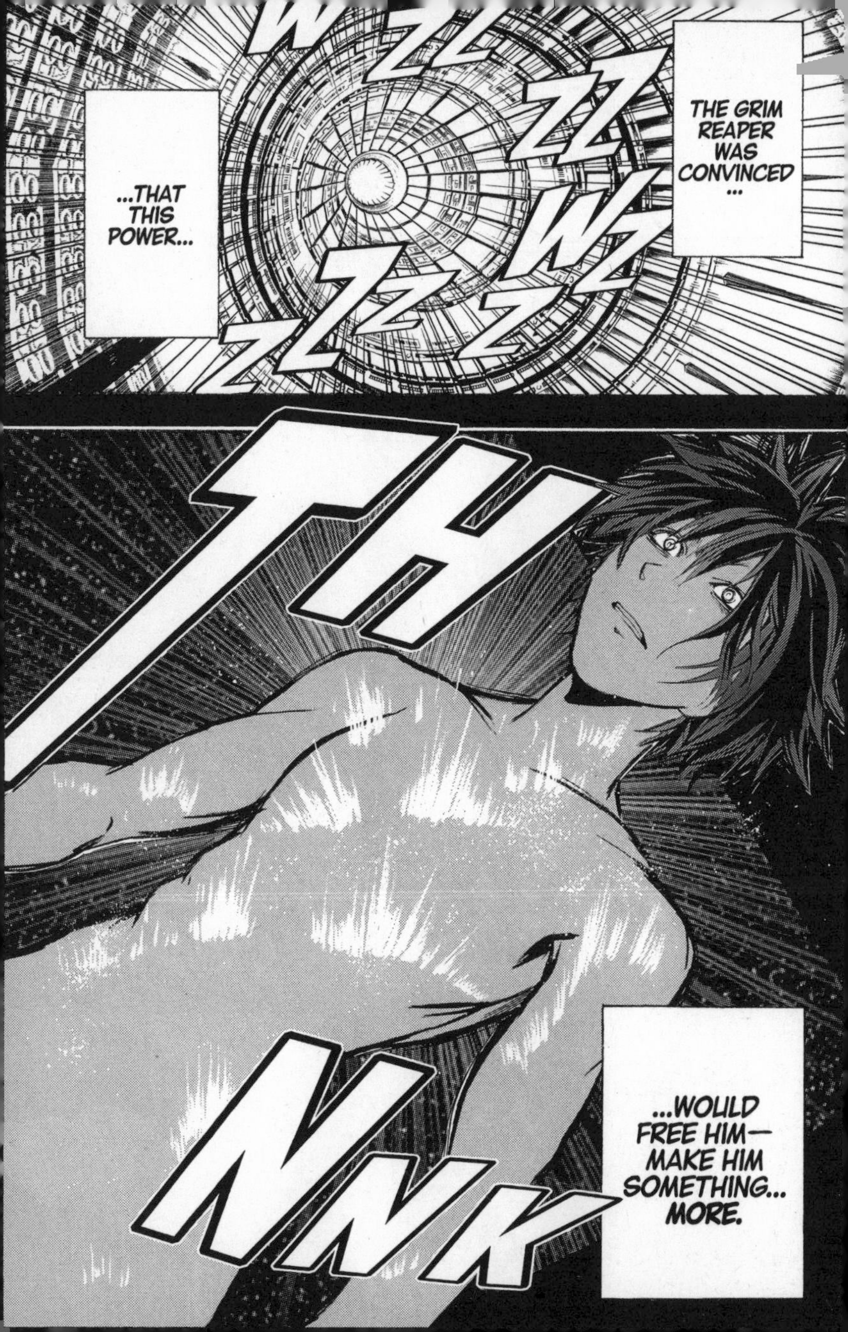
THE GRIM REAPER WAS CONVINCED...
WZZZZ WZZZZZ
...THAT THIS POWER...
THNNK
...WOULD FREE HIM—MAKE HIM SOMETHING... MORE.

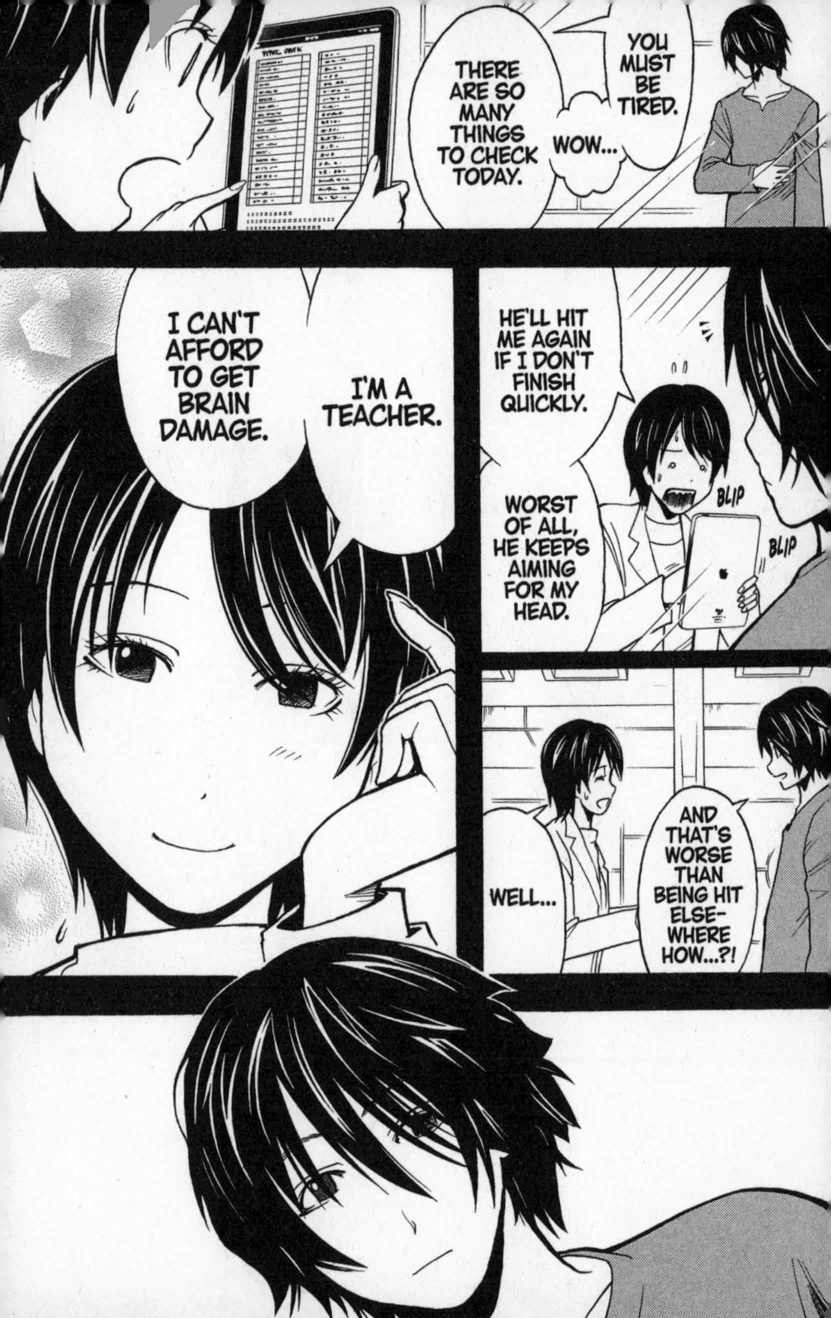
YOU MUST BE TIRED.
WOW...
THERE ARE SO MANY THINGS TO CHECK TODAY.
HE'LL HIT ME AGAIN IF I DON'T FINISH QUICKLY.
BLIP
BLIP
WORST OF ALL, HE KEEPS AIMING FOR MY HEAD.
AND THAT'S WORSE THAN BEING HIT ELSE-WHERE HOW...?!
WELL...
I'M A TEACHER.
I CAN'T AFFORD TO GET BRAIN DAMAGE.

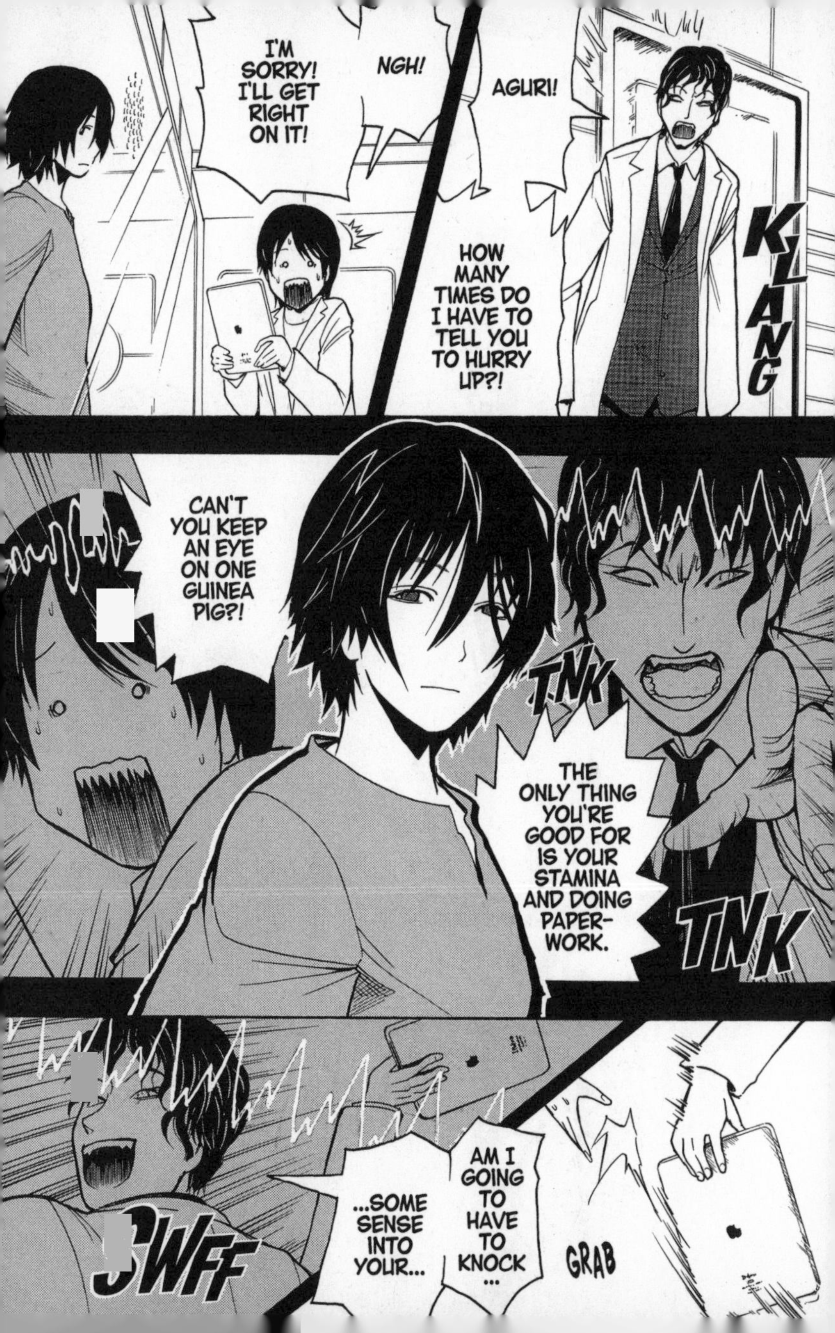
KLANG
AGURI!
HOW MANY TIMES DO I HAVE TO TELL YOU TO HURRY UP?!
NGH!
I'M SORRY! I'LL GET RIGHT ON IT!
CAN'T YOU KEEP AN EYE ON ONE GUINEA PIG?!
TNK
THE ONLY THING YOU'RE GOOD FOR IS YOUR STAMINA AND DOING PAPER-WORK.
TNK
GRAB
AM I GOING TO HAVE TO KNOCK...
...SOME SENSE INTO YOUR...
SWFF

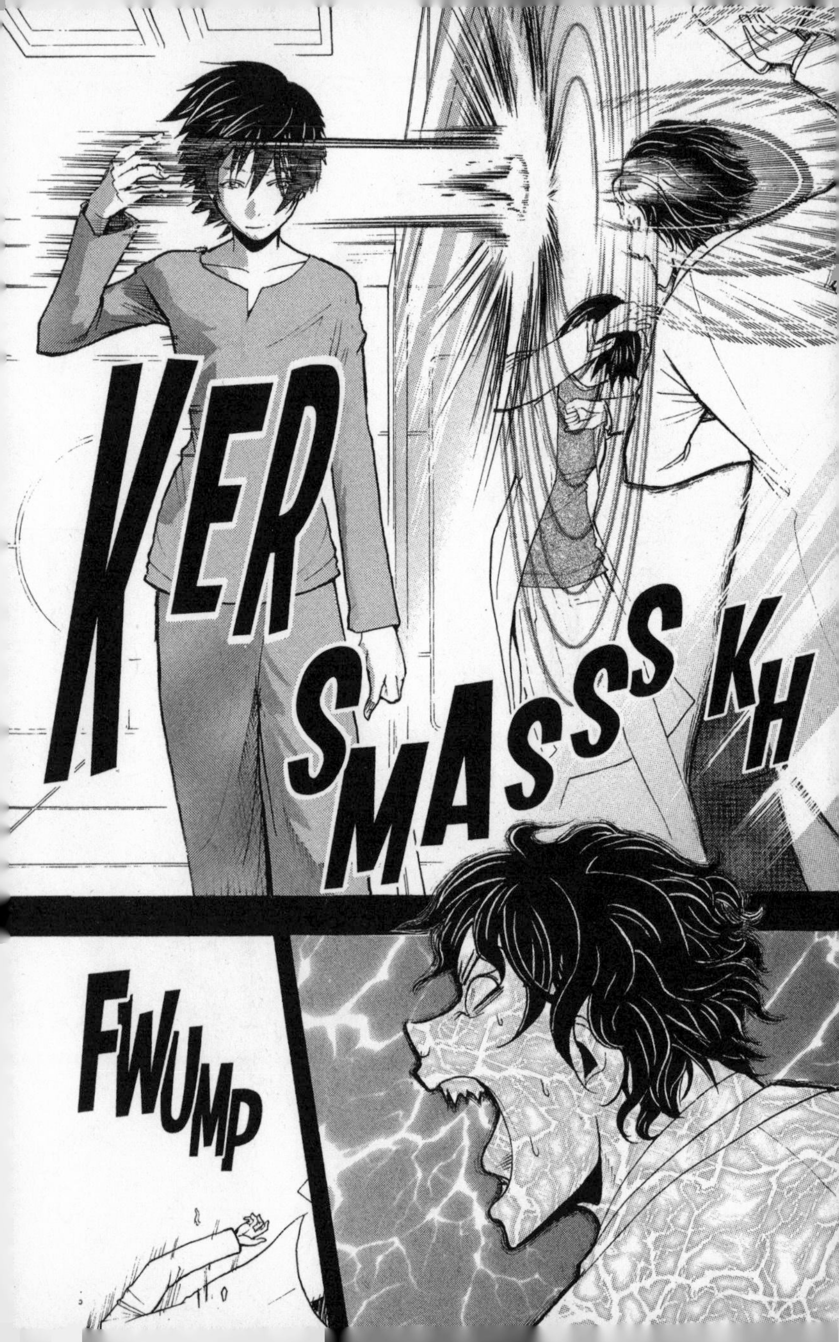
KER
SMASSSKH
FWUMP

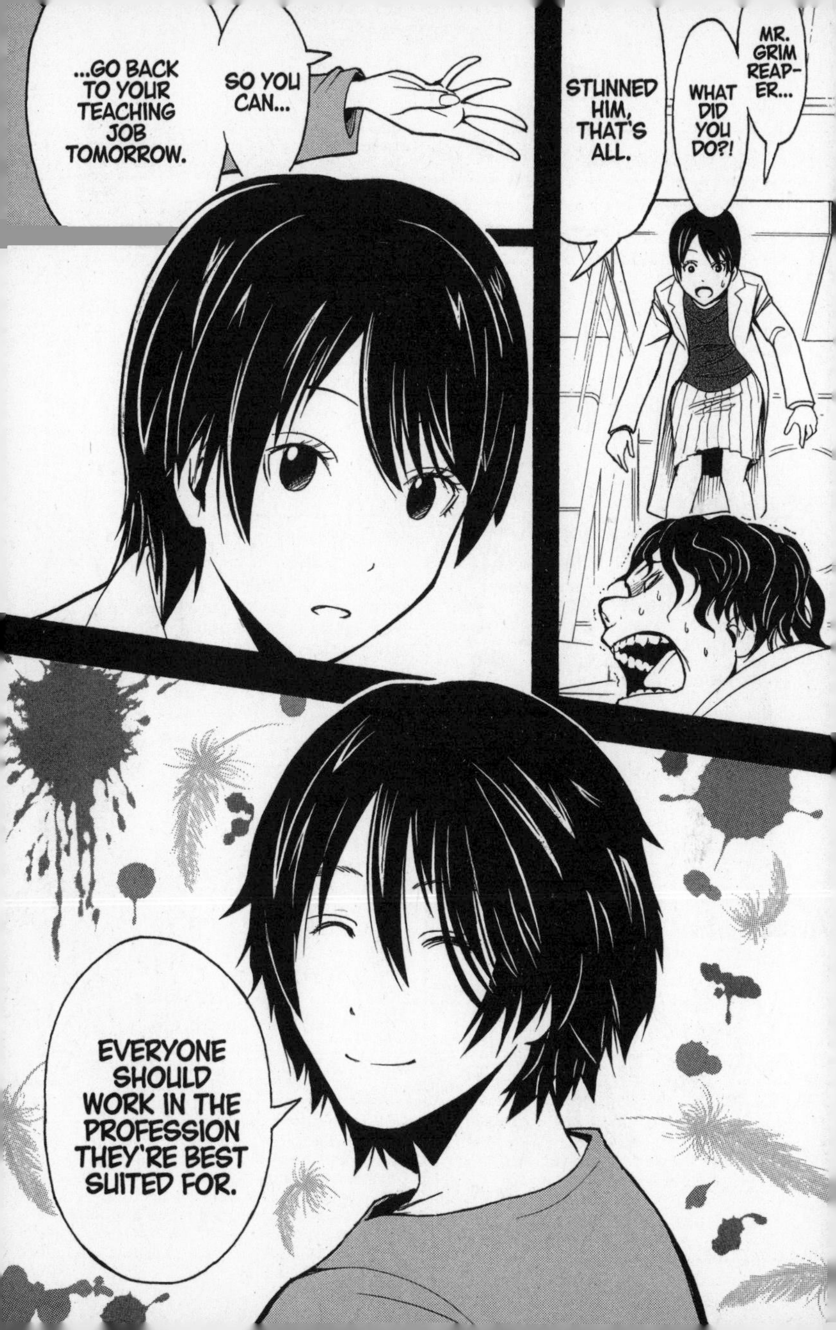
MR. GRIM REAPER...
WHAT DID YOU DO?!
STUNNED HIM, THAT'S ALL.
SO YOU CAN...
...GO BACK TO YOUR TEACHING JOB TOMORROW.
EVERYONE SHOULD WORK IN THE PROFESSION THEY'RE BEST SUITED FOR.

Mr. Karasuma's Report Card ②

Close-Range Assassination

(Scores from the mock assassination drill against Mr. Karasuma from September to December)

Knife Skills (Combination)			Knife Skills (Single)		
1st Place	Yuma Isogai/ Hiroto Maehara	55 Points	1st Place	Hiroto Maehara	38 Points
2nd Place	Tomohito Sugino/ Taiga Okajima	32 Points	2nd Place	Karma Akabane	35 Points
3rd Place	Karma Akabane/ Nagisa Shiota	30 Points	3rd Place	Yuma Isogai	23 Points
4th Place	Taisei Yoshida/ Takuya Muramatsu	26 Points	4th Place	Tomohito Sugino	20 Points
5th Place	Ryoma Terasaka/ Itona Horibe	25 Points	5th Place	Hinata Okano	17 Points
Highlight	Taisei Yoshida/Takuya Muramatsu/ Ryoma Terasaka/Itona Horibe		Highlight	Hiroto Maehara	
These three slackers and the transfer student showed great improvement over the second semester. They have become an important asset to Class E, and have increased the likelihood of a successful assassination.			Capable of wielding two knives at once now. Even I can't take his knife skills lightly anymore. If there were a national tournament for knife fighting, he would be the one I put forward.		

Stealth Skill			High-Speed Assassination		
1st Place	Masayoshi Kimura	8 Points	1st Place	Masayoshi Kimura	16 Points
2nd Place	Meg Kataoka	6 Points	1st Place	Hinata Okano	16 Points
2nd Place	Nagisa Shiota	6 Points	3rd Place	Taiga Okajima	11 Points
4th Place	Tomohito Sugino	5 Points	4th Place	Yuma Isogai	9 Points
5th Place	Koki Mimura	4 Points	5th Place	Hinano Kurahashi	9 Points
Highlight	Masayoshi Kimura		Highlight	Taiga Okajima	
Expertise in the technique of closing in on opponents from their blind side. Being small and nimble, he managed to scratch me with his blade eight times.			Skilled at close-range assassinations in three-dimensional environments containing numerous obstacles. He has flexible hip joints, and there isn't a tree that he can't climb. I prefer not to ask him to, though, given the types of photos he takes from the tops of them.		

CLASS 136 TIME FOR THE PAST—3RD PERIOD

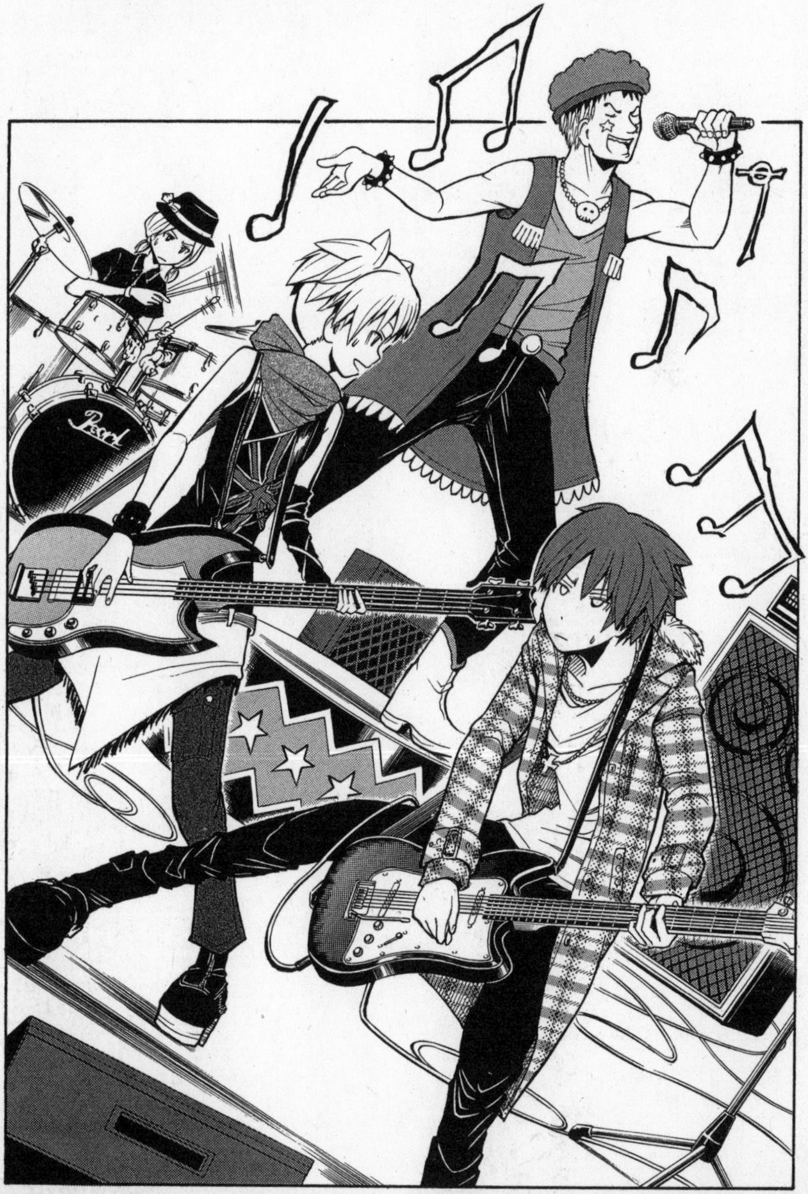
Pearl

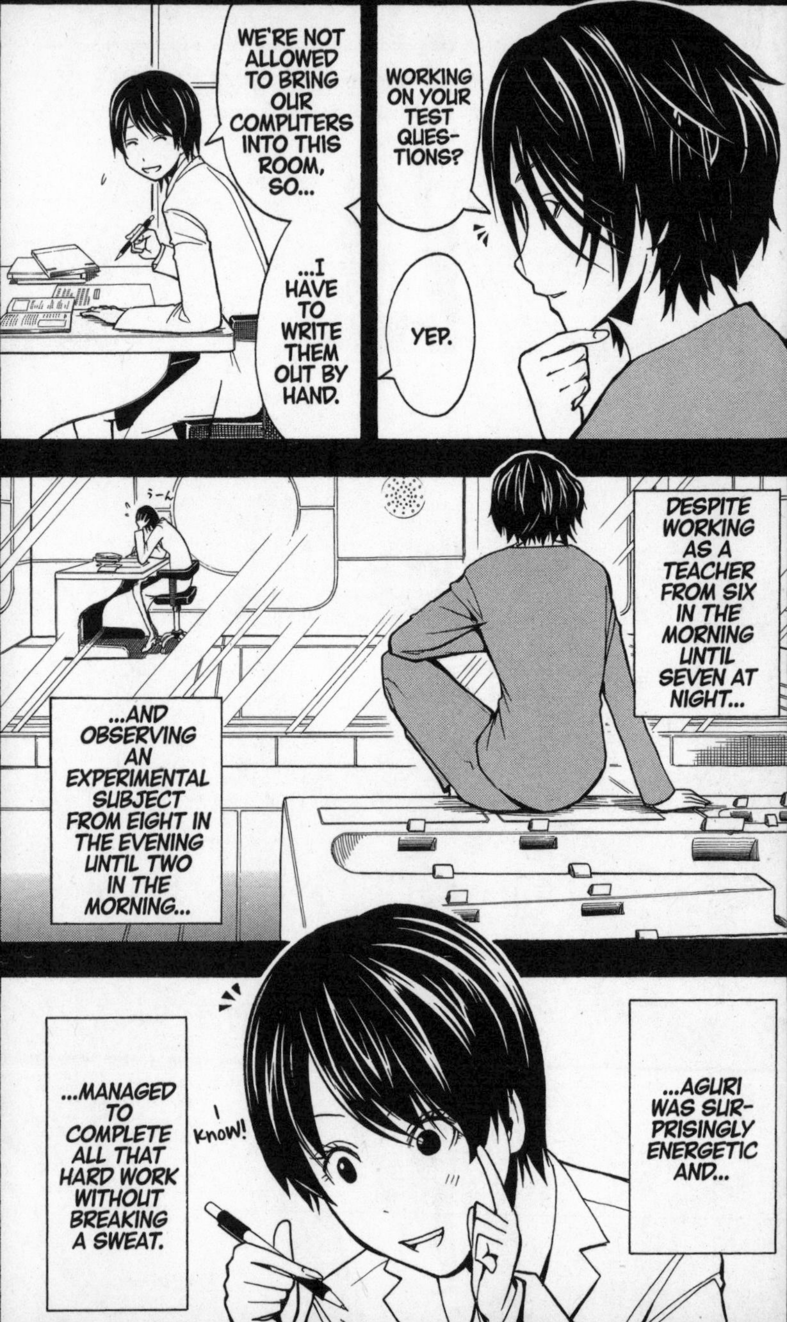
WORKING ON YOUR TEST QUES-TIONS?
YEP.
WE'RE NOT ALLOWED TO BRING OUR COMPUTERS INTO THIS ROOM, SO...
...I HAVE TO WRITE THEM OUT BY HAND.
DESPITE WORKING AS A TEACHER FROM SIX IN THE MORNING UNTIL SEVEN AT NIGHT...
...AND OBSERVING AN EXPERIMENTAL SUBJECT FROM EIGHT IN THE EVENING UNTIL TWO IN THE MORNING...
...AGURI WAS SUR-PRISINGLY ENERGETIC AND...
I KNOW!
...MANAGED TO COMPLETE ALL THAT HARD WORK WITHOUT BREAKING A SWEAT.

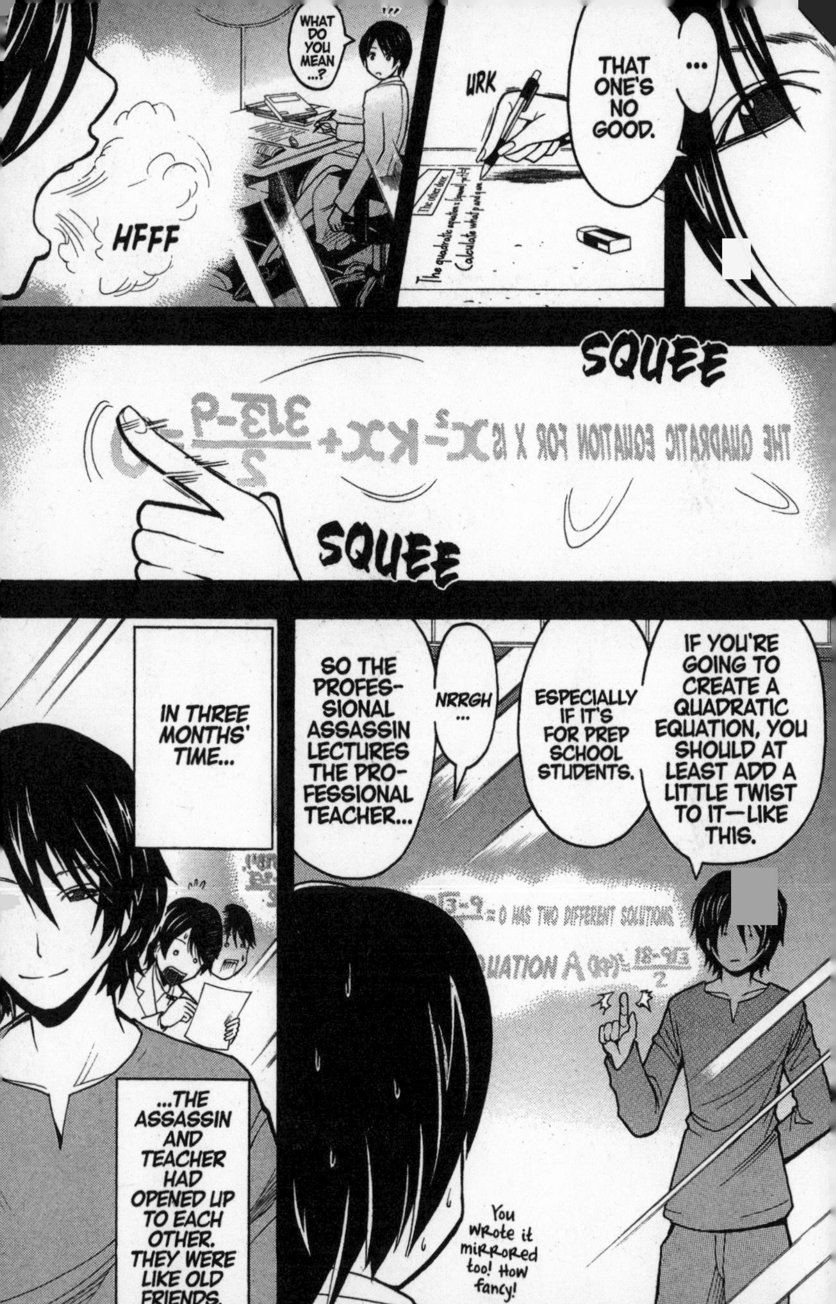
...
THAT ONE'S NO GOOD.
URK
The quadratic equation
Calculate what p and q are
WHAT DO YOU MEAN ...?
HFFF
SQUEE
SQUEE
IF YOU'RE GOING TO CREATE A QUADRATIC EQUATION, YOU SHOULD AT LEAST ADD A LITTLE TWIST TO IT—LIKE THIS.
ESPECIALLY IF IT'S FOR PREP SCHOOL STUDENTS.
NRRGH ...
SO THE PROFESSIONAL ASSASSIN LECTURES THE PROFESSIONAL TEACHER...
= 0 HAS TWO DIFFERENT SOLUTIONS
EQUATION A
You wrote it mirrored too! How fancy!
IN THREE MONTHS' TIME...
...THE ASSASSIN AND TEACHER HAD OPENED UP TO EACH OTHER. THEY WERE LIKE OLD FRIENDS.

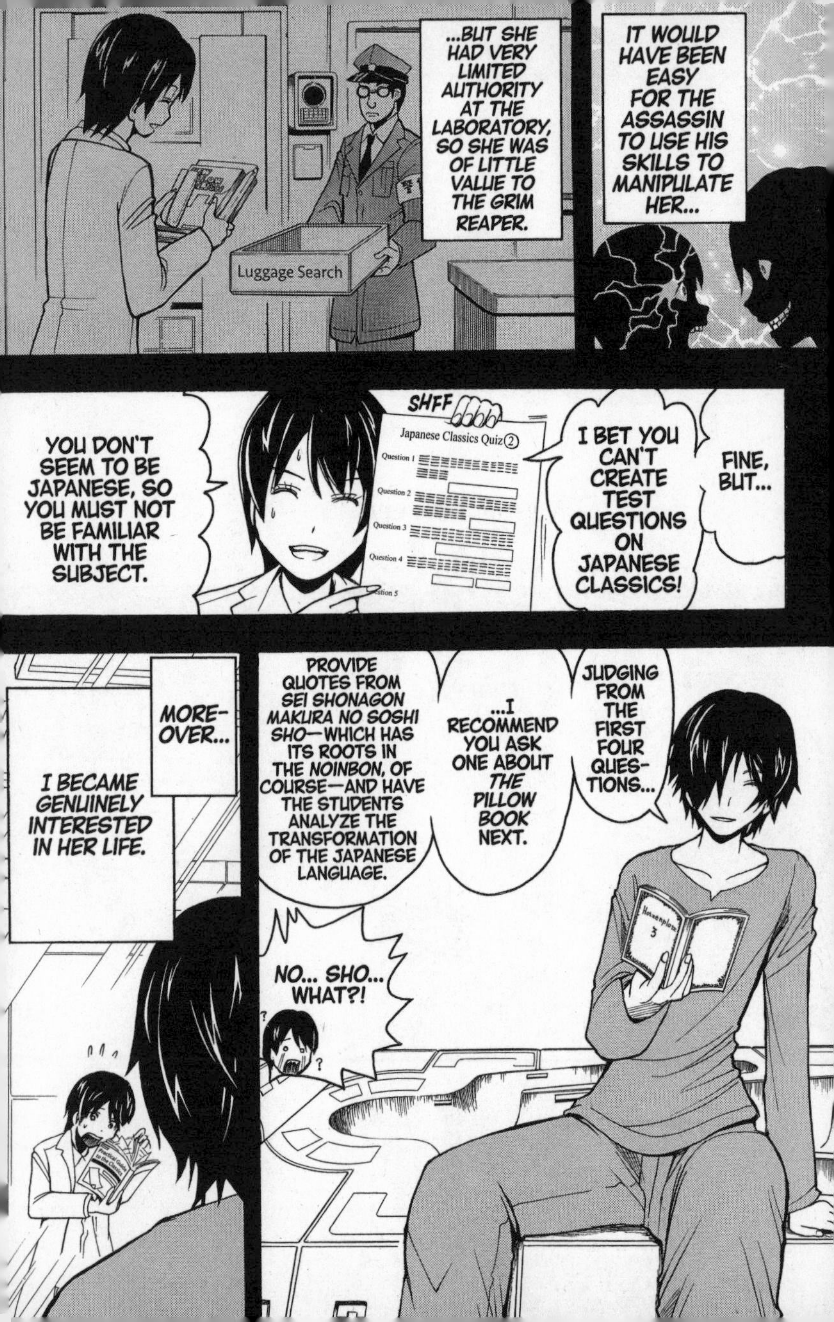
IT WOULD HAVE BEEN EASY FOR THE ASSASSIN TO USE HIS SKILLS TO MANIPULATE HER...
...BUT SHE HAD VERY LIMITED AUTHORITY AT THE LABORATORY, SO SHE WAS OF LITTLE VALUE TO THE GRIM REAPER.
Luggage Search
FINE, BUT...
I BET YOU CAN'T CREATE TEST QUESTIONS ON JAPANESE CLASSICS!
SHFF
Japanese Classics Quiz ②
Question 1
Question 2
Question 3
Question 4
YOU DON'T SEEM TO BE JAPANESE, SO YOU MUST NOT BE FAMILIAR WITH THE SUBJECT.
JUDGING FROM THE FIRST FOUR QUES-TIONS...
...I RECOMMEND YOU ASK ONE ABOUT *THE PILLOW BOOK* NEXT.
PROVIDE QUOTES FROM SEI SHONAGON *MAKURA NO SOSHI SHO*—WHICH HAS ITS ROOTS IN THE *NOINBON*, OF COURSE—AND HAVE THE STUDENTS ANALYZE THE TRANSFORMATION OF THE JAPANESE LANGUAGE.
NO... SHO... WHAT?!
MORE-OVER...
I BECAME GENUINELY INTERESTED IN HER LIFE.

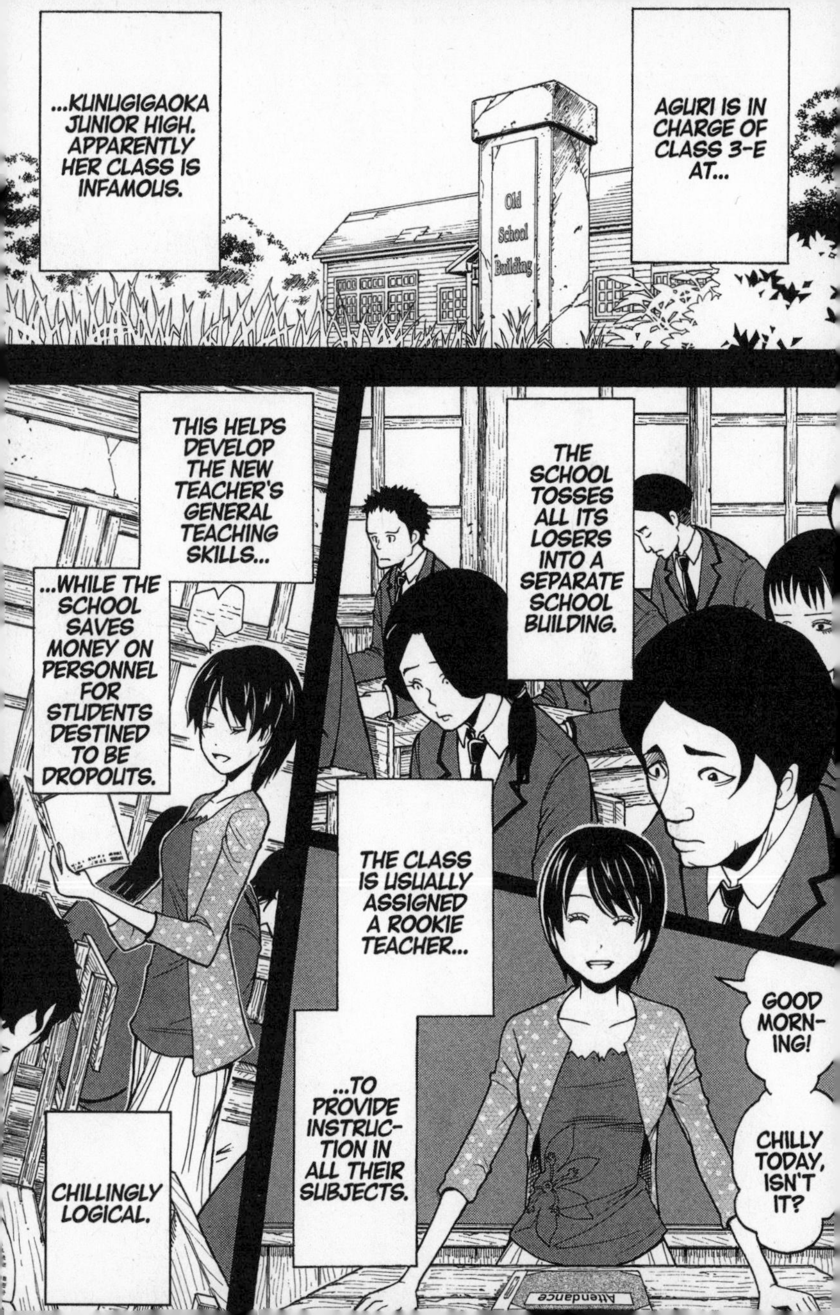
AGURI IS IN CHARGE OF CLASS 3-E AT...
...KUNUGIGAOKA JUNIOR HIGH. APPARENTLY HER CLASS IS INFAMOUS.
Old School Building
THE SCHOOL TOSSES ALL ITS LOSERS INTO A SEPARATE SCHOOL BUILDING.
THE CLASS IS USUALLY ASSIGNED A ROOKIE TEACHER...
...TO PROVIDE INSTRUCTION IN ALL THEIR SUBJECTS.
GOOD MORNING!
CHILLY TODAY, ISN'T IT?
Attendance
THIS HELPS DEVELOP THE NEW TEACHER'S GENERAL TEACHING SKILLS...
...WHILE THE SCHOOL SAVES MONEY ON PERSONNEL FOR STUDENTS DESTINED TO BE DROPOUTS.
CHILLINGLY LOGICAL.

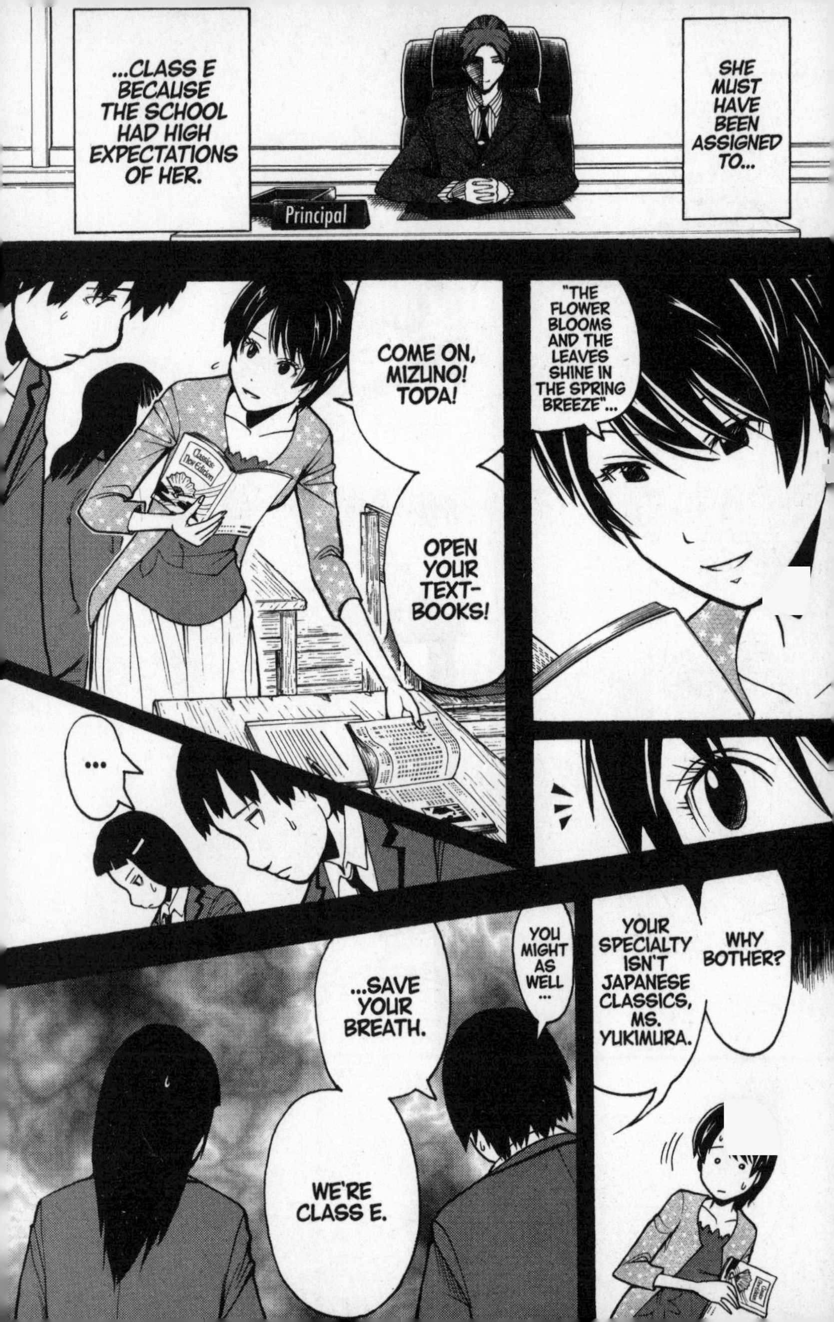
SHE MUST HAVE BEEN ASSIGNED TO...
...CLASS E BECAUSE THE SCHOOL HAD HIGH EXPECTATIONS OF HER.
Principal
"THE FLOWER BLOOMS AND THE LEAVES SHINE IN THE SPRING BREEZE"...
COME ON, MIZUNO! TODA!
OPEN YOUR TEXT-BOOKS!
Classics New Edition
...
WHY BOTHER?
YOUR SPECIALTY ISN'T JAPANESE CLASSICS, MS. YUKIMURA.
YOU MIGHT AS WELL...
...SAVE YOUR BREATH.
WE'RE CLASS E.

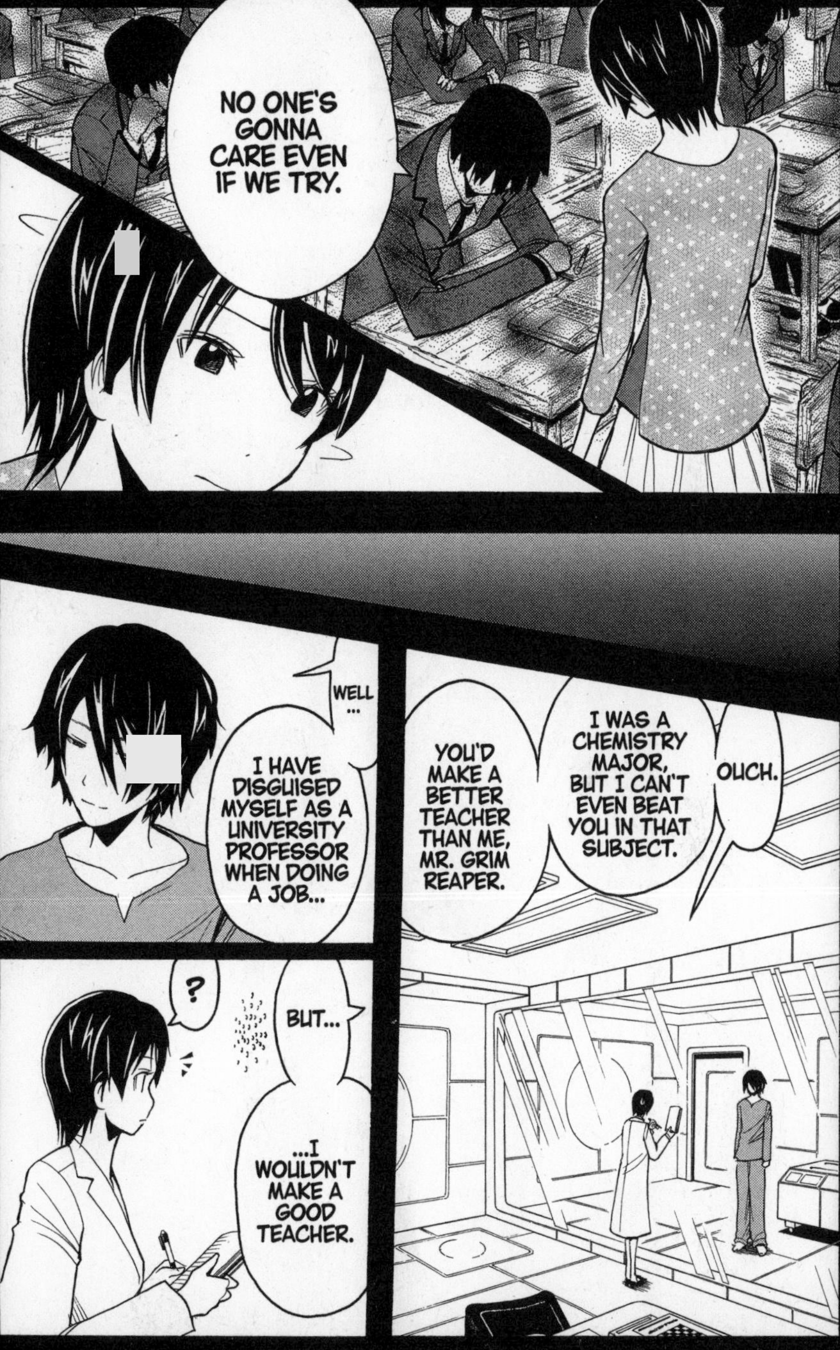
NO ONE'S GONNA CARE EVEN IF WE TRY.
OUCH.
I WAS A CHEMISTRY MAJOR, BUT I CAN'T EVEN BEAT YOU IN THAT SUBJECT.
YOU'D MAKE A BETTER TEACHER THAN ME, MR. GRIM REAPER.
WELL...
I HAVE DISGUISED MYSELF AS A UNIVERSITY PROFESSOR WHEN DOING A JOB...
?
BUT...
...I WOULDN'T MAKE A GOOD TEACHER.

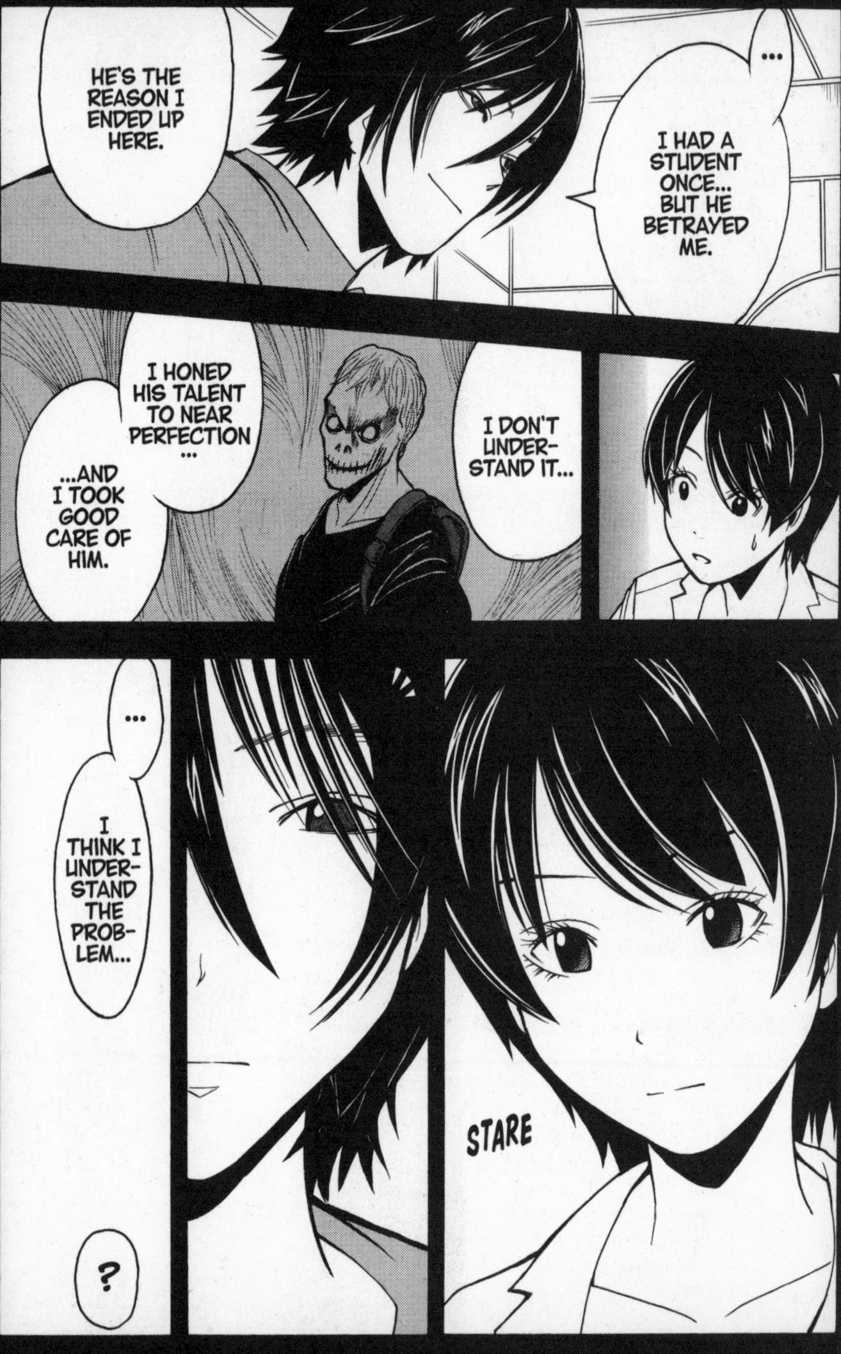
...
I HAD A STUDENT ONCE... BUT HE BETRAYED ME.
HE'S THE REASON I ENDED UP HERE.
I DON'T UNDER-STAND IT...
I HONED HIS TALENT TO NEAR PERFECTION ...
...AND I TOOK GOOD CARE OF HIM.
STARE
...
I THINK I UNDER-STAND THE PROB-LEM...
?

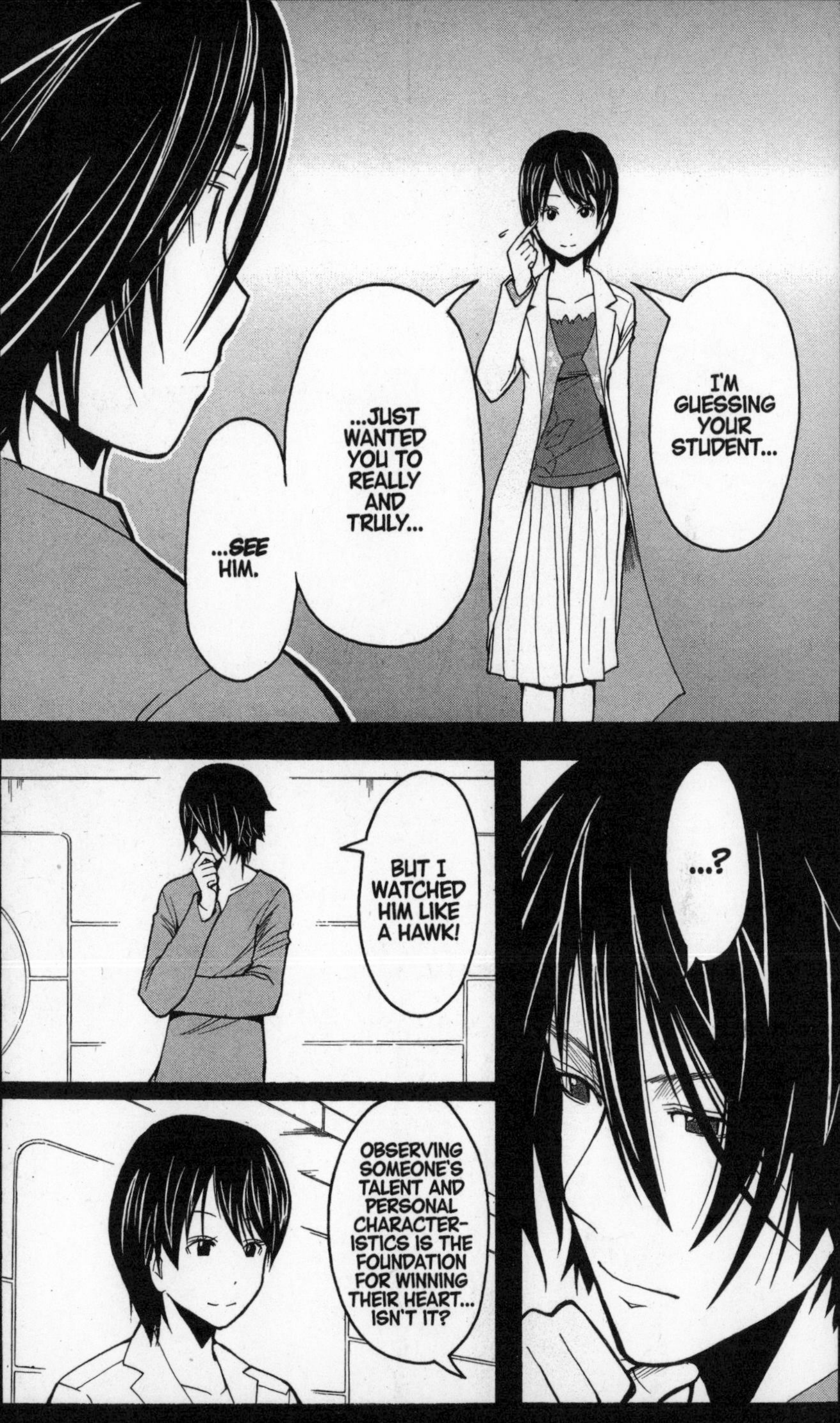
I'M GUESSING YOUR STUDENT...
...JUST WANTED YOU TO REALLY AND TRULY...
...SEE HIM.
...?
BUT I WATCHED HIM LIKE A HAWK!
OBSERVING SOMEONE'S TALENT AND PERSONAL CHARACTER-ISTICS IS THE FOUNDATION FOR WINNING THEIR HEART... ISN'T IT?

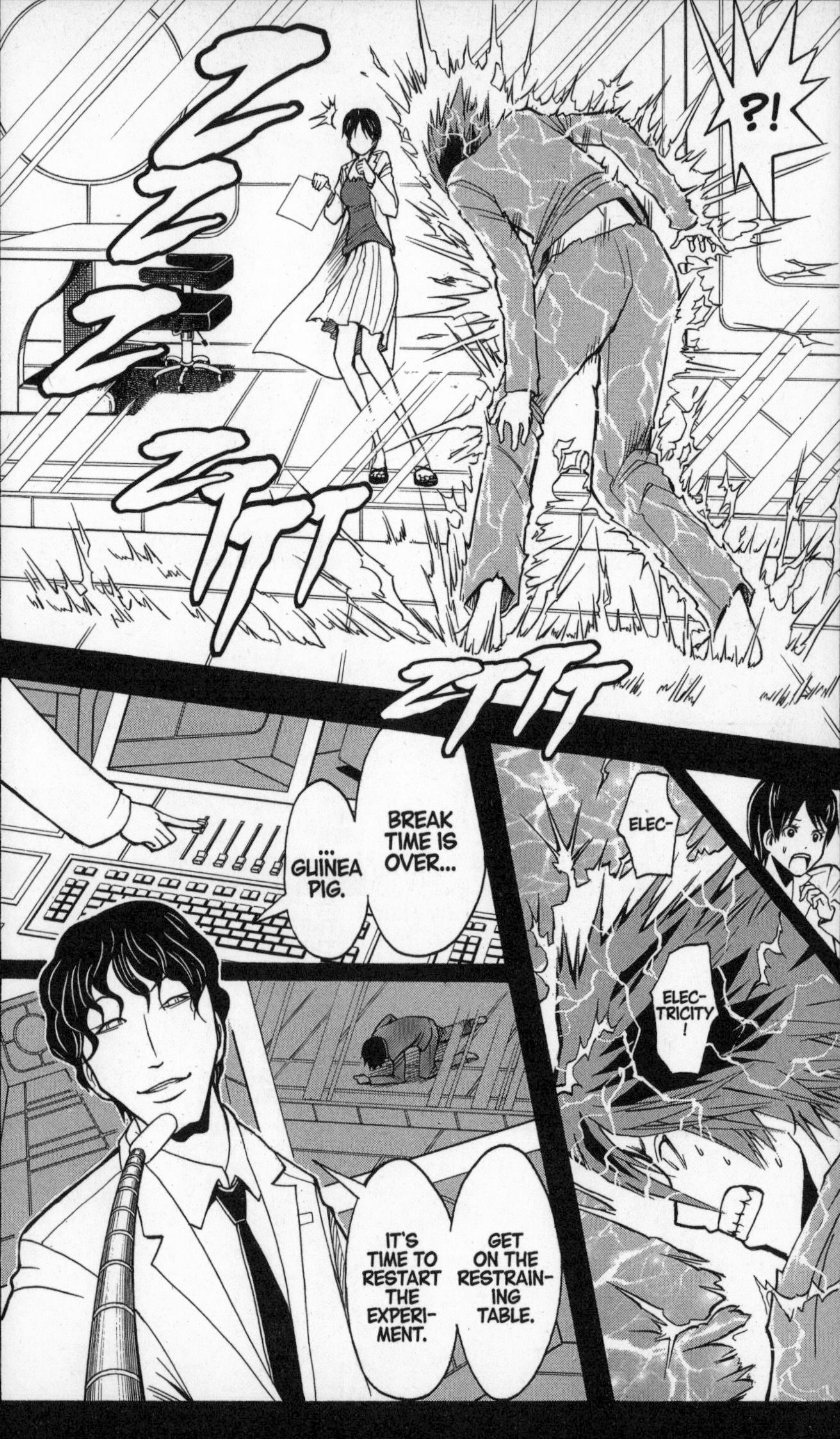
?!
ELEC-
ELEC-TRICITY!
BREAK TIME IS OVER...
... GUINEA PIG.
GET ON THE RESTRAIN-ING TABLE.
IT'S TIME TO RESTART THE EXPERI-MENT.

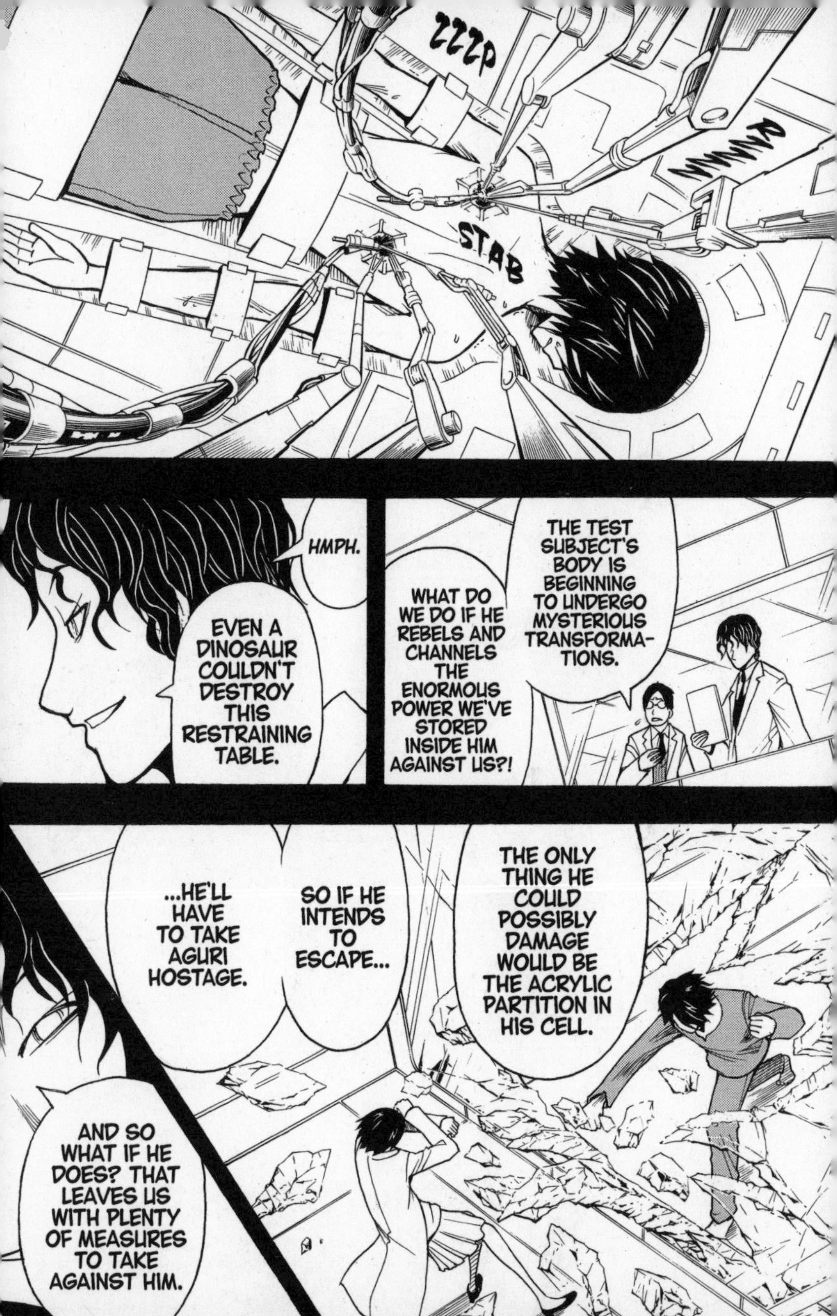
RNNNN
ZZZP
STAB
THE TEST SUBJECT'S BODY IS BEGINNING TO UNDERGO MYSTERIOUS TRANSFORMA-TIONS.
WHAT DO WE DO IF HE REBELS AND CHANNELS THE ENORMOUS POWER WE'VE STORED INSIDE HIM AGAINST US?!
HMPH.
EVEN A DINOSAUR COULDN'T DESTROY THIS RESTRAINING TABLE.
THE ONLY THING HE COULD POSSIBLY DAMAGE WOULD BE THE ACRYLIC PARTITION IN HIS CELL.
SO IF HE INTENDS TO ESCAPE...
...HE'LL HAVE TO TAKE AGURI HOSTAGE.
AND SO WHAT IF HE DOES? THAT LEAVES US WITH PLENTY OF MEASURES TO TAKE AGAINST HIM.

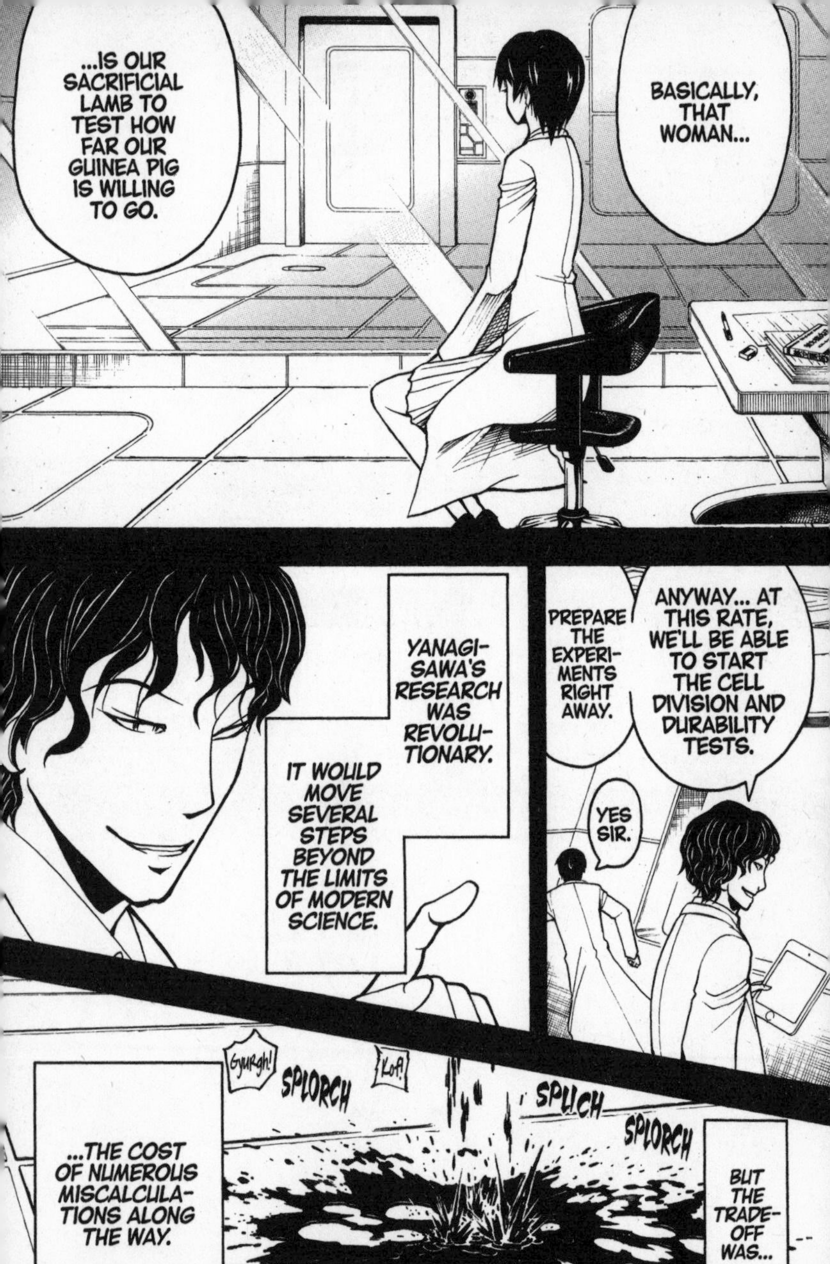
BASICALLY, THAT WOMAN...
...IS OUR SACRIFICIAL LAMB TO TEST HOW FAR OUR GUINEA PIG IS WILLING TO GO.
ANYWAY... AT THIS RATE, WE'LL BE ABLE TO START THE CELL DIVISION AND DURABILITY TESTS.
PREPARE THE EXPERIMENTS RIGHT AWAY.
YES SIR.
YANAGI-SAWA'S RESEARCH WAS REVOLU-TIONARY.
IT WOULD MOVE SEVERAL STEPS BEYOND THE LIMITS OF MODERN SCIENCE.
BUT THE TRADE-OFF WAS...
SPLORCH
SPLUCH
Kof!
SPLORCH
Gyurgh!
...THE COST OF NUMEROUS MISCALCULA-TIONS ALONG THE WAY.

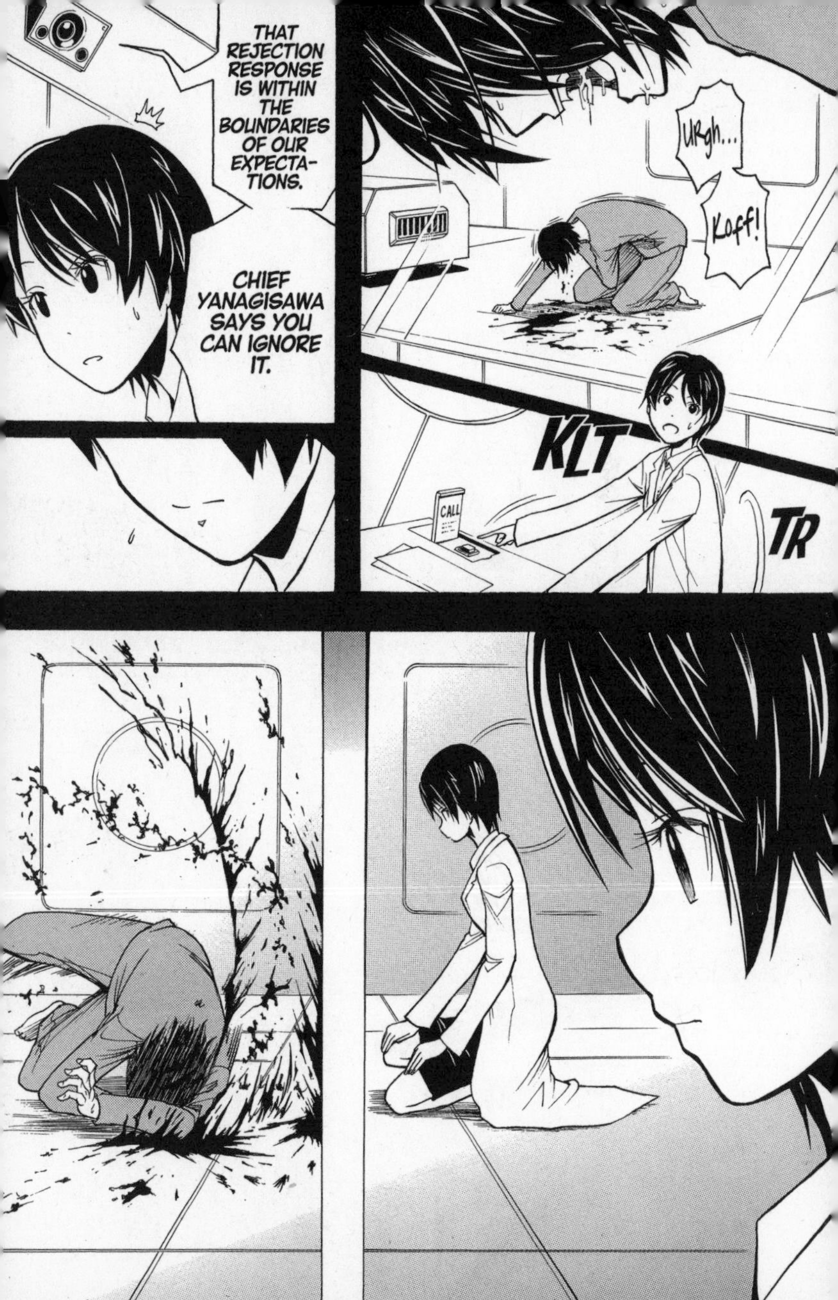
Urgh...
Koff!
THAT REJECTION RESPONSE IS WITHIN THE BOUNDARIES OF OUR EXPECTATIONS.
CHIEF YANAGISAWA SAYS YOU CAN IGNORE IT.
KLT
TR
CALL

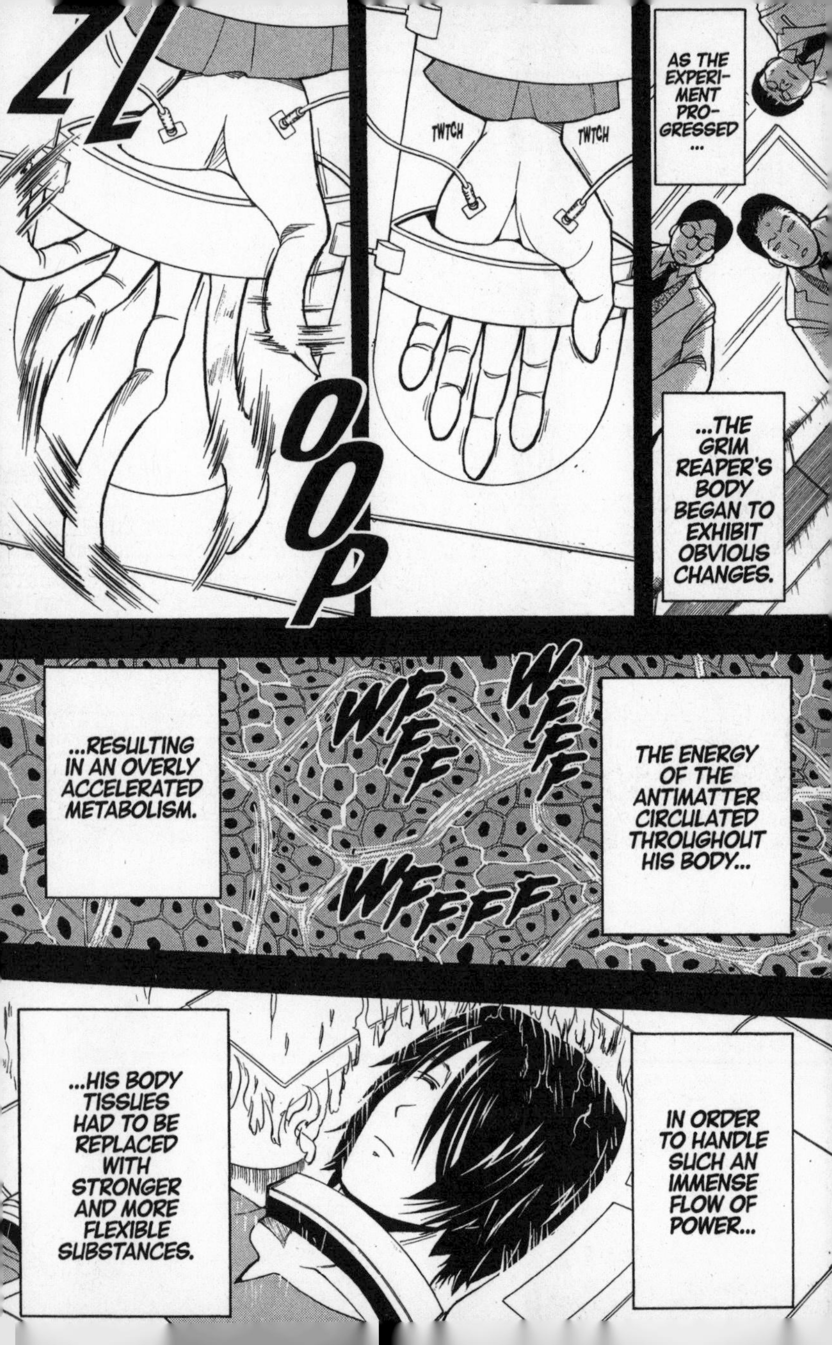
AS THE EXPERIMENT PROGRESSED...
...THE GRIM REAPER'S BODY BEGAN TO EXHIBIT OBVIOUS CHANGES.
TWTCH
TWTCH
ZZOOOP
THE ENERGY OF THE ANTIMATTER CIRCULATED THROUGHOUT HIS BODY...
WEFFF
WEFFF
WFFFFF
...RESULTING IN AN OVERLY ACCELERATED METABOLISM.
IN ORDER TO HANDLE SUCH AN IMMENSE FLOW OF POWER...
...HIS BODY TISSUES HAD TO BE REPLACED WITH STRONGER AND MORE FLEXIBLE SUBSTANCES.

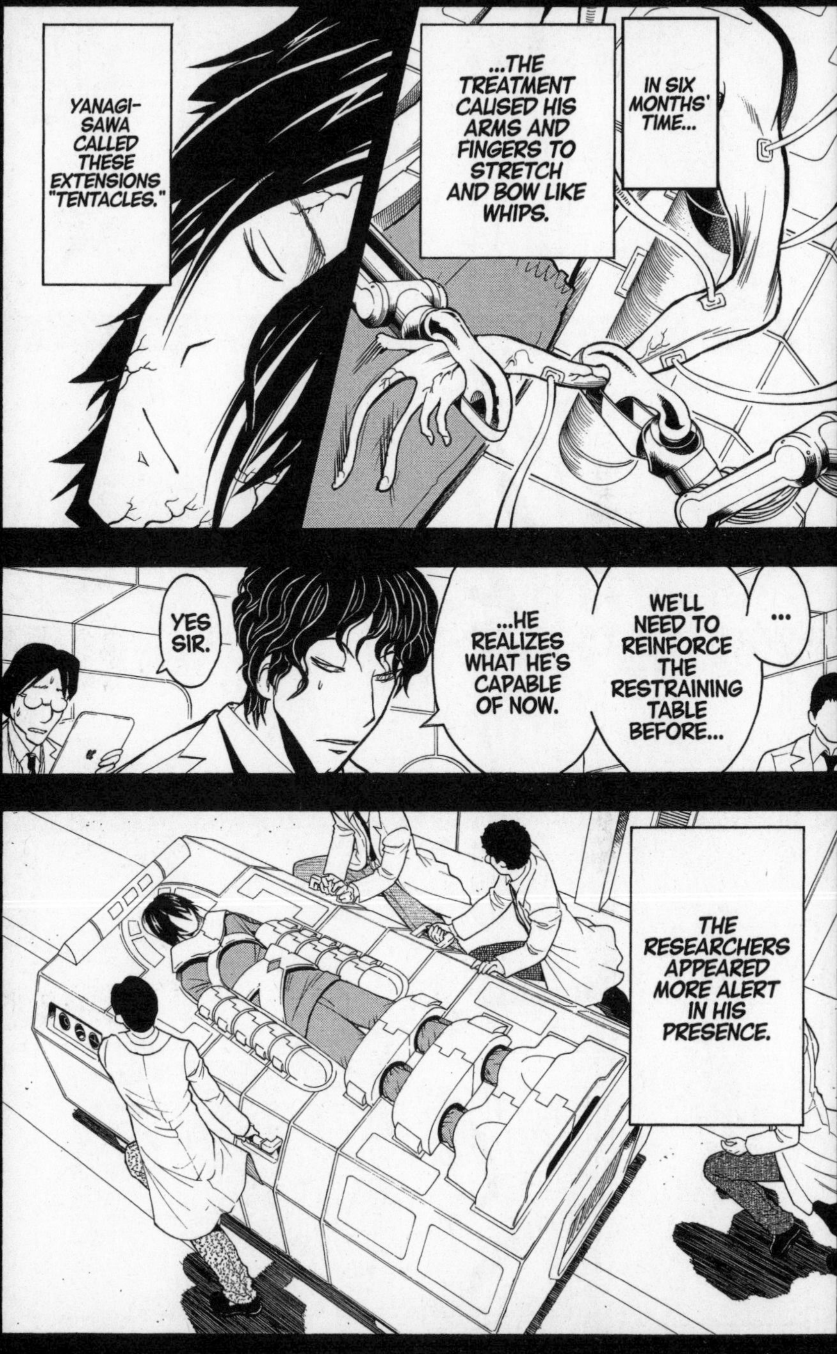
IN SIX MONTHS' TIME...
...THE TREATMENT CAUSED HIS ARMS AND FINGERS TO STRETCH AND BOW LIKE WHIPS.
YANAGI-SAWA CALLED THESE EXTENSIONS "TENTACLES."
...
WE'LL NEED TO REINFORCE THE RESTRAINING TABLE BEFORE...
...HE REALIZES WHAT HE'S CAPABLE OF NOW.
YES SIR.
THE RESEARCHERS APPEARED MORE ALERT IN HIS PRESENCE.

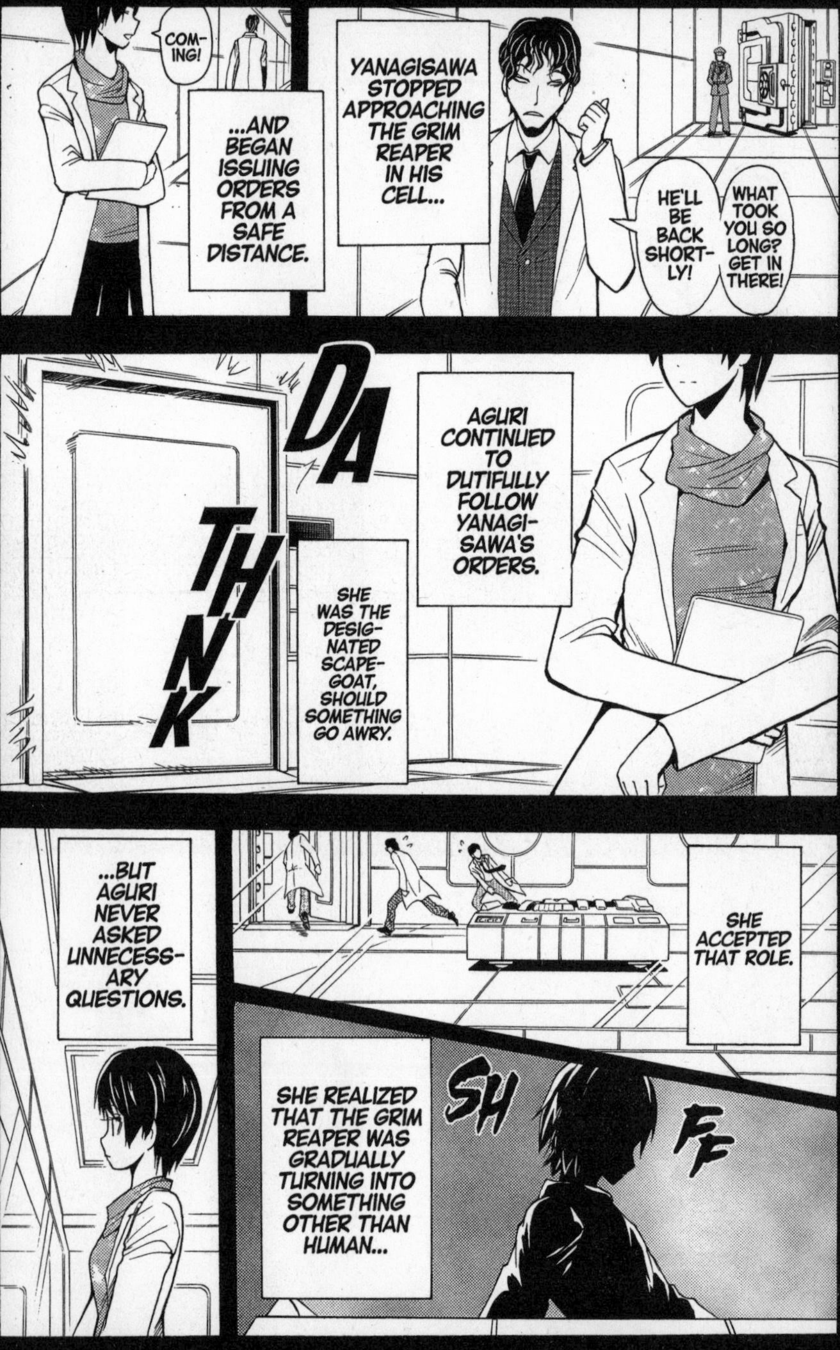
YANAGISAWA STOPPED APPROACHING THE GRIM REAPER IN HIS CELL...
WHAT TOOK YOU SO LONG? GET IN THERE!
HE'LL BE BACK SHORT-LY!
...AND BEGAN ISSUING ORDERS FROM A SAFE DISTANCE.
COM-ING!
AGURI CONTINUED TO DUTIFULLY FOLLOW YANAGI-SAWA'S ORDERS.
SHE WAS THE DESIG-NATED SCAPE-GOAT, SHOULD SOMETHING GO AWRY.
DA
THNK
SHE ACCEPTED THAT ROLE.
...BUT AGURI NEVER ASKED UNNECESS-ARY QUESTIONS.
SHFF
SHE REALIZED THAT THE GRIM REAPER WAS GRADUALLY TURNING INTO SOMETHING OTHER THAN HUMAN...

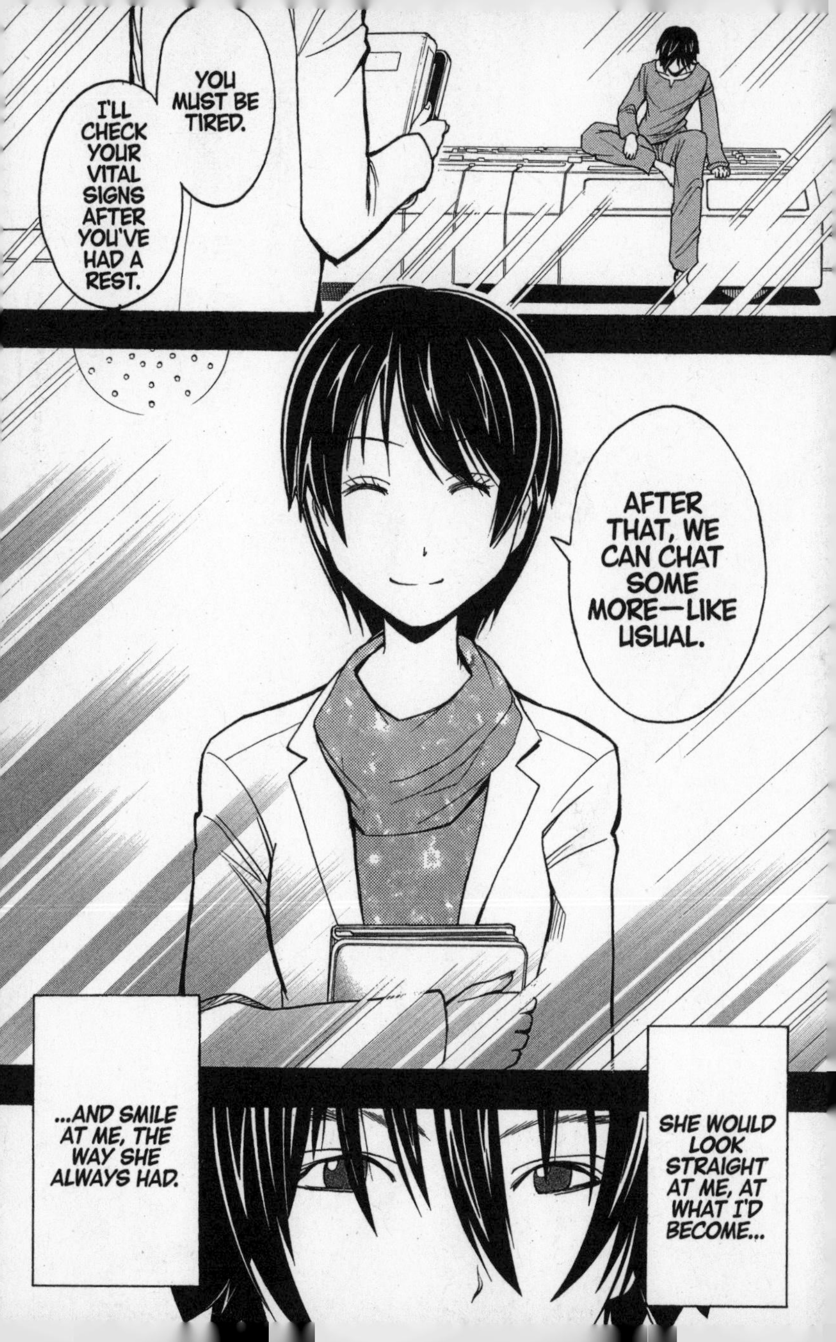
YOU MUST BE TIRED.
I'LL CHECK YOUR VITAL SIGNS AFTER YOU'VE HAD A REST.
AFTER THAT, WE CAN CHAT SOME MORE—LIKE USUAL.
SHE WOULD LOOK STRAIGHT AT ME, AT WHAT I'D BECOME...
...AND SMILE AT ME, THE WAY SHE ALWAYS HAD.

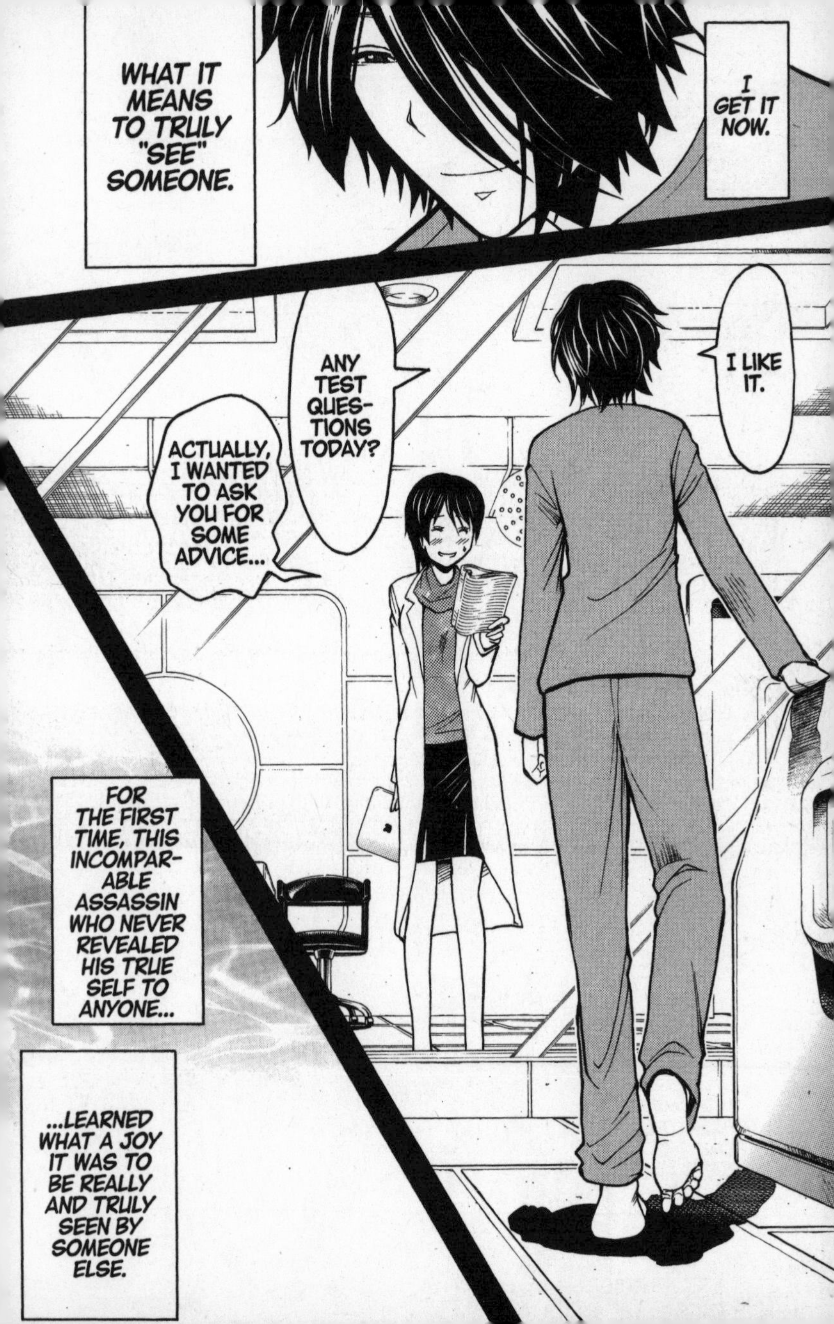
I GET IT NOW.
WHAT IT MEANS TO TRULY "SEE" SOMEONE.
I LIKE IT.
ANY TEST QUESTIONS TODAY?
ACTUALLY, I WANTED TO ASK YOU FOR SOME ADVICE...
FOR THE FIRST TIME, THIS INCOMPARABLE ASSASSIN WHO NEVER REVEALED HIS TRUE SELF TO ANYONE...
...LEARNED WHAT A JOY IT WAS TO BE REALLY AND TRULY SEEN BY SOMEONE ELSE.

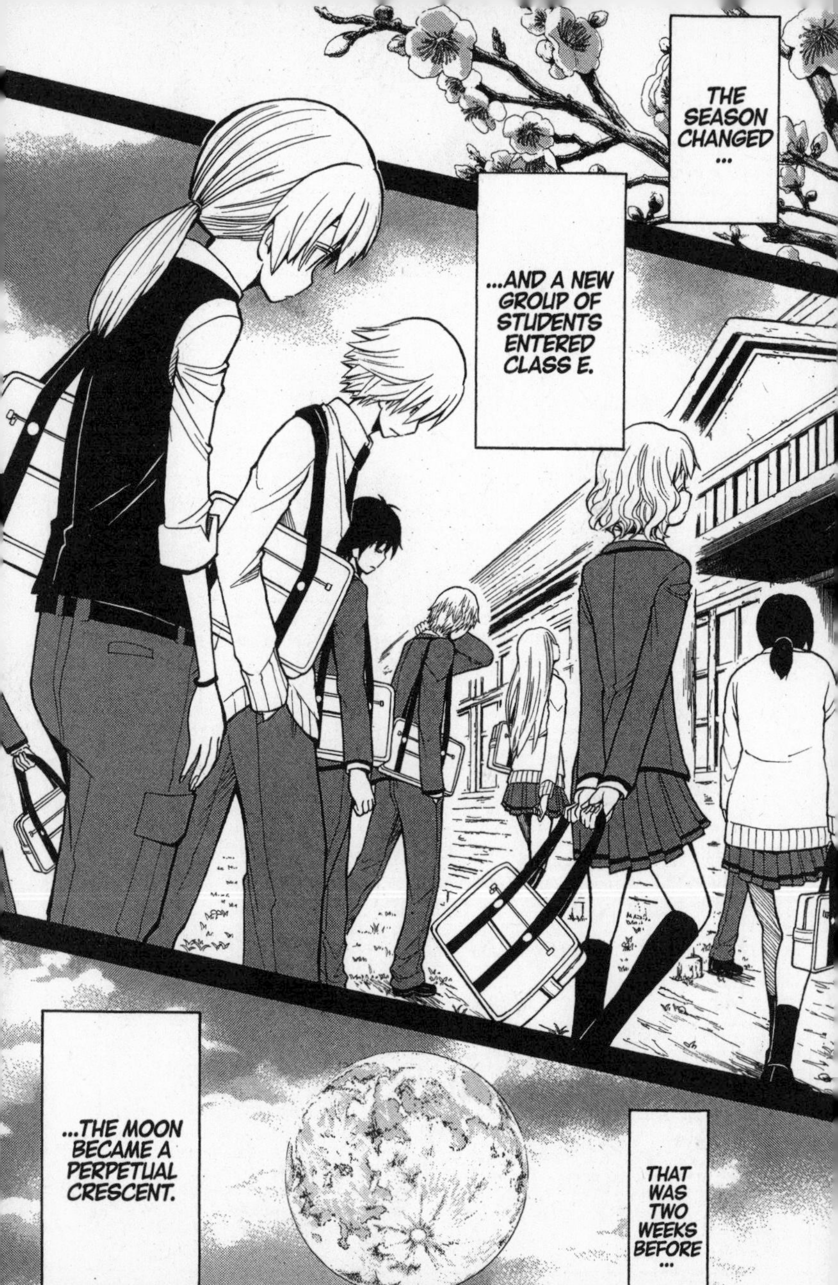
THE SEASON CHANGED ...
...AND A NEW GROUP OF STUDENTS ENTERED CLASS E.
THAT WAS TWO WEEKS BEFORE ...
...THE MOON BECAME A PERPETUAL CRESCENT.

Mr. Karasuma's Report Card ③

Trap Making	(Evaluated by Mr. Karasuma in terms of knowledge, skill, and creativity with a maximum of 10 points)

Camouflaged Traps

Place		Points
1st Place	Sosuke Sugaya	10 Points
2nd Place	Hinano Kurahashi	8 Points
3rd Place	Taisei Yoshida	7 Points
4th Place	Kirara Hazama	5 Points
4th Place	Koki Mimura	5 Points

Highlight Sosuke Sugaya

The camouflage he applies to his traps literally makes them invisible. You could even call the effect an optical illusion. His traps often deceive his opponents. His work is a good reminder to me as an instructor to teach the effectiveness of the use of color in an assassination.

Wire & Net Traps

Place		Points
1st Place	Sumire Hara	10 Points
2nd Place	Toka Yada	8 Points
3rd Place	Kaede Kayano	7 Points
4th Place	Koki Mimura	6 Points
4th Place	Kotaro Takebayashi	6 Points

Highlight Sumire Hara

Students skilled in handicrafts tend to excel at this type of trap. Note: the whereabouts of the boar she caught is classified.

Specialty Traps

Place		
1st Place	Kotaro Takebayashi	10 Points (Explosives)
1st Place	Manami Okuda	10 Points (Chemicals)
3rd Place	Koki Mimura	8 Points (Video Images)
4th Place	Hinano Kurahashi	7 Points (Living Creatures)
4th Place	Taiga Okajima	7 Points (Book Layout)

Highlight Kotaro Takebayashi

A student with a unique trapping skill that no one else can replicate. His expertise in explosives has reduced my burden as I no longer need to handle them myself, and has made him an essential member of the assassination team.

Mechanical Tricks

Place		Points
1st Place	Itona Horibe	10 Points
1st Place	Autonomous Intelligence Fixed Artillery	10 Points
3rd Place	Taisei Yoshida	8 Points
4th Place	Taiga Okajima	6 Points
4th Place	Rio Nakamura	6 Points

Highlight Itona Horibe

Ritsu handles the digital design and Yoshida the larger mechanics, but it's Horibe who gives form to the clever ideas of these expert techies. There is no doubt that this transfer student has strengthened the bonds in Class E.

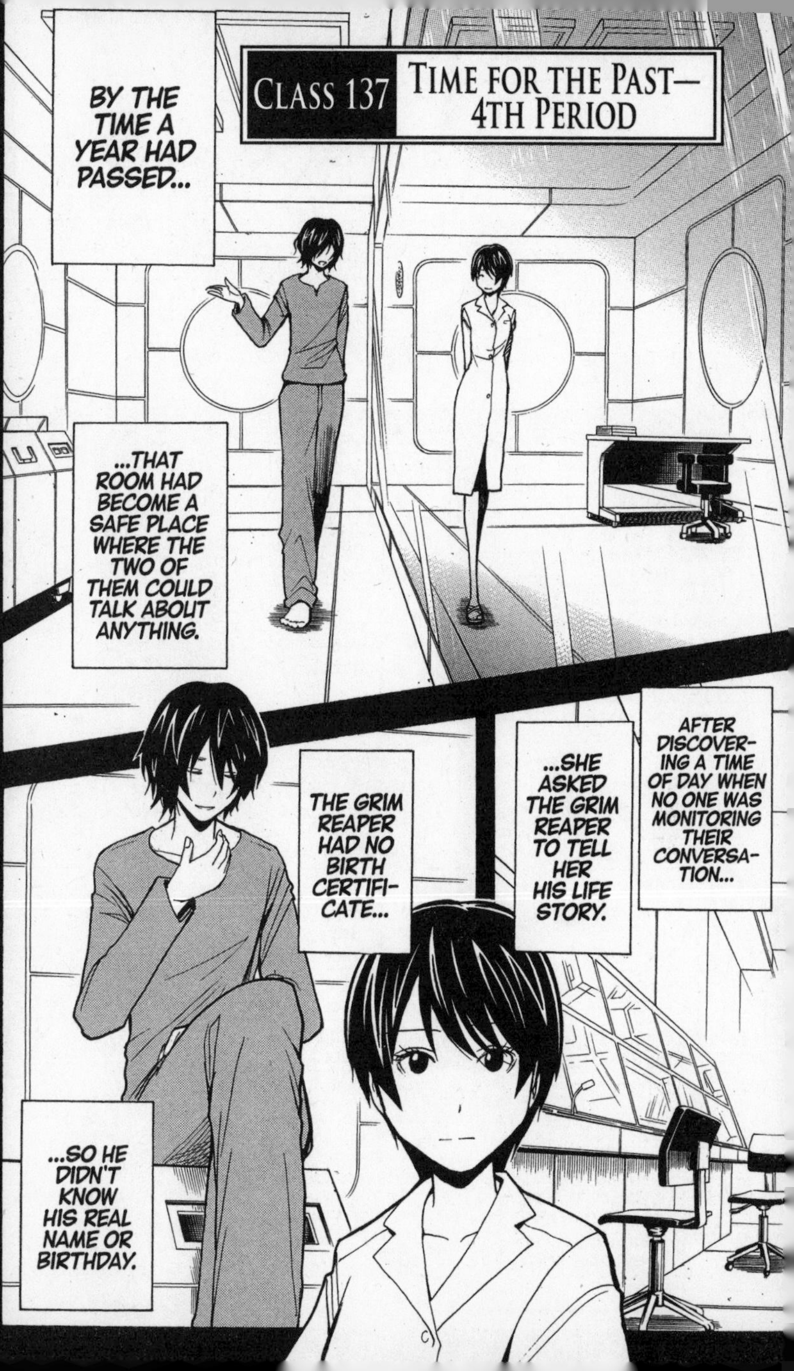
CLASS 137 TIME FOR THE PAST— 4TH PERIOD
BY THE TIME A YEAR HAD PASSED...
...THAT ROOM HAD BECOME A SAFE PLACE WHERE THE TWO OF THEM COULD TALK ABOUT ANYTHING.
AFTER DISCOVERING A TIME OF DAY WHEN NO ONE WAS MONITORING THEIR CONVERSATION...
...SHE ASKED THE GRIM REAPER TO TELL HER HIS LIFE STORY.
THE GRIM REAPER HAD NO BIRTH CERTIFICATE...
...SO HE DIDN'T KNOW HIS REAL NAME OR BIRTHDAY.

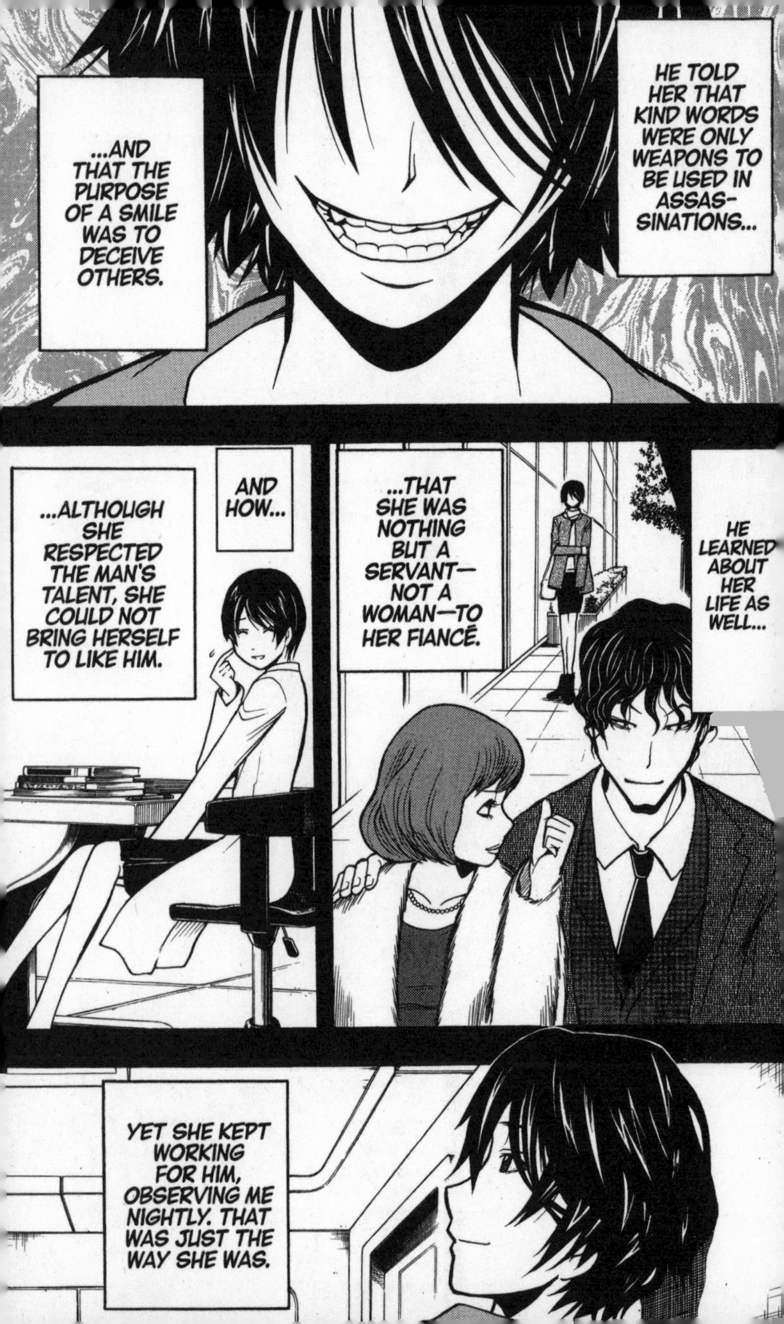
HE TOLD HER THAT KIND WORDS WERE ONLY WEAPONS TO BE USED IN ASSAS-SINATIONS...
...AND THAT THE PURPOSE OF A SMILE WAS TO DECEIVE OTHERS.
HE LEARNED ABOUT HER LIFE AS WELL...
...THAT SHE WAS NOTHING BUT A SERVANT—NOT A WOMAN—TO HER FIANCÉ.
AND HOW...
...ALTHOUGH SHE RESPECTED THE MAN'S TALENT, SHE COULD NOT BRING HERSELF TO LIKE HIM.
YET SHE KEPT WORKING FOR HIM, OBSERVING ME NIGHTLY. THAT WAS JUST THE WAY SHE WAS.

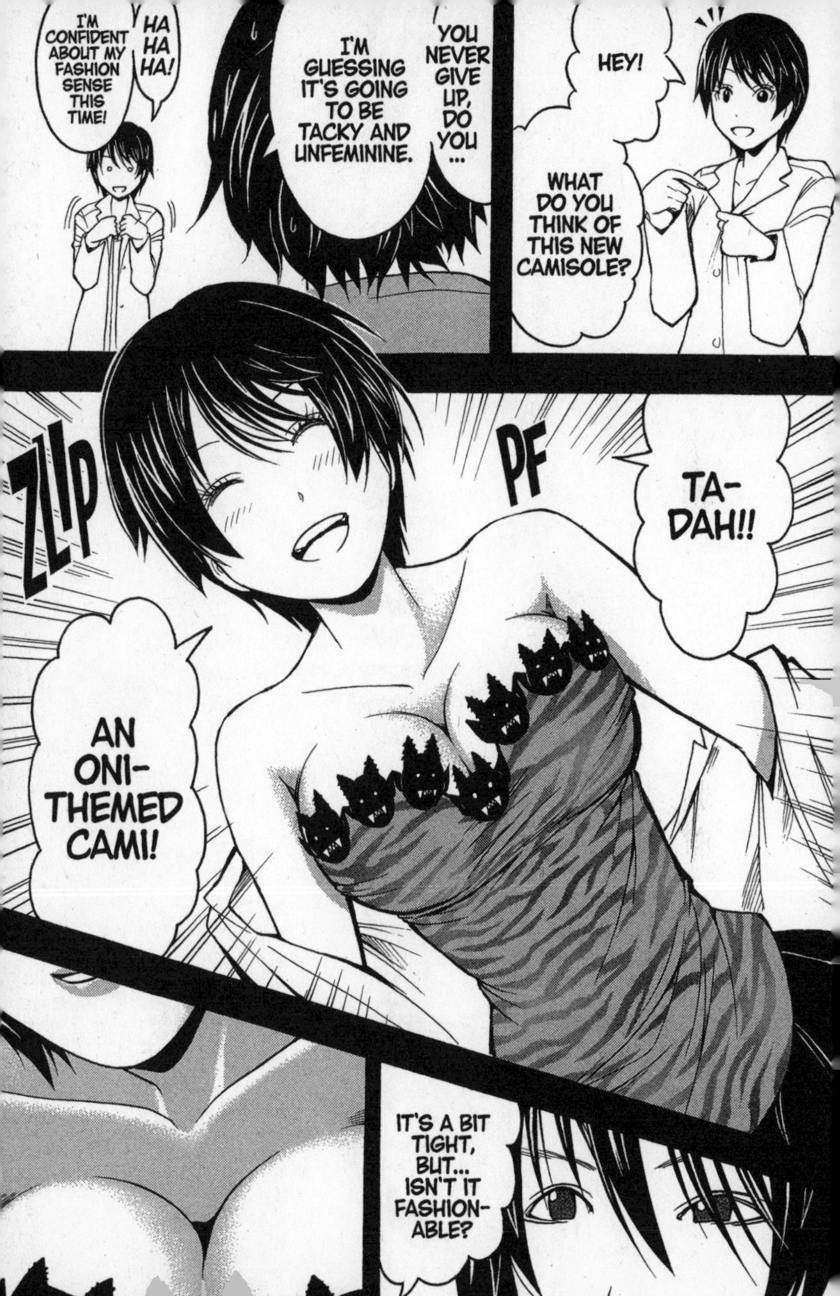
HEY!
WHAT DO YOU THINK OF THIS NEW CAMISOLE?
YOU NEVER GIVE UP, DO YOU...
I'M GUESSING IT'S GOING TO BE TACKY AND UNFEMININE.
HA HA HA!
I'M CONFIDENT ABOUT MY FASHION SENSE THIS TIME!
TA-DAH!!
PF
ZZIP
AN ONI-THEMED CAMI!
IT'S A BIT TIGHT, BUT... ISN'T IT FASHIONABLE?

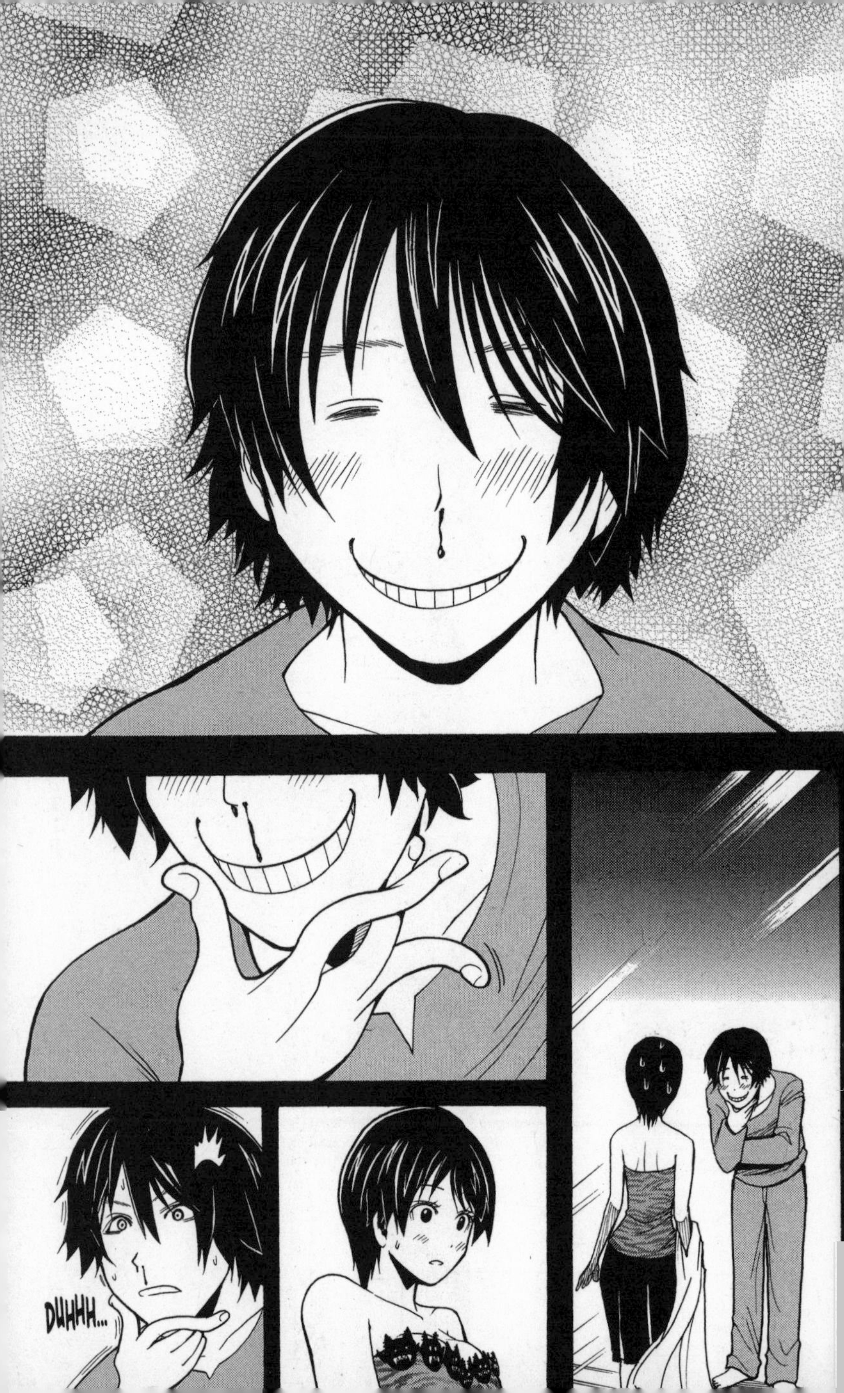
DUHHH...

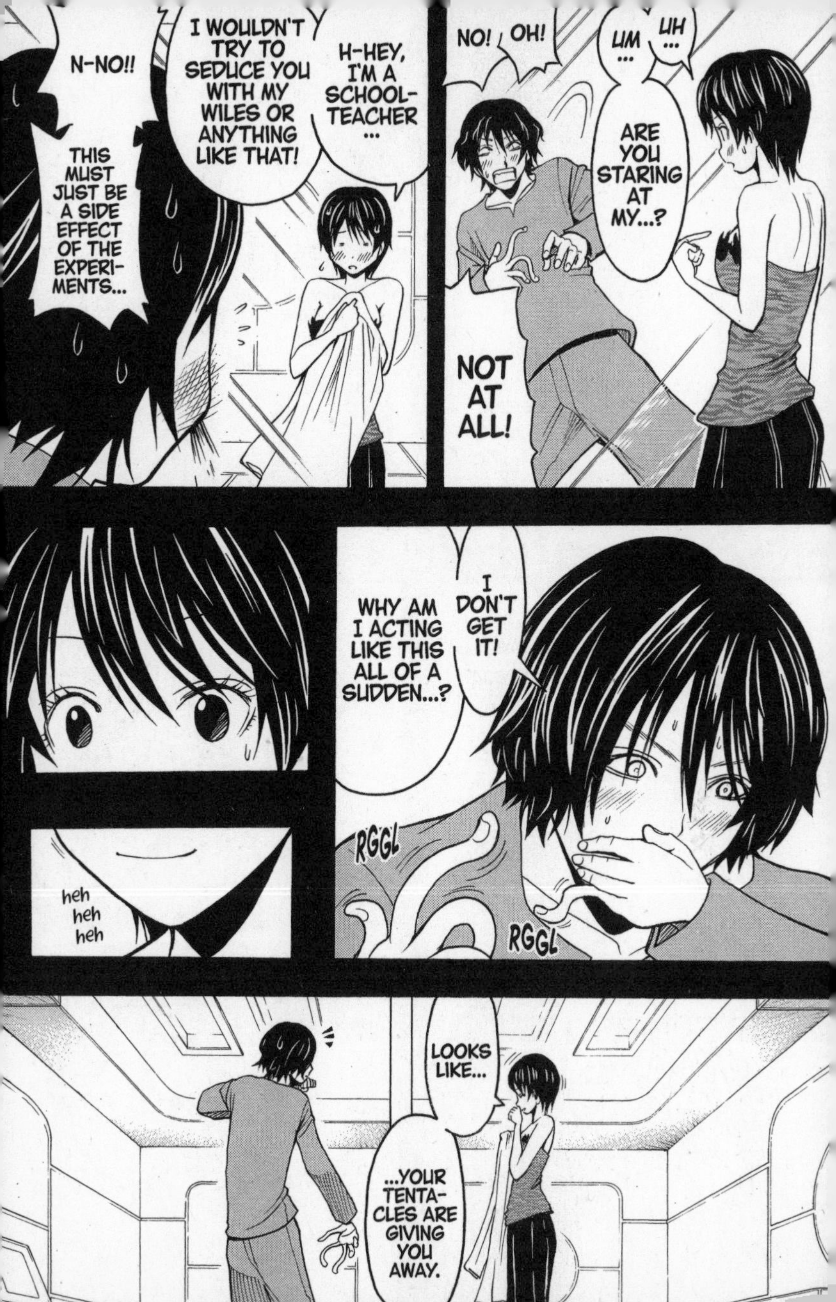
UH ...
UM ...
ARE YOU STARING AT MY...?
NO! OH!
NOT AT ALL!
H-HEY, I'M A SCHOOL-TEACHER ...
I WOULDN'T TRY TO SEDUCE YOU WITH MY WILES OR ANYTHING LIKE THAT!
N-NO!!
THIS MUST JUST BE A SIDE EFFECT OF THE EXPERI-MENTS...
I DON'T GET IT!
WHY AM I ACTING LIKE THIS ALL OF A SUDDEN...?
RGGL
RGGL
heh heh heh
LOOKS LIKE...
...YOUR TENTA-CLES ARE GIVING YOU AWAY.

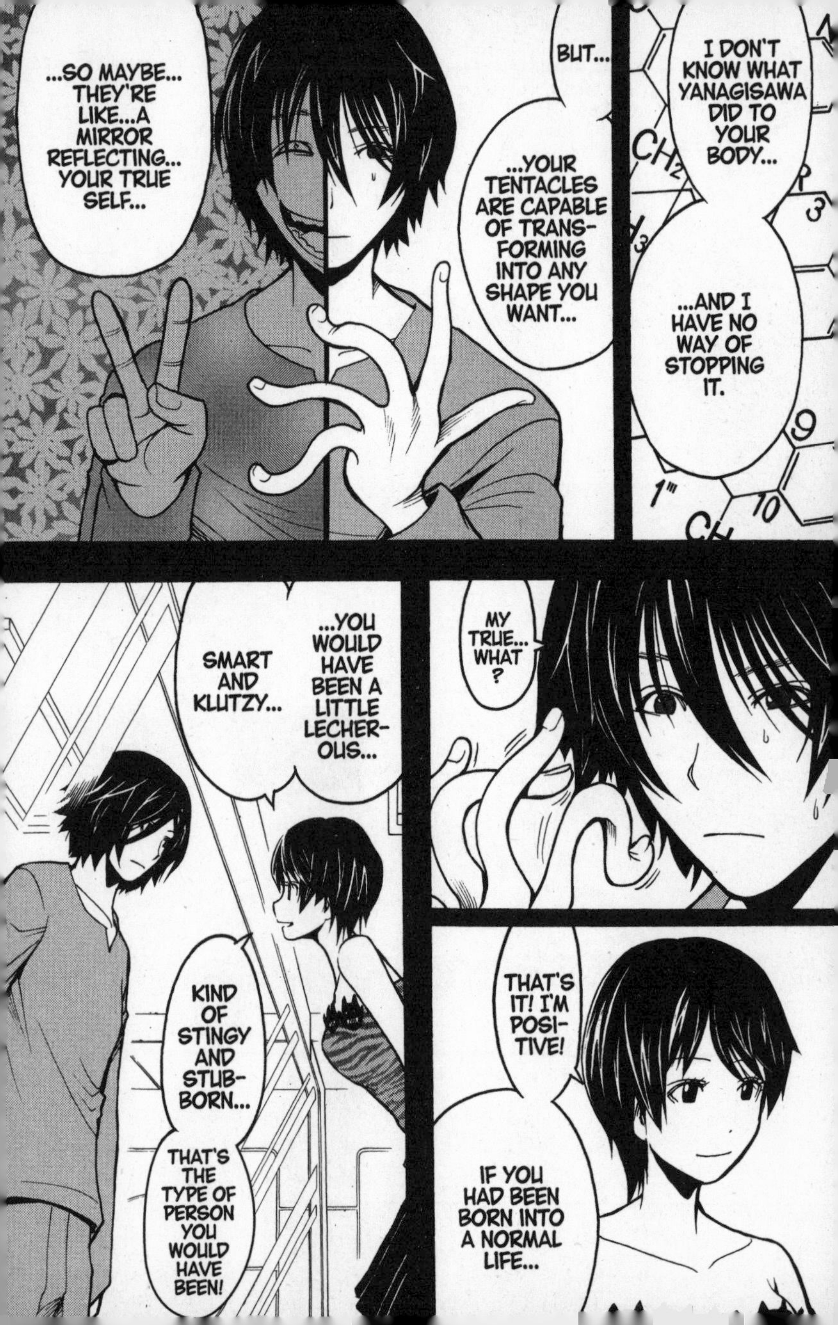
I DON'T KNOW WHAT YANAGISAWA DID TO YOUR BODY...
...AND I HAVE NO WAY OF STOPPING IT.
BUT...
...YOUR TENTACLES ARE CAPABLE OF TRANSFORMING INTO ANY SHAPE YOU WANT...
...SO MAYBE... THEY'RE LIKE...A MIRROR REFLECTING... YOUR TRUE SELF...
MY TRUE... WHAT?
THAT'S IT! I'M POSITIVE!
IF YOU HAD BEEN BORN INTO A NORMAL LIFE...
...YOU WOULD HAVE BEEN A LITTLE LECHEROUS...
SMART AND KLUTZY...
KIND OF STINGY AND STUBBORN...
THAT'S THE TYPE OF PERSON YOU WOULD HAVE BEEN!

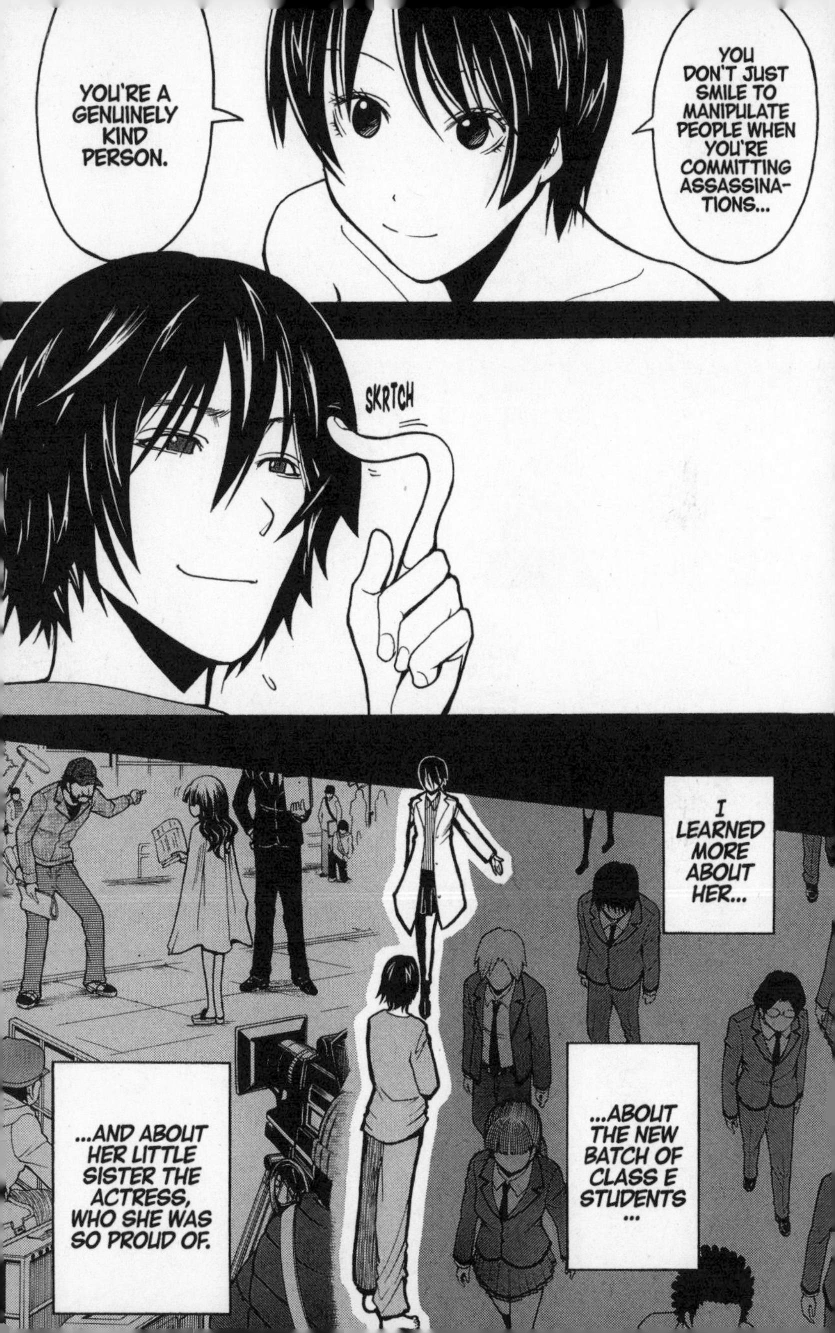
YOU DON'T JUST SMILE TO MANIPULATE PEOPLE WHEN YOU'RE COMMITTING ASSASSINA-TIONS...
YOU'RE A GENUINELY KIND PERSON.
SKRTCH
I LEARNED MORE ABOUT HER...
...ABOUT THE NEW BATCH OF CLASS E STUDENTS...
...AND ABOUT HER LITTLE SISTER THE ACTRESS, WHO SHE WAS SO PROUD OF.

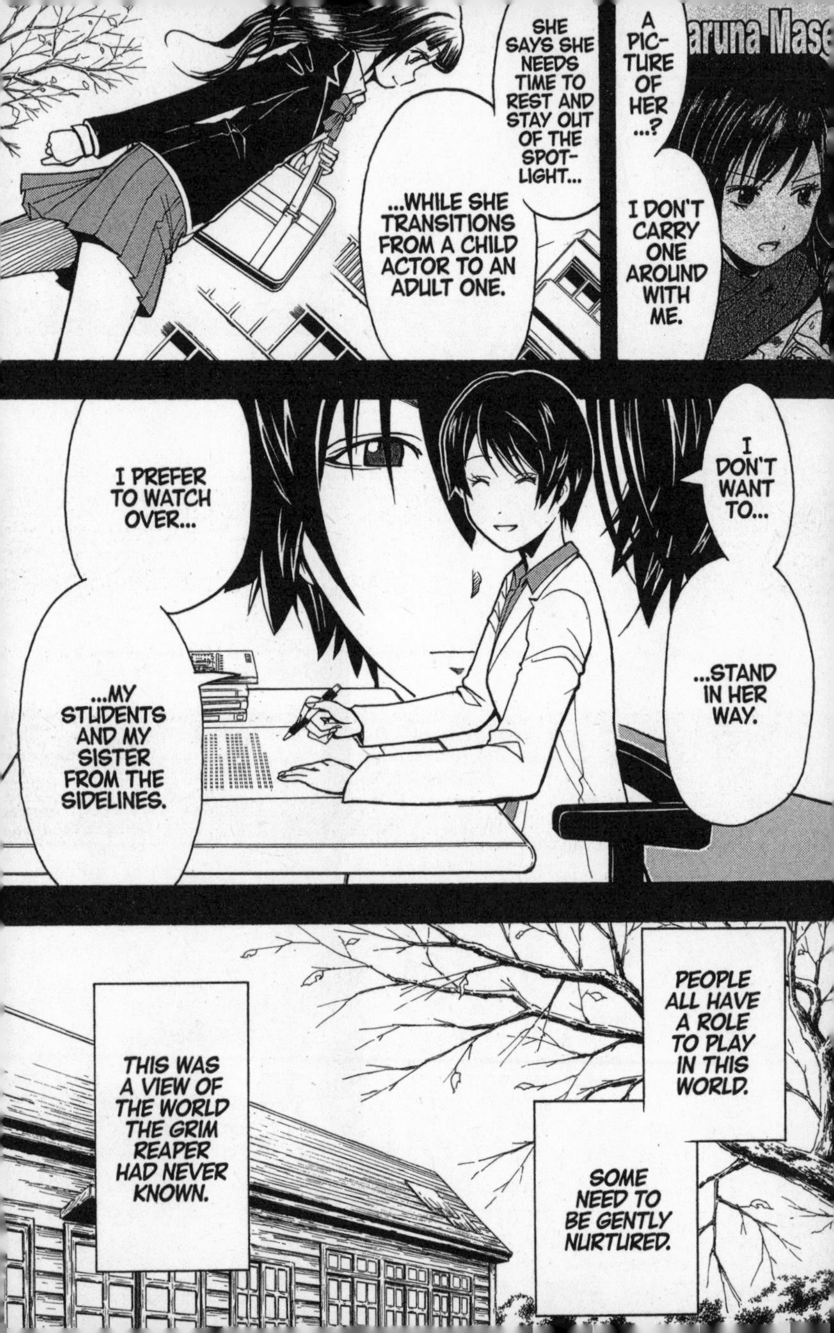
aruna Mase
A PICTURE OF HER...?
I DON'T CARRY ONE AROUND WITH ME.
SHE SAYS SHE NEEDS TIME TO REST AND STAY OUT OF THE SPOTLIGHT...
...WHILE SHE TRANSITIONS FROM A CHILD ACTOR TO AN ADULT ONE.
I DON'T WANT TO...
...STAND IN HER WAY.
I PREFER TO WATCH OVER...
...MY STUDENTS AND MY SISTER FROM THE SIDELINES.
PEOPLE ALL HAVE A ROLE TO PLAY IN THIS WORLD.
SOME NEED TO BE GENTLY NURTURED.
THIS WAS A VIEW OF THE WORLD THE GRIM REAPER HAD NEVER KNOWN.

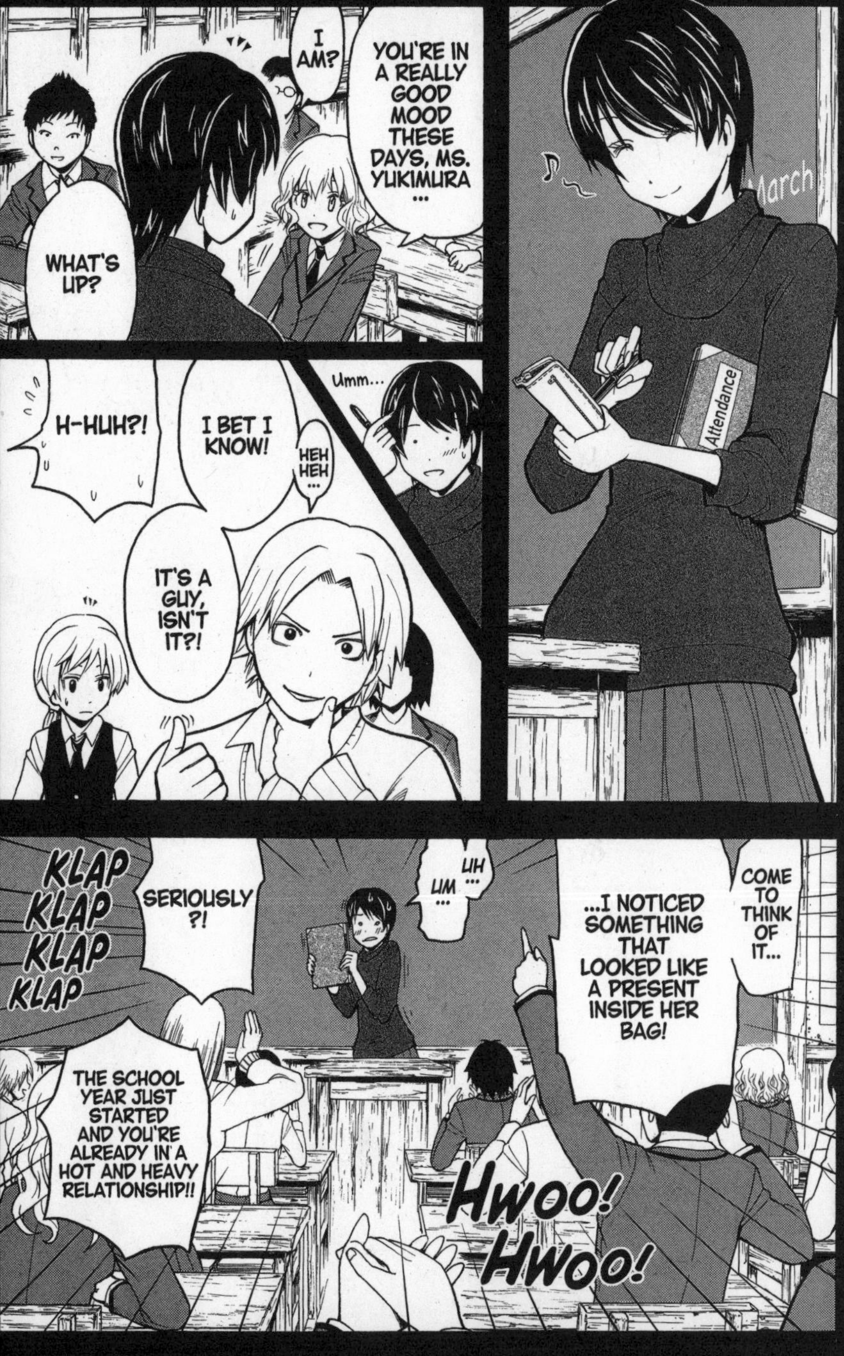
March
Attendance
YOU'RE IN A REALLY GOOD MOOD THESE DAYS, MS. YUKIMURA...
I AM?
WHAT'S UP?
Umm...
HEH HEH...
I BET I KNOW!
H-HUH?!
IT'S A GUY, ISN'T IT?!
COME TO THINK OF IT...
...I NOTICED SOMETHING THAT LOOKED LIKE A PRESENT INSIDE HER BAG!
UH...
UM...
SERIOUSLY?!
KLAP KLAP KLAP KLAP
THE SCHOOL YEAR JUST STARTED AND YOU'RE ALREADY IN A HOT AND HEAVY RELATIONSHIP!!
HWOO! HWOO!

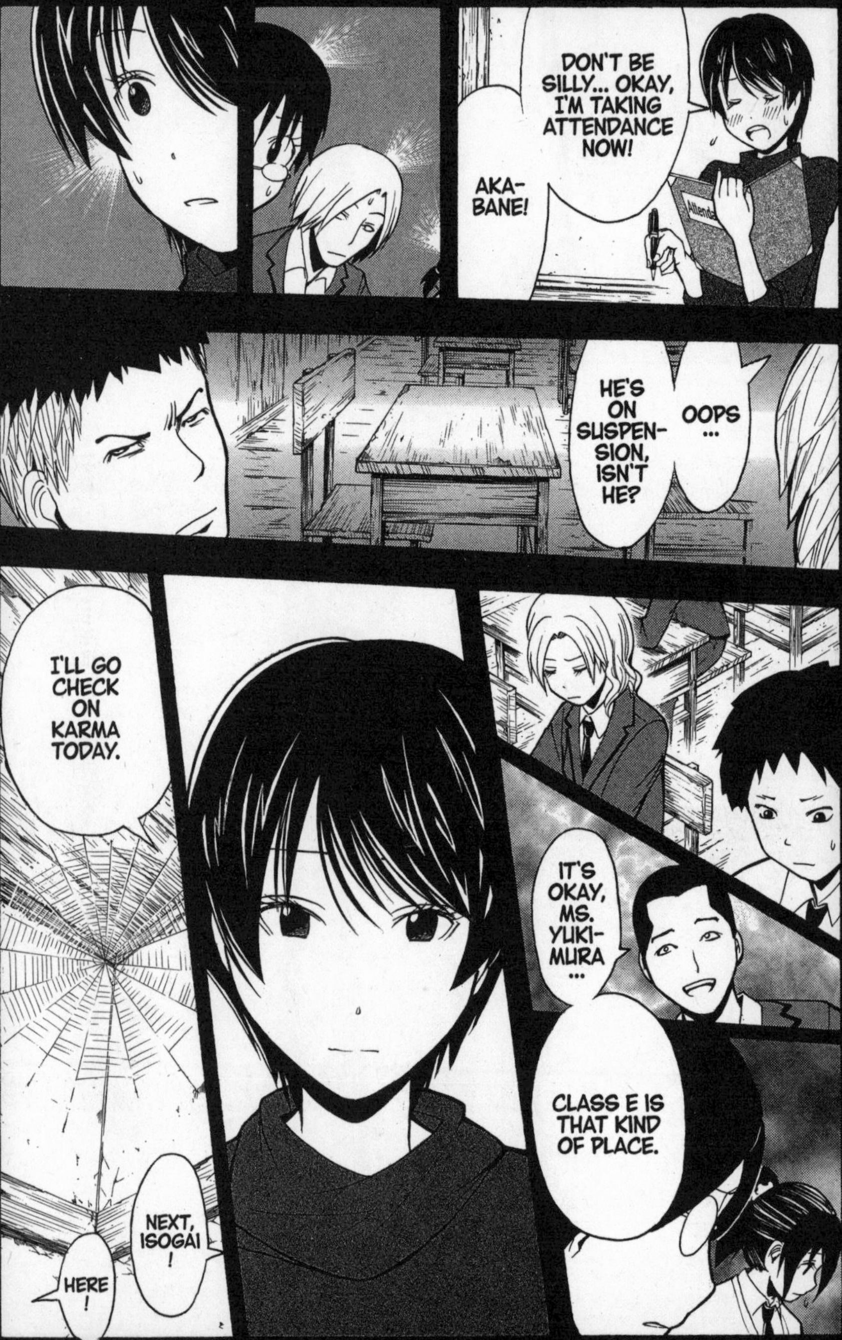

DON'T BE SILLY... OKAY, I'M TAKING ATTENDANCE NOW!
AKABANE!
OOPS...
HE'S ON SUSPENSION, ISN'T HE?
IT'S OKAY, MS. YUKIMURA...
CLASS E IS THAT KIND OF PLACE.
NEXT, ISOGAI!
I'LL GO CHECK ON KARMA TODAY.
HERE!

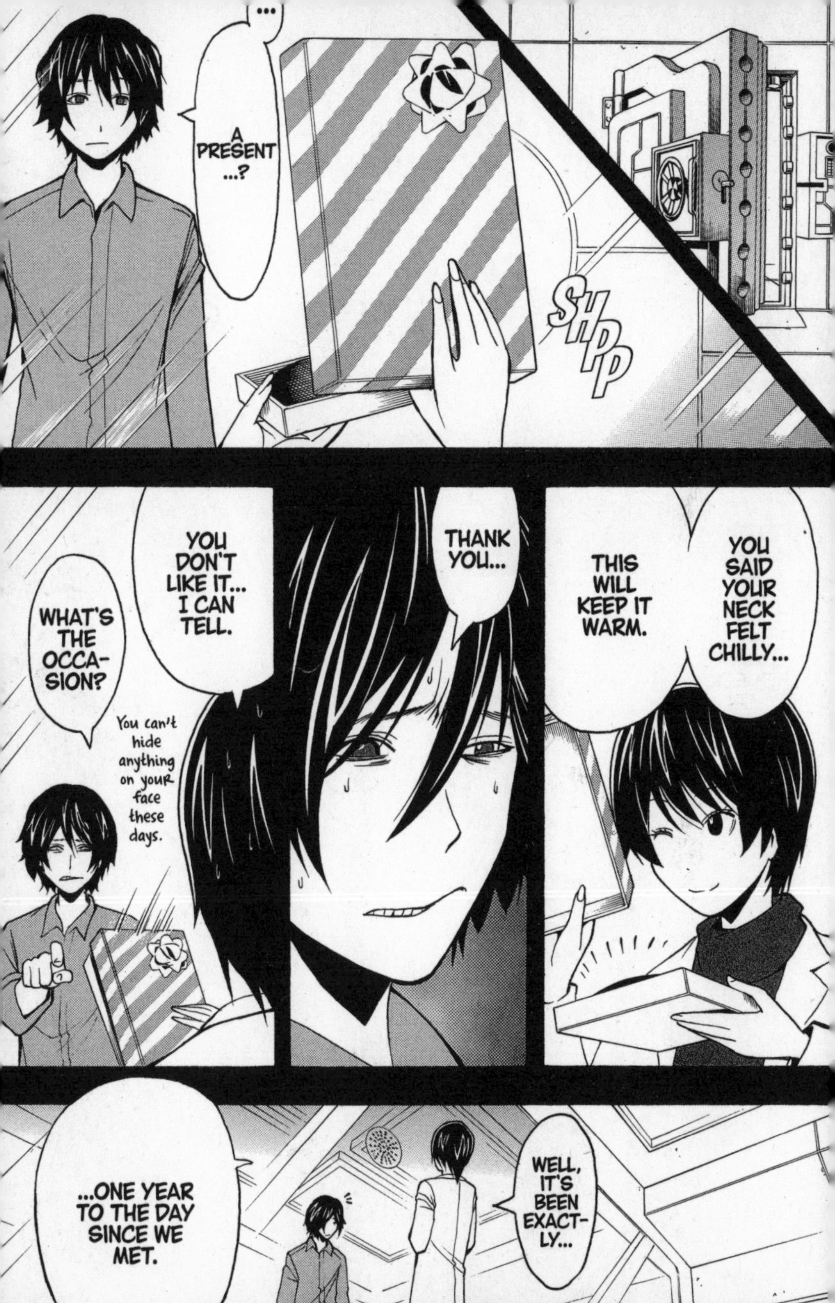
SHPP
...
A PRESENT ...?
YOU SAID YOUR NECK FELT CHILLY...
THIS WILL KEEP IT WARM.
THANK YOU...
YOU DON'T LIKE IT... I CAN TELL.
WHAT'S THE OCCASION?
You can't hide anything on your face these days.
WELL, IT'S BEEN EXACTLY...
...ONE YEAR TO THE DAY SINCE WE MET.

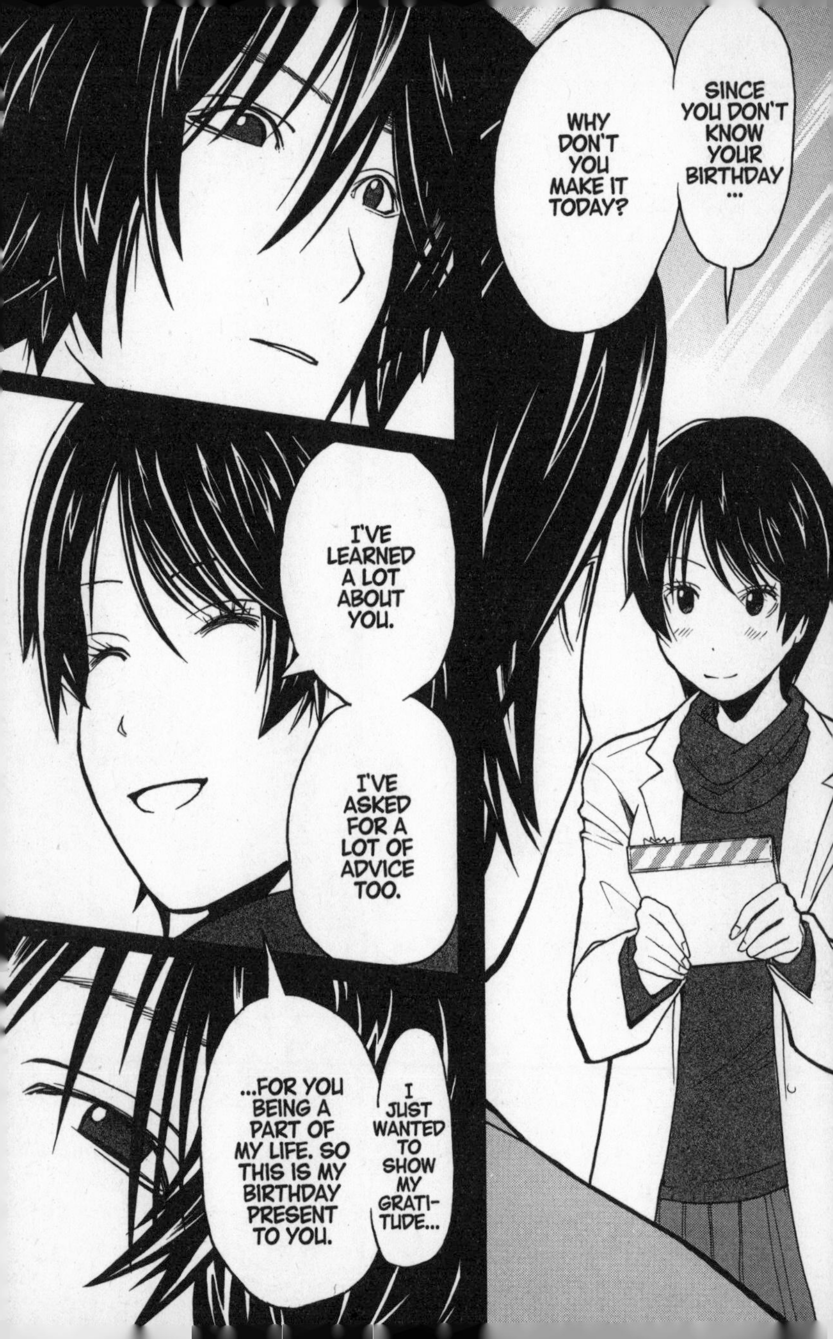
SINCE YOU DON'T KNOW YOUR BIRTHDAY ...
WHY DON'T YOU MAKE IT TODAY?
I'VE LEARNED A LOT ABOUT YOU.
I'VE ASKED FOR A LOT OF ADVICE TOO.
I JUST WANTED TO SHOW MY GRATITUDE...
...FOR YOU BEING A PART OF MY LIFE. SO THIS IS MY BIRTHDAY PRESENT TO YOU.

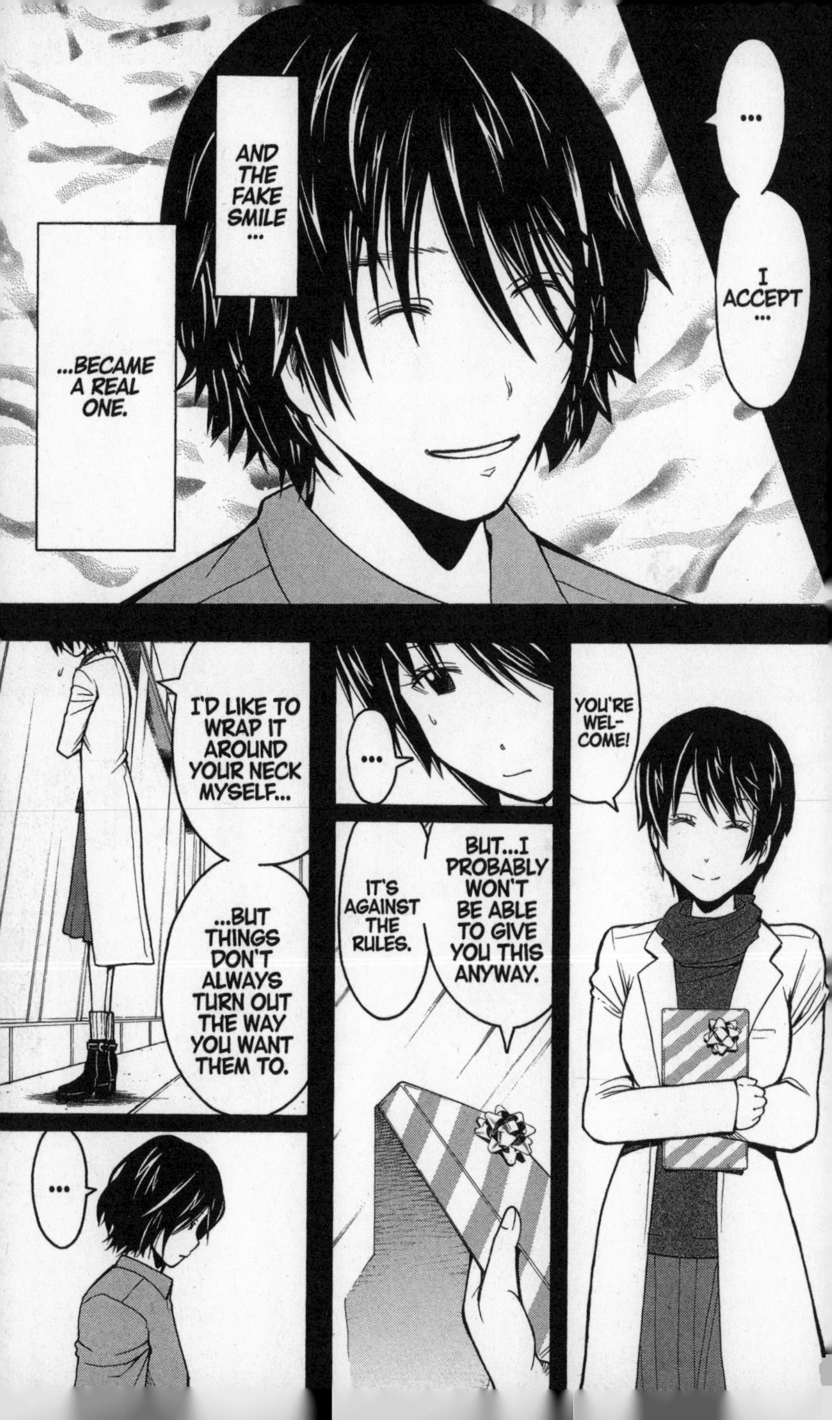
...
I ACCEPT...
AND THE FAKE SMILE...
...BECAME A REAL ONE.
YOU'RE WEL-COME!
...
BUT...I PROBABLY WON'T BE ABLE TO GIVE YOU THIS ANYWAY.
IT'S AGAINST THE RULES.
I'D LIKE TO WRAP IT AROUND YOUR NECK MYSELF...
...BUT THINGS DON'T ALWAYS TURN OUT THE WAY YOU WANT THEM TO.
...

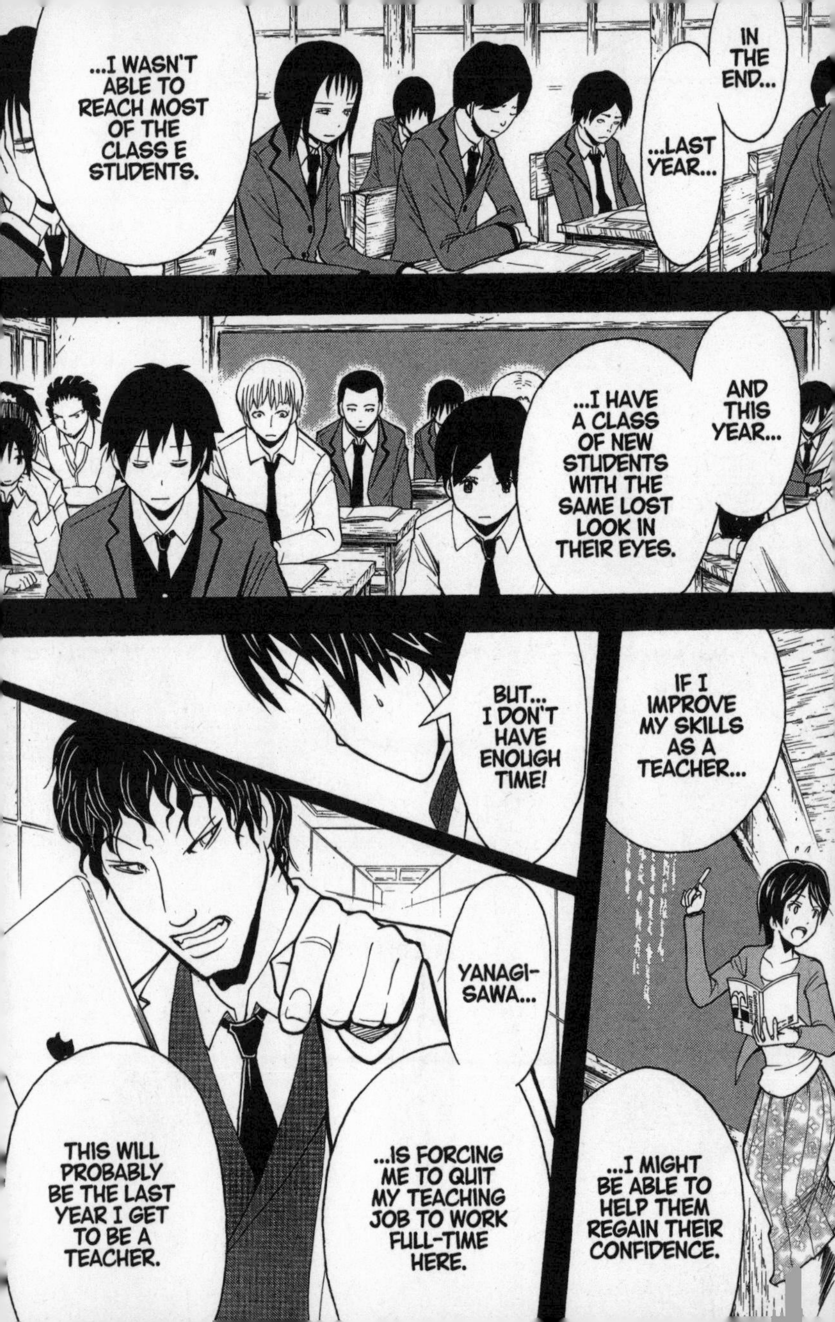
IN THE END...
...LAST YEAR...
...I WASN'T ABLE TO REACH MOST OF THE CLASS E STUDENTS.
AND THIS YEAR...
...I HAVE A CLASS OF NEW STUDENTS WITH THE SAME LOST LOOK IN THEIR EYES.
IF I IMPROVE MY SKILLS AS A TEACHER...
...I MIGHT BE ABLE TO HELP THEM REGAIN THEIR CONFIDENCE.
BUT... I DON'T HAVE ENOUGH TIME!
YANAGI-SAWA...
...IS FORCING ME TO QUIT MY TEACHING JOB TO WORK FULL-TIME HERE.
THIS WILL PROBABLY BE THE LAST YEAR I GET TO BE A TEACHER.

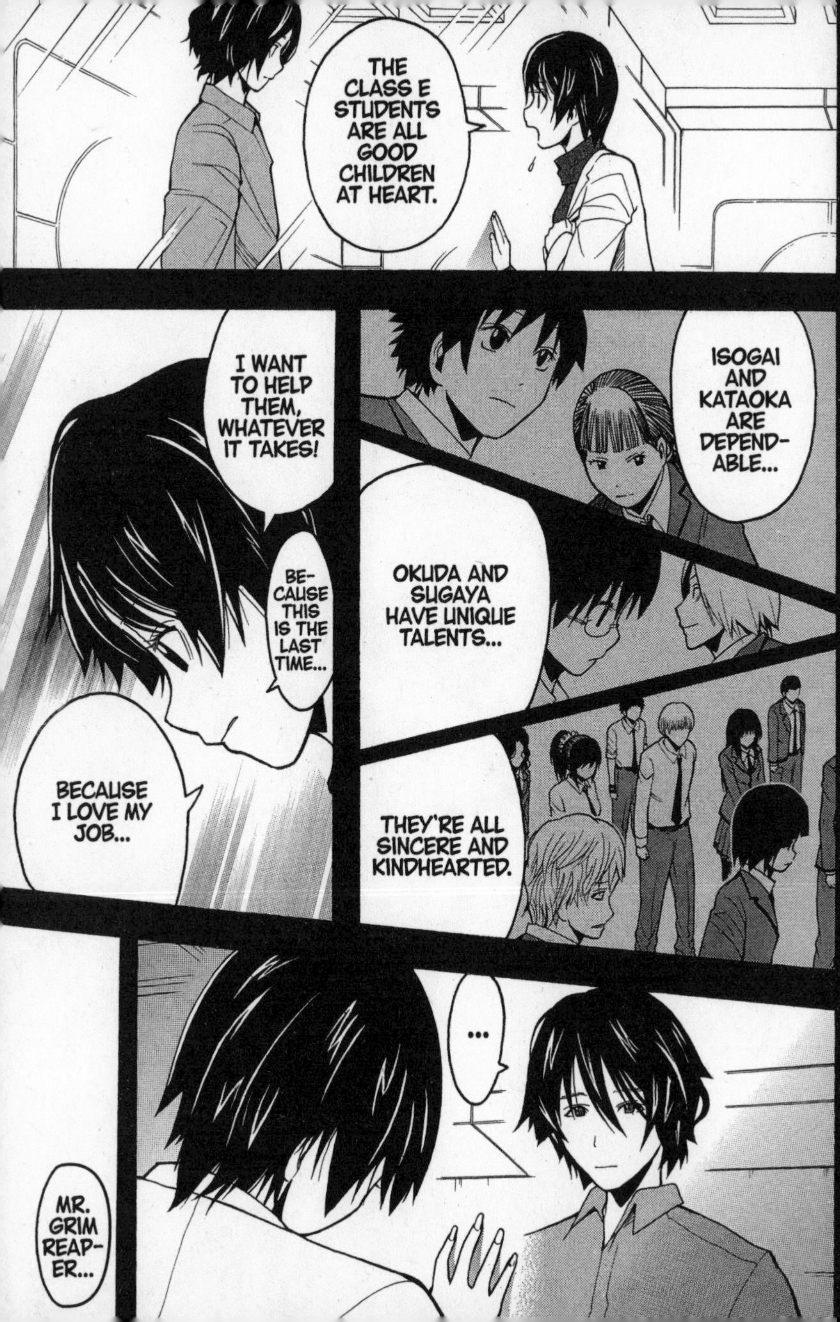
THE CLASS E STUDENTS ARE ALL GOOD CHILDREN AT HEART.
ISOGAI AND KATAOKA ARE DEPEND-ABLE...
OKUDA AND SUGAYA HAVE UNIQUE TALENTS...
THEY'RE ALL SINCERE AND KINDHEARTED.
I WANT TO HELP THEM, WHATEVER IT TAKES!
BE-CAUSE THIS IS THE LAST TIME...
BECAUSE I LOVE MY JOB...
...
MR. GRIM REAP-ER...

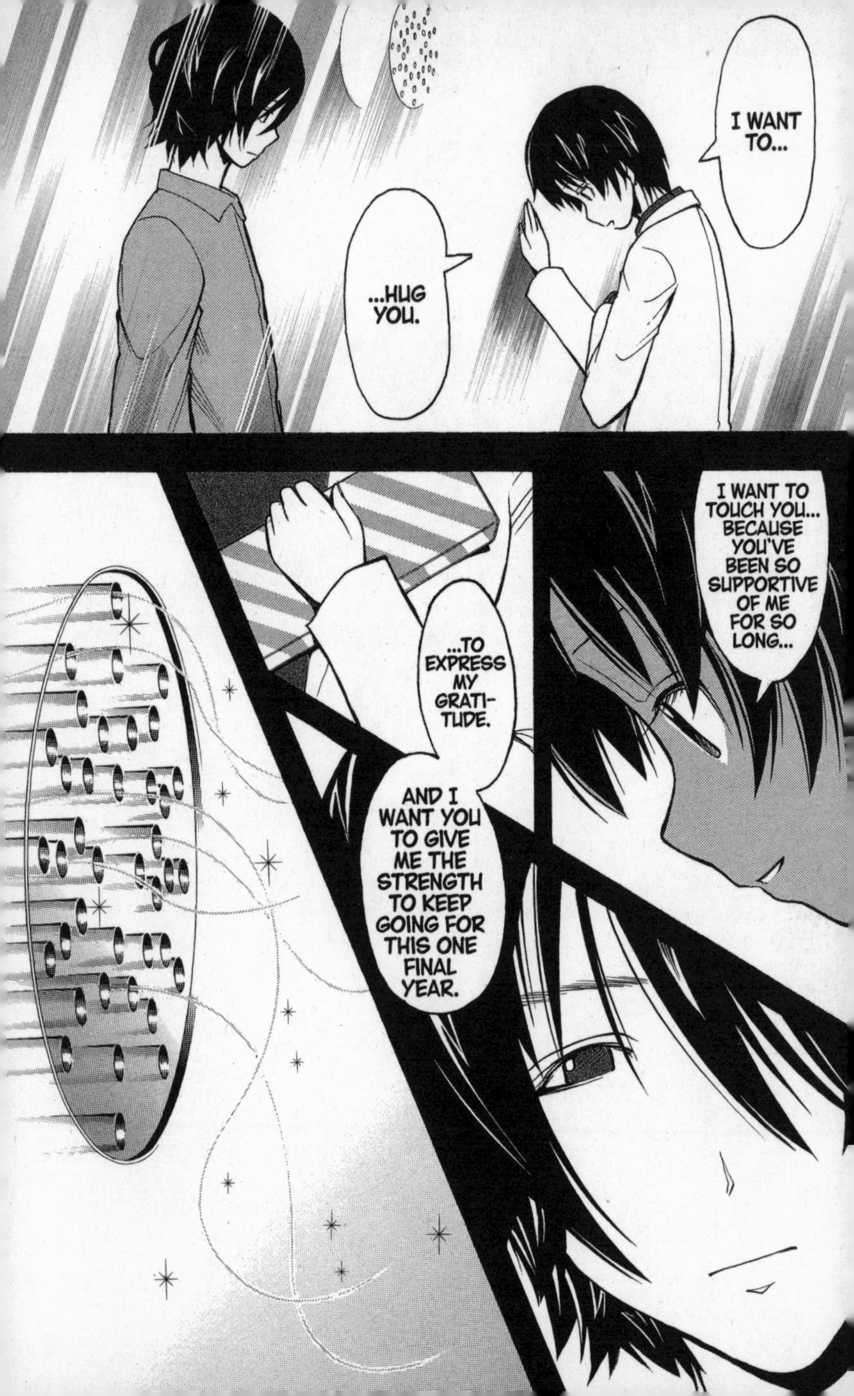
I WANT TO...
...HUG YOU.
I WANT TO TOUCH YOU... BECAUSE YOU'VE BEEN SO SUPPORTIVE OF ME FOR SO LONG...
...TO EXPRESS MY GRATI-TUDE.
AND I WANT YOU TO GIVE ME THE STRENGTH TO KEEP GOING FOR THIS ONE FINAL YEAR.

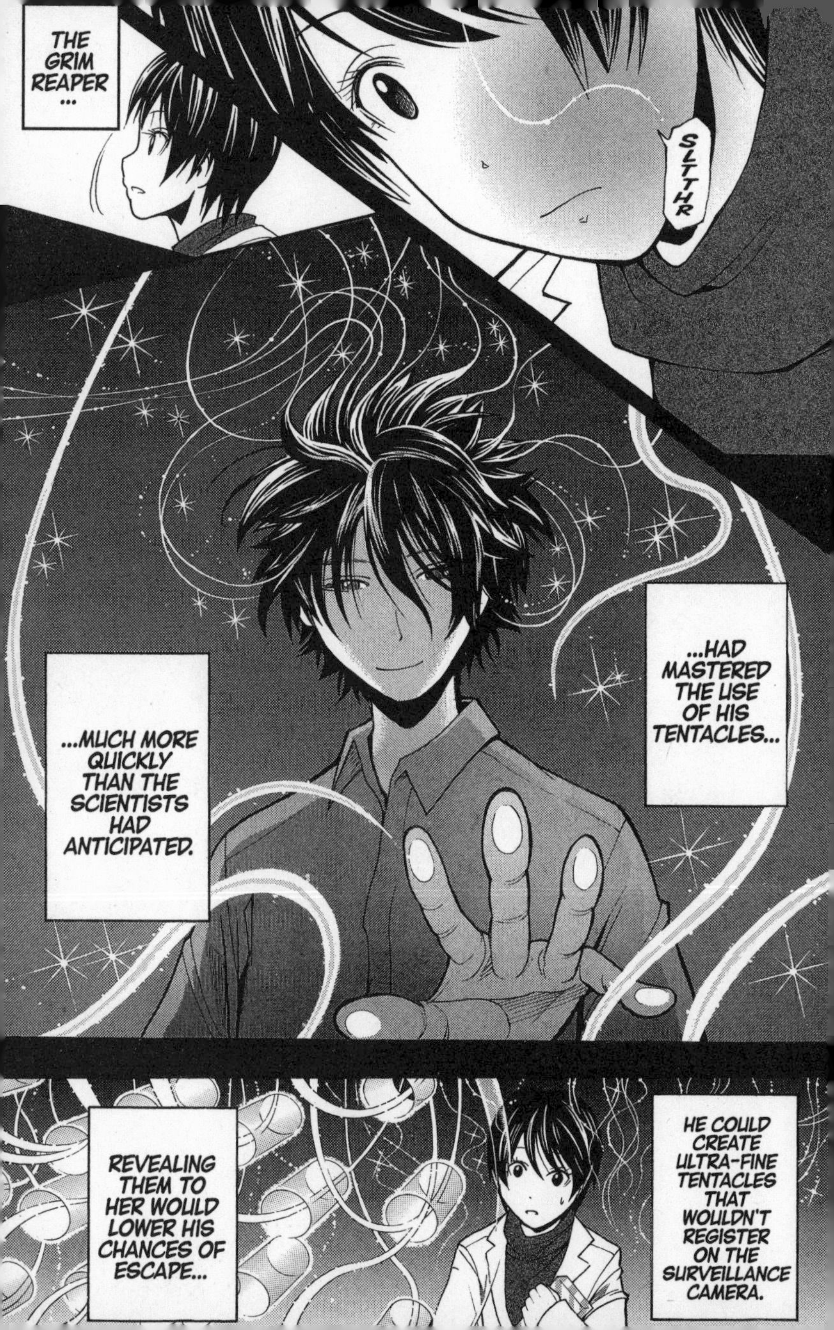
SLTTHR
THE GRIM REAPER...
...HAD MASTERED THE USE OF HIS TENTACLES...
...MUCH MORE QUICKLY THAN THE SCIENTISTS HAD ANTICIPATED.
HE COULD CREATE ULTRA-FINE TENTACLES THAT WOULDN'T REGISTER ON THE SURVEILLANCE CAMERA.
REVEALING THEM TO HER WOULD LOWER HIS CHANCES OF ESCAPE...

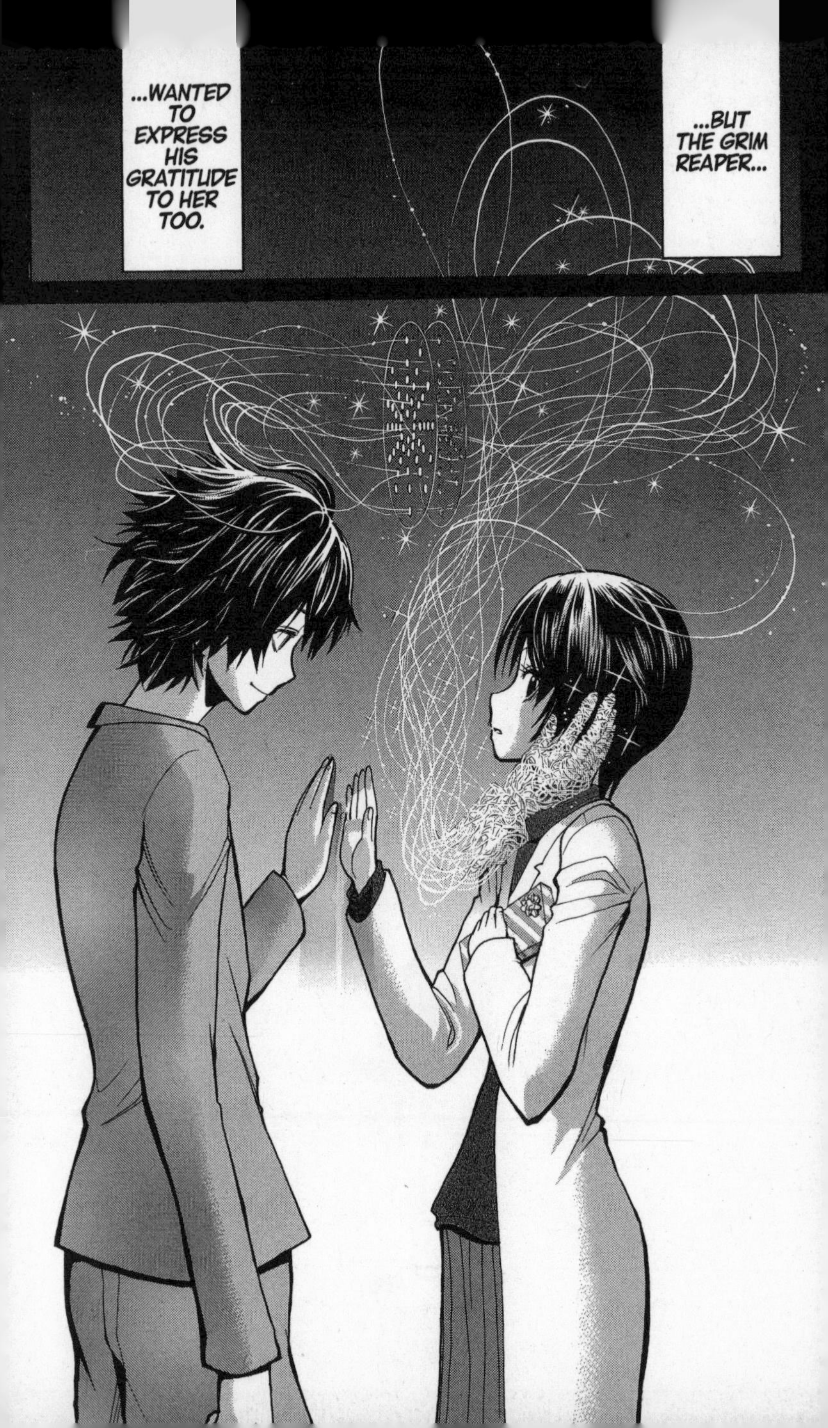
...BUT THE GRIM REAPER...
...WANTED TO EXPRESS HIS GRATITUDE TO HER TOO.

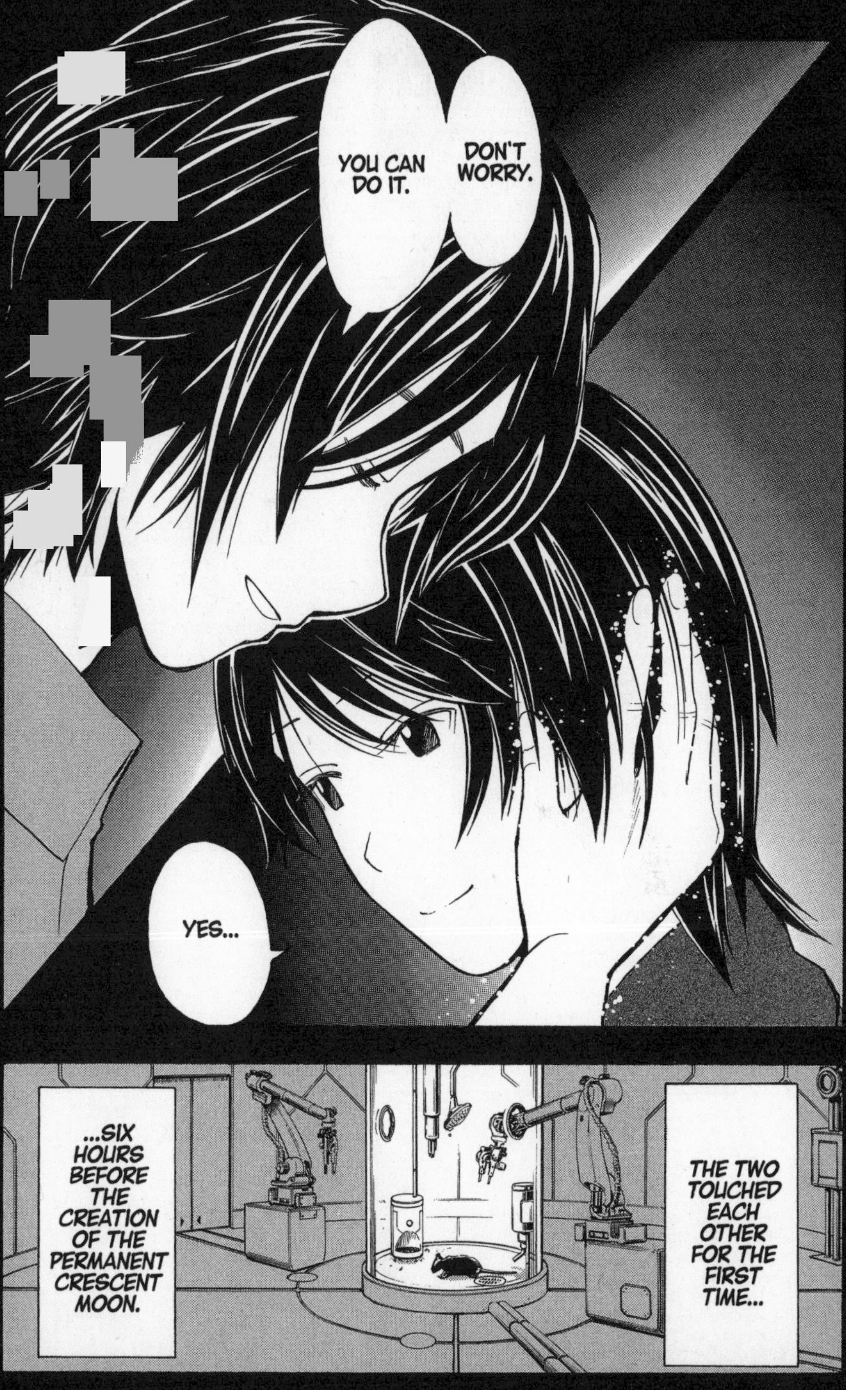
DON'T WORRY.
YOU CAN DO IT.
YES...
THE TWO TOUCHED EACH OTHER FOR THE FIRST TIME...
...SIX HOURS BEFORE THE CREATION OF THE PERMANENT CRESCENT MOON.

Mr. Karasuma's Report Card ④

Miscellaneous (Skills not directly connected to assassinations that nevertheless boost the assassination success of the class as a whole. Evaluated by Mr. Karasuma with a maximum of 10 points.)

Information Analysis		
1st Place	Autonomous Intelligence Fixed Artillery	10 Points
2nd Place	Yuzuki Fuwa	9 Points
3rd Place	Kotaro Takebayashi	8 Points
3rd Place	Karma Akabane	8 Points
5th Place	Rio Nakamura	7 Points

Highlight: Yuzuki Fuwa

Amassing vast amounts of information isn't that useful in and of itself, but she is also capable of selecting relevant data, making connections and drawing useful conclusions. That's something only a handful of agents are good at.

Leadership		
1st Place	Yuma Isogai	10 Points
2nd Place	Meg Kataoka	10 Points
3rd Place	Karma Akabane	9 Points
4th Place	Ryoma Terasaka	6 Points
4th Place	Koki Mimura	6 Points

Highlight: Karma Akabane

The leadership skills of the two students at the top are clear, but Karma Akabane is hiding his talent. He may rise to his true potential when things get critical.

Language Arts		
1st Place	Kirara Hazama	9 Points
1st Place	Karma Akabane	9 Points
3rd Place	Yuma Isogai	7 Points
3rd Place	Sumire Hara	7 Points
5th Place	Rio Nakamura	6 Points

Highlight: Kirara Hazama

Communications skills are important in every area of assassination—to deceive, agitate, calm and persuade a target. And at times her stream of abuse can damage the target more than a bullet.

Medical/Pharmaceutical Knowledge		
1st Place	Manami Okuda	10 Points
1st Place	Kotaro Takebayashi	10 Points
3rd Place	Yukiko Kanzaki	6 Points
4th Place	Hinano Kurahashi	5 Points
4th Place	Kaede Kayano	5 Points

Highlight: Manami Okuda

It's not easy for a junior high school student to be knowledgeable enough in this category to apply it to assassinations, but she already knows a lot more about these subjects than I do.

Negotiation		
1st Place	Toka Yada	10 Points
2nd Place	Hinano Kurahashi	8 Points
2nd Place	Karma Akabane	8 Points
4th Place	Nagisa Shiota	6 Points
4th Place	Kaede Kayano	6 Points

Highlight: Kaede Kayano

She is the only student who needs to be evaluated with fresh eyes, since her acting skills were only revealed at the end of the semester. Thus my evaluation of her might change during the third semester.

CLASS 138 TIME FOR THE PAST–5TH PERIOD

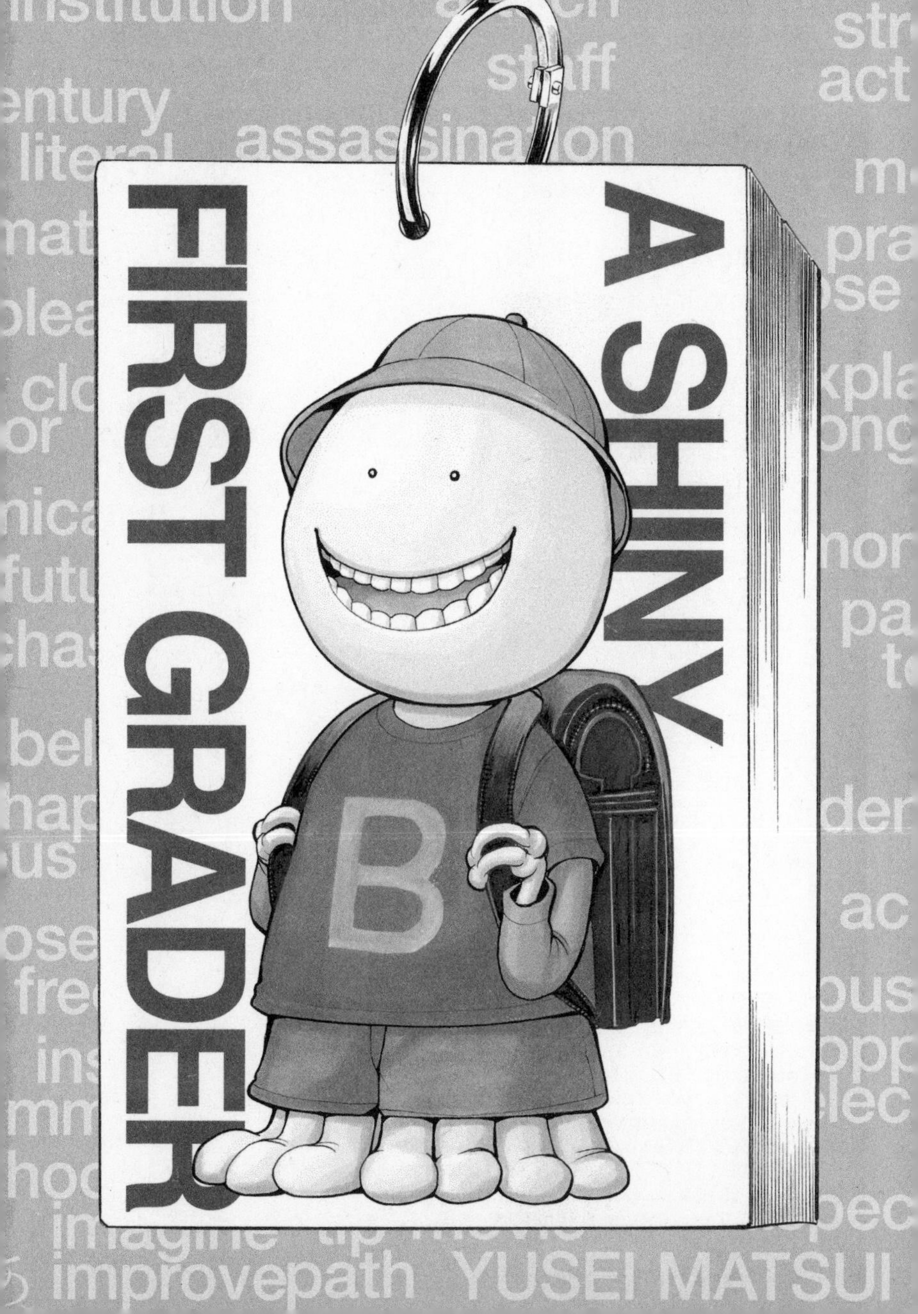
A SHINY
FIRST GRADER
B
YUSEI MATSUI

Ms. Yukimura's favorite brand: Rotten Manten

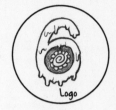

Logo

SCREAM
Brossiere
I had
Caviar
For Centipedes
Small Intestine
Large Intestine
Appendix
ease Stand Back

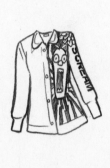

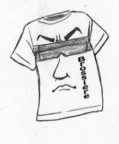

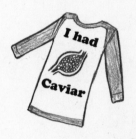

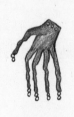

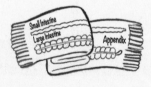

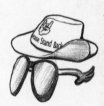

A relatively cheap clothing brand despite their unique designs and many enthusiastic fans. They also offer small accessories. Ms. Yukimura has been a huge fan of this line ever since she saw her sister's colleague, Akari, wearing it. Yanagisawa slaps her when he sees her wearing these clothes, so she usually conceals them under her outerwear.

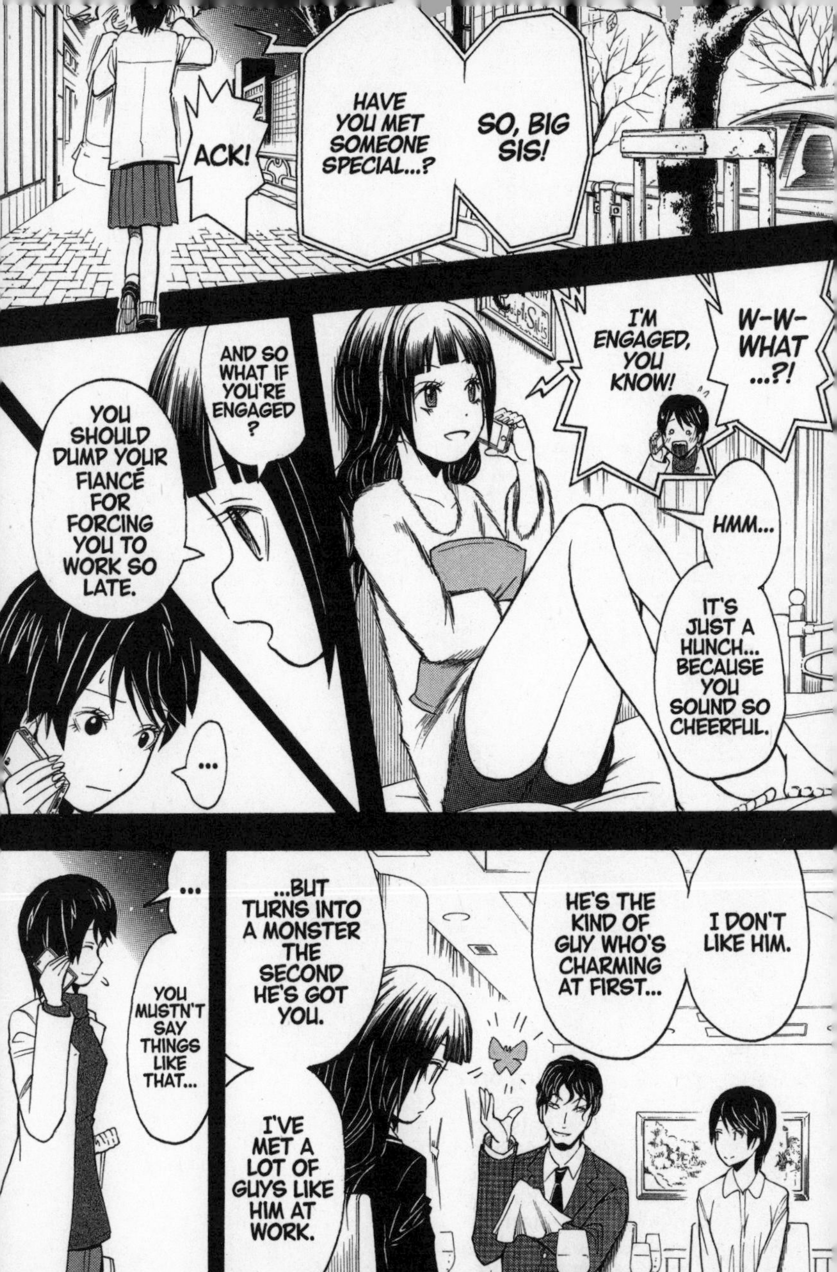
SO, BIG SIS!
HAVE YOU MET SOMEONE SPECIAL...?
ACK!
W-W-WHAT ...?!
I'M ENGAGED, YOU KNOW!
HMM...
IT'S JUST A HUNCH... BECAUSE YOU SOUND SO CHEERFUL.
AND SO WHAT IF YOU'RE ENGAGED?
YOU SHOULD DUMP YOUR FIANCÉ FOR FORCING YOU TO WORK SO LATE.
...
I DON'T LIKE HIM.
HE'S THE KIND OF GUY WHO'S CHARMING AT FIRST...
...BUT TURNS INTO A MONSTER THE SECOND HE'S GOT YOU.
I'VE MET A LOT OF GUYS LIKE HIM AT WORK.
...
YOU MUSTN'T SAY THINGS LIKE THAT...

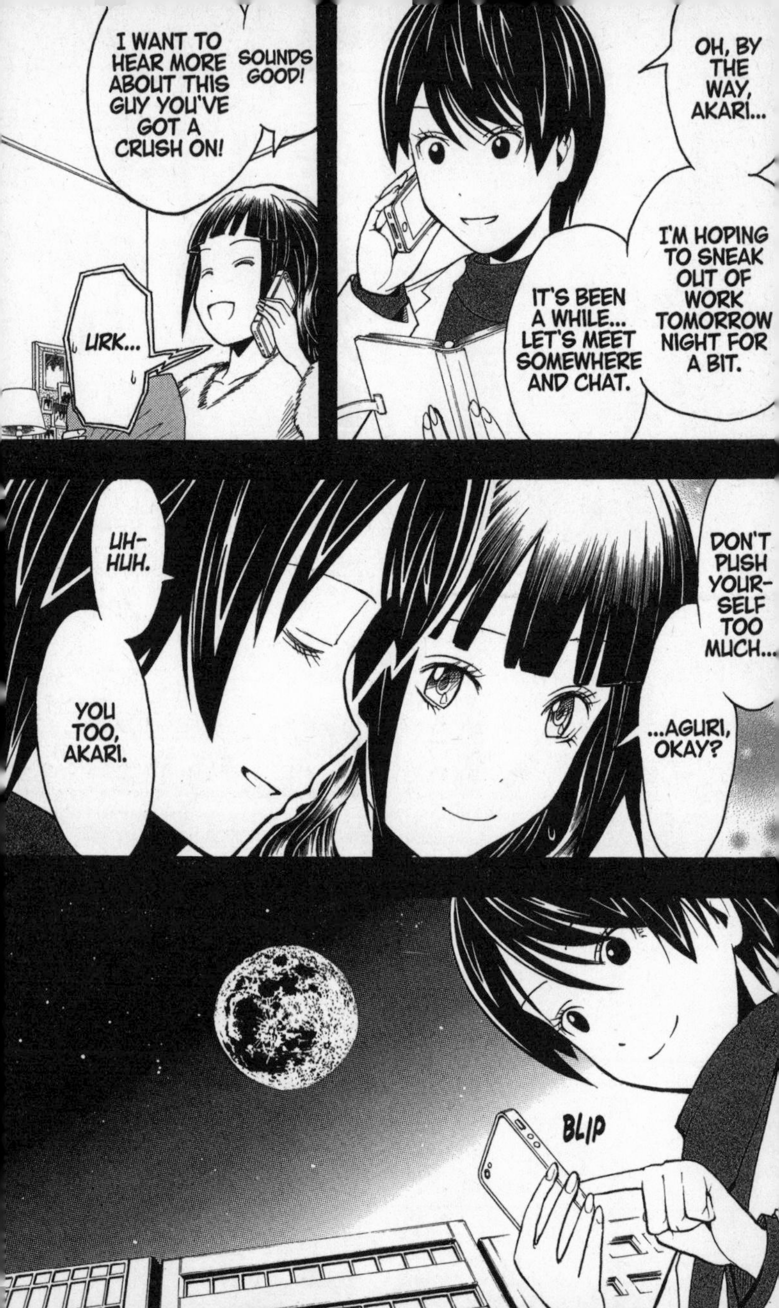
OH, BY THE WAY, AKARI...
I'M HOPING TO SNEAK OUT OF WORK TOMORROW NIGHT FOR A BIT.
IT'S BEEN A WHILE... LET'S MEET SOMEWHERE AND CHAT.
SOUNDS GOOD!
I WANT TO HEAR MORE ABOUT THIS GUY YOU'VE GOT A CRUSH ON!
URK...
DON'T PUSH YOURSELF TOO MUCH...
...AGURI, OKAY?
UH-HUH.
YOU TOO, AKARI.
BLIP

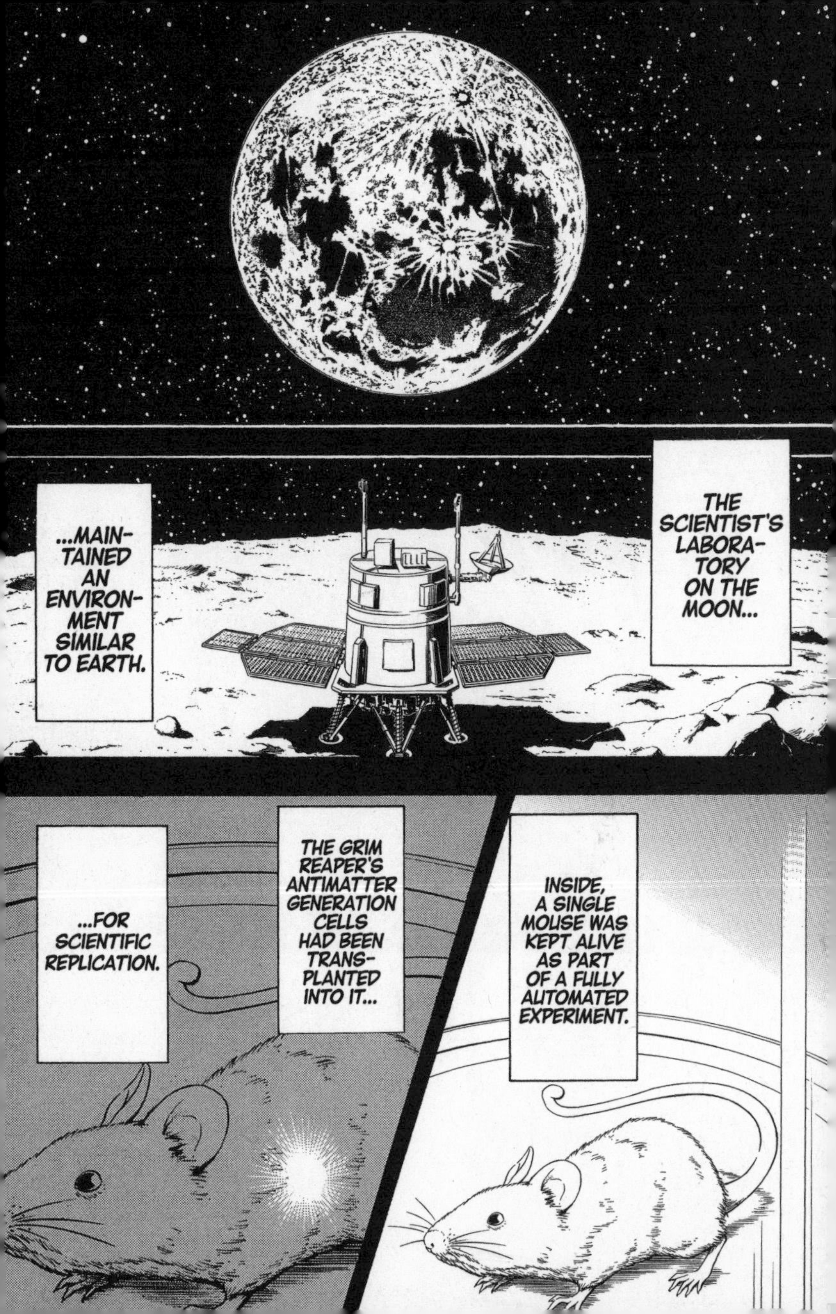
THE SCIENTIST'S LABORATORY ON THE MOON...
...MAINTAINED AN ENVIRONMENT SIMILAR TO EARTH.
INSIDE, A SINGLE MOUSE WAS KEPT ALIVE AS PART OF A FULLY AUTOMATED EXPERIMENT.
THE GRIM REAPER'S ANTIMATTER GENERATION CELLS HAD BEEN TRANSPLANTED INTO IT...
...FOR SCIENTIFIC REPLICATION.

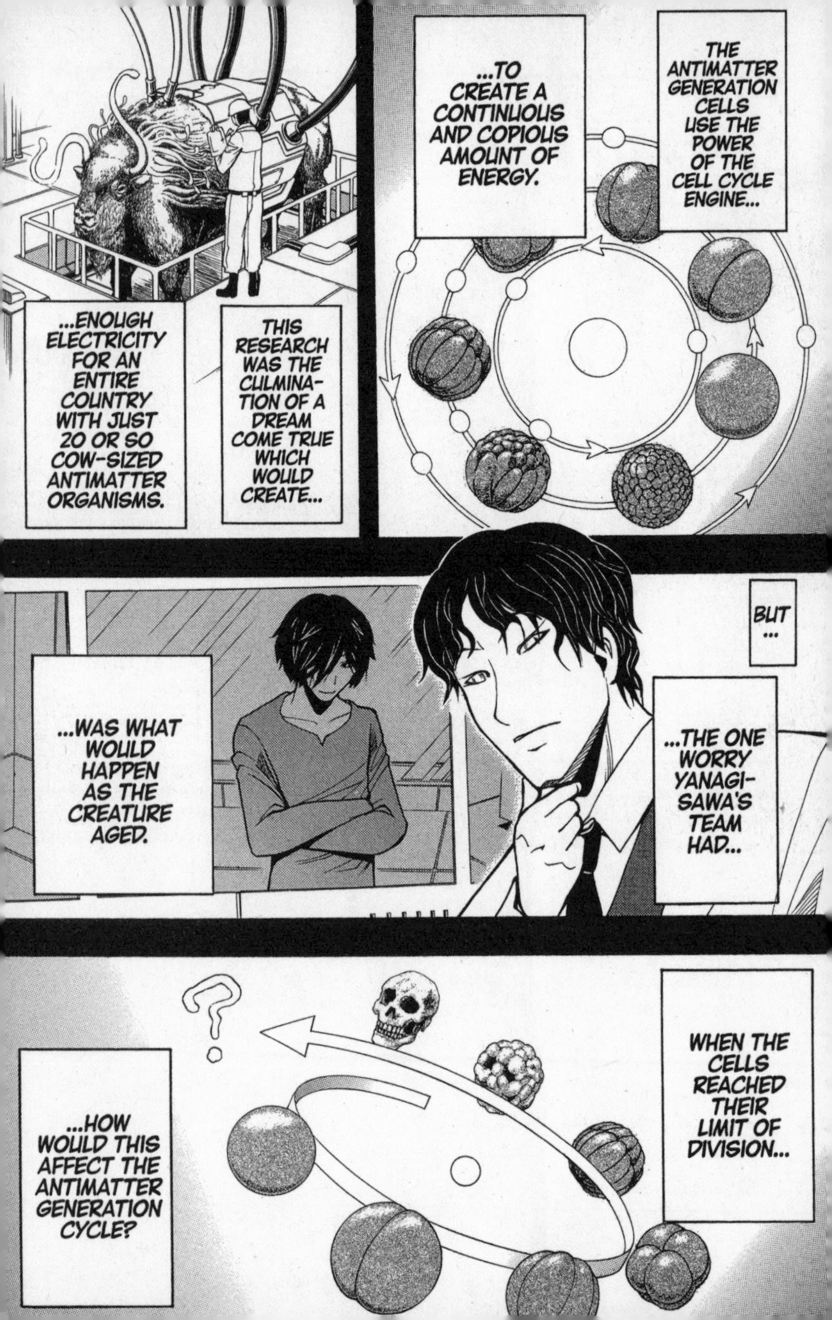
THE ANTIMATTER GENERATION CELLS USE THE POWER OF THE CELL CYCLE ENGINE...
...TO CREATE A CONTINUOUS AND COPIOUS AMOUNT OF ENERGY.
THIS RESEARCH WAS THE CULMINATION OF A DREAM COME TRUE WHICH WOULD CREATE...
...ENOUGH ELECTRICITY FOR AN ENTIRE COUNTRY WITH JUST 20 OR SO COW-SIZED ANTIMATTER ORGANISMS.
BUT ...
...THE ONE WORRY YANAGI-SAWA'S TEAM HAD...
...WAS WHAT WOULD HAPPEN AS THE CREATURE AGED.
WHEN THE CELLS REACHED THEIR LIMIT OF DIVISION...
...HOW WOULD THIS AFFECT THE ANTIMATTER GENERATION CYCLE?

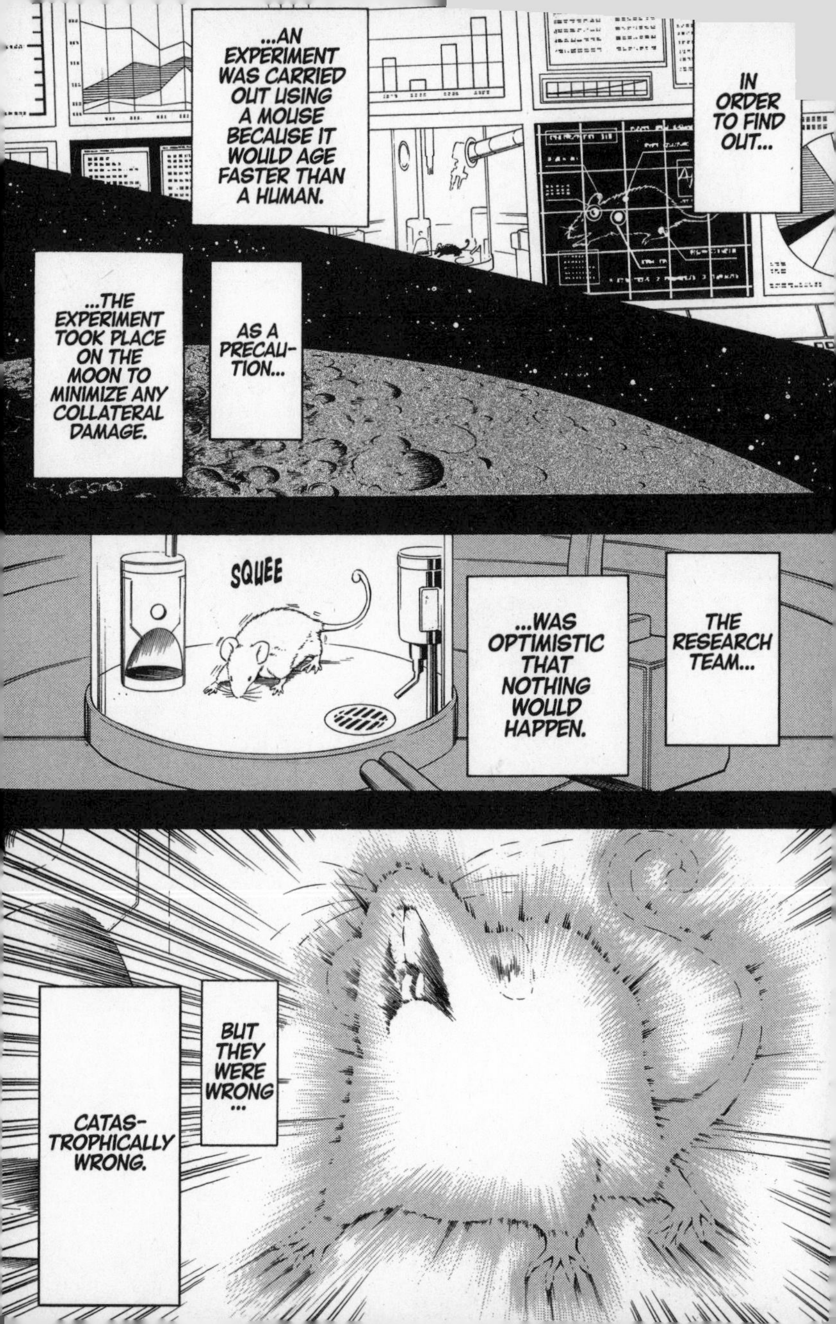
IN ORDER TO FIND OUT...
...AN EXPERIMENT WAS CARRIED OUT USING A MOUSE BECAUSE IT WOULD AGE FASTER THAN A HUMAN.
AS A PRECAUTION...
...THE EXPERIMENT TOOK PLACE ON THE MOON TO MINIMIZE ANY COLLATERAL DAMAGE.
THE RESEARCH TEAM...
...WAS OPTIMISTIC THAT NOTHING WOULD HAPPEN.
SQUEE
BUT THEY WERE WRONG...
CATASTROPHICALLY WRONG.

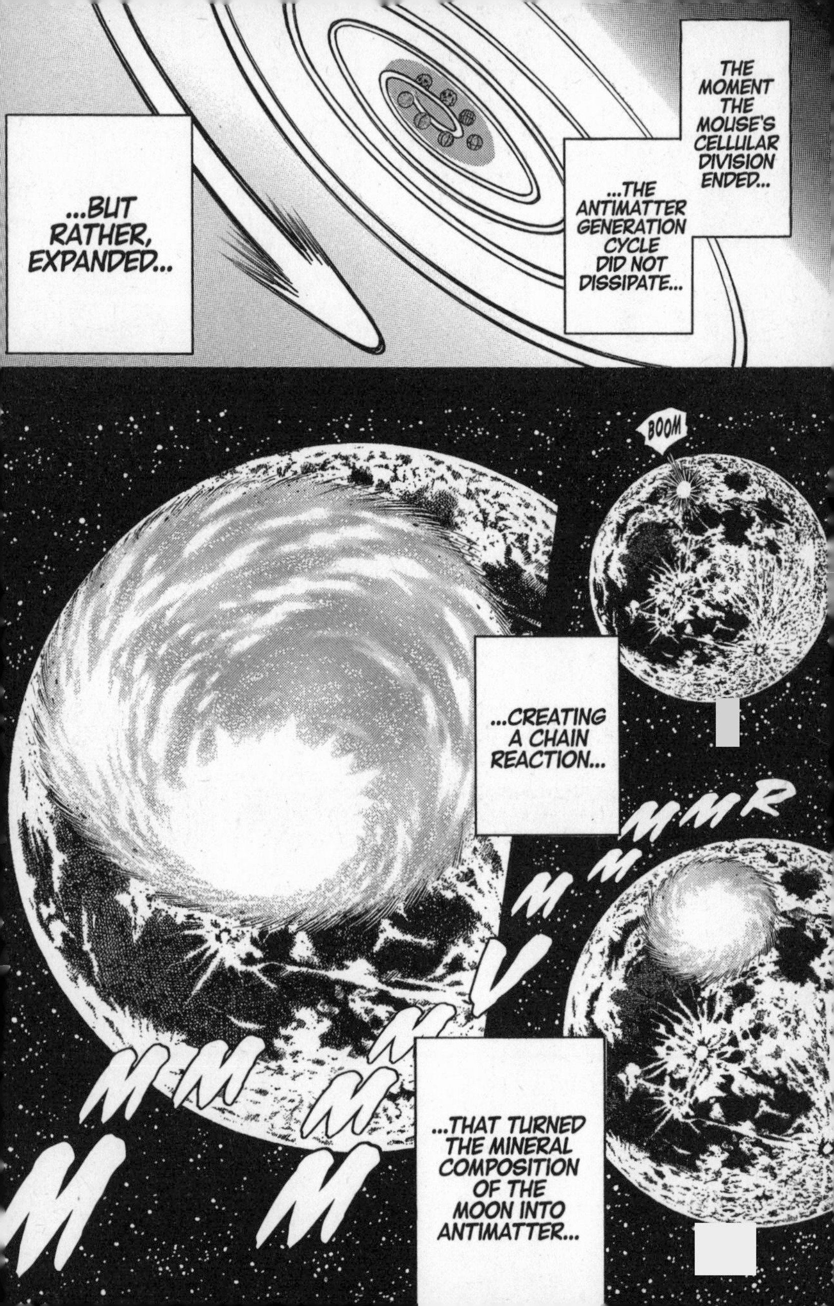
THE MOMENT THE MOUSE'S CELLULAR DIVISION ENDED...
...THE ANTIMATTER GENERATION CYCLE DID NOT DISSIPATE...
...BUT RATHER, EXPANDED...
BOOM
...CREATING A CHAIN REACTION...
MMMMR
...THAT TURNED THE MINERAL COMPOSITION OF THE MOON INTO ANTIMATTER...

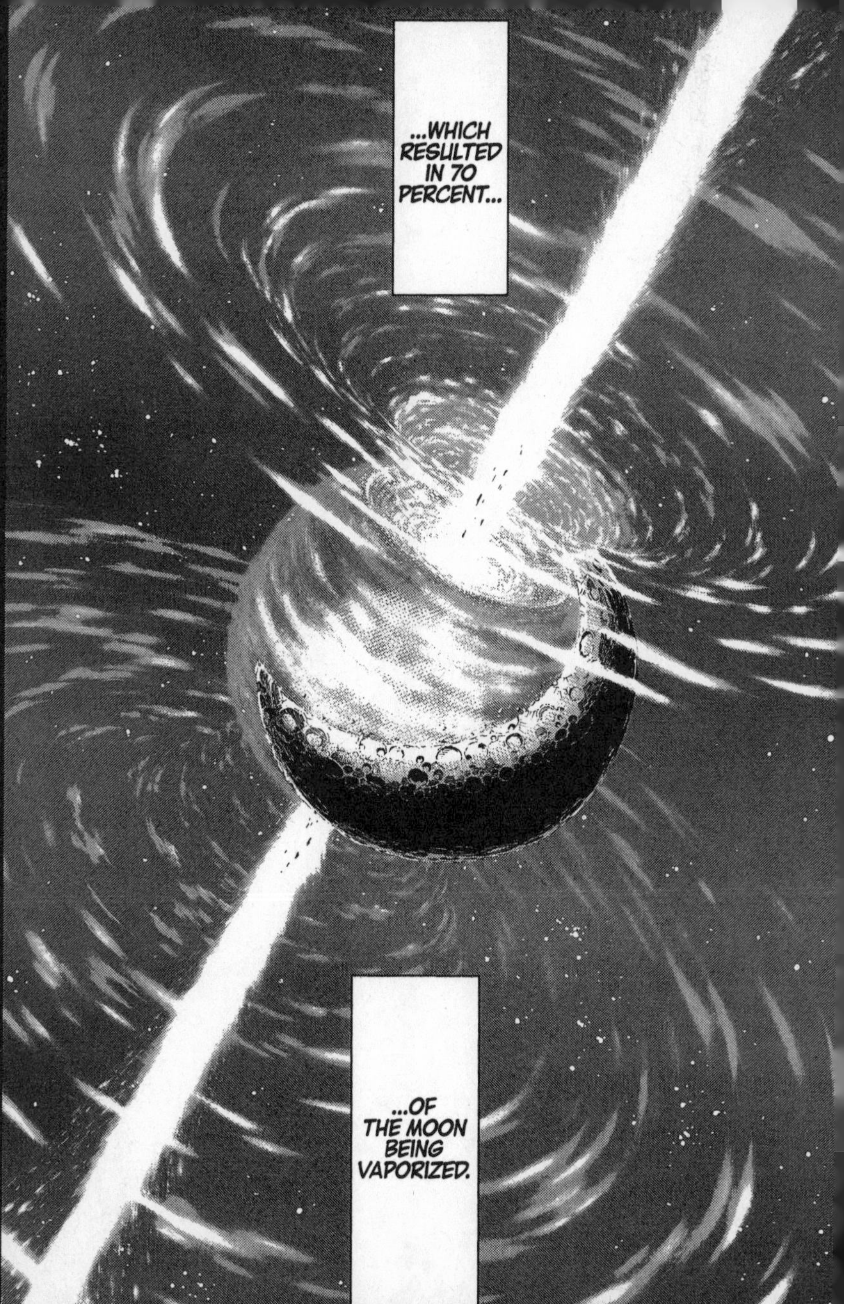
...WHICH RESULTED IN 70 PERCENT...
...OF THE MOON BEING VAPORIZED.

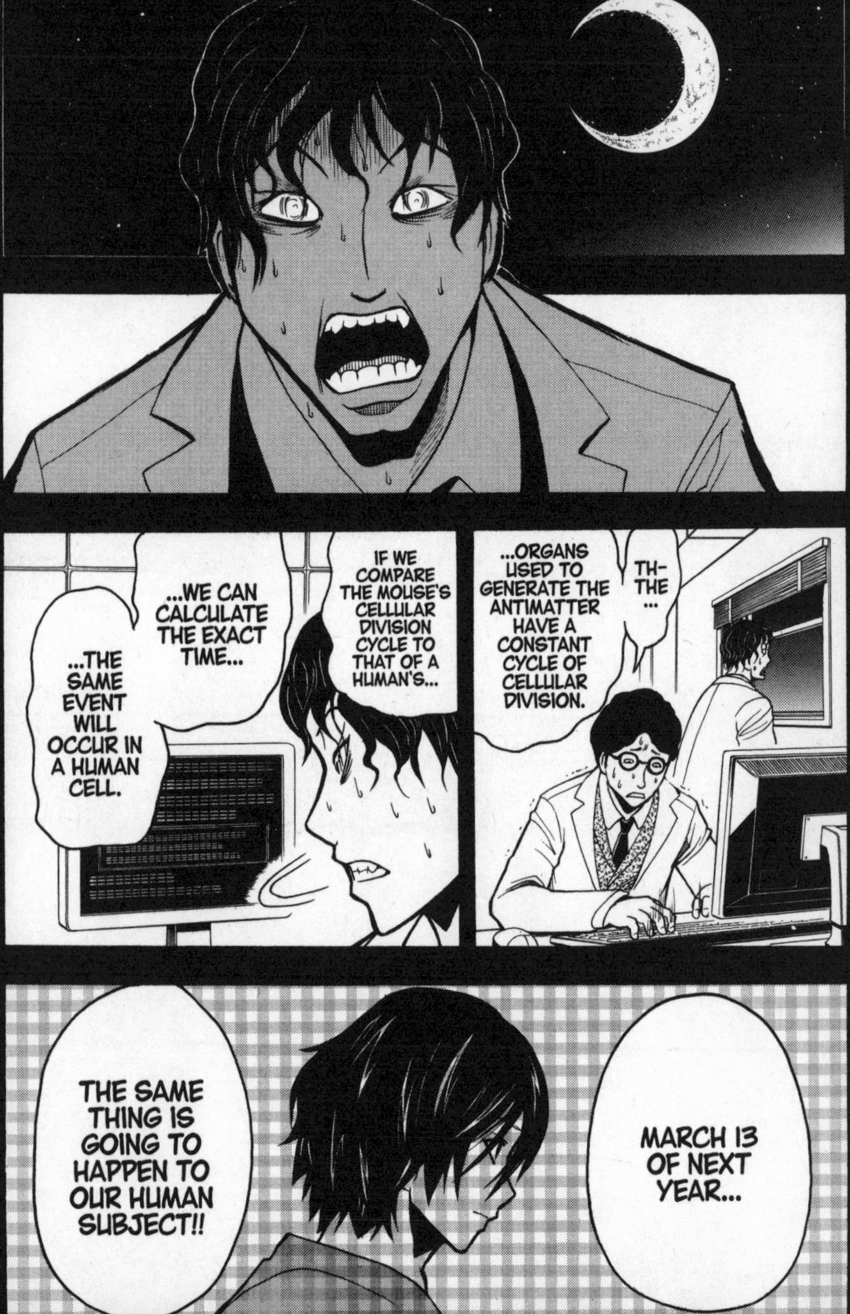
TH-THE ...
...ORGANS USED TO GENERATE THE ANTIMATTER HAVE A CONSTANT CYCLE OF CELLULAR DIVISION.
IF WE COMPARE THE MOUSE'S CELLULAR DIVISION CYCLE TO THAT OF A HUMAN'S...
...WE CAN CALCULATE THE EXACT TIME...
...THE SAME EVENT WILL OCCUR IN A HUMAN CELL.
MARCH 13 OF NEXT YEAR...
THE SAME THING IS GOING TO HAPPEN TO OUR HUMAN SUBJECT!!

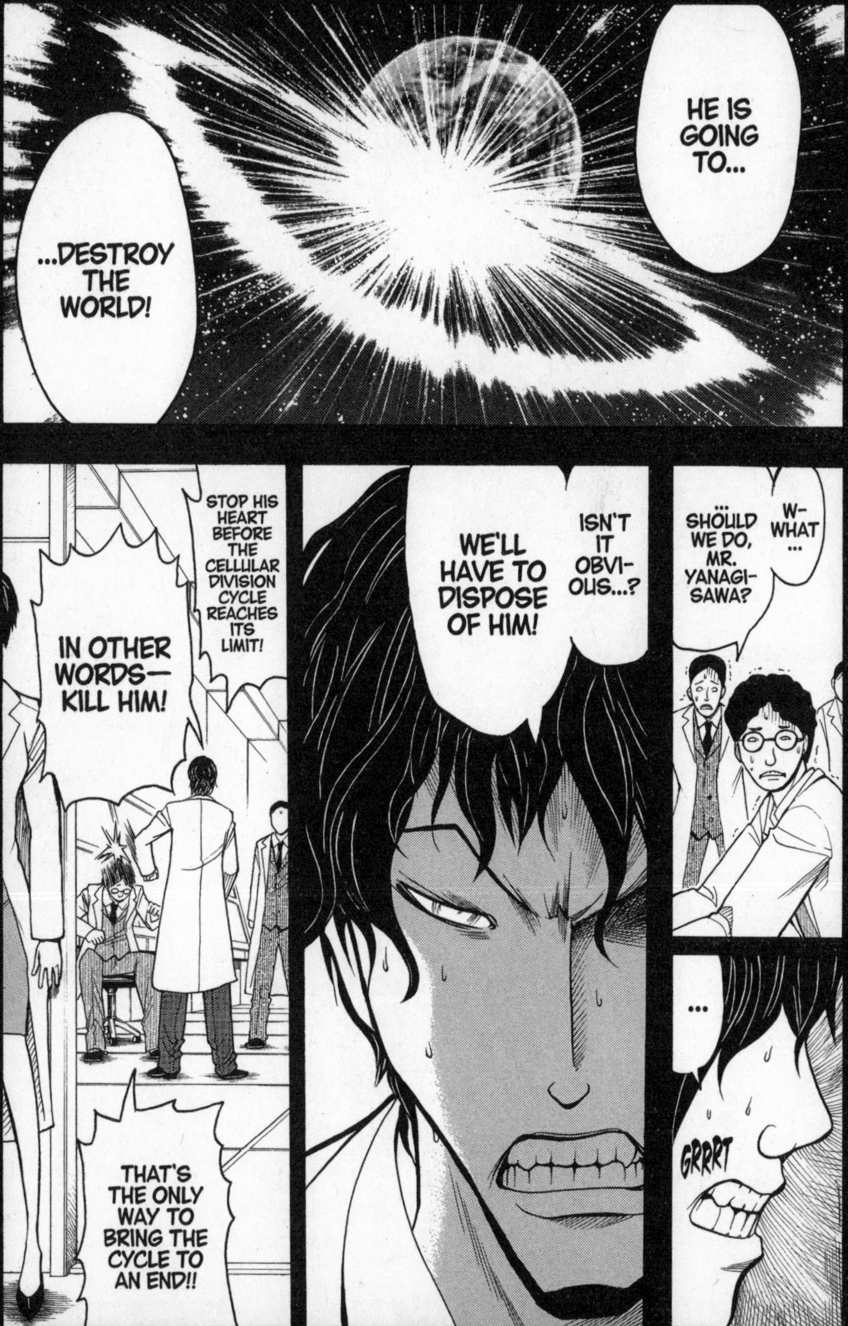
HE IS GOING TO...
...DESTROY THE WORLD!
W-WHAT ...
...SHOULD WE DO, MR. YANAGI-SAWA?
...
GRRRT
ISN'T IT OBVI-OUS...?
WE'LL HAVE TO DISPOSE OF HIM!
STOP HIS HEART BEFORE THE CELLULAR DIVISION CYCLE REACHES ITS LIMIT!
IN OTHER WORDS—KILL HIM!
THAT'S THE ONLY WAY TO BRING THE CYCLE TO AN END!!

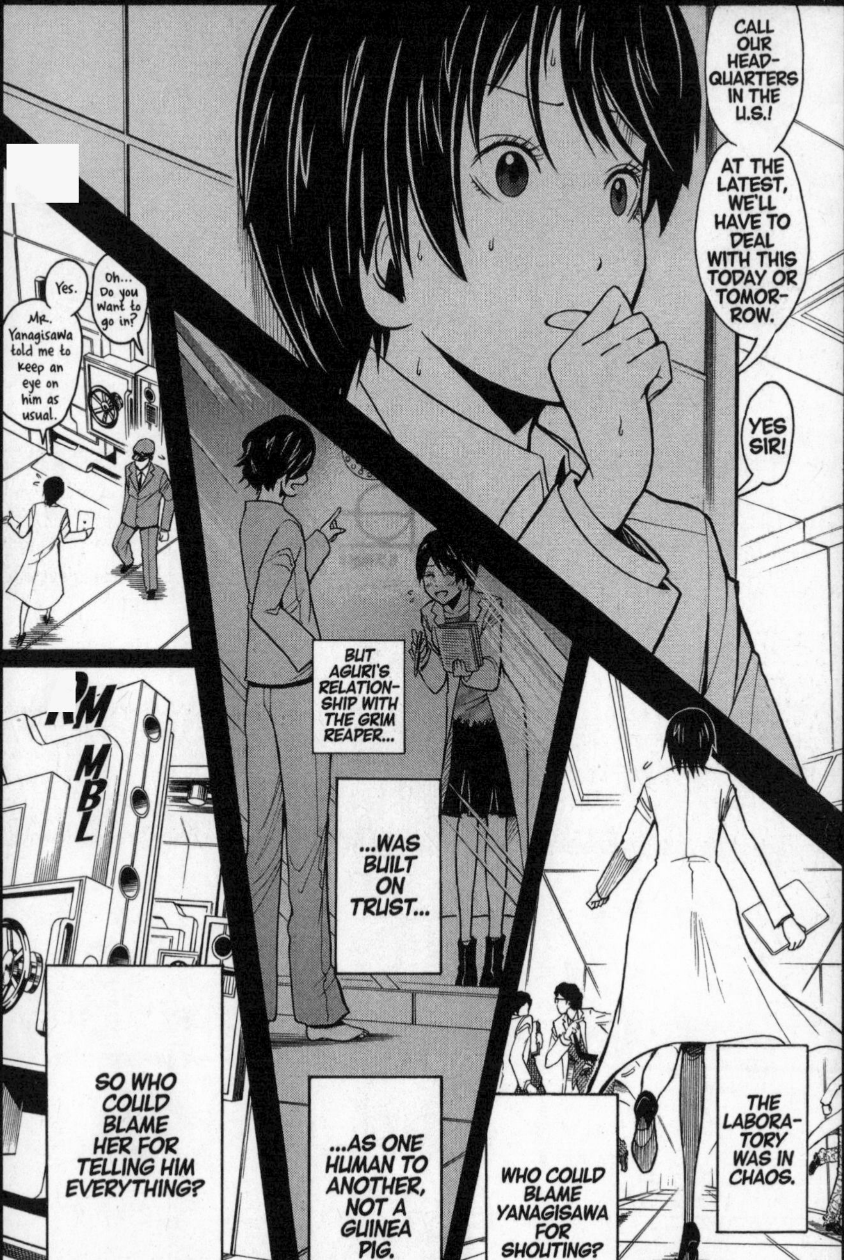
CALL OUR HEAD-QUARTERS IN THE U.S.!
AT THE LATEST, WE'LL HAVE TO DEAL WITH THIS TODAY OR TOMOR-ROW.
YES SIR!
Oh... Do you want to go in?
Yes.
Mr. Yanagisawa told me to keep an eye on him as usual.
THE LABORA-TORY WAS IN CHAOS.
WHO COULD BLAME YANAGISAWA FOR SHOUTING?
BUT AGURI'S RELATION-SHIP WITH THE GRIM REAPER...
...WAS BUILT ON TRUST...
...AS ONE HUMAN TO ANOTHER, NOT A GUINEA PIG.
MBL
SO WHO COULD BLAME HER FOR TELLING HIM EVERYTHING?

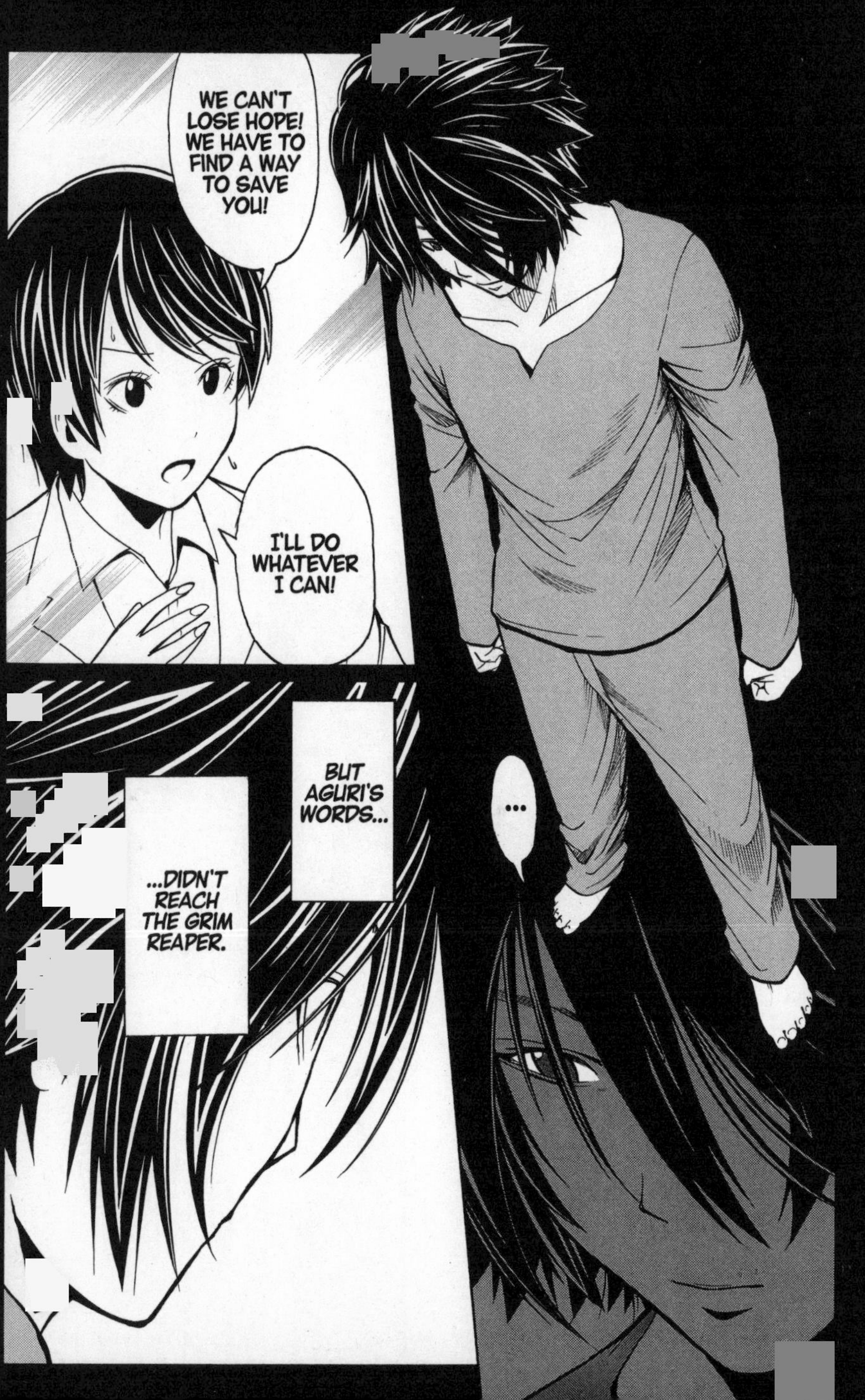
...
WE CAN'T LOSE HOPE! WE HAVE TO FIND A WAY TO SAVE YOU!
I'LL DO WHATEVER I CAN!
BUT AGURI'S WORDS...
...DIDN'T REACH THE GRIM REAPER.

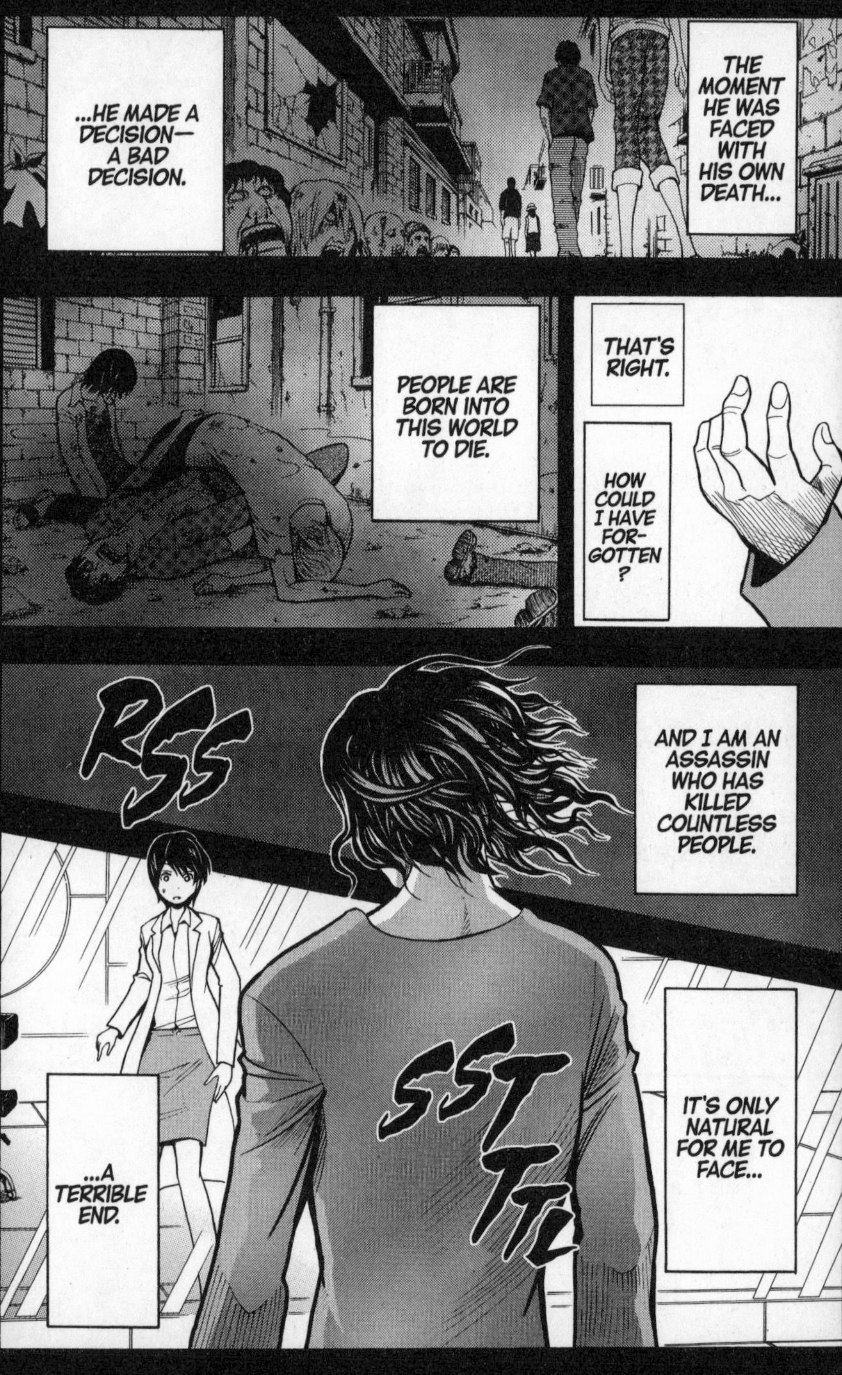
THE MOMENT HE WAS FACED WITH HIS OWN DEATH...
...HE MADE A DECISION— A BAD DECISION.
THAT'S RIGHT.
HOW COULD I HAVE FOR-GOTTEN?
PEOPLE ARE BORN INTO THIS WORLD TO DIE.
AND I AM AN ASSASSIN WHO HAS KILLED COUNTLESS PEOPLE.
RSS
IT'S ONLY NATURAL FOR ME TO FACE...
SST TTL
...A TERRIBLE END.

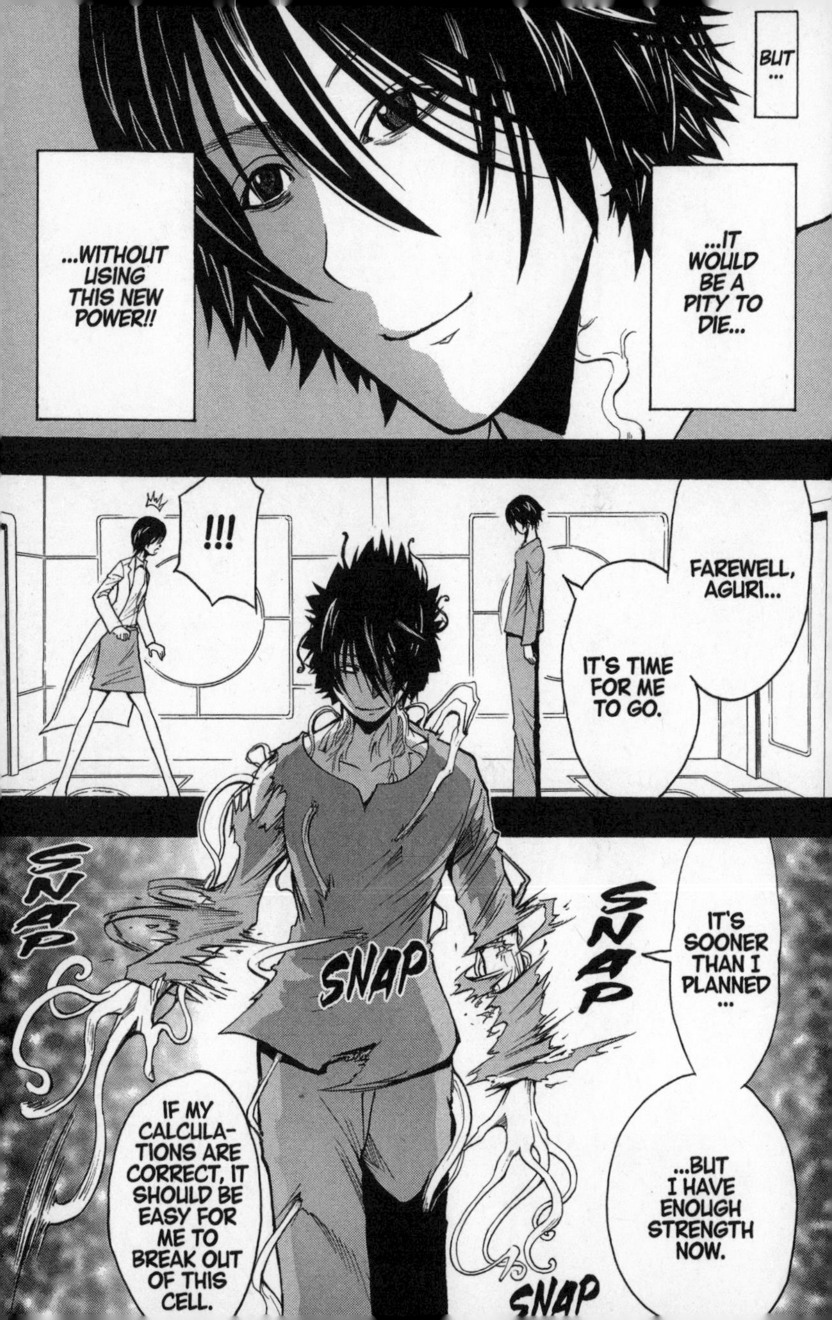
BUT ...
...IT WOULD BE A PITY TO DIE...
...WITHOUT USING THIS NEW POWER!!
FAREWELL, AGURI...
IT'S TIME FOR ME TO GO.
!!!
SNAP
IT'S SOONER THAN I PLANNED ...
...BUT I HAVE ENOUGH STRENGTH NOW.
SNAP
SNAP
SNAP
IF MY CALCULATIONS ARE CORRECT, IT SHOULD BE EASY FOR ME TO BREAK OUT OF THIS CELL.

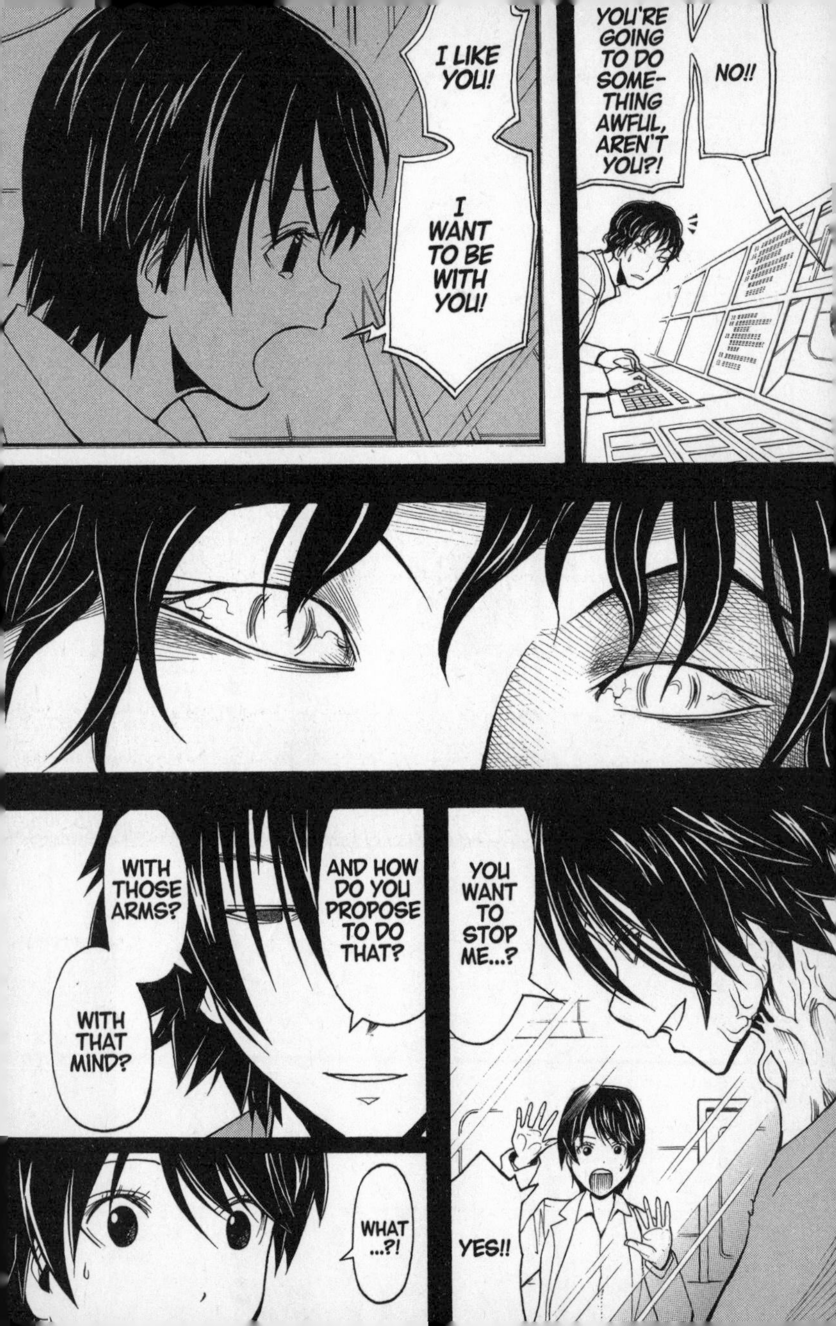
NO!!
YOU'RE GOING TO DO SOME-THING AWFUL, AREN'T YOU?!
I LIKE YOU!
I WANT TO BE WITH YOU!
YOU WANT TO STOP ME...?
YES!!
AND HOW DO YOU PROPOSE TO DO THAT?
WITH THOSE ARMS?
WITH THAT MIND?
WHAT ...?!

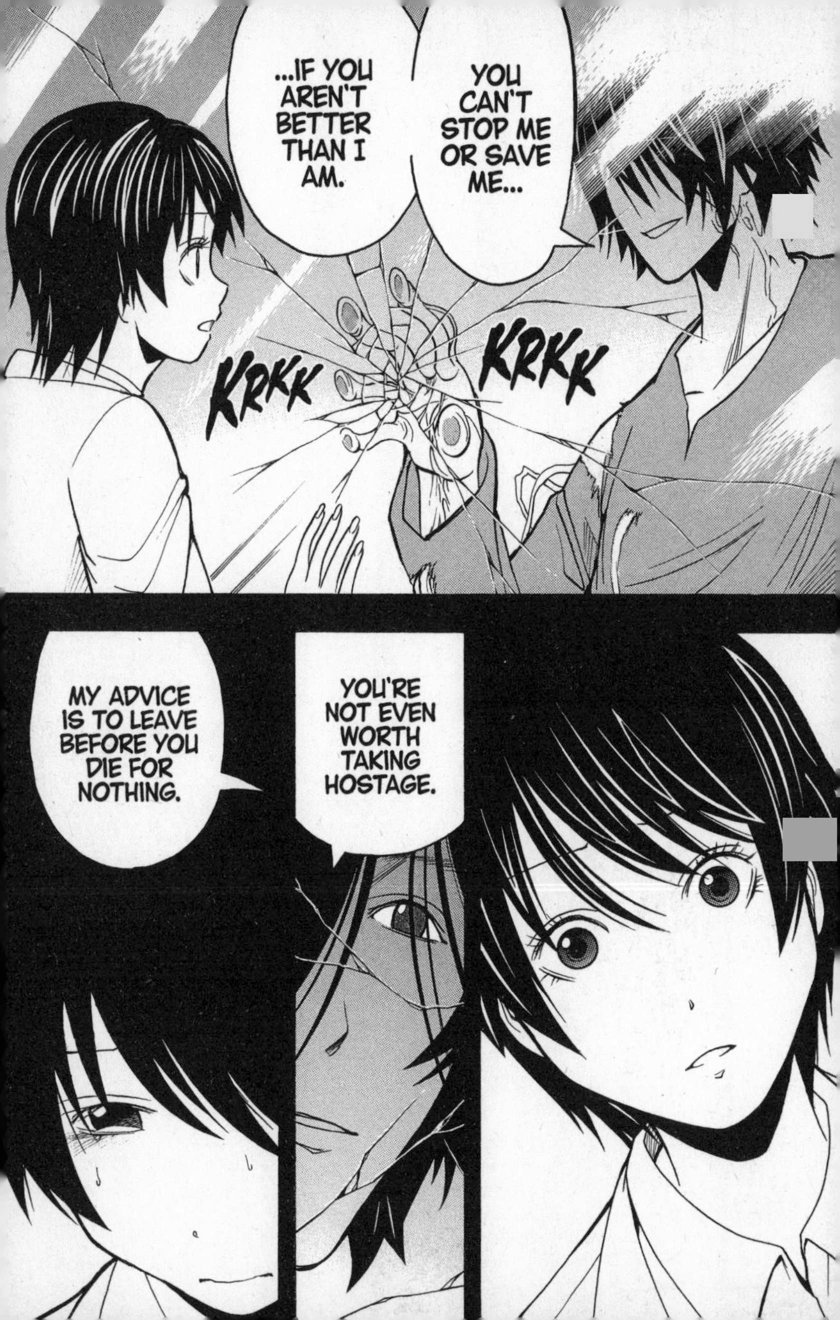
YOU CAN'T STOP ME OR SAVE ME...
...IF YOU AREN'T BETTER THAN I AM.
KRKK
KRKK
YOU'RE NOT EVEN WORTH TAKING HOSTAGE.
MY ADVICE IS TO LEAVE BEFORE YOU DIE FOR NOTHING.

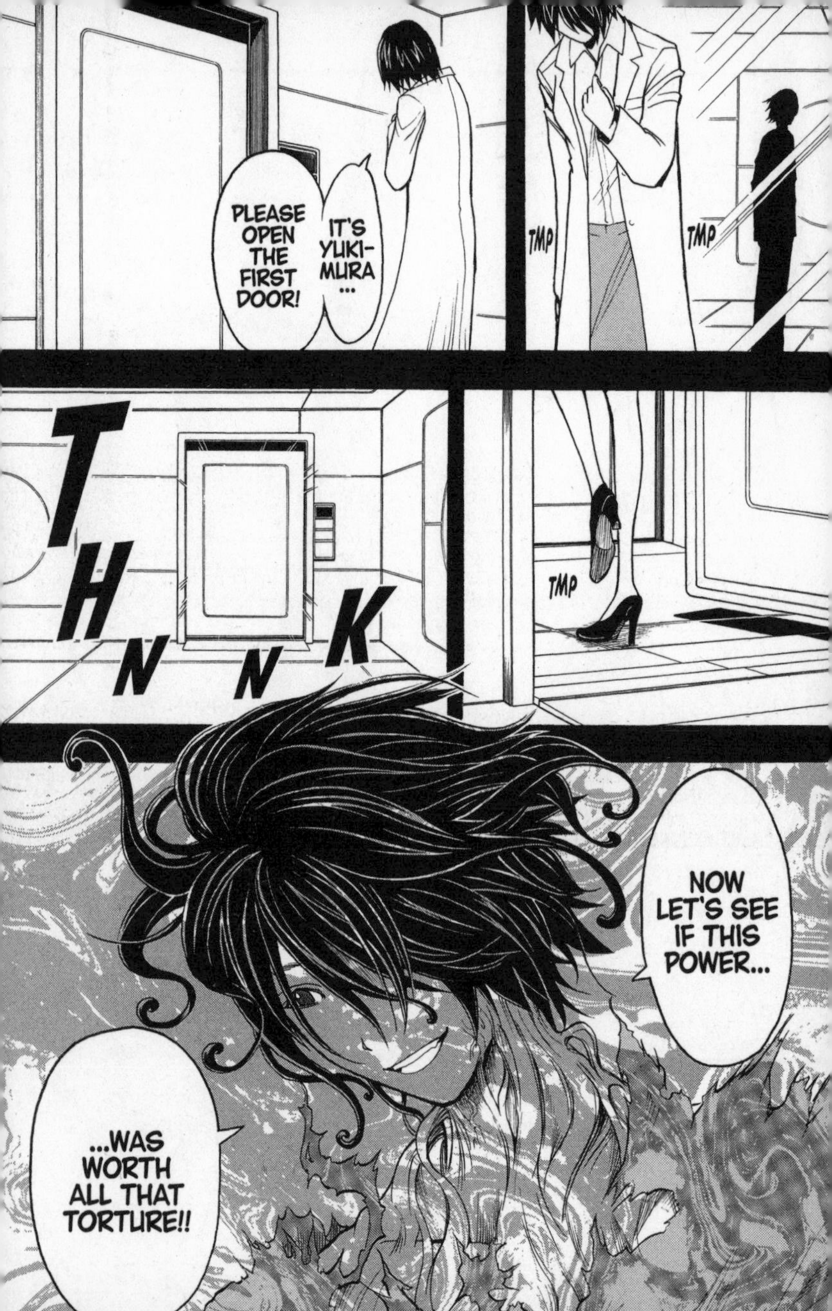
TMP
TMP
IT'S YUKI-MURA...
PLEASE OPEN THE FIRST DOOR!
TMP
THNNK
NOW LET'S SEE IF THIS POWER...
...WAS WORTH ALL THAT TORTURE!!

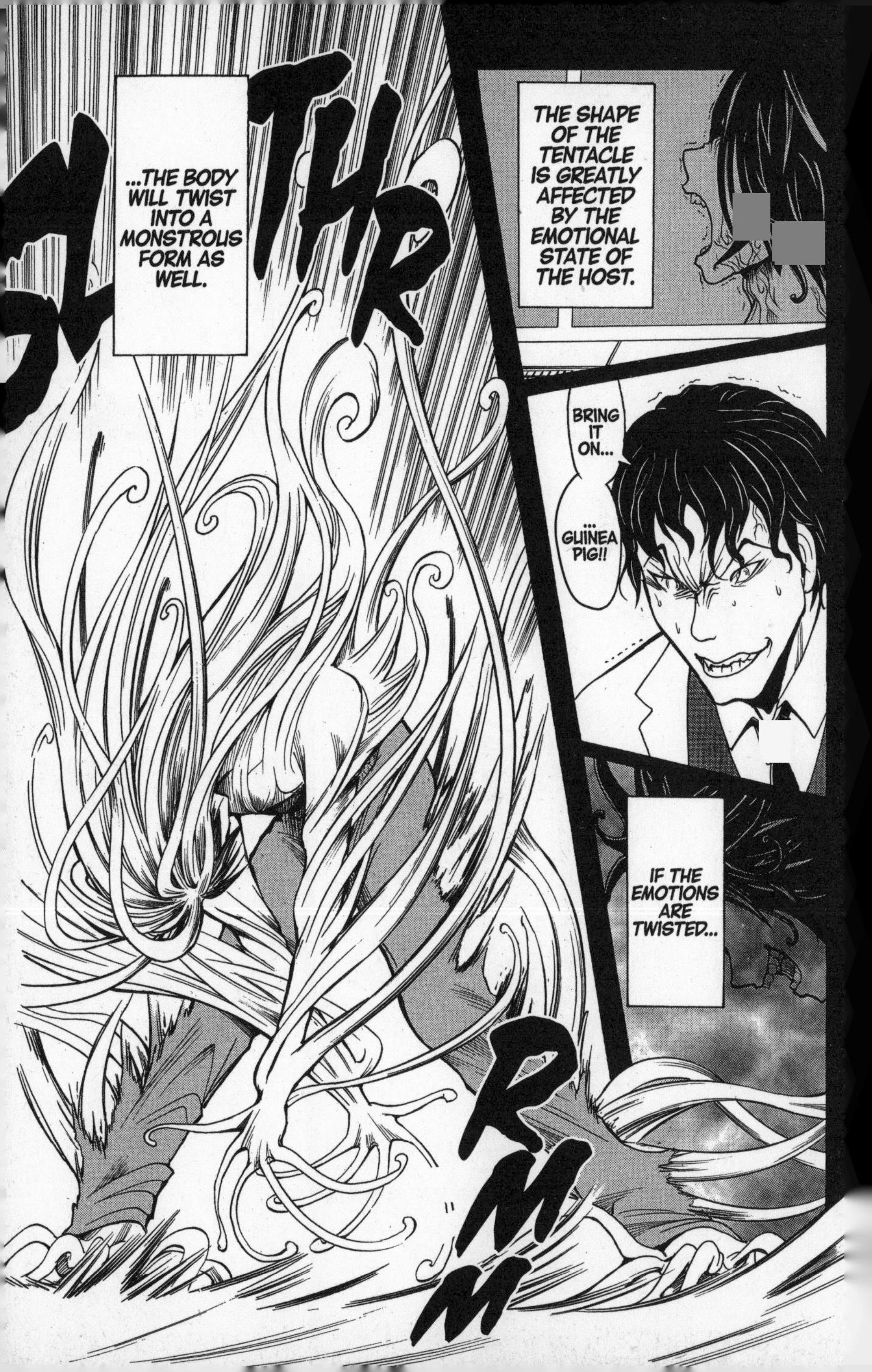
THE SHAPE OF THE TENTACLE IS GREATLY AFFECTED BY THE EMOTIONAL STATE OF THE HOST.
BRING IT ON...
...GUINEA PIG!!
IF THE EMOTIONS ARE TWISTED...
...THE BODY WILL TWIST INTO A MONSTROUS FORM AS WELL.
THR
RMM

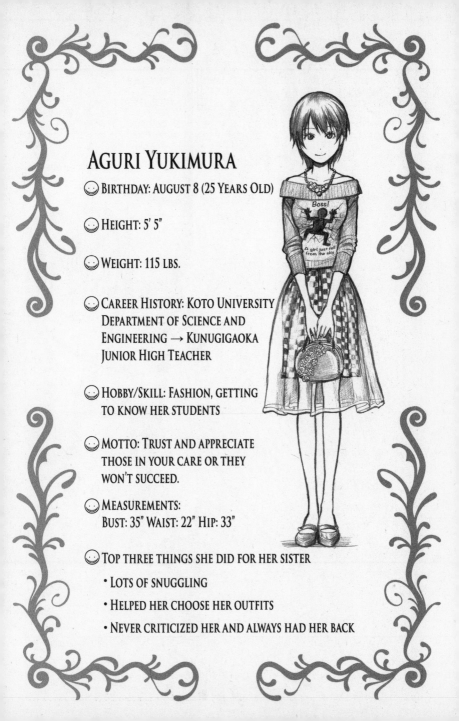

Aguri Yukimura

Boss!
A girl just fell from the sky

- Birthday: August 8 (25 Years Old)
- Height: 5' 5"
- Weight: 115 lbs.
- Career History: Koto University Department of Science and Engineering → Kunugigaoka Junior High Teacher
- Hobby/Skill: Fashion, getting to know her students
- Motto: Trust and appreciate those in your care or they won't succeed.
- Measurements:
  Bust: 35" Waist: 22" Hip: 33"
- Top three things she did for her sister
  - Lots of snuggling
  - Helped her choose her outfits
  - Never criticized her and always had her back

Class 139 Time for the Past—6th Period

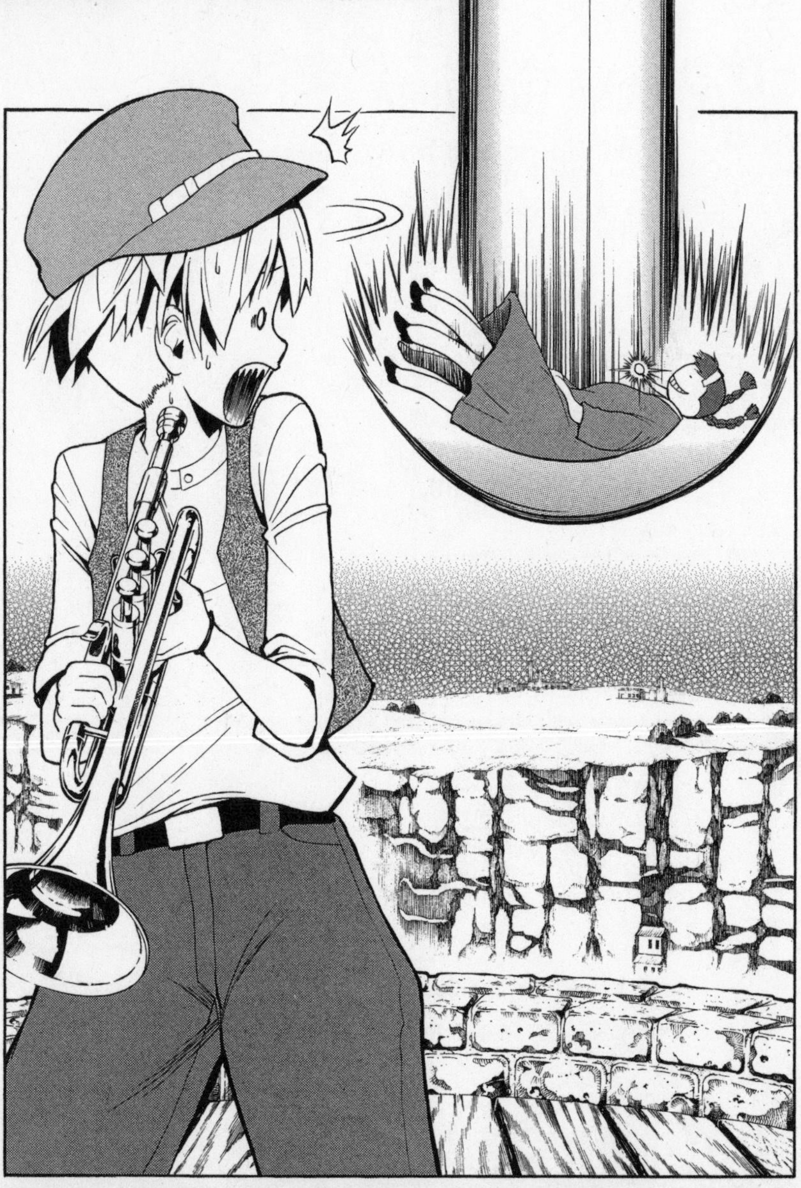

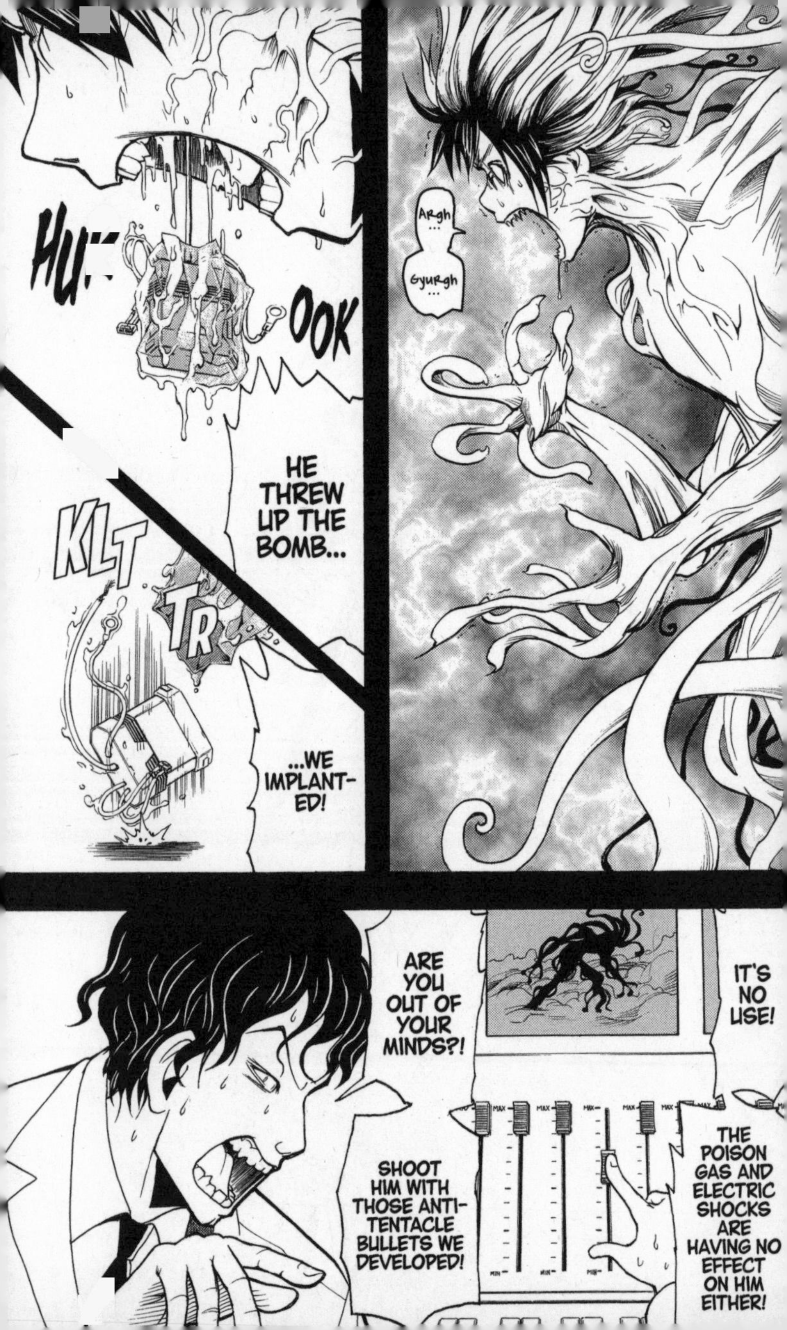
Argh...
Gyurgh...
HU
OOK
HE THREW UP THE BOMB...
KLT
TR
...WE IMPLANT-ED!
IT'S NO USE!
THE POISON GAS AND ELECTRIC SHOCKS ARE HAVING NO EFFECT ON HIM EITHER!
ARE YOU OUT OF YOUR MINDS?!
SHOOT HIM WITH THOSE ANTI-TENTACLE BULLETS WE DEVELOPED!

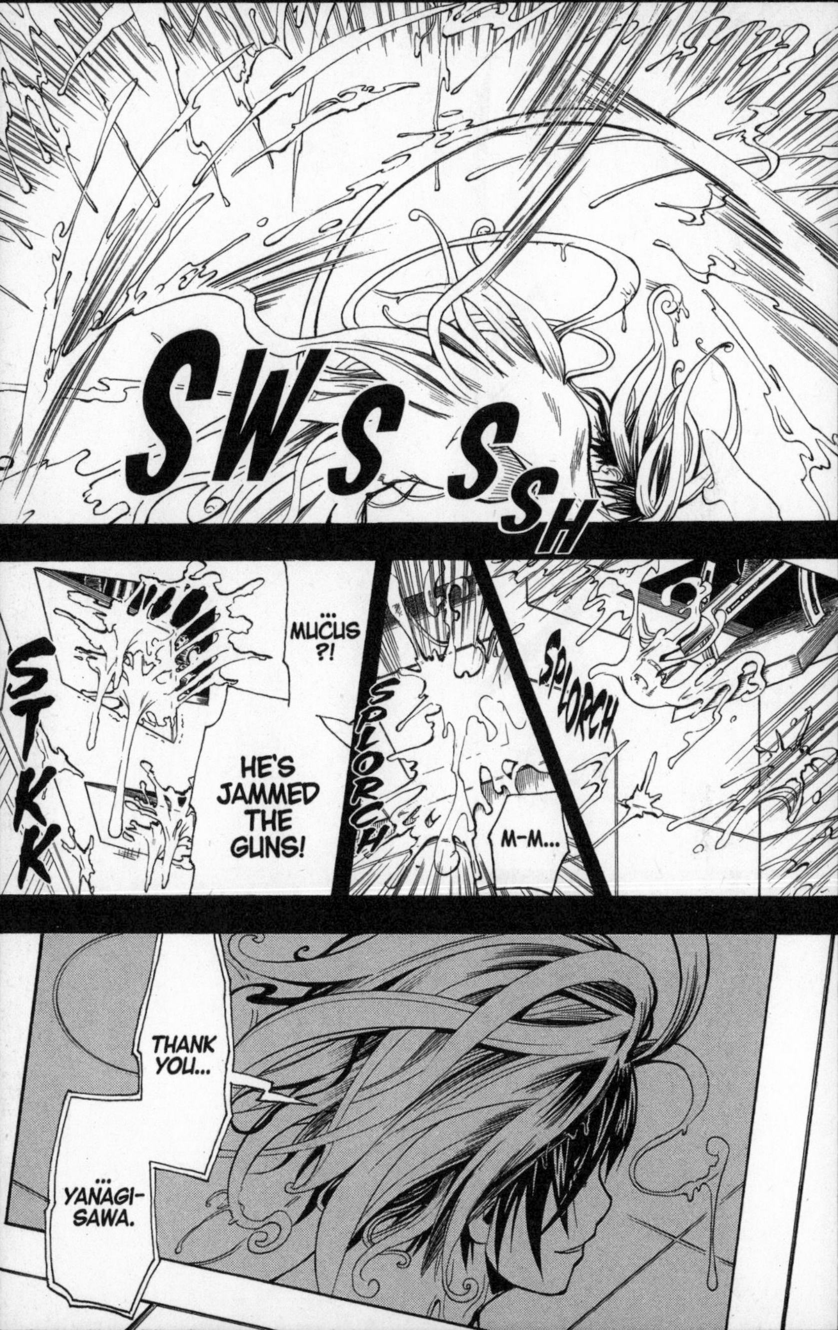
SWSSSSH
SPLORCH
SPLORCH
M-M...
... MUCUS ?!
STKK
HE'S JAMMED THE GUNS!
THANK YOU...
... YANAGI-SAWA.

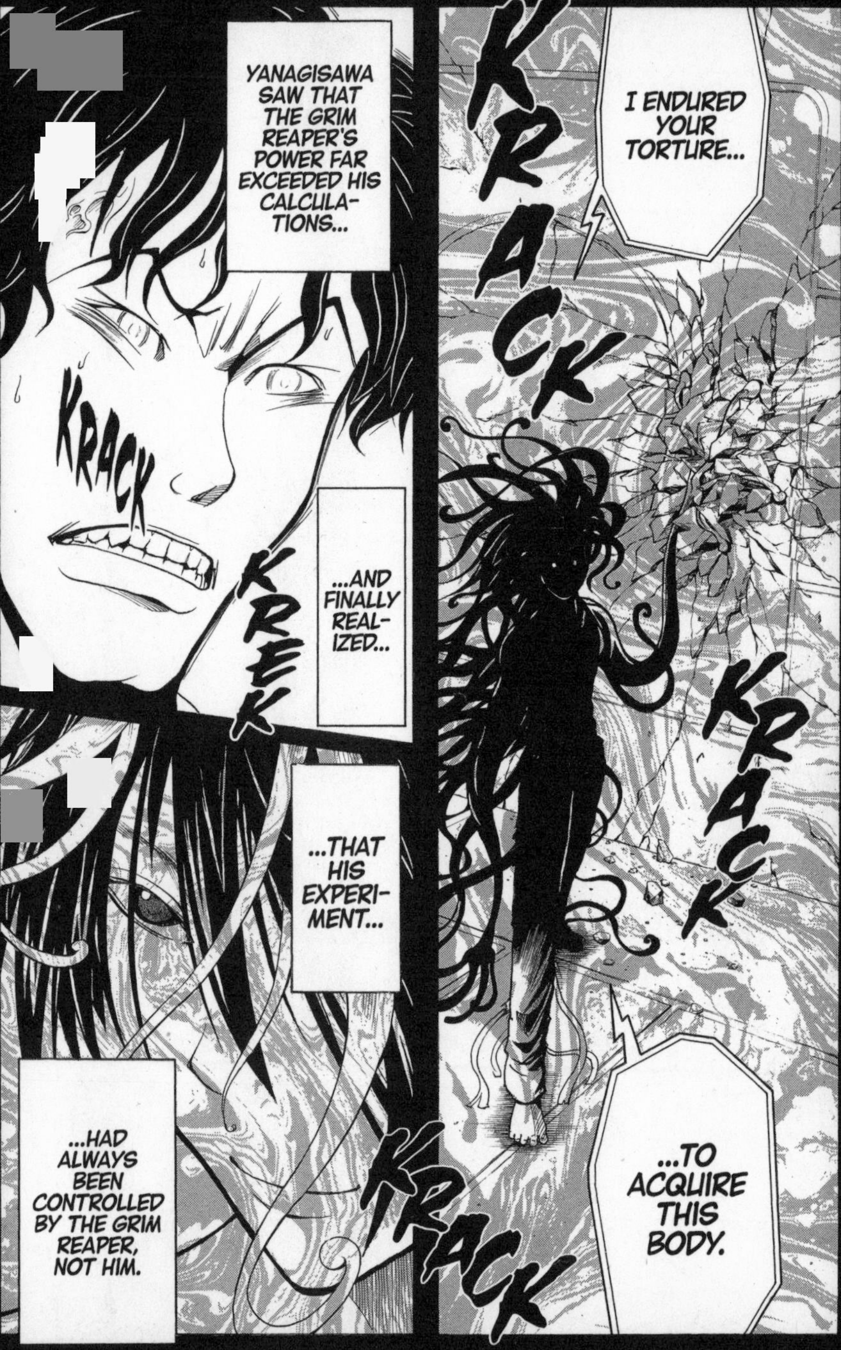
KRACK
I ENDURED YOUR TORTURE...
KRACK
...TO ACQUIRE THIS BODY.
YANAGISAWA SAW THAT THE GRIM REAPER'S POWER FAR EXCEEDED HIS CALCULATIONS...
KRACK
...AND FINALLY REALIZED...
KREK
...THAT HIS EXPERIMENT...
...HAD ALWAYS BEEN CONTROLLED BY THE GRIM REAPER, NOT HIM.
KRACK

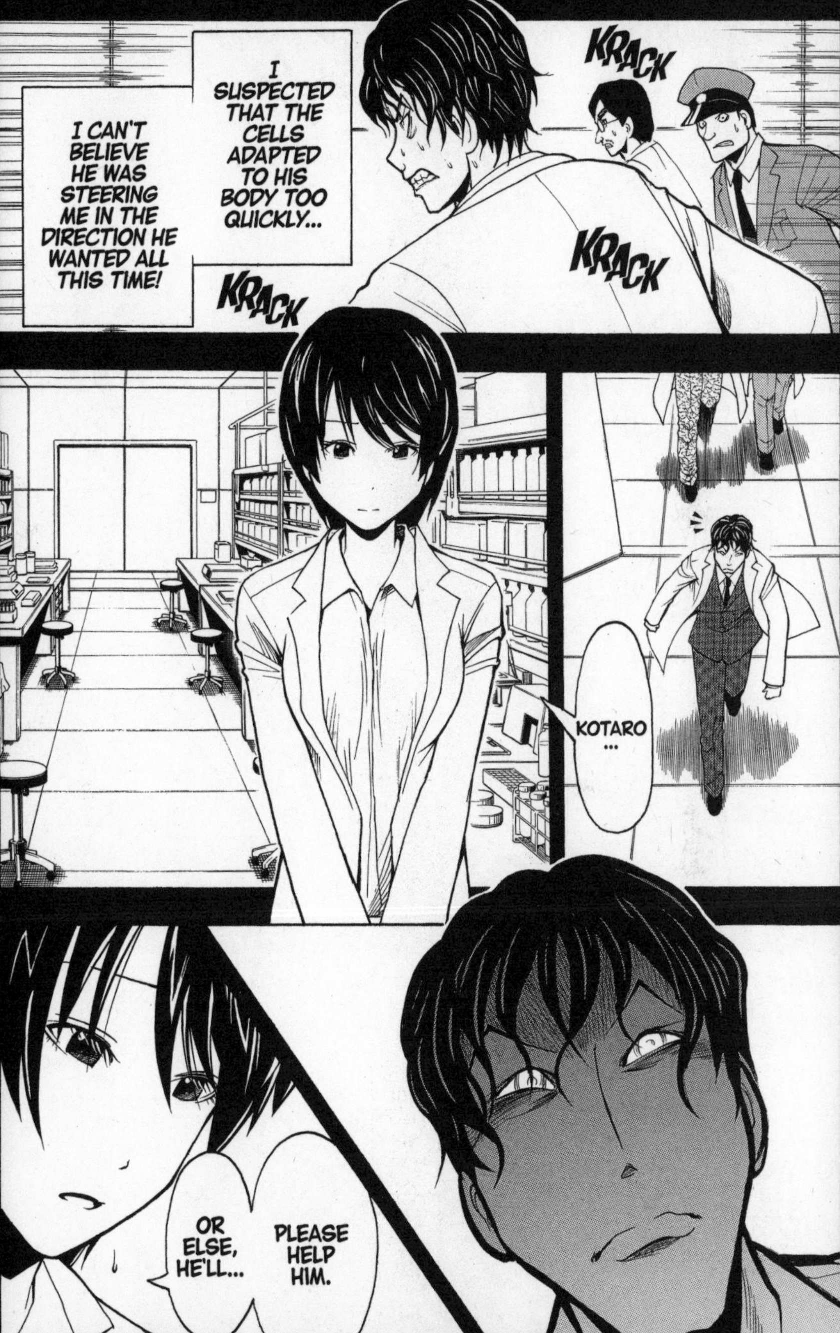
KRACK
I SUSPECTED THAT THE CELLS ADAPTED TO HIS BODY TOO QUICKLY...
I CAN'T BELIEVE HE WAS STEERING ME IN THE DIRECTION HE WANTED ALL THIS TIME!
KRACK
KRACK
KOTARO...
PLEASE HELP HIM.
OR ELSE, HE'LL...

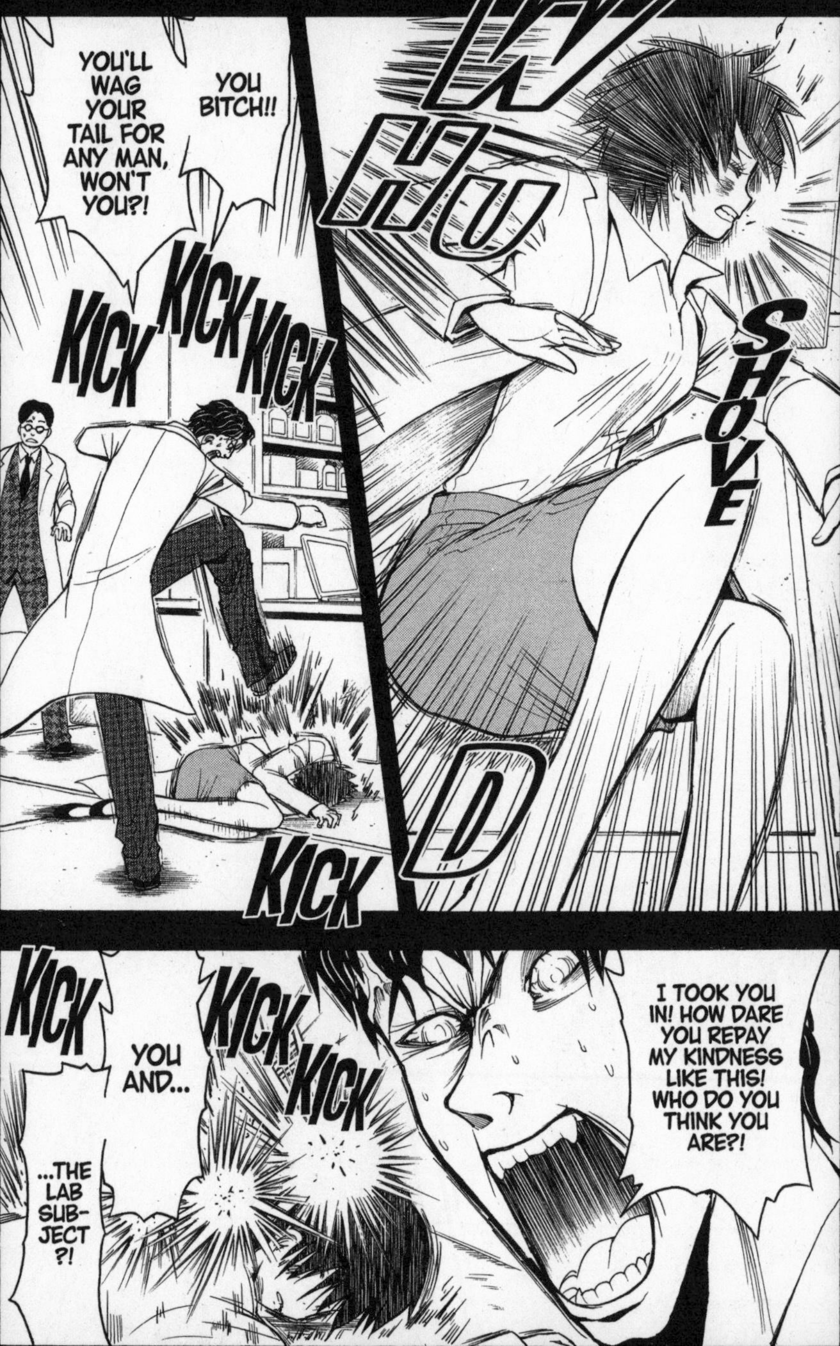
WHUD
SHOVE
YOU BITCH!!
YOU'LL WAG YOUR TAIL FOR ANY MAN, WON'T YOU?!
KICK KICK KICK
KICK
I TOOK YOU IN! HOW DARE YOU REPAY MY KINDNESS LIKE THIS! WHO DO YOU THINK YOU ARE?!
KICK KICK
YOU AND...
KICK
...THE LAB SUB-JECT?!

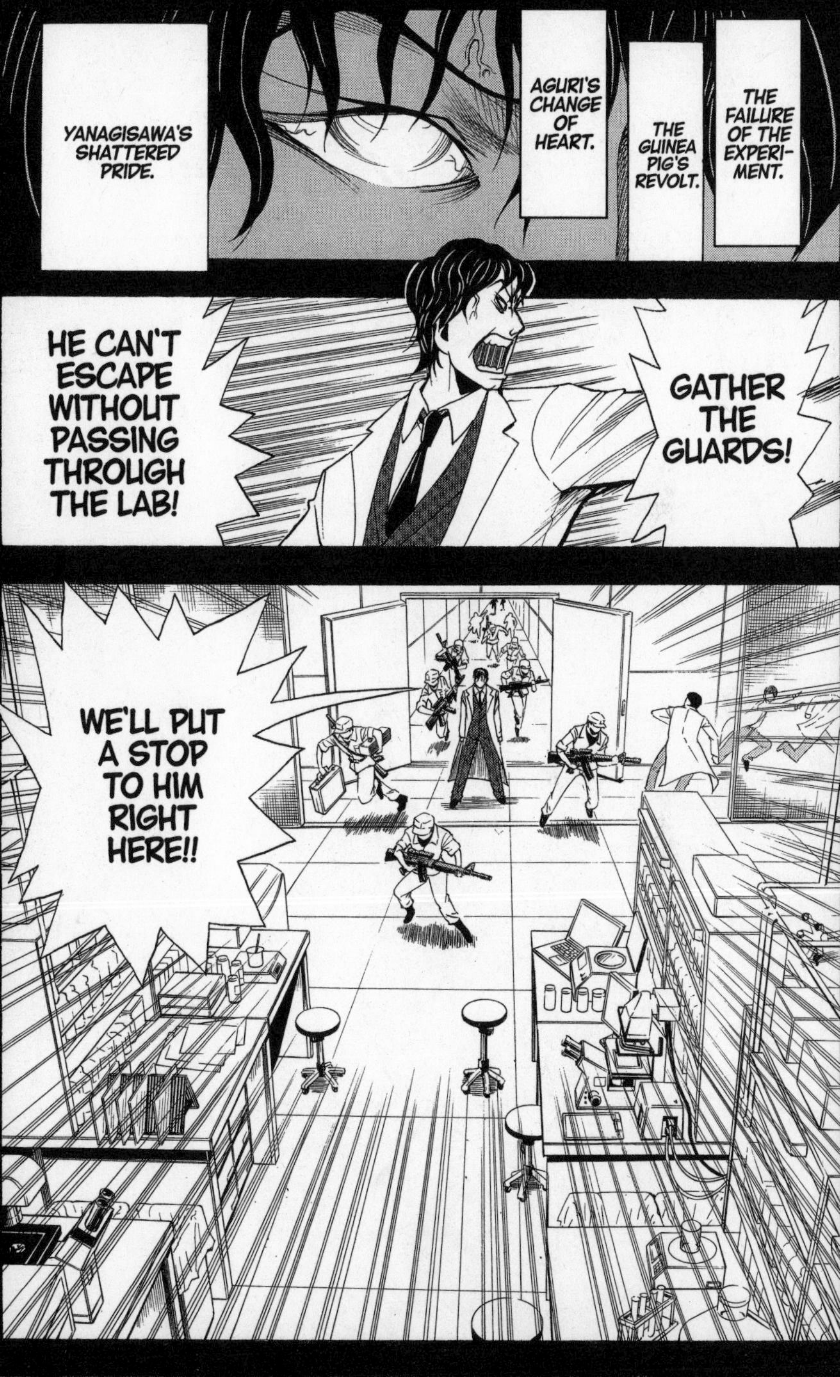
THE FAILURE OF THE EXPERI- MENT.
THE GUINEA PIG'S REVOLT.
AGURI'S CHANGE OF HEART.
YANAGISAWA'S SHATTERED PRIDE.
GATHER THE GUARDS!
HE CAN'T ESCAPE WITHOUT PASSING THROUGH THE LAB!
WE'LL PUT A STOP TO HIM RIGHT HERE!!

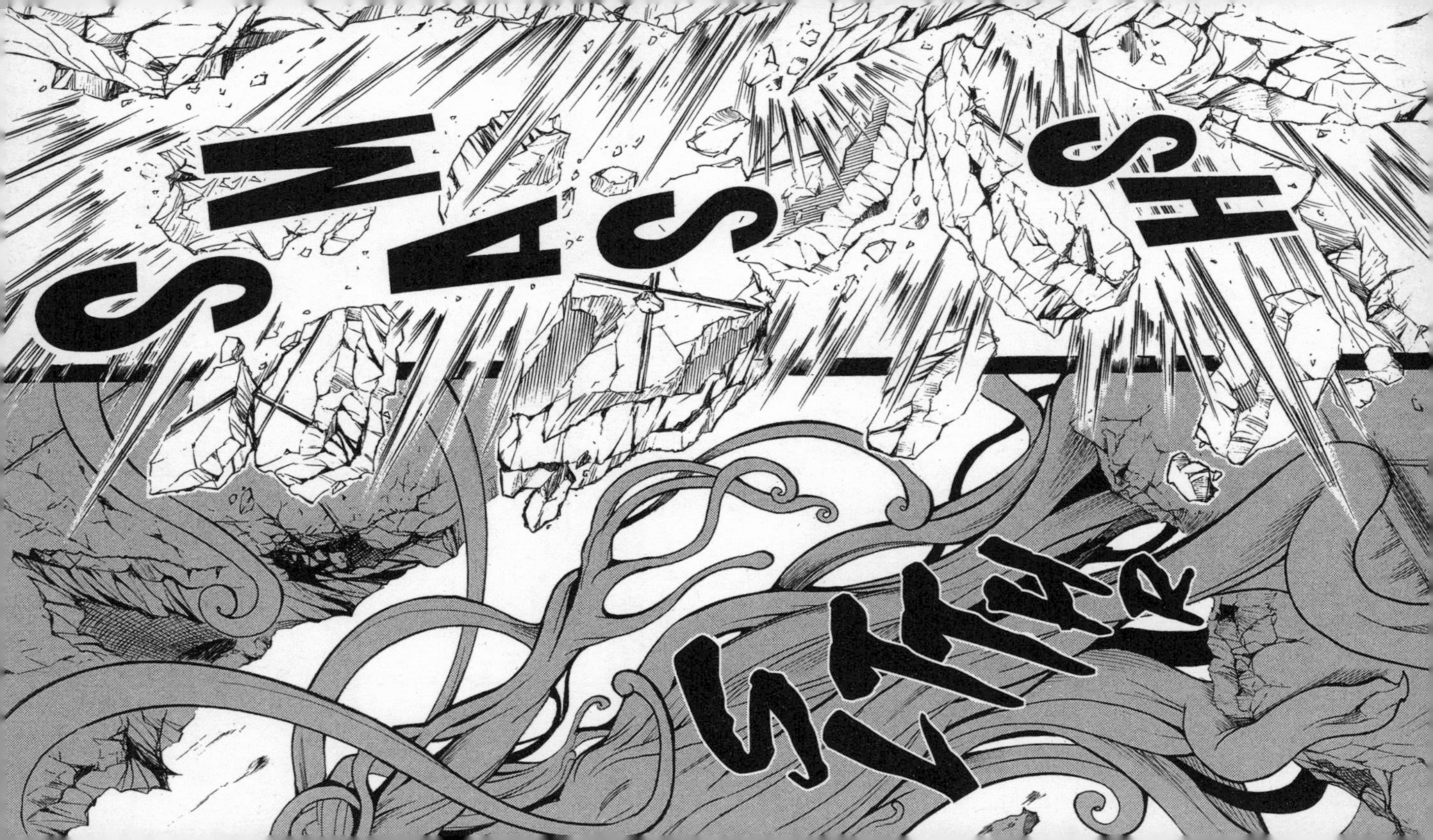
SMASH
SLITHR

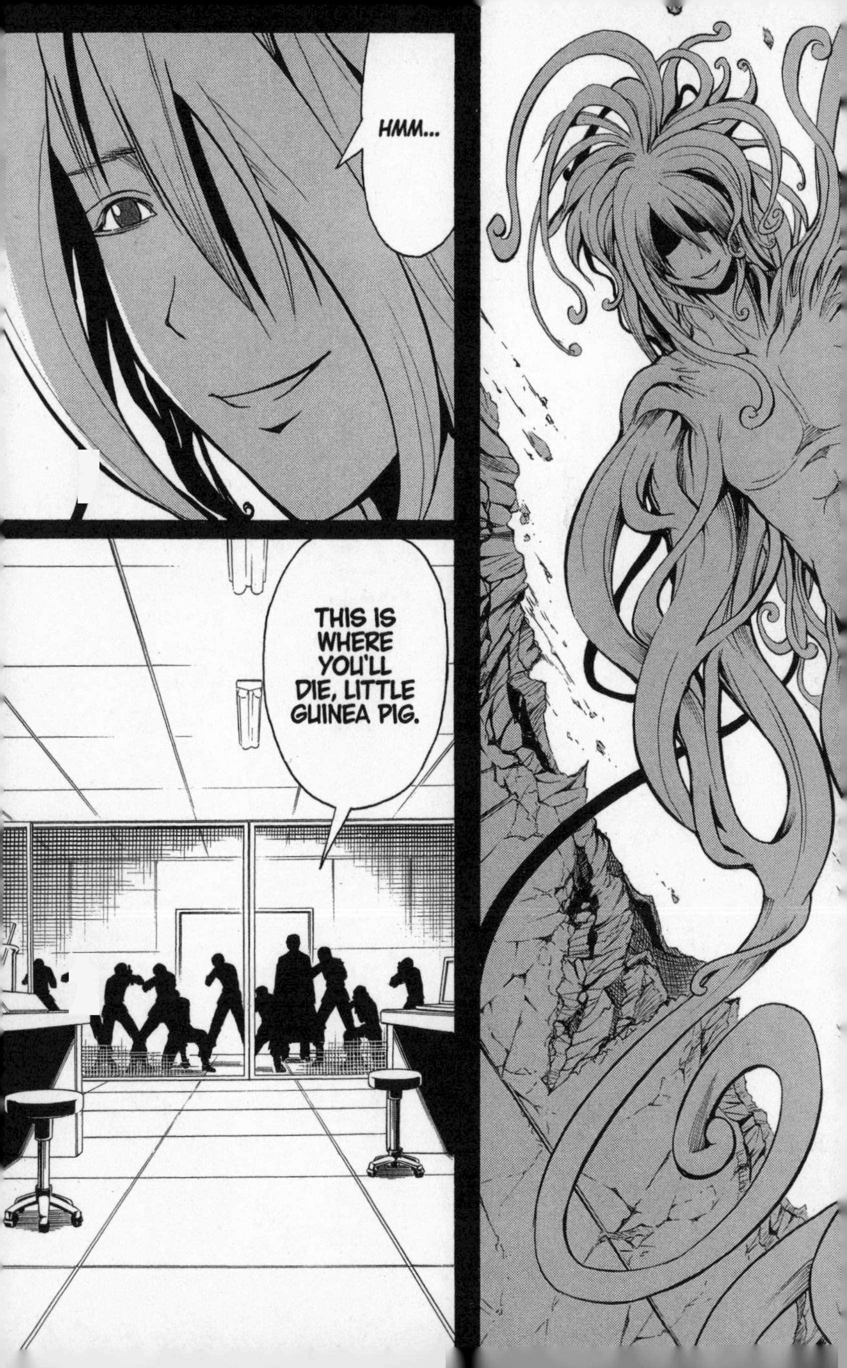
HMM...
THIS IS WHERE YOU'LL DIE, LITTLE GUINEA PIG.

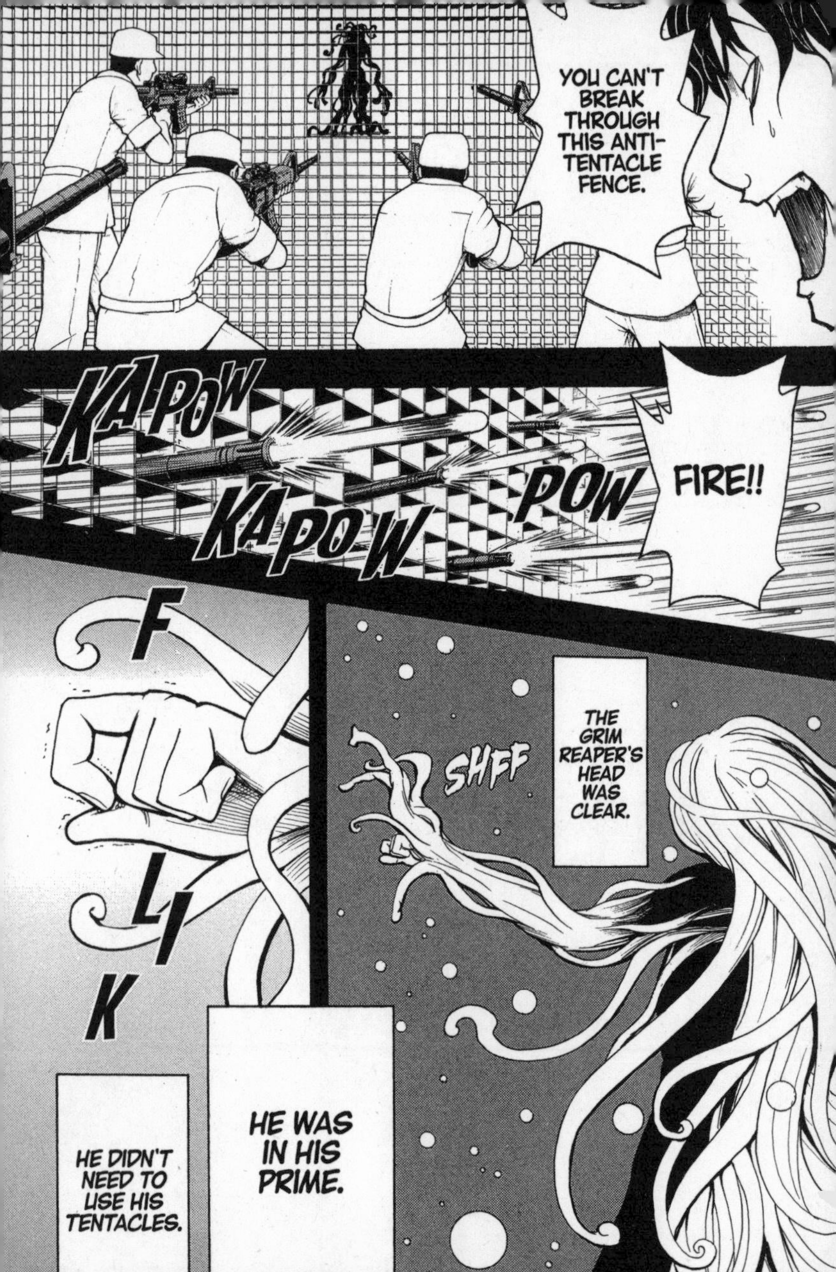
YOU CAN'T BREAK THROUGH THIS ANTI-TENTACLE FENCE.
FIRE!!
POW
KAPOW
KAPOW
THE GRIM REAPER'S HEAD WAS CLEAR.
SHFF
FLIK
HE WAS IN HIS PRIME.
HE DIDN'T NEED TO USE HIS TENTACLES.

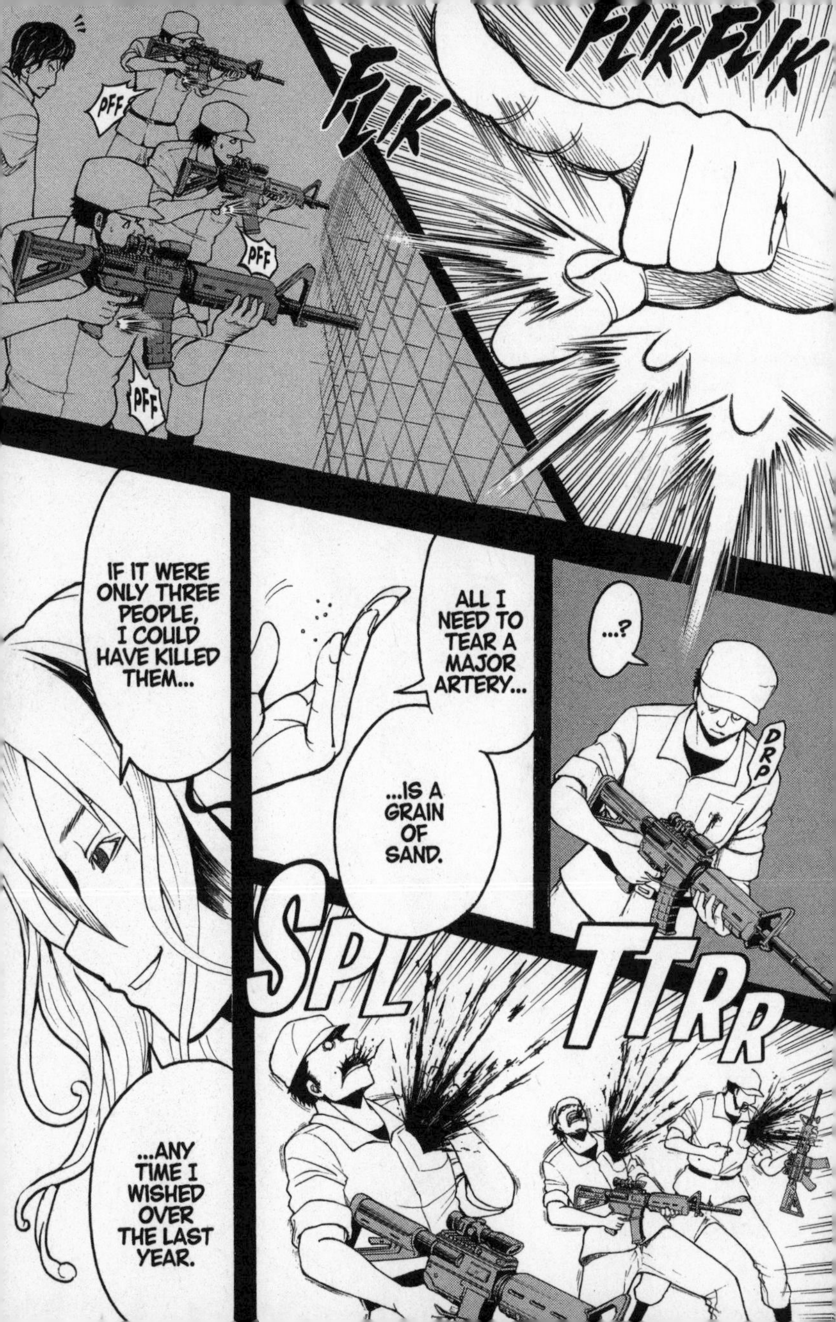
FLIK FLIK
FLIK
PFF
PFF
PFF
...?
DRP
ALL I NEED TO TEAR A MAJOR ARTERY...
...IS A GRAIN OF SAND.
SPL
TTRR
IF IT WERE ONLY THREE PEOPLE, I COULD HAVE KILLED THEM...
...ANY TIME I WISHED OVER THE LAST YEAR.

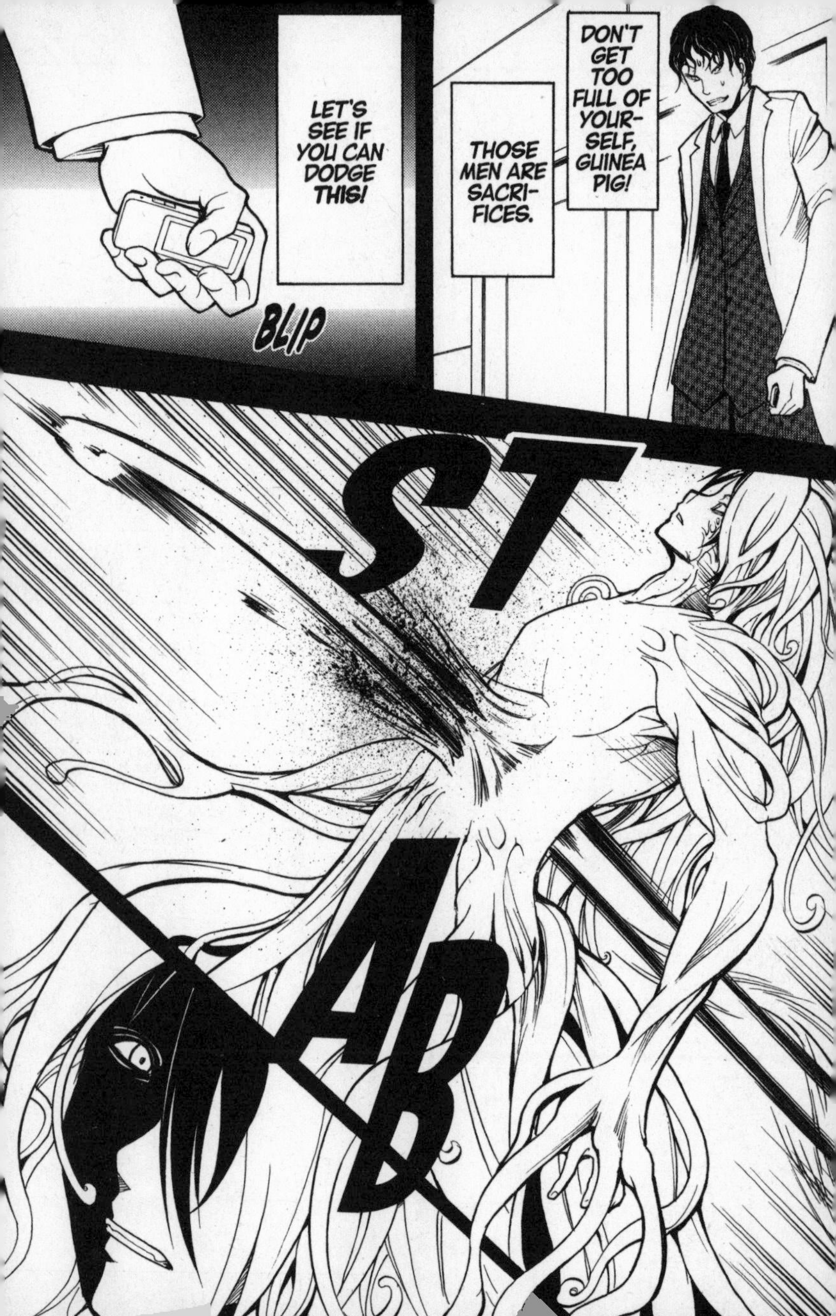
DON'T GET TOO FULL OF YOUR-SELF, GUINEA PIG!
THOSE MEN ARE SACRI-FICES.
LET'S SEE IF YOU CAN DODGE THIS!
BLIP
STAB

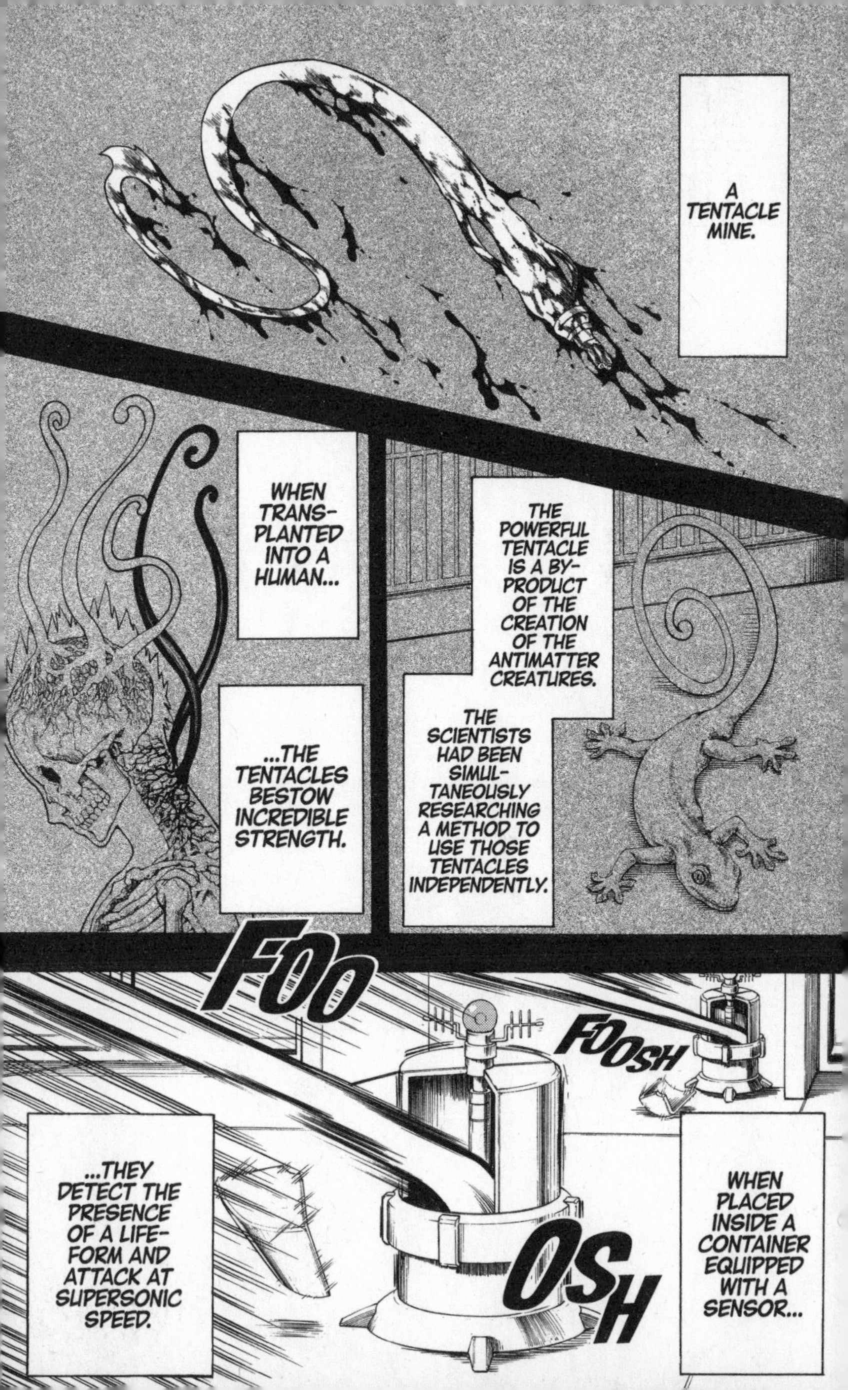
A TENTACLE MINE.
THE POWERFUL TENTACLE IS A BY-PRODUCT OF THE CREATION OF THE ANTIMATTER CREATURES.
THE SCIENTISTS HAD BEEN SIMULTANEOUSLY RESEARCHING A METHOD TO USE THOSE TENTACLES INDEPENDENTLY.
WHEN TRANSPLANTED INTO A HUMAN...
...THE TENTACLES BESTOW INCREDIBLE STRENGTH.
WHEN PLACED INSIDE A CONTAINER EQUIPPED WITH A SENSOR...
FOOSH
FOOOSH
...THEY DETECT THE PRESENCE OF A LIFE-FORM AND ATTACK AT SUPERSONIC SPEED.

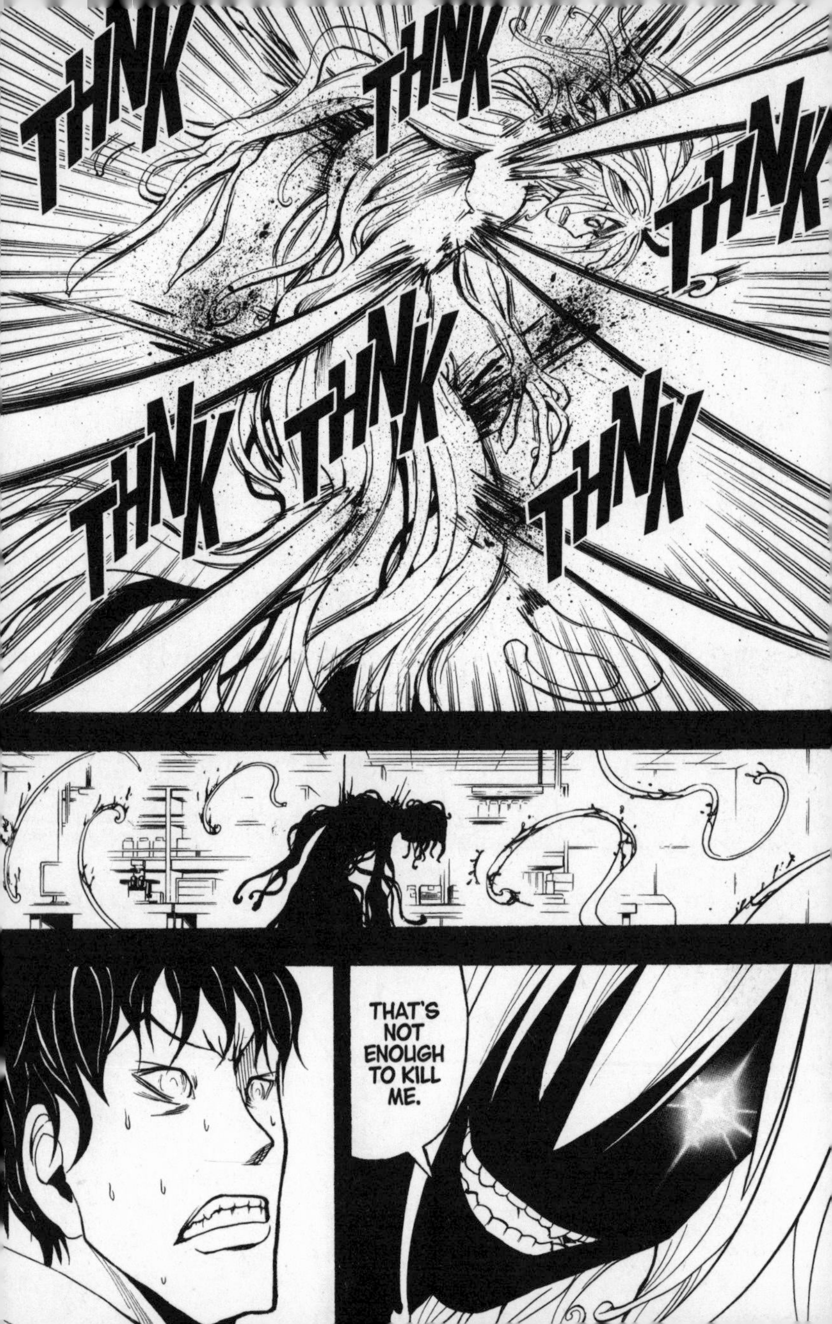
THNK
THNK
THNK
THNK
THNK
THNK
THAT'S NOT ENOUGH TO KILL ME.

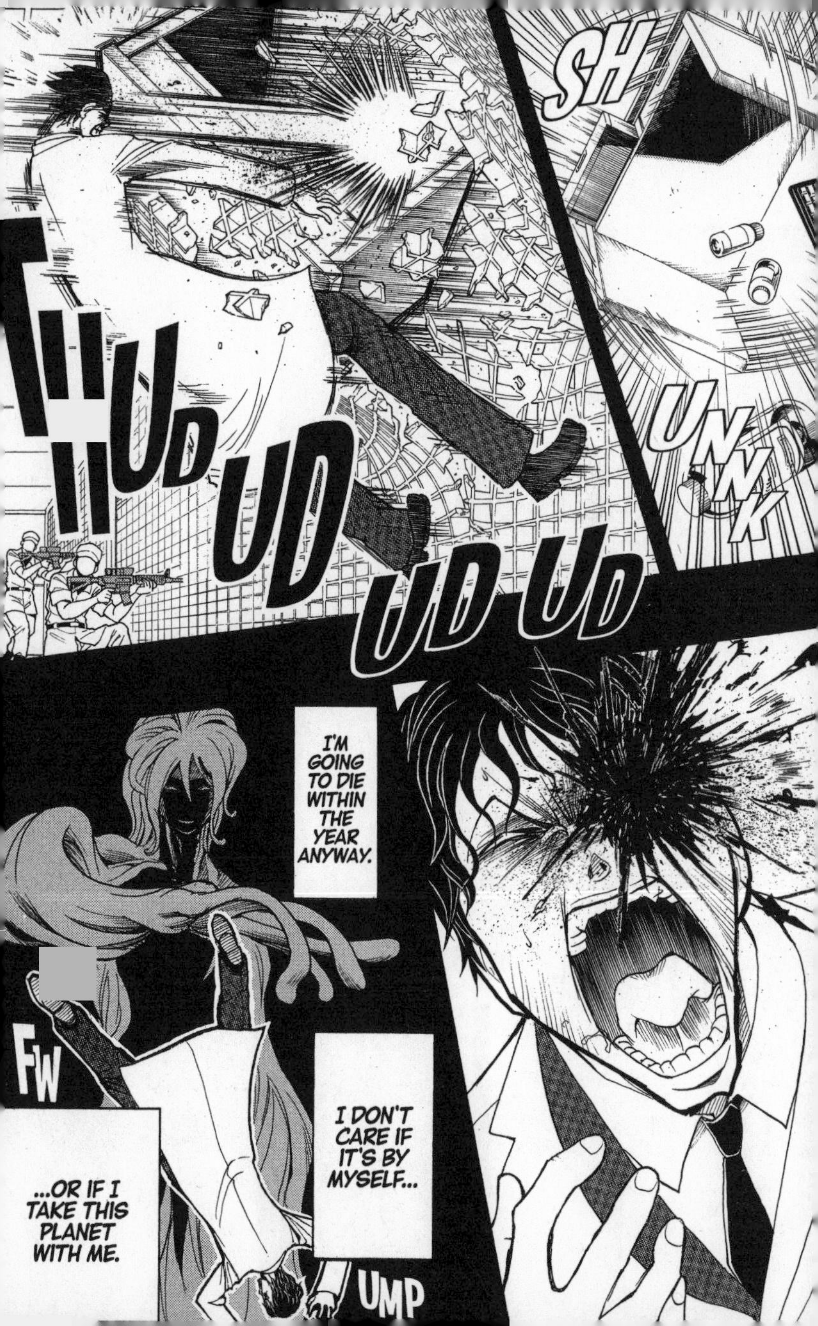
SH
UNNK
THUD UD UD UD
I'M GOING TO DIE WITHIN THE YEAR ANYWAY.
FW
I DON'T CARE IF IT'S BY MYSELF...
...OR IF I TAKE THIS PLANET WITH ME.
UMP

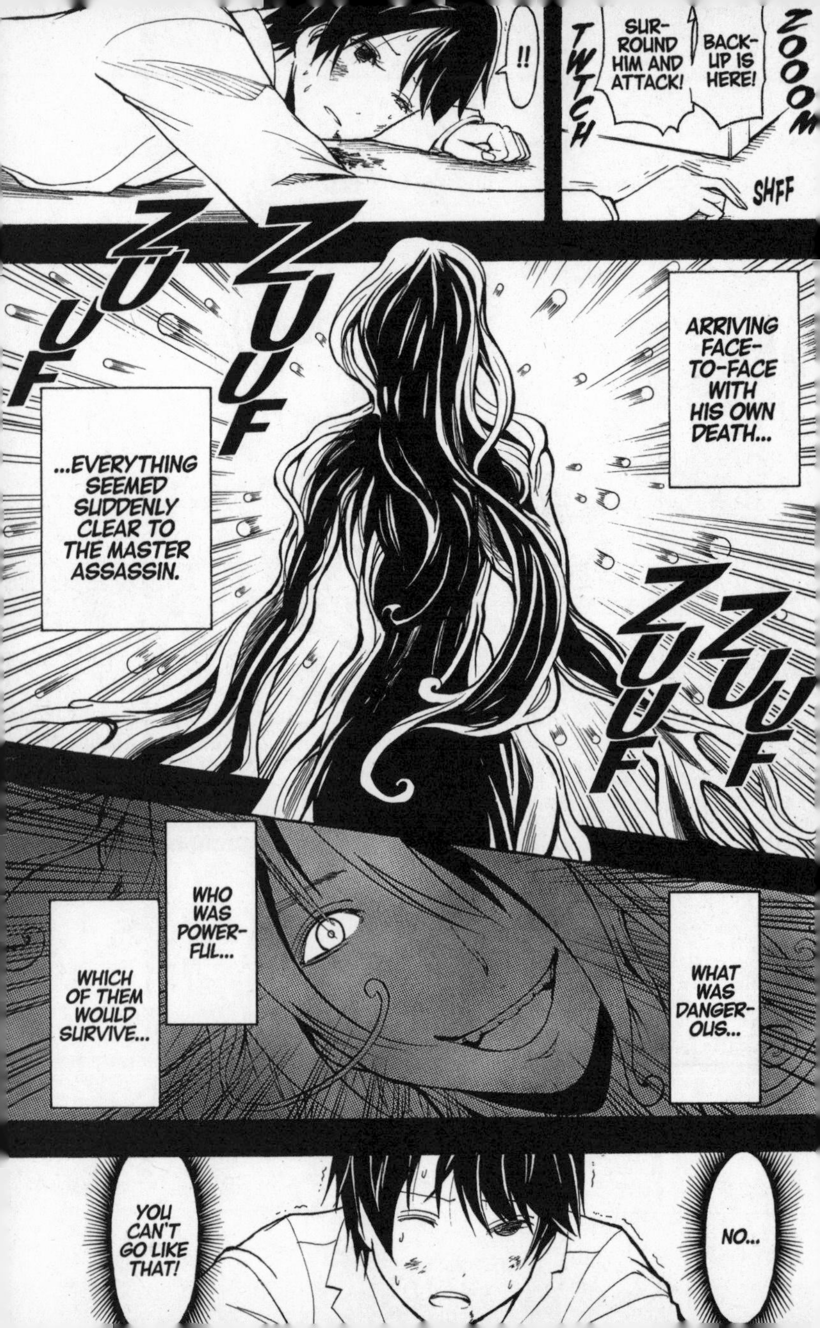
ZOOOM
BACK-UP IS HERE!
SUR-ROUND HIM AND ATTACK!
TWTCH
SHFF
!!
ARRIVING FACE-TO-FACE WITH HIS OWN DEATH...
ZUUF
ZUUF
...EVERYTHING SEEMED SUDDENLY CLEAR TO THE MASTER ASSASSIN.
ZUUF
ZUUF
WHAT WAS DANGER-OUS...
WHO WAS POWER-FUL...
WHICH OF THEM WOULD SURVIVE...
NO...
YOU CAN'T GO LIKE THAT!

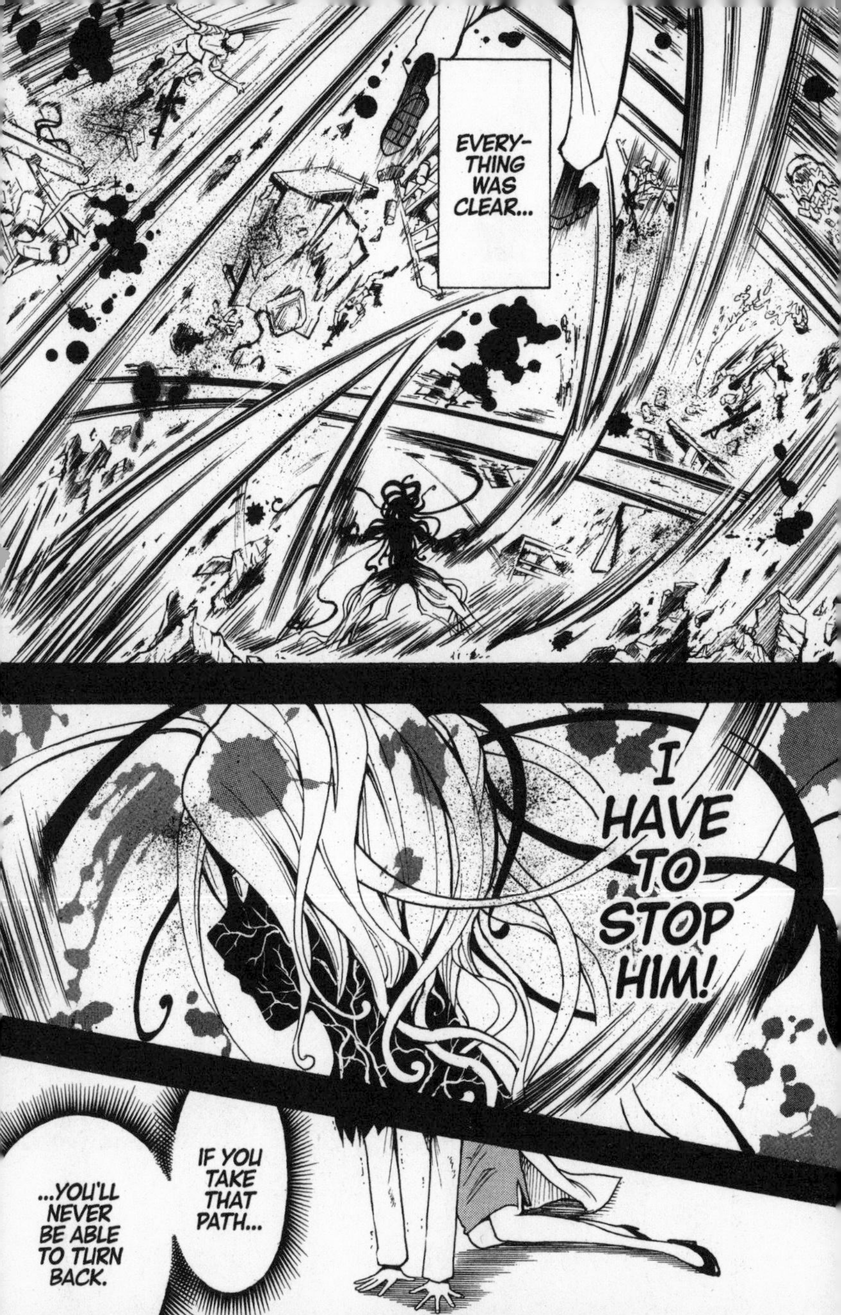
EVERY-THING WAS CLEAR...
I HAVE TO STOP HIM!
IF YOU TAKE THAT PATH...
...YOU'LL NEVER BE ABLE TO TURN BACK.

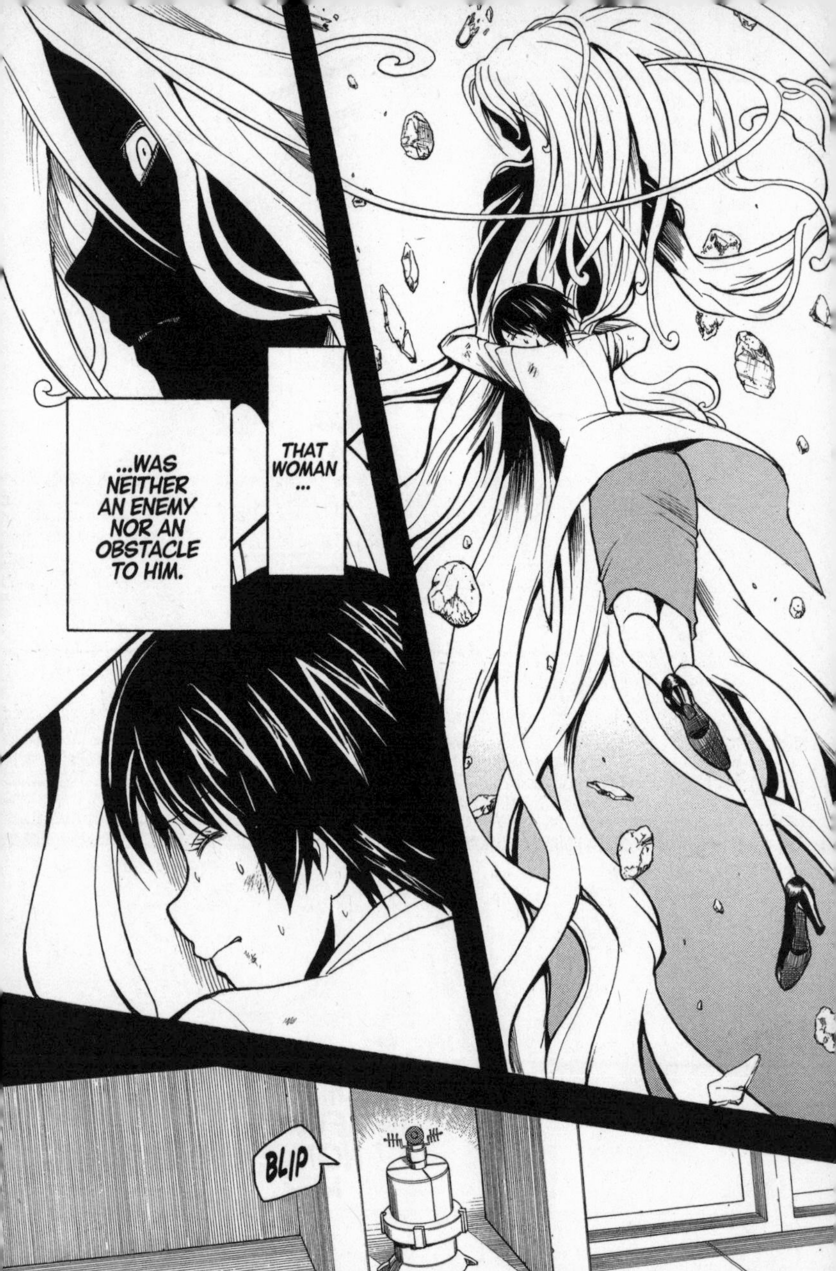
THAT WOMAN ...
...WAS NEITHER AN ENEMY NOR AN OBSTACLE TO HIM.
BLIP

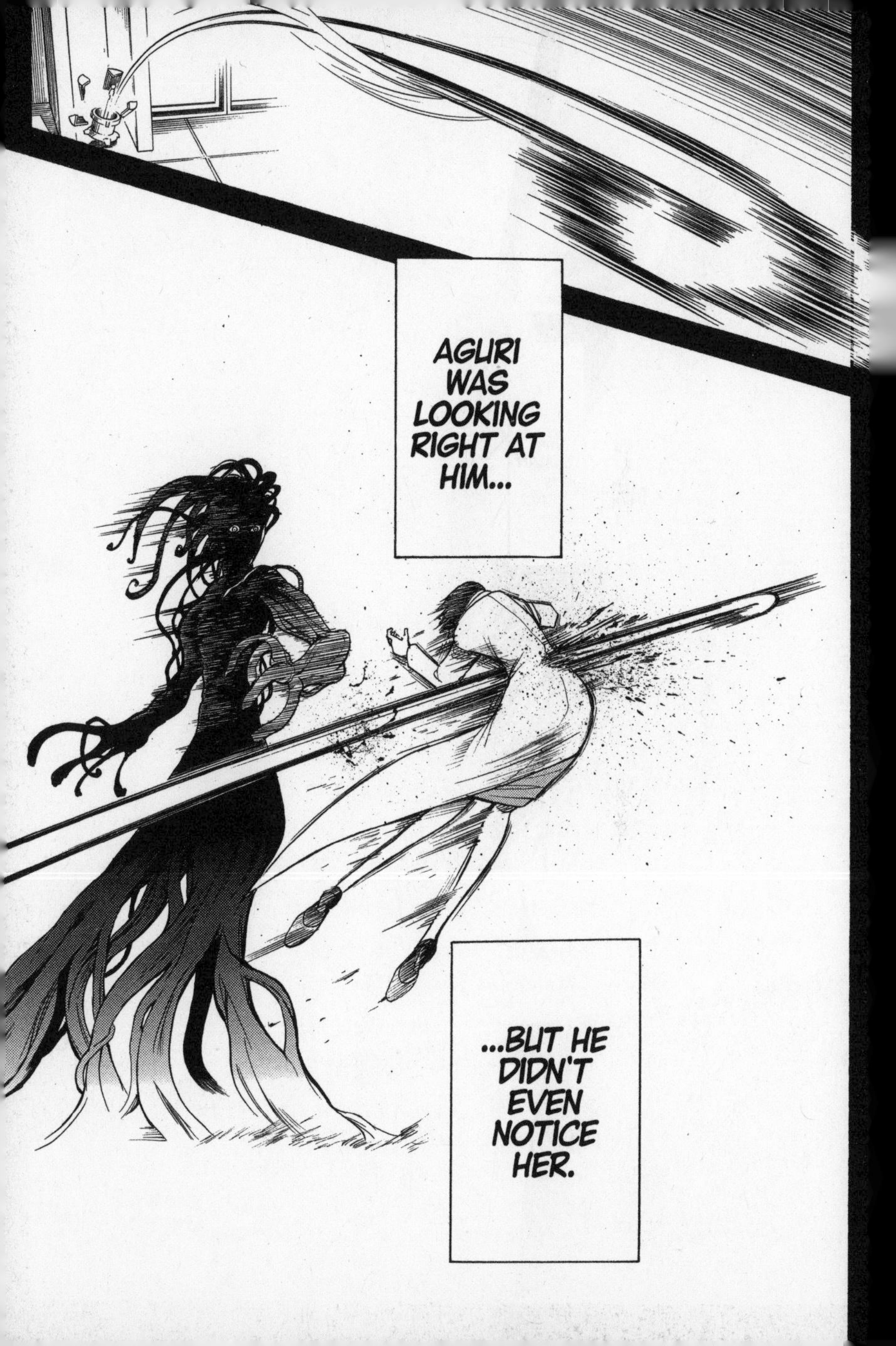
AGURI WAS LOOKING RIGHT AT HIM...
...BUT HE DIDN'T EVEN NOTICE HER.

KOTARO YANAGISANA

- 😊 BIRTHDAY: DECEMBER 10 (34 YEARS OLD)
- 😊 HEIGHT: 5' 8"
- 😊 WEIGHT: 132 LBS.
- 😊 CAREER: KOTO UNIVERSITY BIOENERGETICS RESEARCH LAB
  → INTERNATIONAL ENERGY RESEARCH INSTITUTE
- 😊 HOBBY/SKILL: MAGIC, NETWORKING
- 😊 MOTTO: A GENIUS'S MOMENT OF INSPIRATION IS GREATER
  THAN AN AVERAGE JOE'S ENTIRE LIFE.
- 😊 FIELDS OF EXPERTISE: QUANTUM MECHANICS,
  BIOCHEMISTRY, PHYSICAL CHEMISTRY
- 😊 THE WORDS OF A FAMOUS SCIENTIST WHO MET HIM:
  "IF ONLY THERE WERE AN IMPLANT FOR ETHICS. HE
  WOULD BE PERFECT AFTER THAT."

Class 140 Time for the Past—7th Period

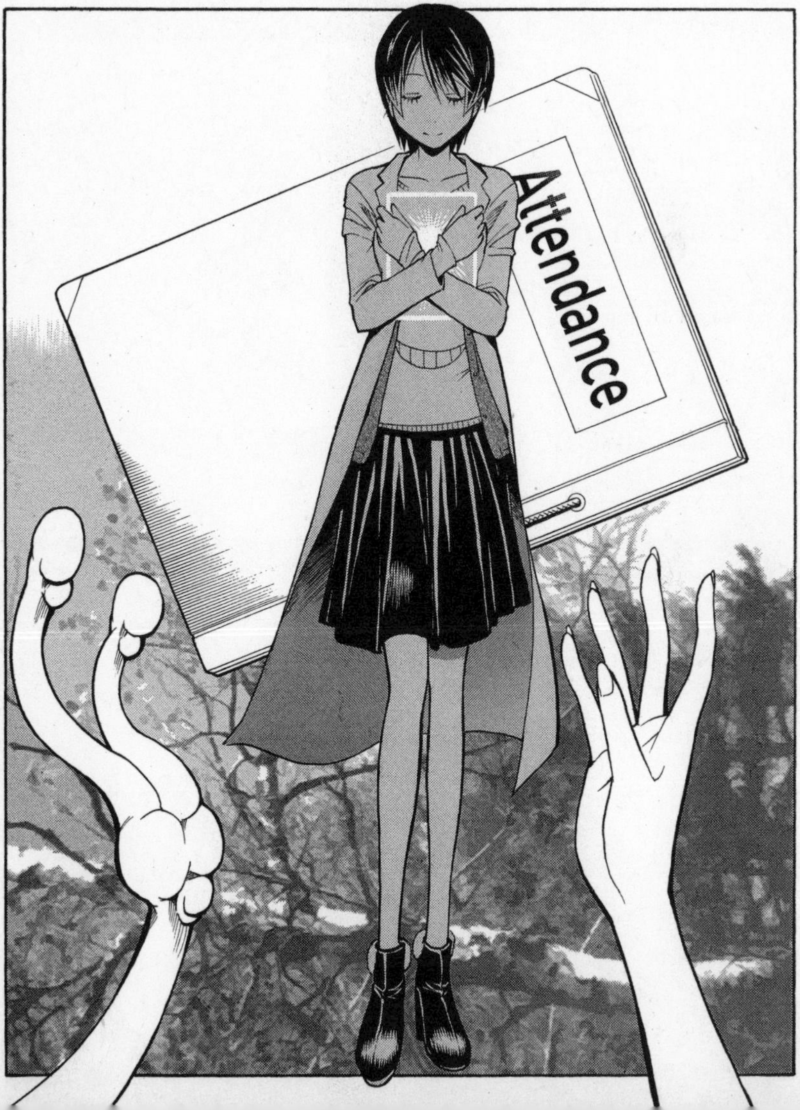
Attendance

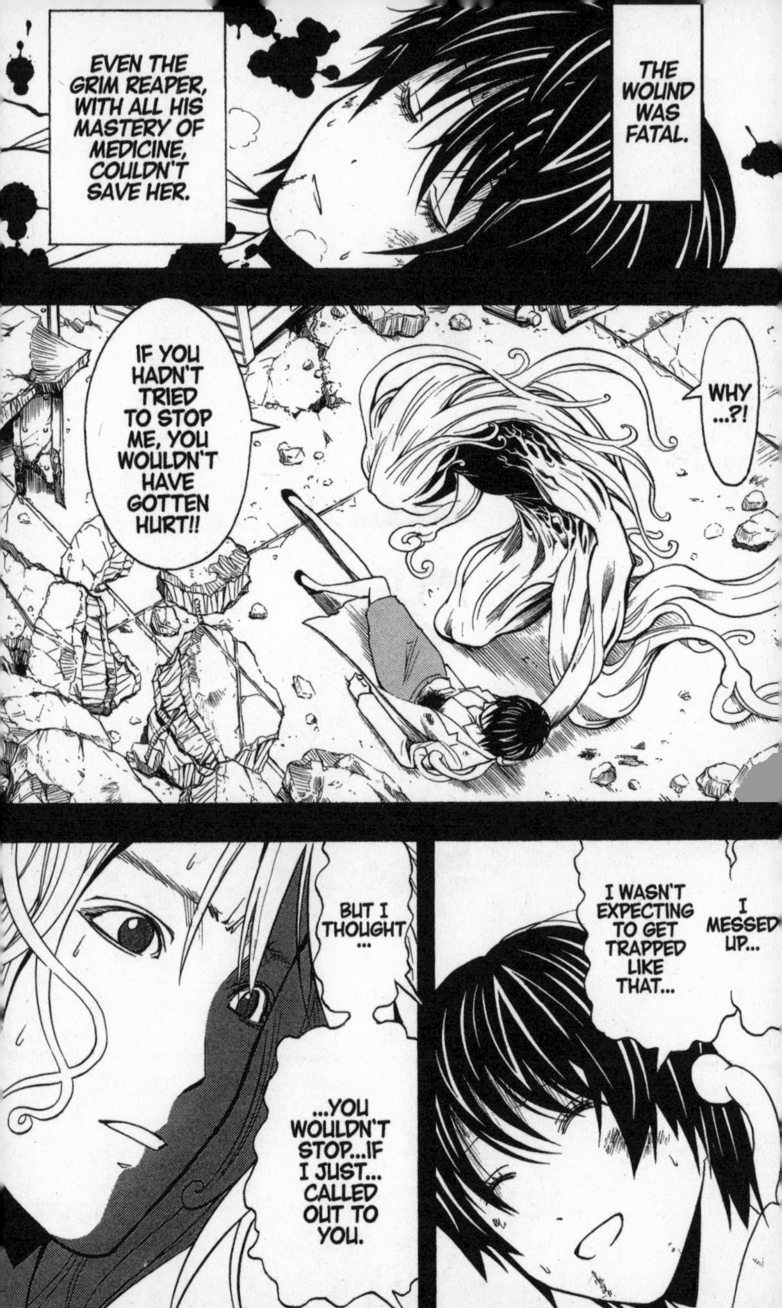
THE WOUND WAS FATAL.
EVEN THE GRIM REAPER, WITH ALL HIS MASTERY OF MEDICINE, COULDN'T SAVE HER.
WHY ...?!
IF YOU HADN'T TRIED TO STOP ME, YOU WOULDN'T HAVE GOTTEN HURT!!
I MESSED UP...
I WASN'T EXPECTING TO GET TRAPPED LIKE THAT...
BUT I THOUGHT ...
...YOU WOULDN'T STOP...IF I JUST... CALLED OUT TO YOU.

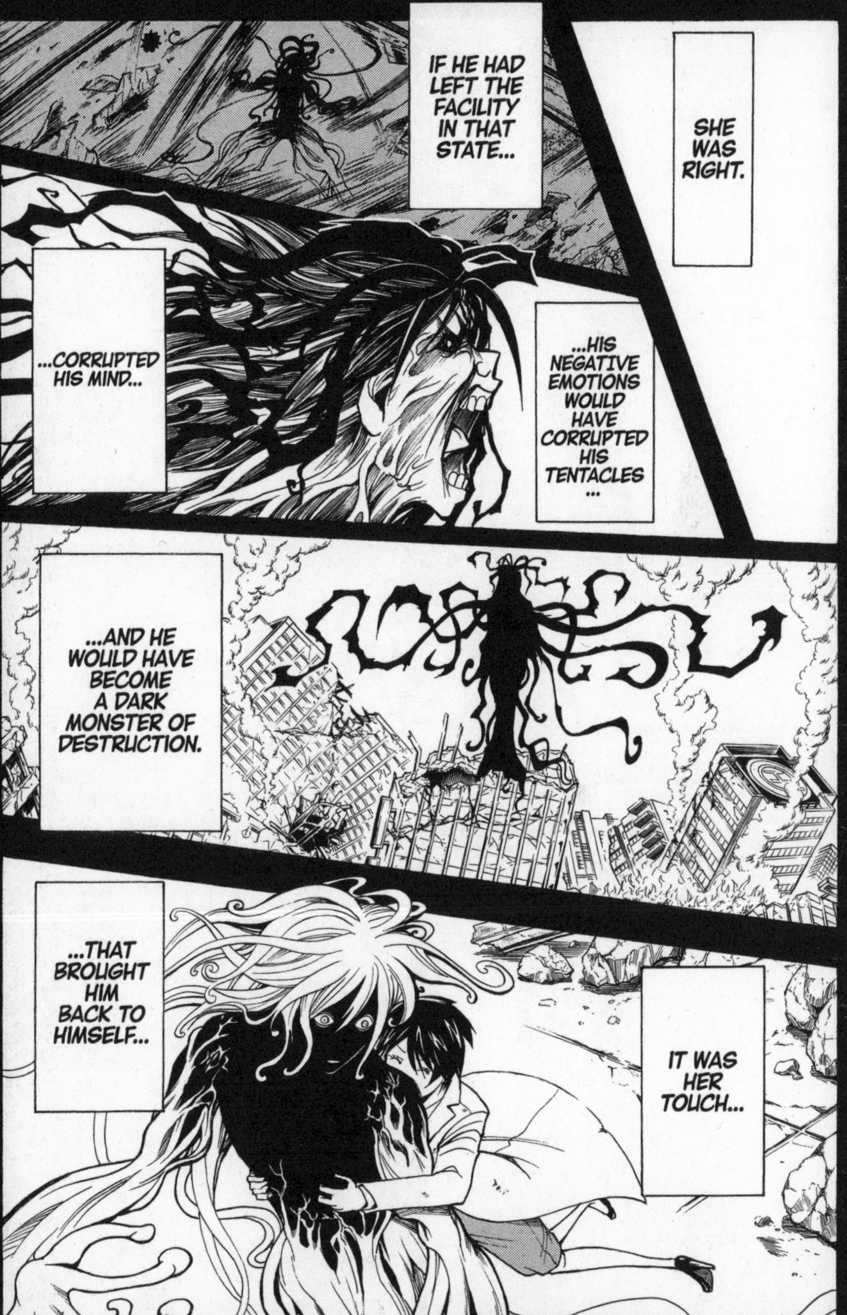
SHE WAS RIGHT.
IF HE HAD LEFT THE FACILITY IN THAT STATE...
...HIS NEGATIVE EMOTIONS WOULD HAVE CORRUPTED HIS TENTACLES ...
...CORRUPTED HIS MIND...
...AND HE WOULD HAVE BECOME A DARK MONSTER OF DESTRUCTION.
IT WAS HER TOUCH...
...THAT BROUGHT HIM BACK TO HIMSELF...

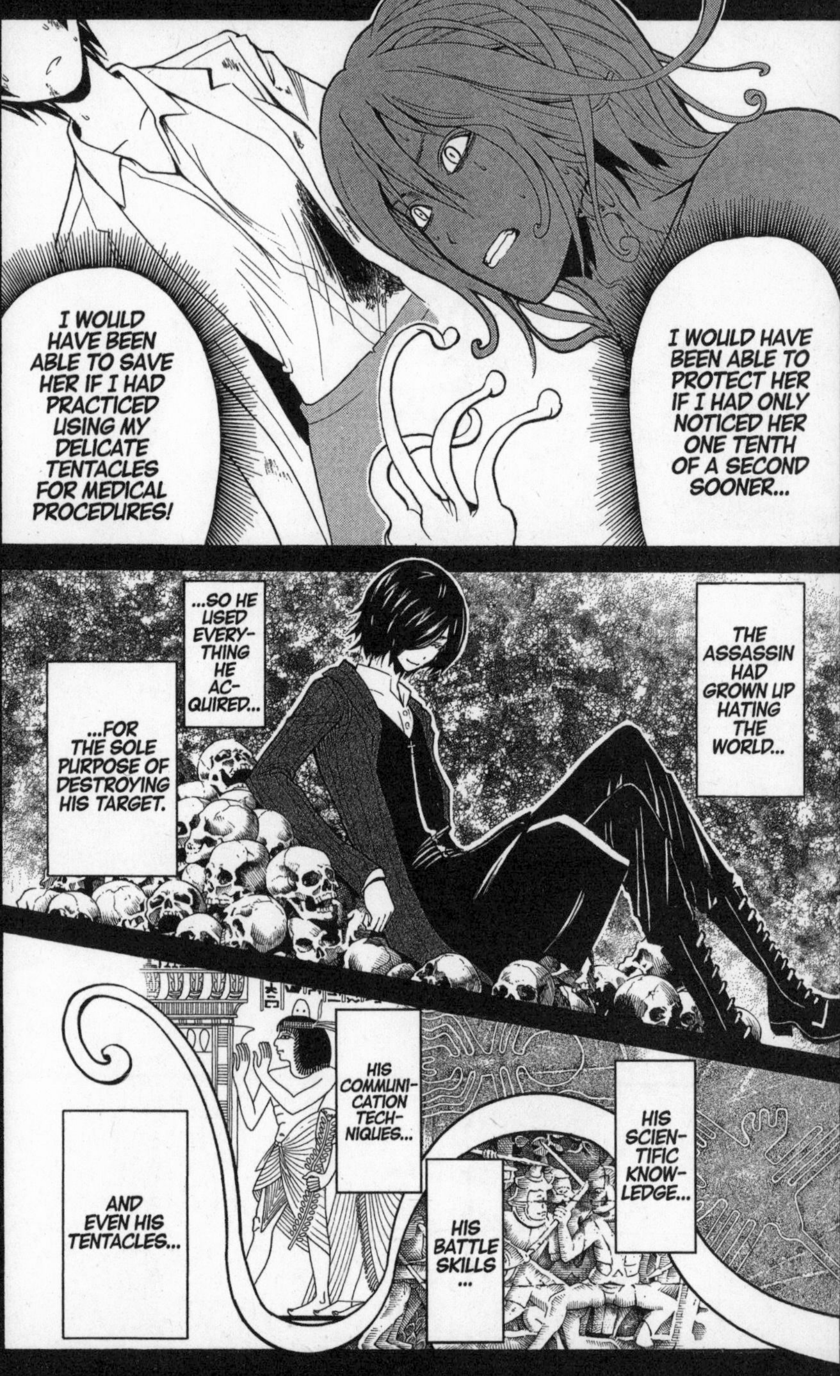
I WOULD HAVE BEEN ABLE TO PROTECT HER IF I HAD ONLY NOTICED HER ONE TENTH OF A SECOND SOONER...
I WOULD HAVE BEEN ABLE TO SAVE HER IF I HAD PRACTICED USING MY DELICATE TENTACLES FOR MEDICAL PROCEDURES!
THE ASSASSIN HAD GROWN UP HATING THE WORLD...
...SO HE USED EVERY-THING HE AC-QUIRED...
...FOR THE SOLE PURPOSE OF DESTROYING HIS TARGET.
HIS SCIEN-TIFIC KNOW-LEDGE...
HIS COMMUNI-CATION TECH-NIQUES...
HIS BATTLE SKILLS...
AND EVEN HIS TENTACLES...

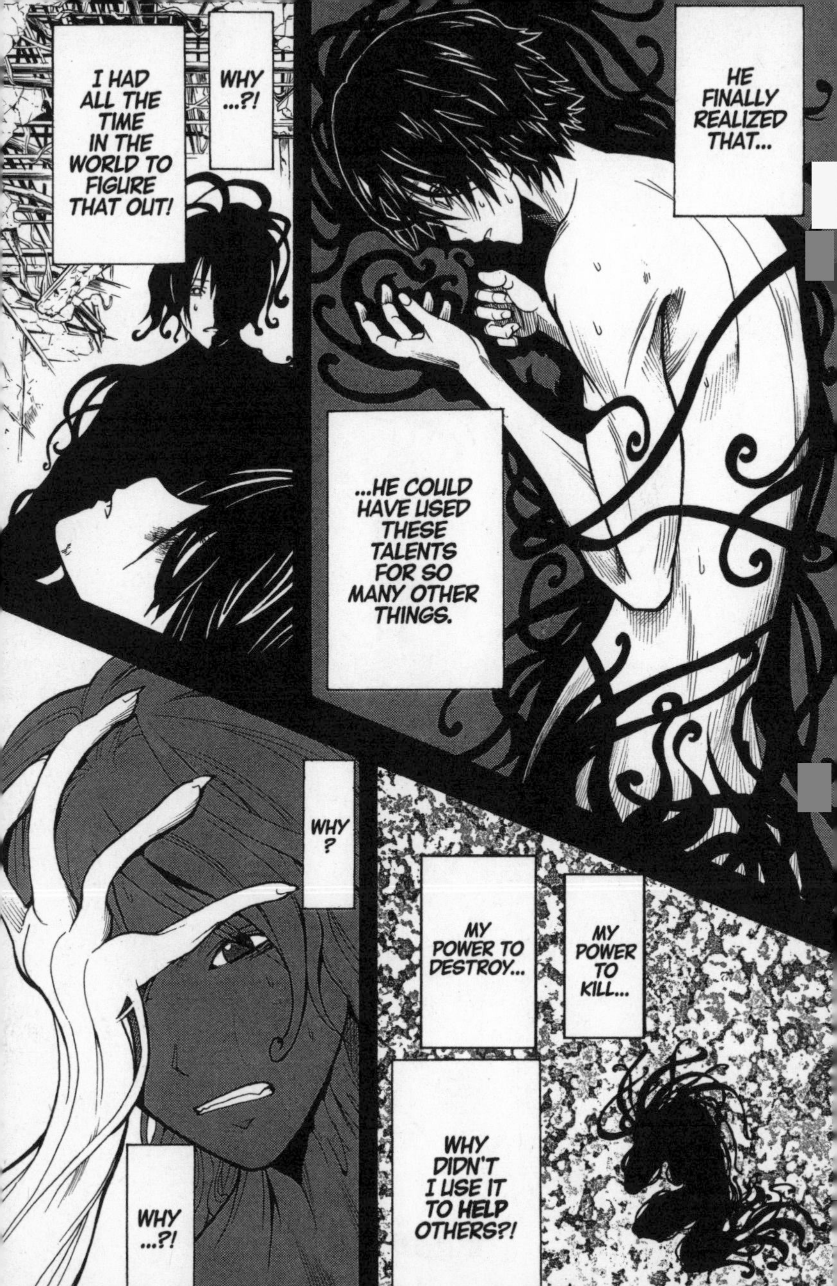
HE FINALLY REALIZED THAT...
...HE COULD HAVE USED THESE TALENTS FOR SO MANY OTHER THINGS.
WHY ...?!
I HAD ALL THE TIME IN THE WORLD TO FIGURE THAT OUT!
MY POWER TO KILL...
MY POWER TO DESTROY...
WHY DIDN'T I USE IT TO HELP OTHERS?!
WHY ?
WHY ...?!

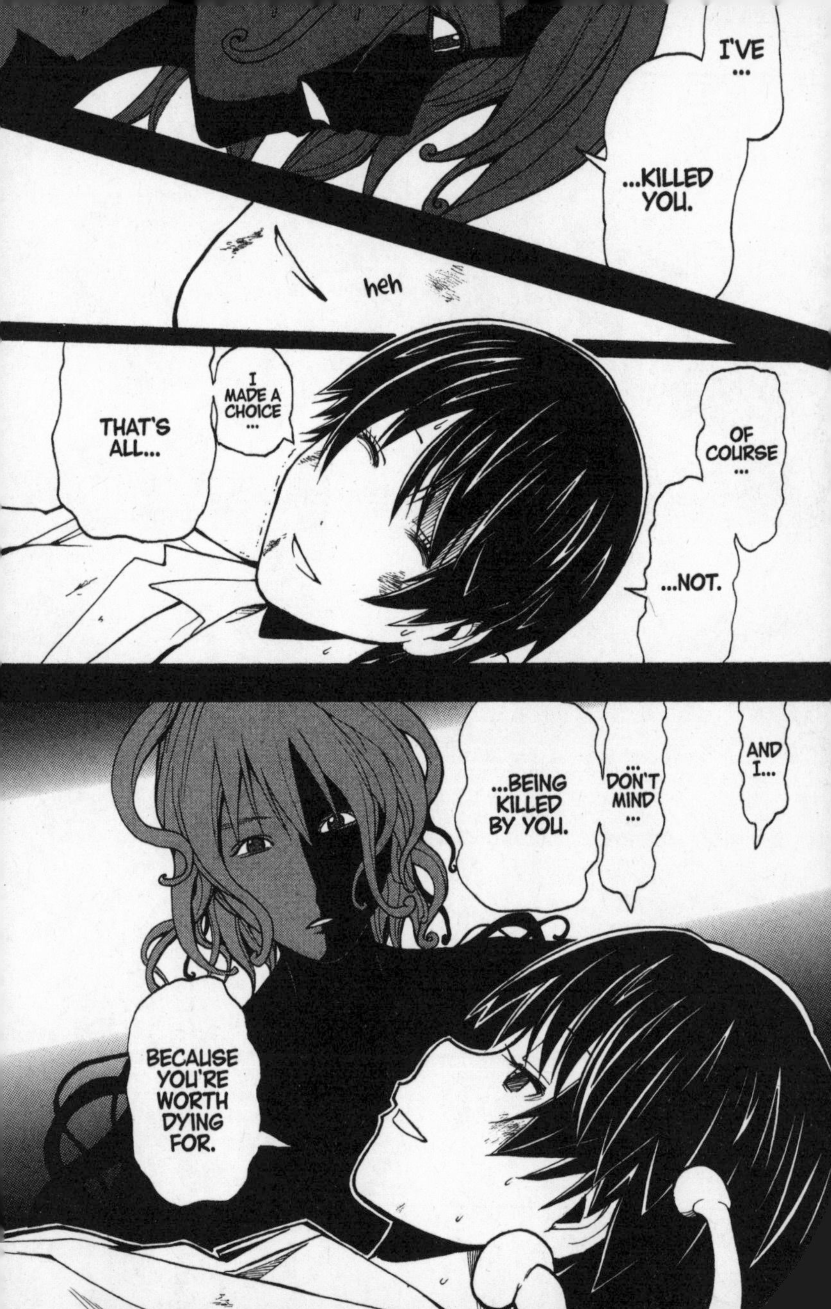
I'VE ...
...KILLED YOU.
heh
OF COURSE ...
...NOT.
I MADE A CHOICE ...
THAT'S ALL...
AND I...
... DON'T MIND ...
...BEING KILLED BY YOU.
BECAUSE YOU'RE WORTH DYING FOR.

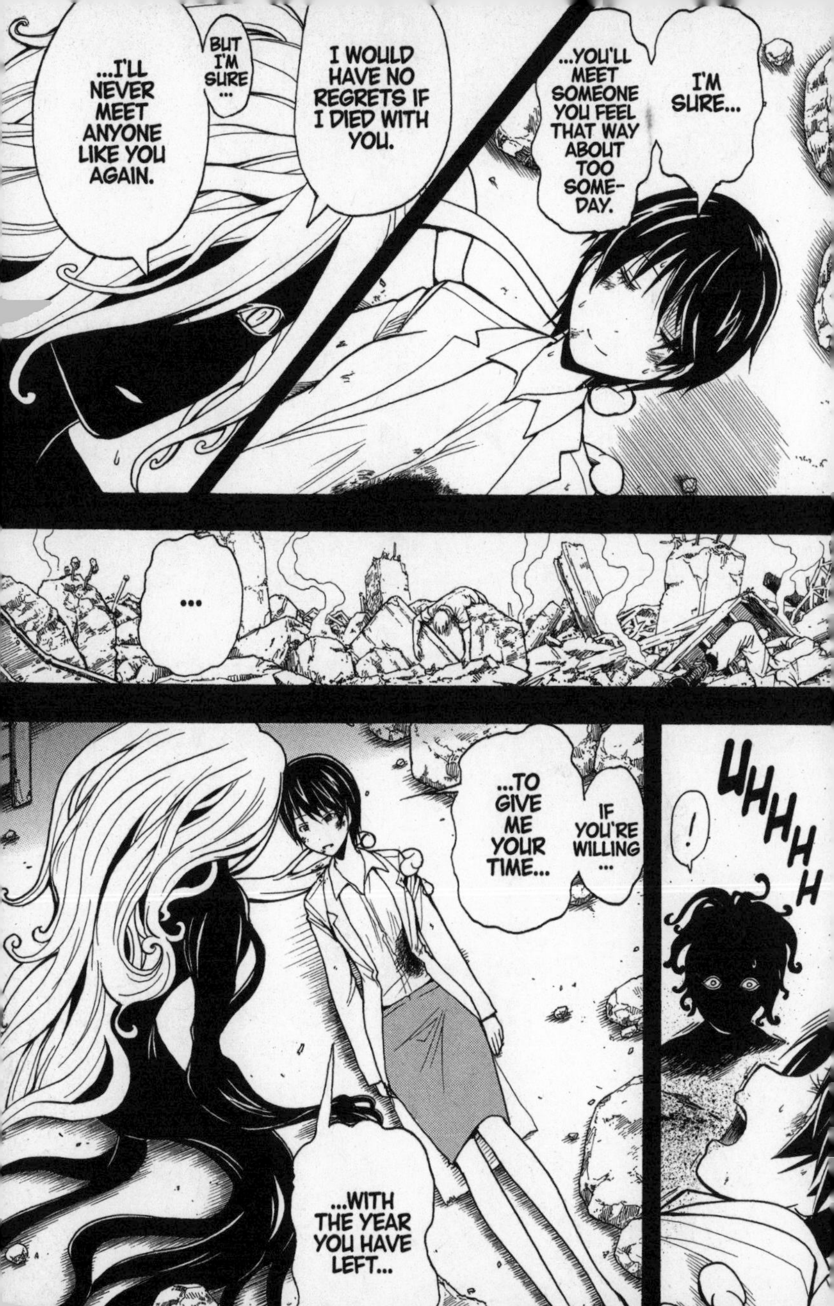
I'M SURE...
...YOU'LL MEET SOMEONE YOU FEEL THAT WAY ABOUT TOO SOME-DAY.
I WOULD HAVE NO REGRETS IF I DIED WITH YOU.
BUT I'M SURE...
...I'LL NEVER MEET ANYONE LIKE YOU AGAIN.
...
UHHHHH
!
IF YOU'RE WILLING...
...TO GIVE ME YOUR TIME...
...WITH THE YEAR YOU HAVE LEFT...

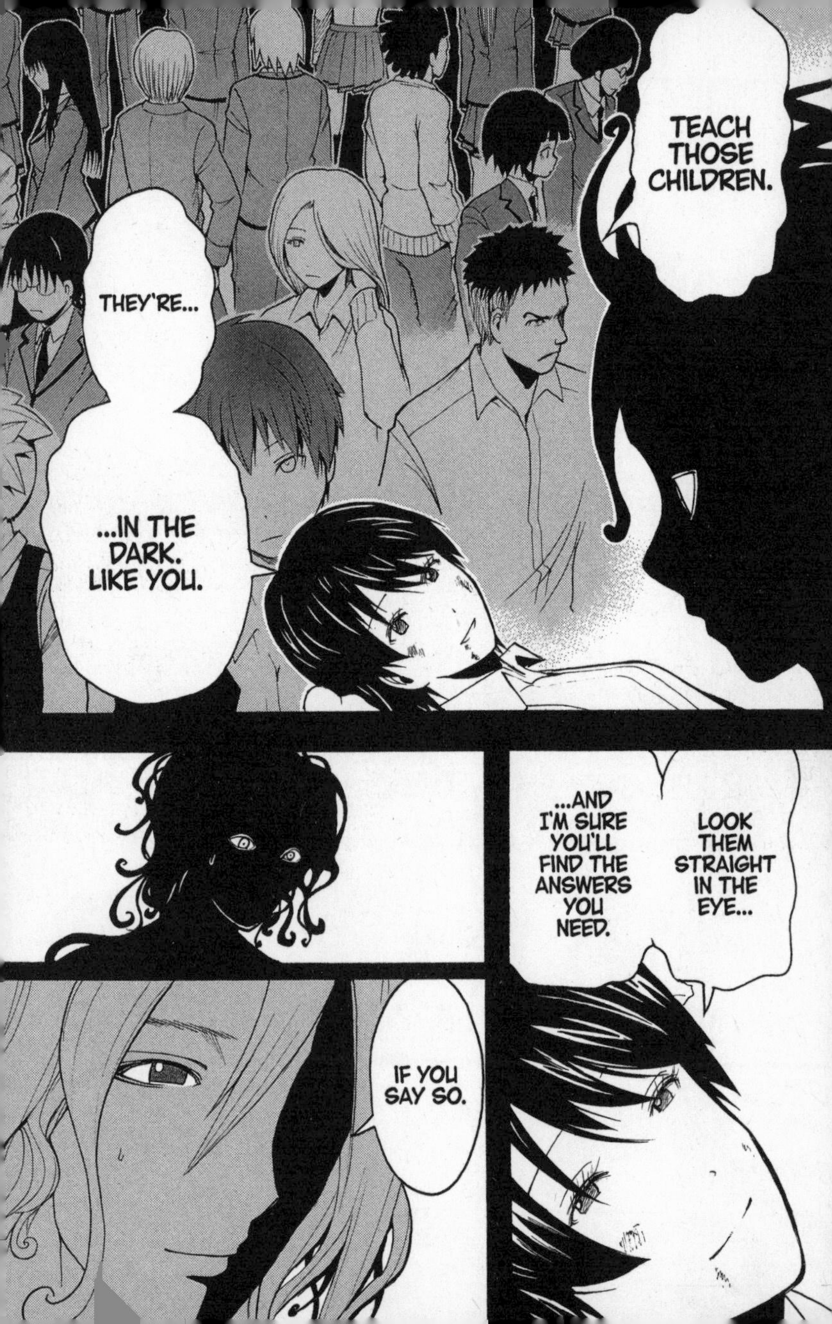
TEACH THOSE CHILDREN.
THEY'RE...
...IN THE DARK. LIKE YOU.
LOOK THEM STRAIGHT IN THE EYE...
...AND I'M SURE YOU'LL FIND THE ANSWERS YOU NEED.
IF YOU SAY SO.

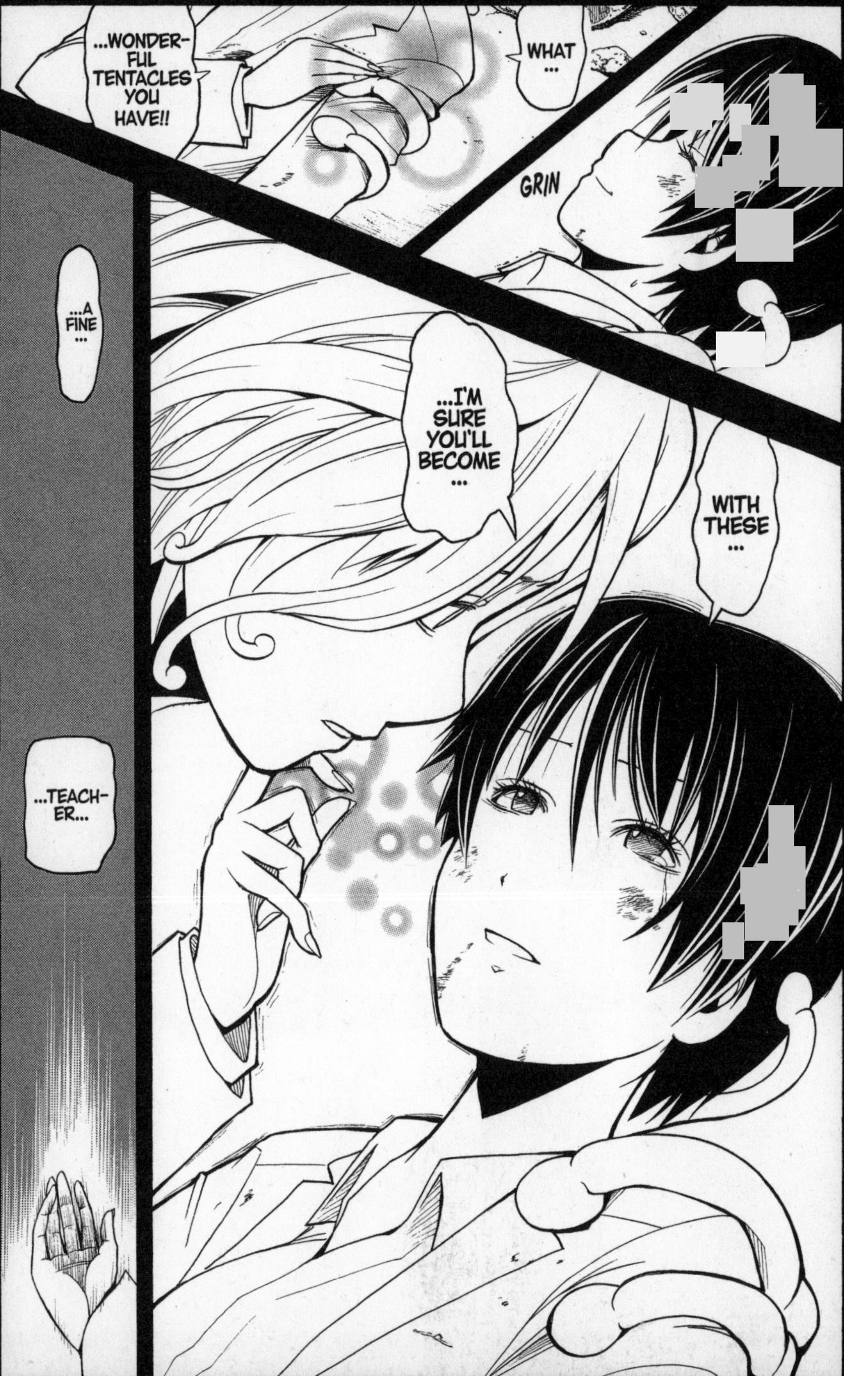
GRIN
WHAT...
...WONDERFUL TENTACLES YOU HAVE!!
WITH THESE...
...I'M SURE YOU'LL BECOME...
...A FINE...
...TEACHER...

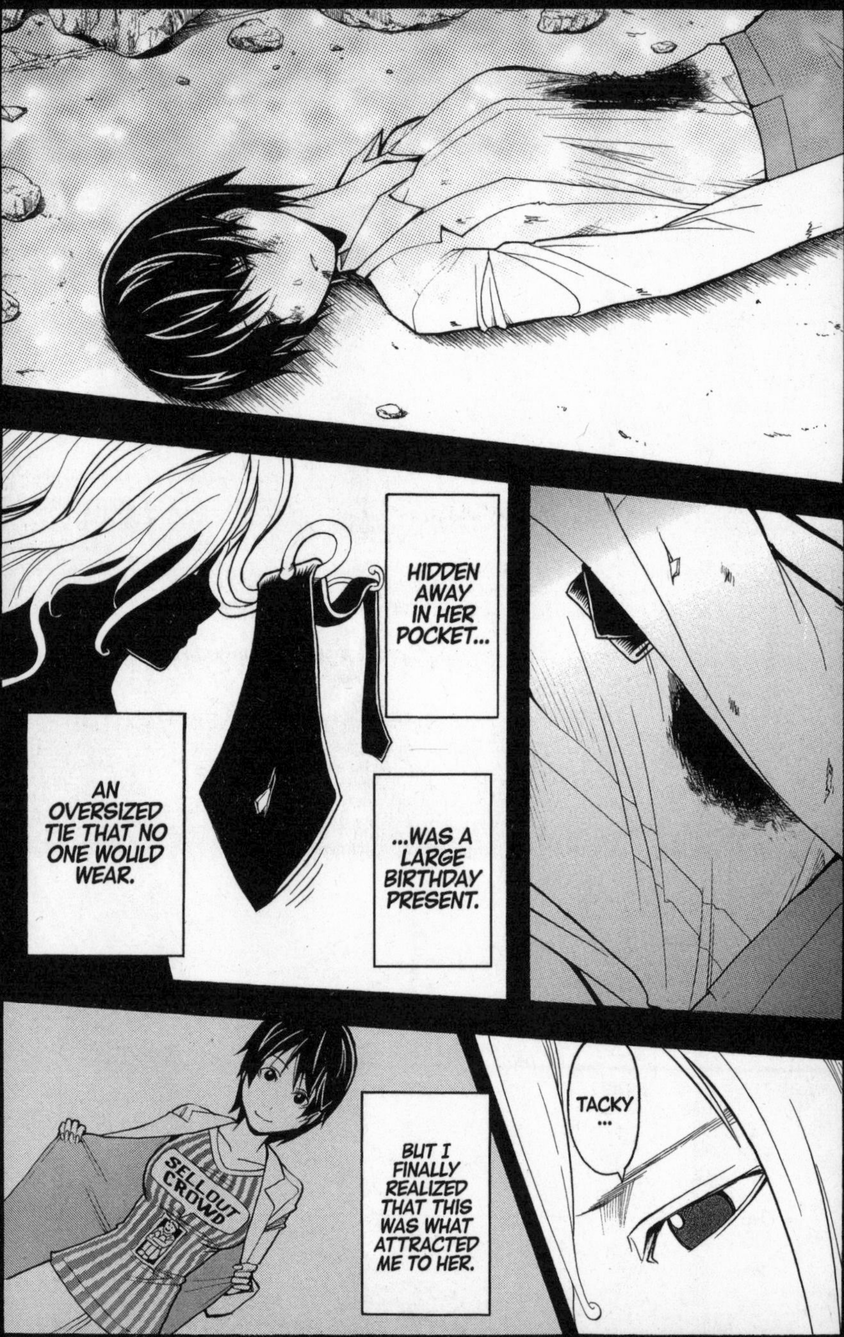
HIDDEN AWAY IN HER POCKET...
...WAS A LARGE BIRTHDAY PRESENT.
AN OVERSIZED TIE THAT NO ONE WOULD WEAR.
TACKY ...
BUT I FINALLY REALIZED THAT THIS WAS WHAT ATTRACTED ME TO HER.
SELLOUT CROWD

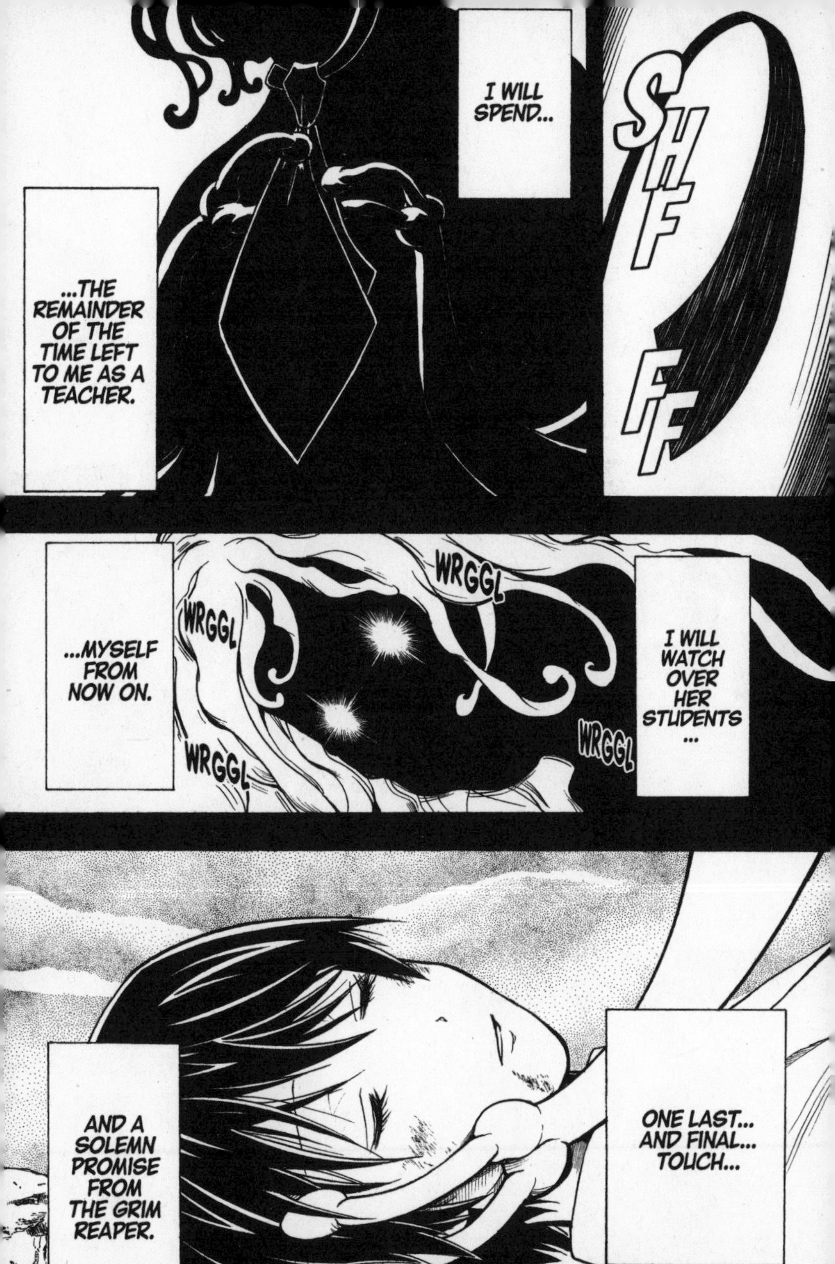
SHFFF
I WILL SPEND...
...THE REMAINDER OF THE TIME LEFT TO ME AS A TEACHER.
I WILL WATCH OVER HER STUDENTS ...
WRGGL
WRGGL
WRGGL
WRGGL
...MYSELF FROM NOW ON.
ONE LAST... AND FINAL... TOUCH...
AND A SOLEMN PROMISE FROM THE GRIM REAPER.

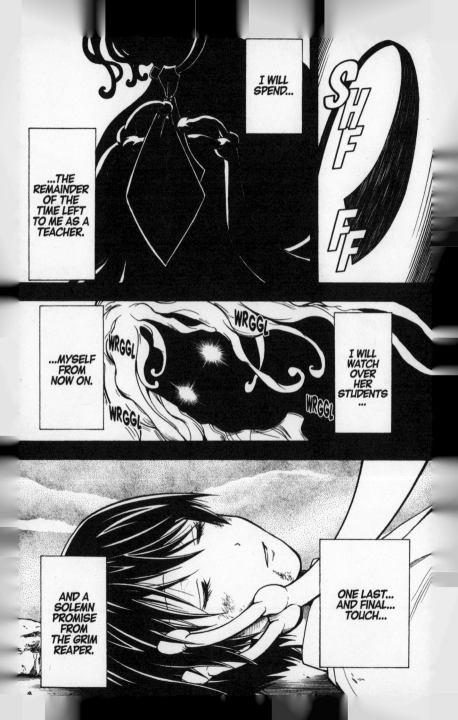

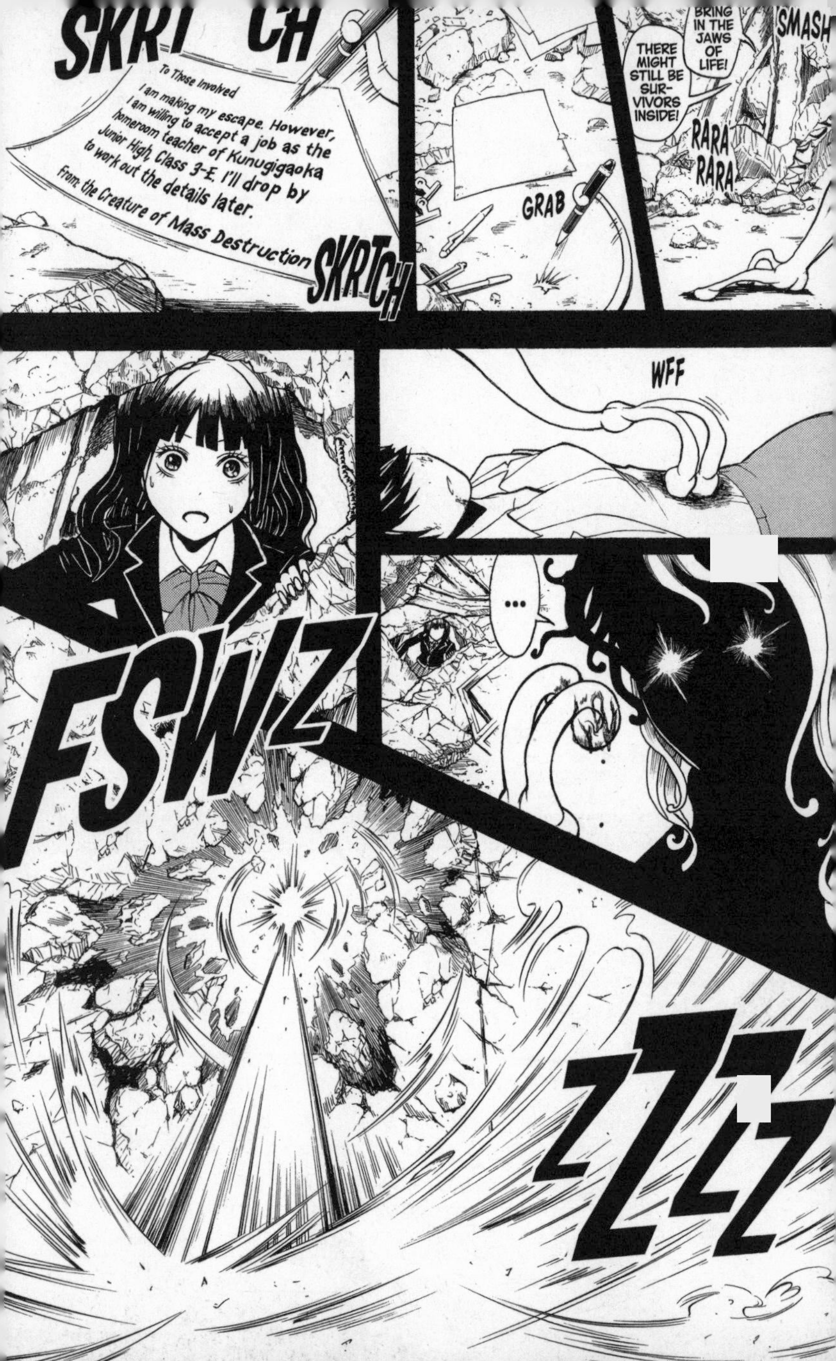
SMASH
BRING IN THE JAWS OF LIFE!
THERE MIGHT STILL BE SUR-VIVORS INSIDE!
RARA RARA
GRAB
SKRI CH
To Those Involved
I am making my escape. However, I am willing to accept a job as the homeroom teacher of Kunugigaoka Junior High, Class 3-E. I'll drop by to work out the details later.
From: the Creature of Mass Destruction
SKRTCH
WFF
...
FSWZ
ZZZ

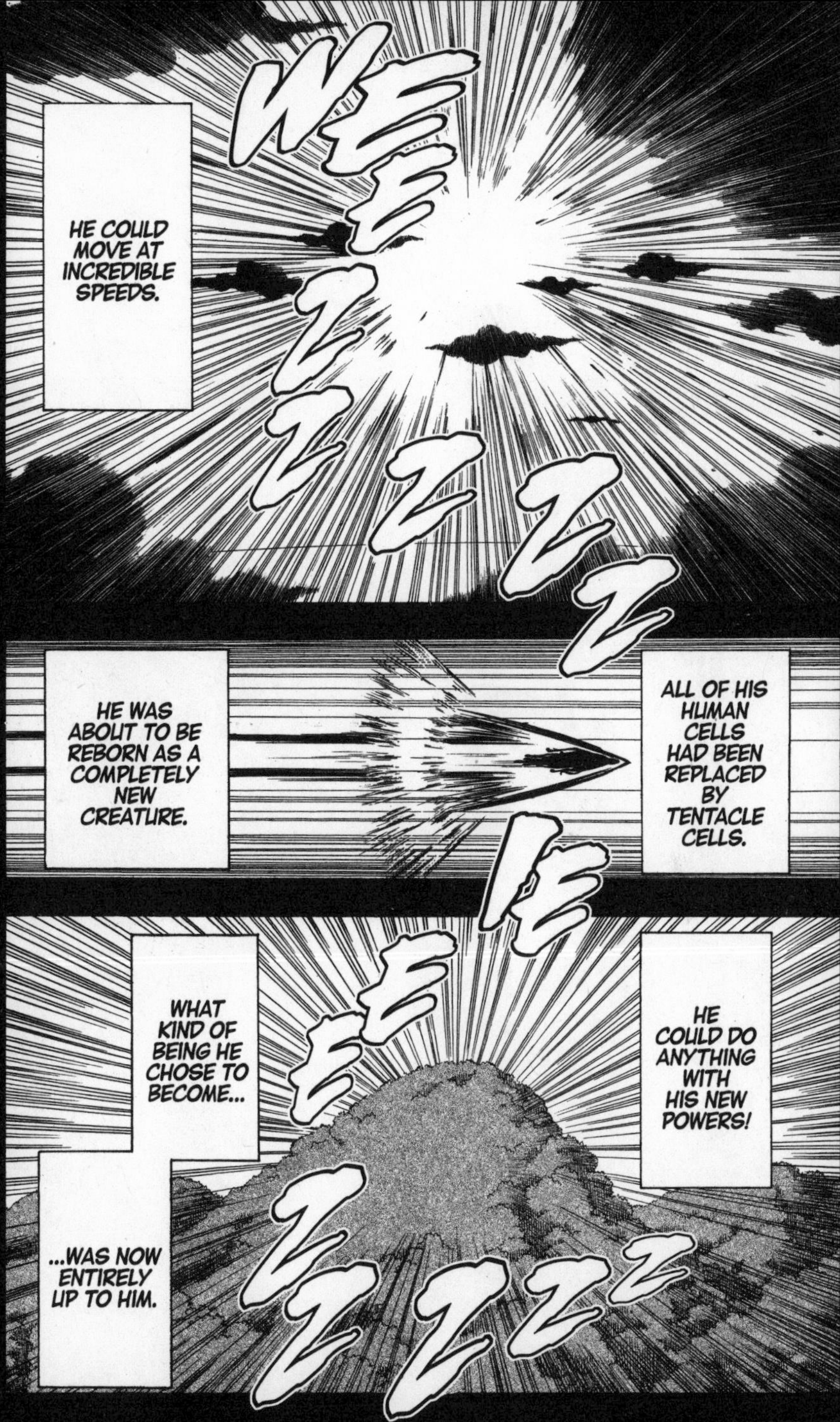
WEEEZZZZZZZ
HE COULD MOVE AT INCREDIBLE SPEEDS.
ALL OF HIS HUMAN CELLS HAD BEEN REPLACED BY TENTACLE CELLS.
HE WAS ABOUT TO BE REBORN AS A COMPLETELY NEW CREATURE.
IEEEZZZZZZ
HE COULD DO ANYTHING WITH HIS NEW POWERS!
WHAT KIND OF BEING HE CHOSE TO BECOME...
...WAS NOW ENTIRELY UP TO HIM.

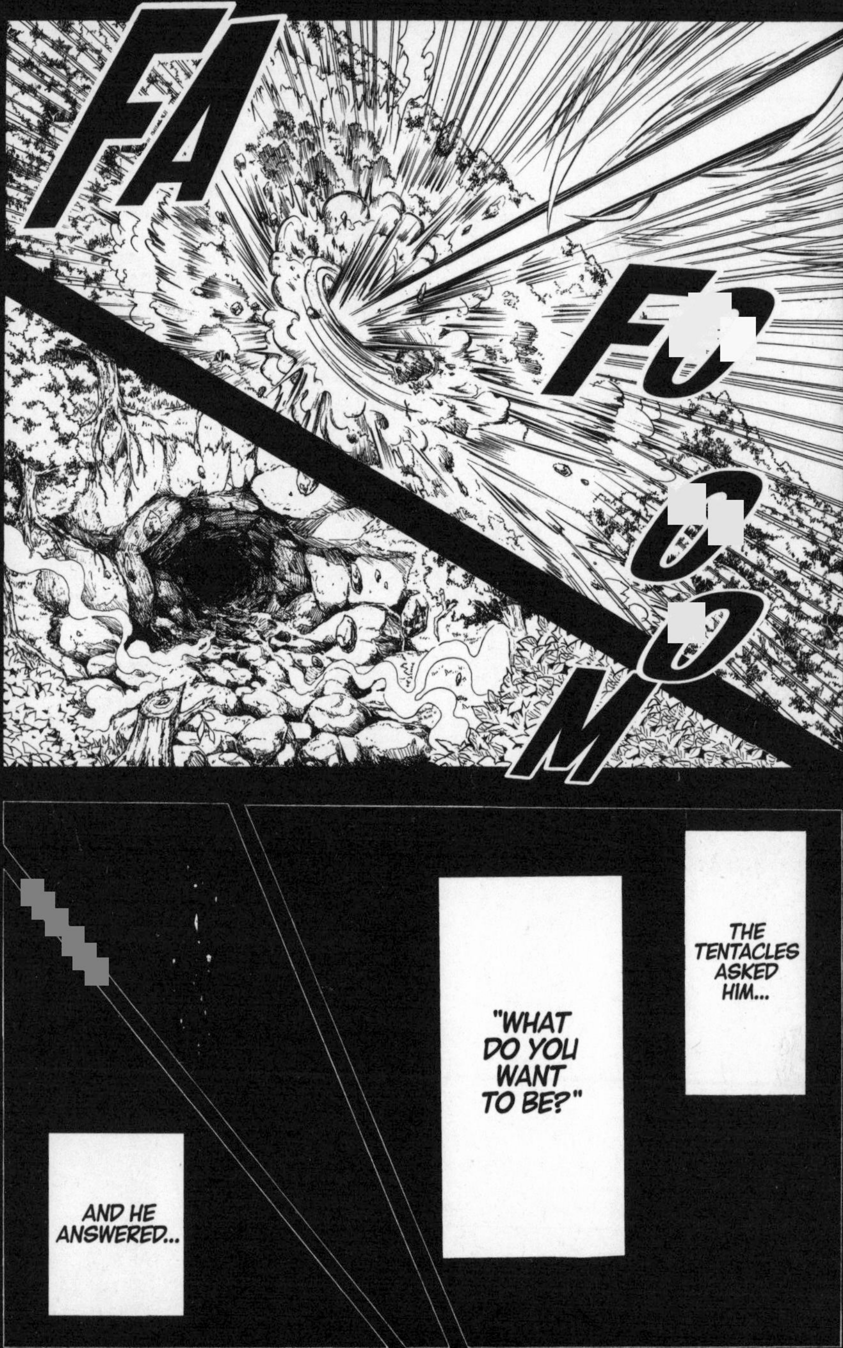
FA
FOOOM
THE TENTACLES ASKED HIM...
"WHAT DO YOU WANT TO BE?"
AND HE ANSWERED...

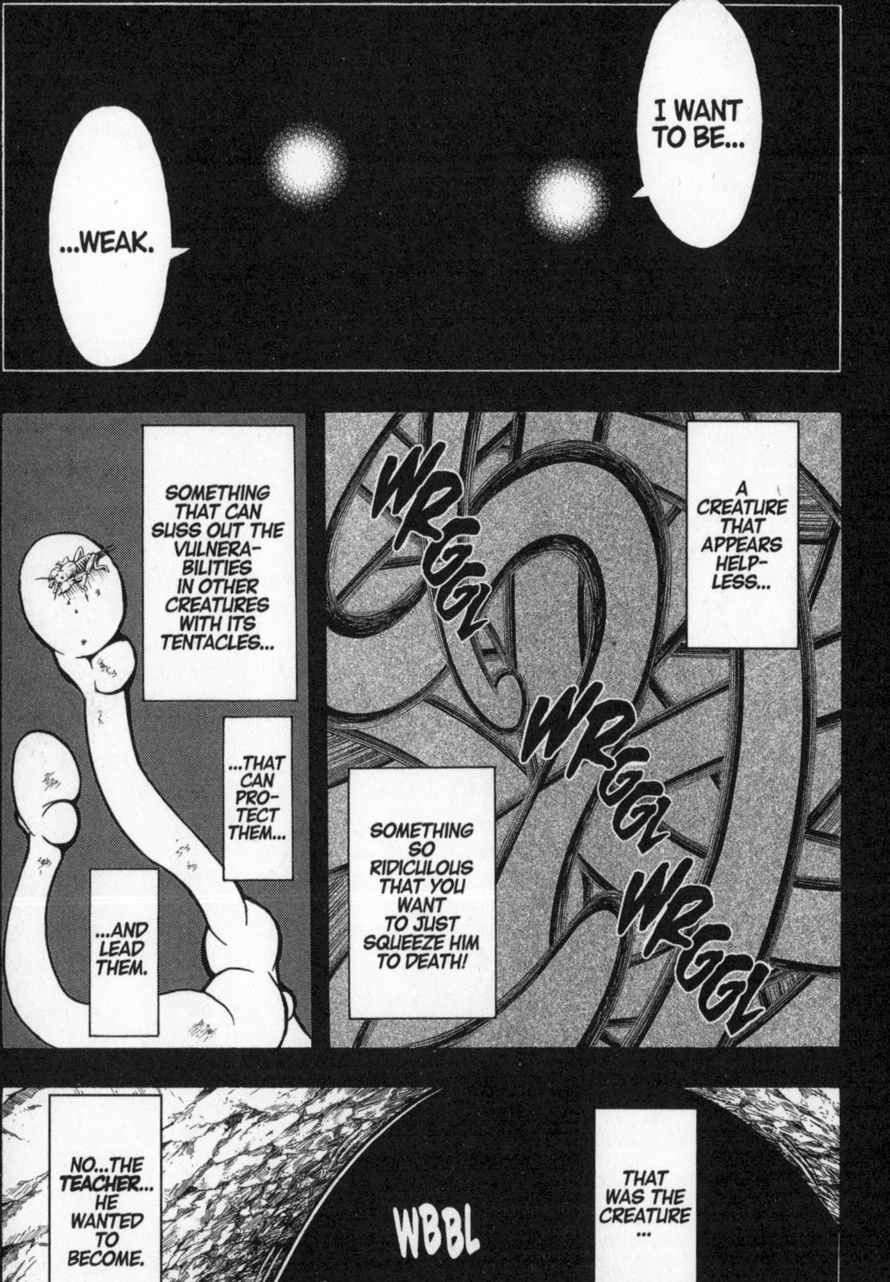

I WANT TO BE...
...WEAK.
A CREATURE THAT APPEARS HELPLESS...
WRGGL
WRGGL
WRGGL
WRGGL
SOMETHING SO RIDICULOUS THAT YOU WANT TO JUST SQUEEZE HIM TO DEATH!
SOMETHING THAT CAN SUSS OUT THE VULNERABILITIES IN OTHER CREATURES WITH ITS TENTACLES...
...THAT CAN PROTECT THEM...
...AND LEAD THEM.
THAT WAS THE CREATURE ...
WBBL
NO...THE TEACHER... HE WANTED TO BECOME.

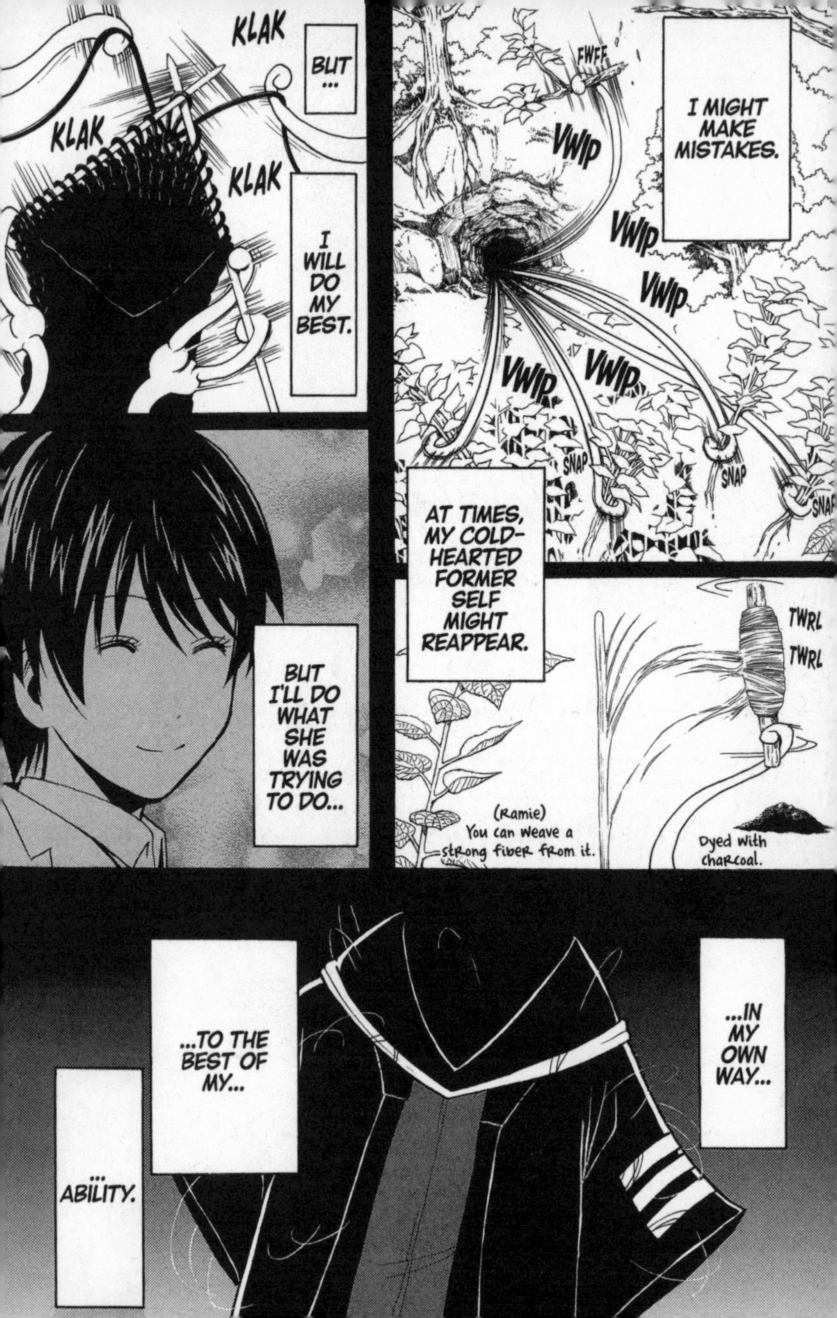
I MIGHT MAKE MISTAKES.
FWFF
VWIP
VWIP
VWIP
VWIP
VWIP
SNAP
SNAP
SNAP
AT TIMES, MY COLD-HEARTED FORMER SELF MIGHT REAPPEAR.
TWRL
TWRL
Dyed with charcoal.
(Ramie)
You can weave a strong fiber from it.
BUT ...
KLAK
KLAK
KLAK
I WILL DO MY BEST.
BUT I'LL DO WHAT SHE WAS TRYING TO DO...
...IN MY OWN WAY...
...TO THE BEST OF MY...
... ABILITY.

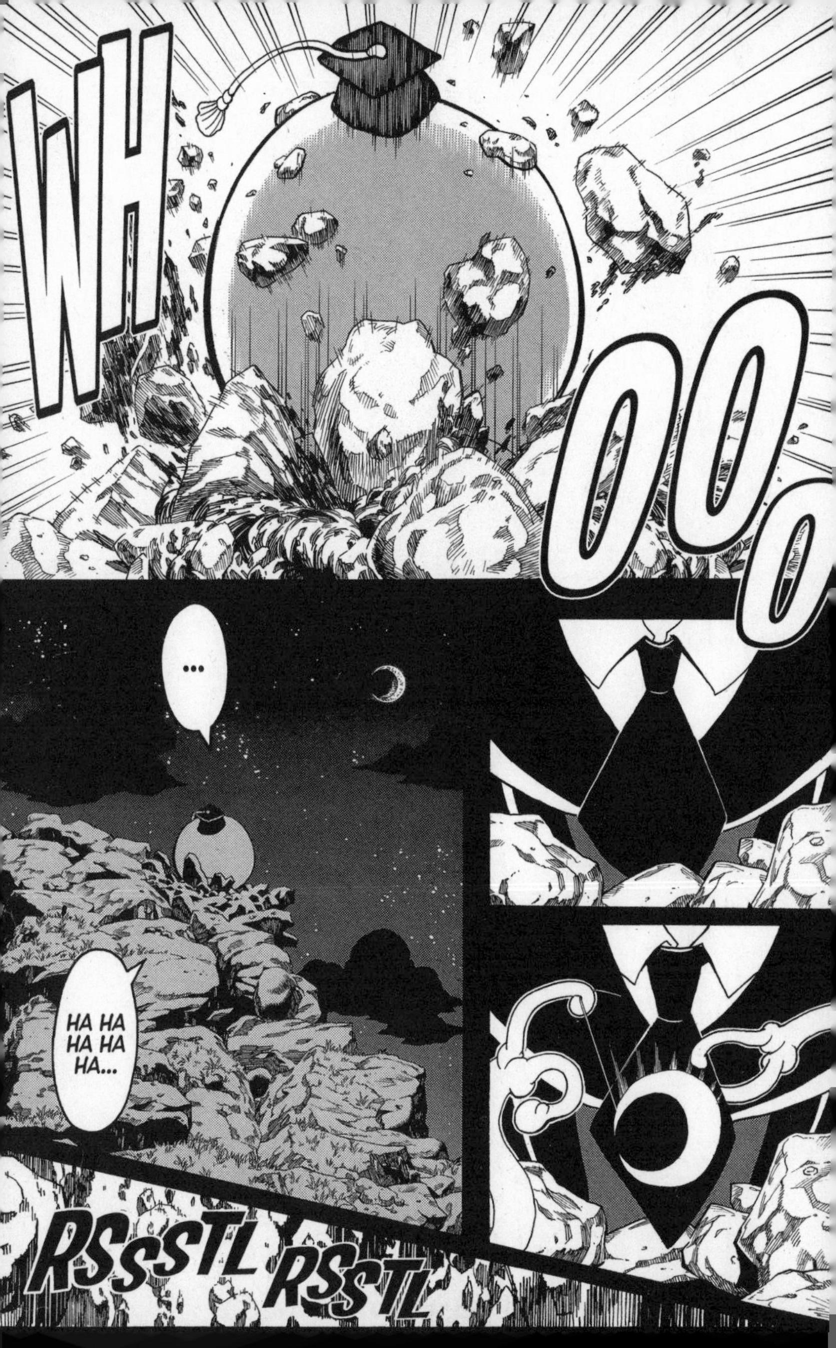
WHOOOO
...
HA HA HA HA HA...
RSSSTL RSSTL

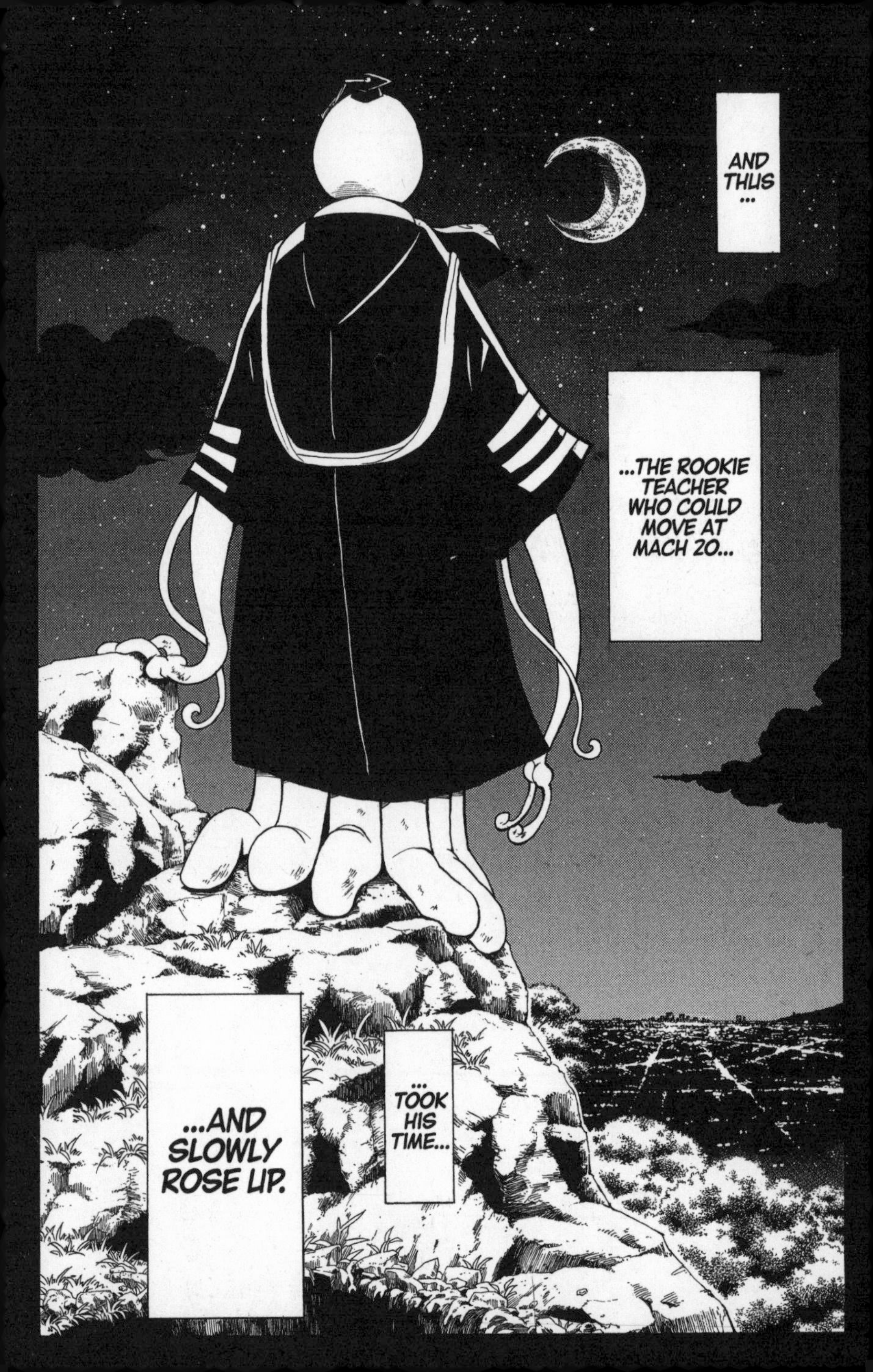
AND THUS ...
...THE ROOKIE TEACHER WHO COULD MOVE AT MACH 20...
... TOOK HIS TIME...
...AND SLOWLY ROSE UP.

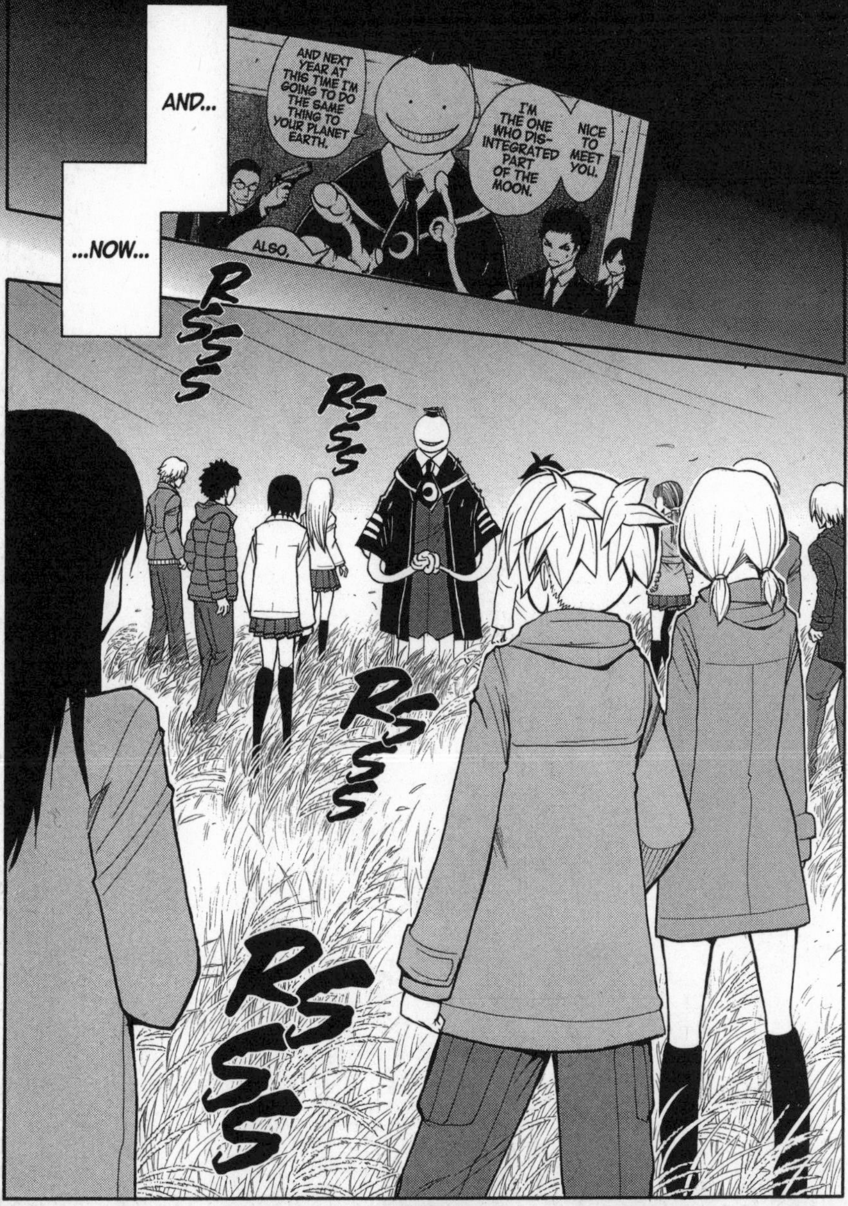
NICE TO MEET YOU.
I'M THE ONE WHO DIS-INTEGRATED PART OF THE MOON.
AND NEXT YEAR AT THIS TIME I'M GOING TO DO THE SAME THING TO YOUR PLANET EARTH.
ALSO,
AND...
...NOW...
RSSSS
RSSSS
RSSSS
RSSSS

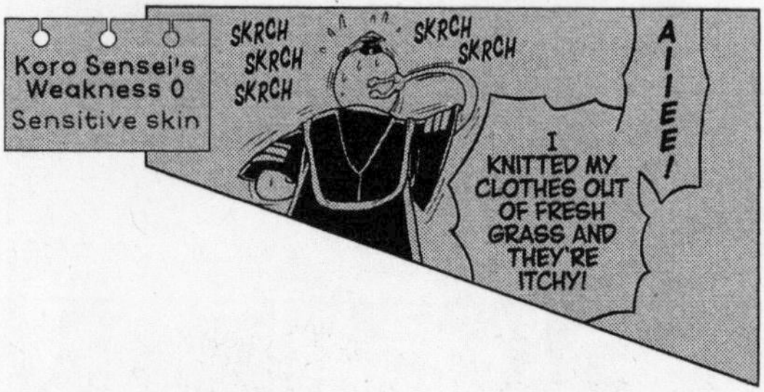
Koro Sensei's Weakness 0
Sensitive skin
AIIEE!
SKRCH SKRCH
SKRCH SKRCH SKRCH
I KNITTED MY CLOTHES OUT OF FRESH GRASS AND THEY'RE ITCHY!

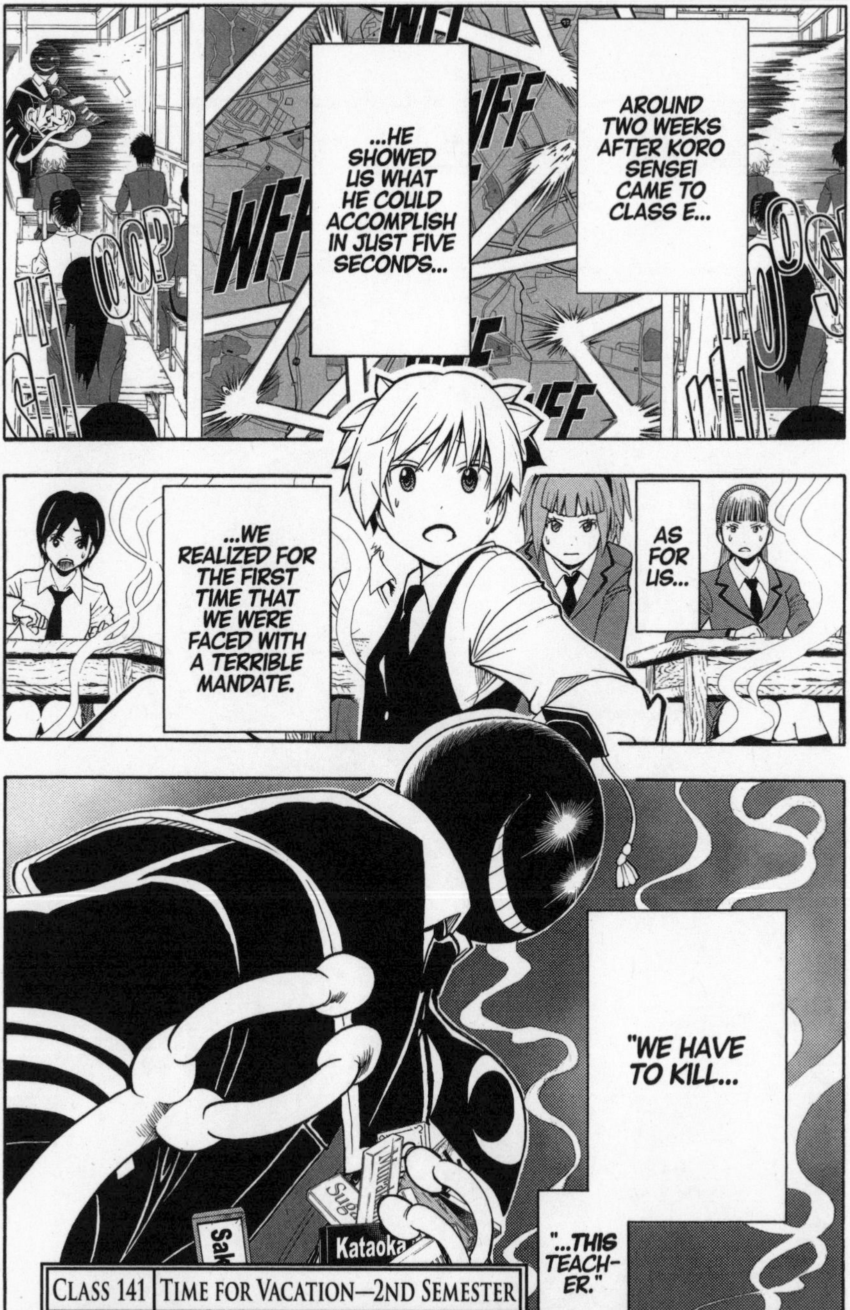
AROUND TWO WEEKS AFTER KORO SENSEI CAME TO CLASS E...
...HE SHOWED US WHAT HE COULD ACCOMPLISH IN JUST FIVE SECONDS...
WFF
WFF
AS FOR US...
...WE REALIZED FOR THE FIRST TIME THAT WE WERE FACED WITH A TERRIBLE MANDATE.
"WE HAVE TO KILL...
"...THIS TEACHER."
Kataoka

Class 141 Time for Vacation—2nd Semester

CLASS 141 TIME FOR VACATION—2ND SEMESTER

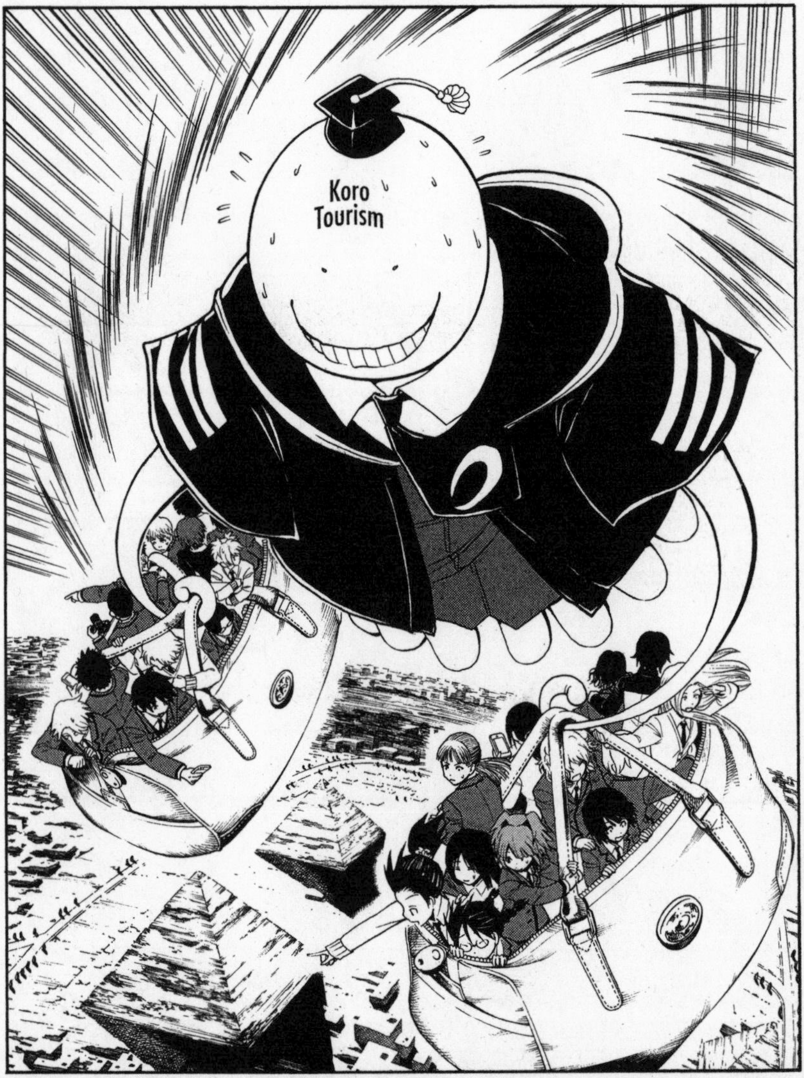
Koro Tourism

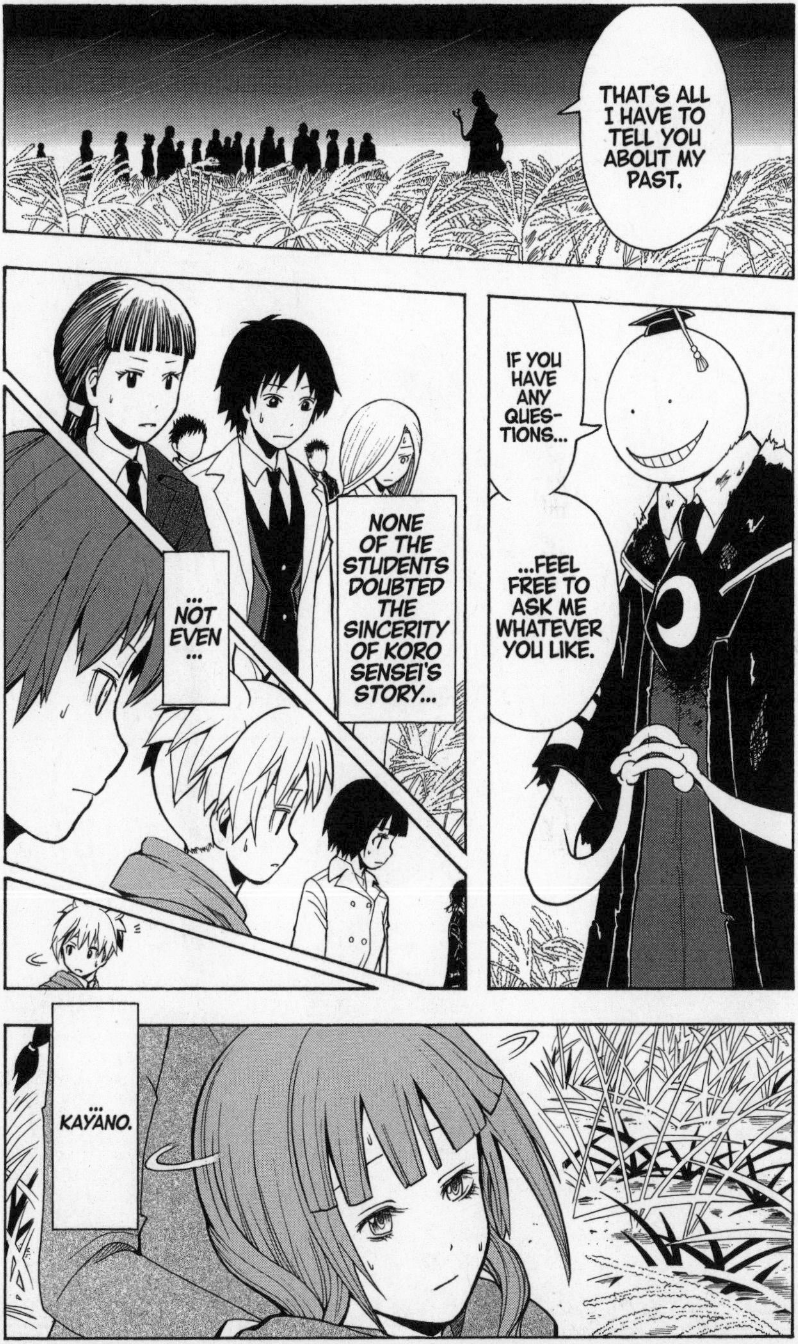
THAT'S ALL I HAVE TO TELL YOU ABOUT MY PAST.
IF YOU HAVE ANY QUES-TIONS...
...FEEL FREE TO ASK ME WHATEVER YOU LIKE.
NONE OF THE STUDENTS DOUBTED THE SINCERITY OF KORO SENSEI'S STORY...
...NOT EVEN...
...KAYANO.

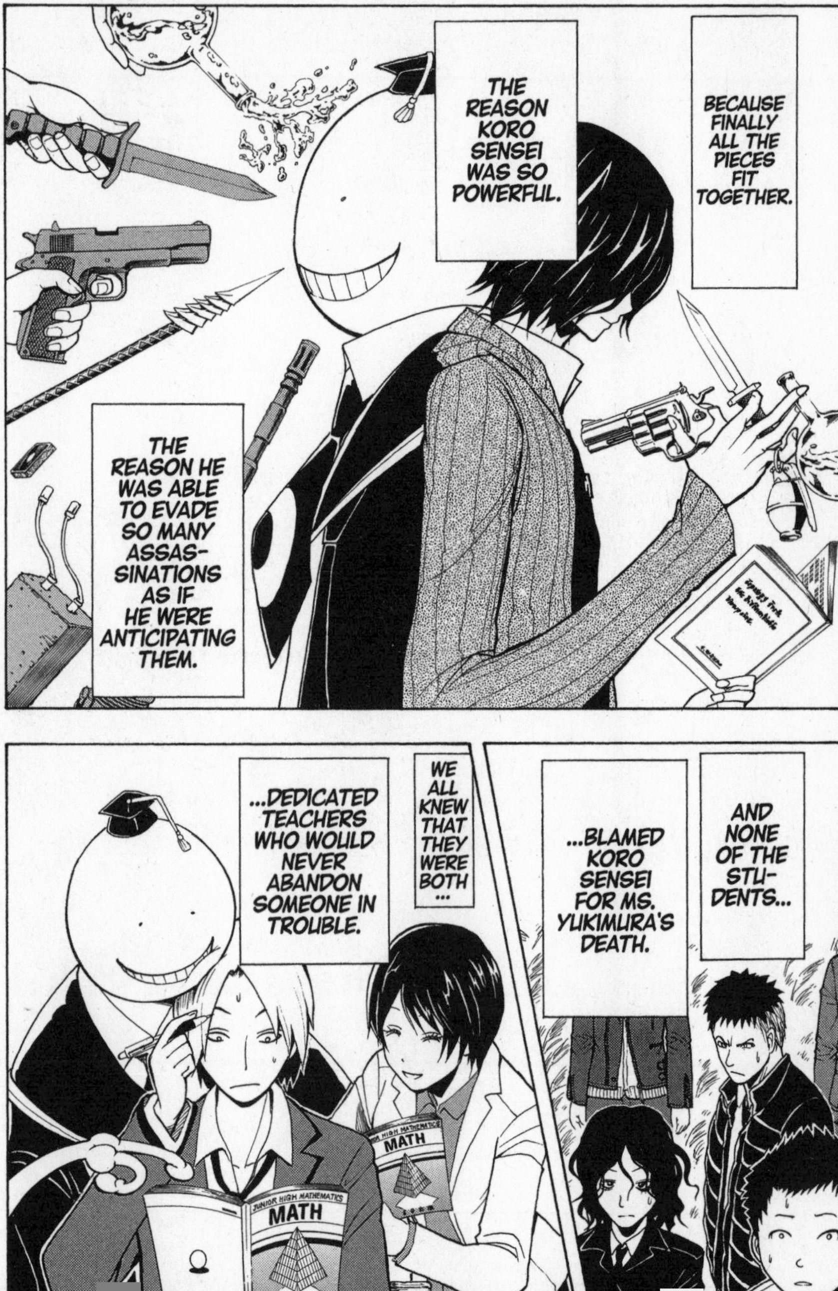
BECAUSE FINALLY ALL THE PIECES FIT TOGETHER.
THE REASON KORO SENSEI WAS SO POWERFUL.
THE REASON HE WAS ABLE TO EVADE SO MANY ASSAS-SINATIONS AS IF HE WERE ANTICIPATING THEM.
AND NONE OF THE STU-DENTS...
...BLAMED KORO SENSEI FOR MS. YUKIMURA'S DEATH.
WE ALL KNEW THAT THEY WERE BOTH...
...DEDICATED TEACHERS WHO WOULD NEVER ABANDON SOMEONE IN TROUBLE.
MATH
JUNIOR HIGH MATHEMATICS
MATH

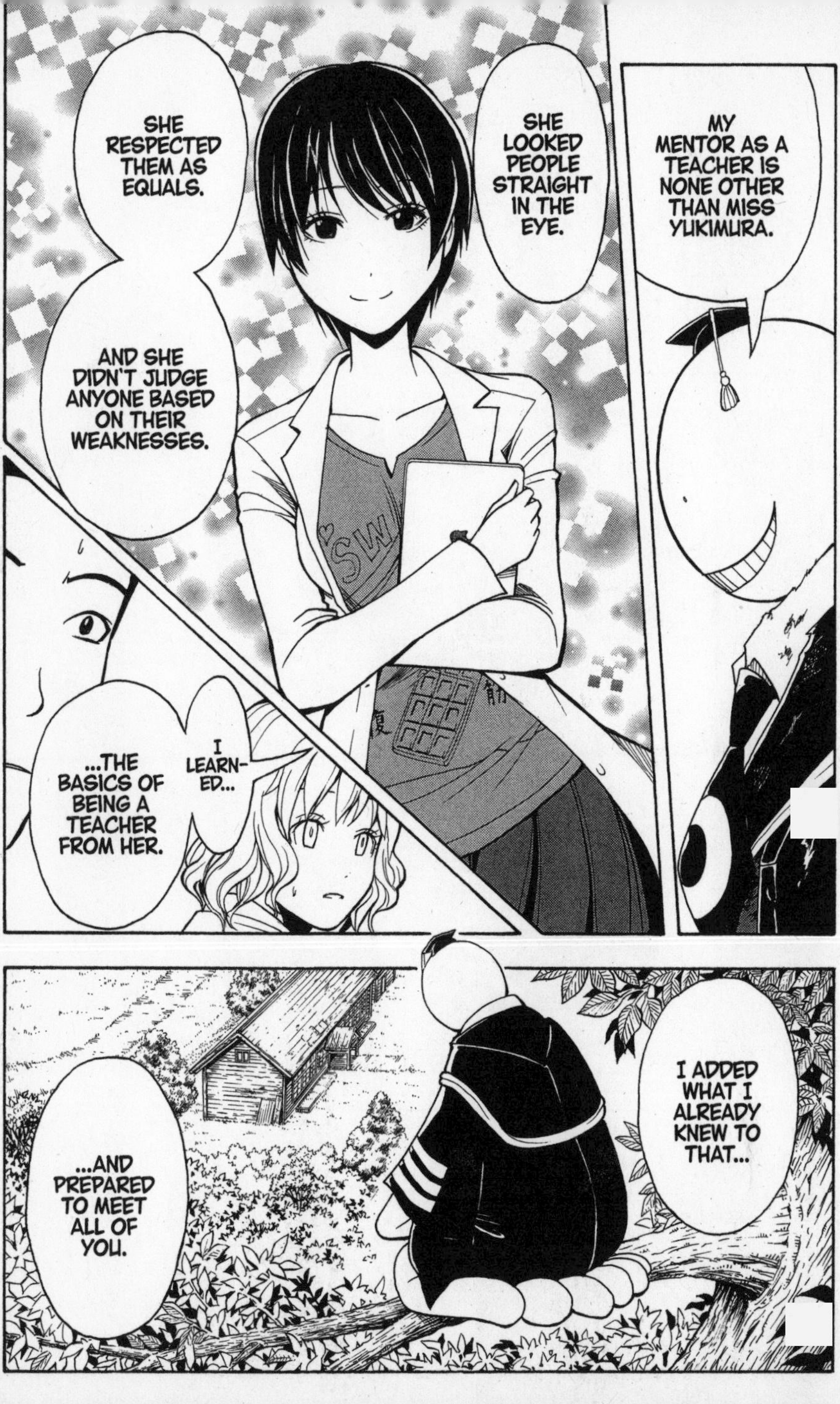
MY MENTOR AS A TEACHER IS NONE OTHER THAN MISS YUKIMURA.
SHE LOOKED PEOPLE STRAIGHT IN THE EYE.
SHE RESPECTED THEM AS EQUALS.
AND SHE DIDN'T JUDGE ANYONE BASED ON THEIR WEAKNESSES.
I LEARN-ED...
...THE BASICS OF BEING A TEACHER FROM HER.
I ADDED WHAT I ALREADY KNEW TO THAT...
...AND PREPARED TO MEET ALL OF YOU.

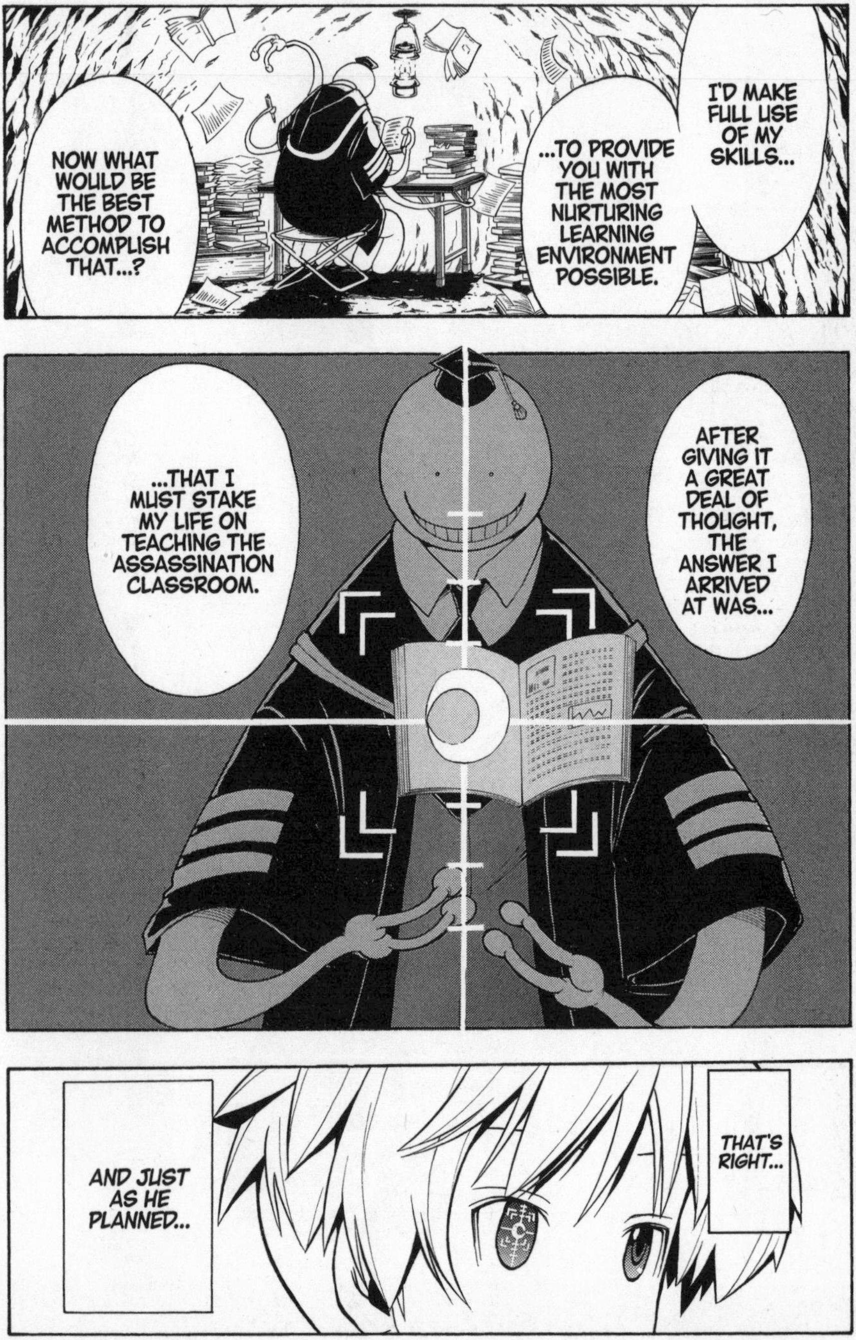
I'D MAKE FULL USE OF MY SKILLS...
...TO PROVIDE YOU WITH THE MOST NURTURING LEARNING ENVIRONMENT POSSIBLE.
NOW WHAT WOULD BE THE BEST METHOD TO ACCOMPLISH THAT...?
AFTER GIVING IT A GREAT DEAL OF THOUGHT, THE ANSWER I ARRIVED AT WAS...
...THAT I MUST STAKE MY LIFE ON TEACHING THE ASSASSINATION CLASSROOM.
THAT'S RIGHT...
AND JUST AS HE PLANNED...

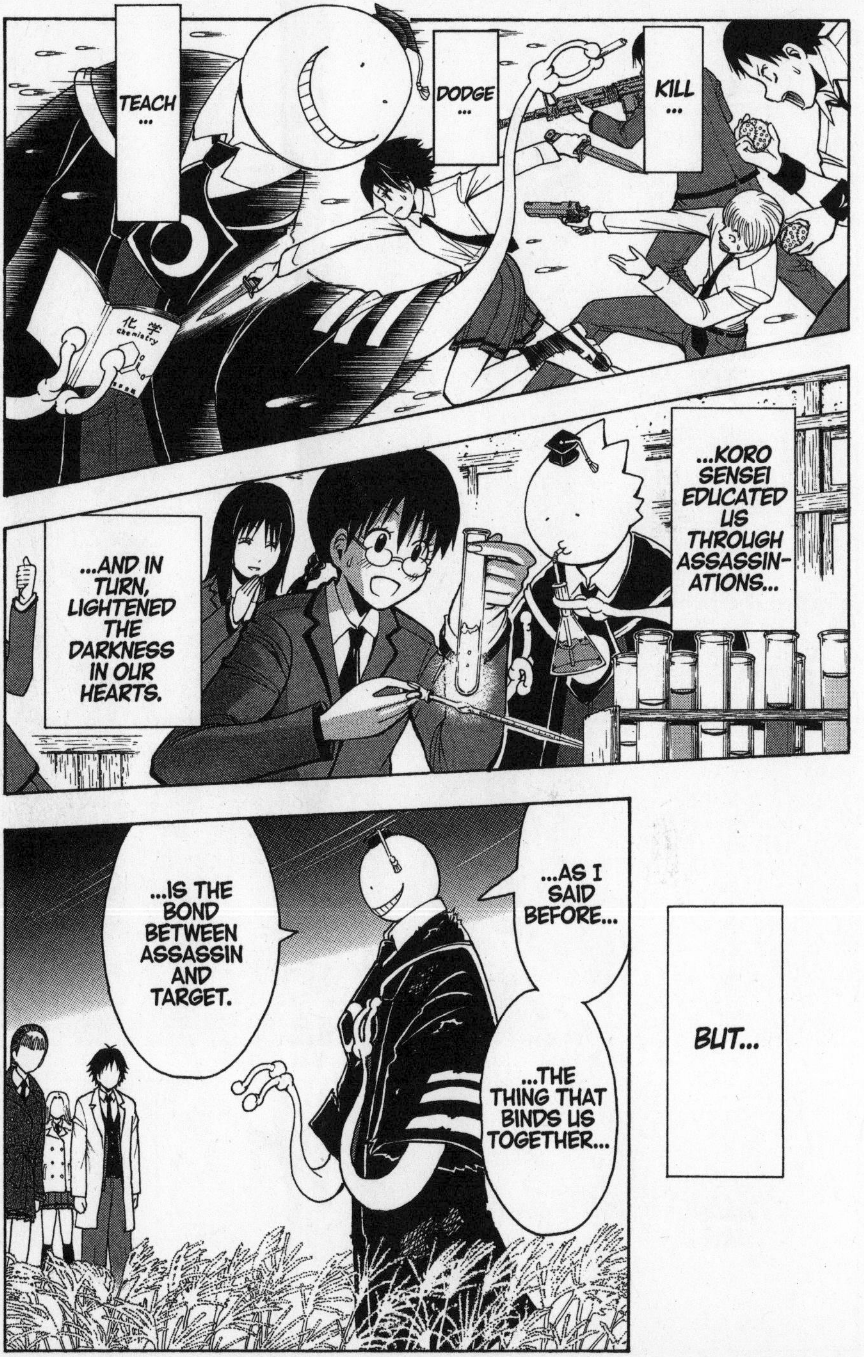
KILL...
DODGE...
TEACH...
化学
chemistry
...KORO SENSEI EDUCATED US THROUGH ASSASSIN-ATIONS...
...AND IN TURN, LIGHTENED THE DARKNESS IN OUR HEARTS.
BUT...
...AS I SAID BEFORE...
...THE THING THAT BINDS US TOGETHER...
...IS THE BOND BETWEEN ASSASSIN AND TARGET.

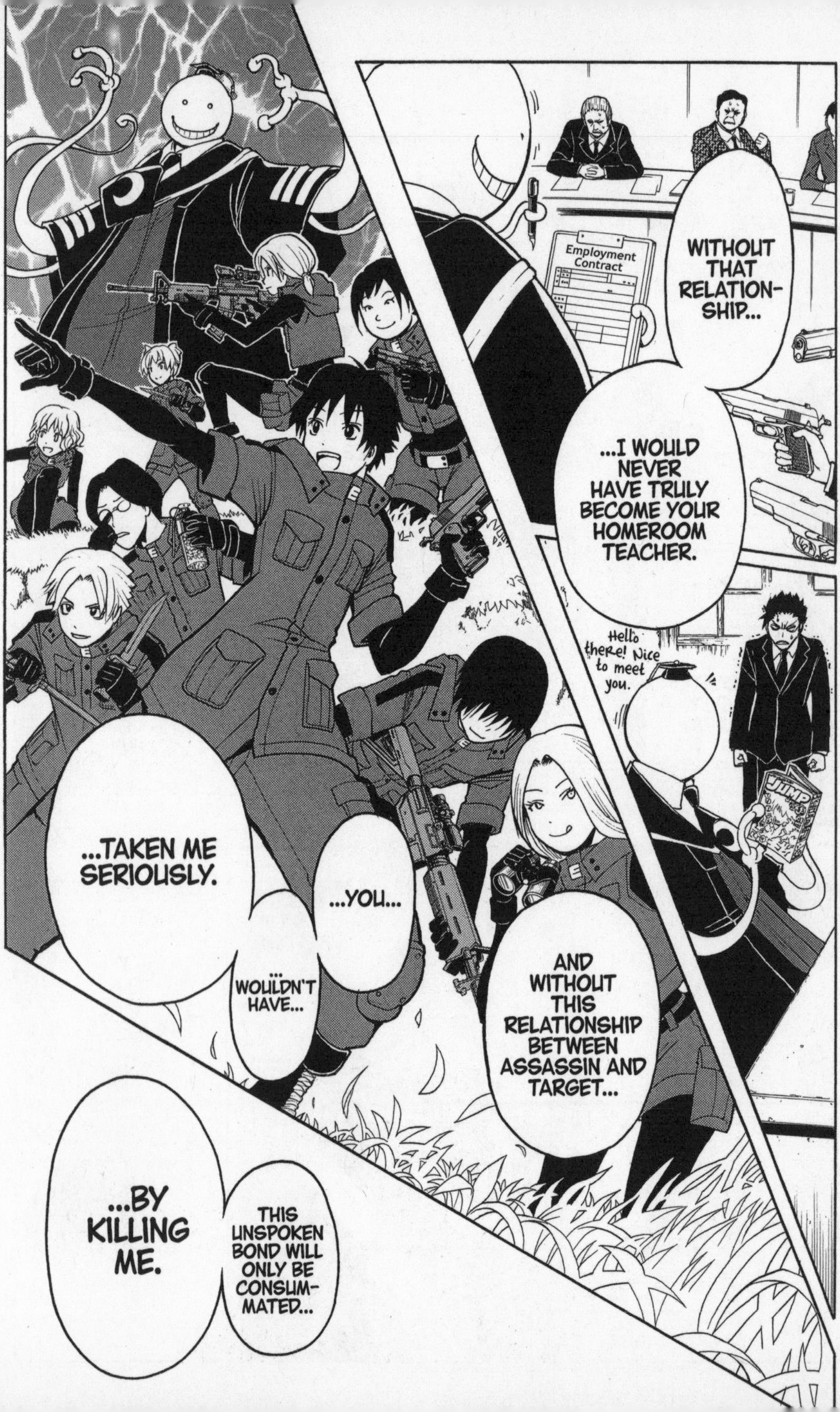
Employment Contract
WITHOUT THAT RELATIONSHIP...
...I WOULD NEVER HAVE TRULY BECOME YOUR HOMEROOM TEACHER.
Hello there! Nice to meet you.
JUMP
AND WITHOUT THIS RELATIONSHIP BETWEEN ASSASSIN AND TARGET...
...YOU...
...WOULDN'T HAVE...
...TAKEN ME SERIOUSLY.
THIS UNSPOKEN BOND WILL ONLY BE CONSUMMATED...
...BY KILLING ME.

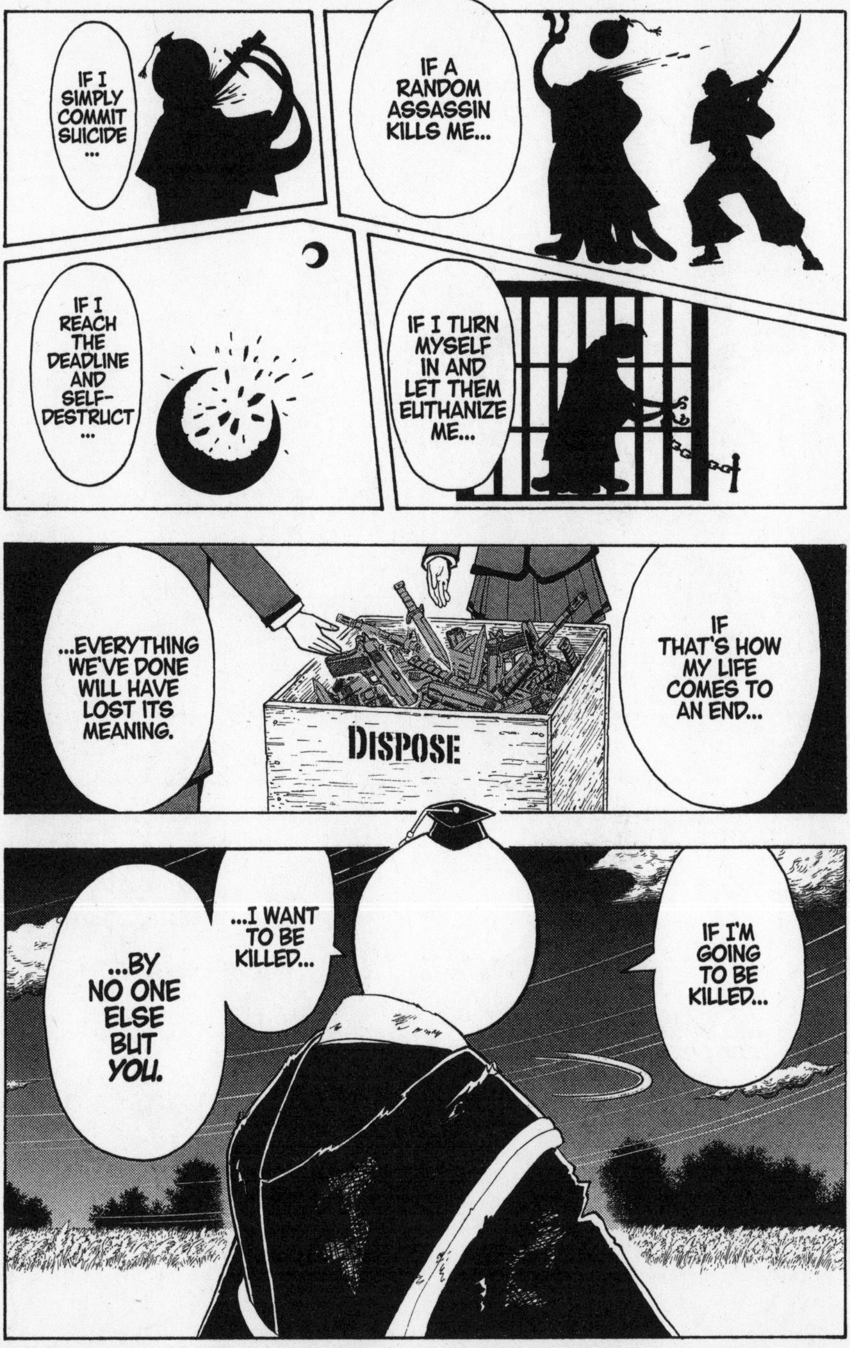
IF A RANDOM ASSASSIN KILLS ME...
IF I SIMPLY COMMIT SUICIDE...
IF I TURN MYSELF IN AND LET THEM EUTHANIZE ME...
IF I REACH THE DEADLINE AND SELF-DESTRUCT...
IF THAT'S HOW MY LIFE COMES TO AN END...
DISPOSE
...EVERYTHING WE'VE DONE WILL HAVE LOST ITS MEANING.
IF I'M GOING TO BE KILLED...
...I WANT TO BE KILLED...
...BY NO ONE ELSE BUT YOU.

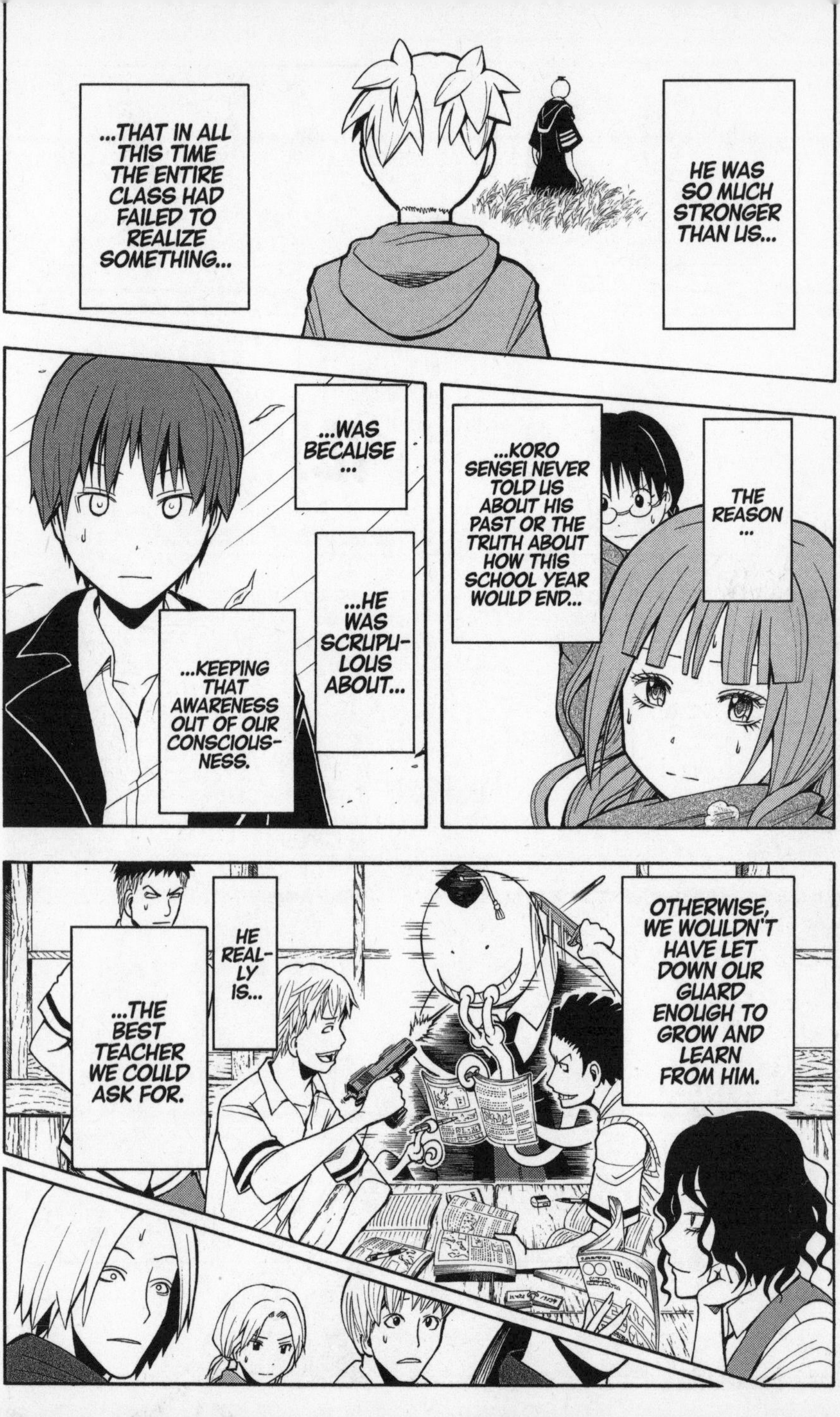
HE WAS SO MUCH STRONGER THAN US...
...THAT IN ALL THIS TIME THE ENTIRE CLASS HAD FAILED TO REALIZE SOMETHING...
THE REASON...
...KORO SENSEI NEVER TOLD US ABOUT HIS PAST OR THE TRUTH ABOUT HOW THIS SCHOOL YEAR WOULD END...
...WAS BECAUSE...
...HE WAS SCRUPULOUS ABOUT...
...KEEPING THAT AWARENESS OUT OF OUR CONSCIOUSNESS.
OTHERWISE, WE WOULDN'T HAVE LET DOWN OUR GUARD ENOUGH TO GROW AND LEARN FROM HIM.
HE REALLY IS...
...THE BEST TEACHER WE COULD ASK FOR.
History

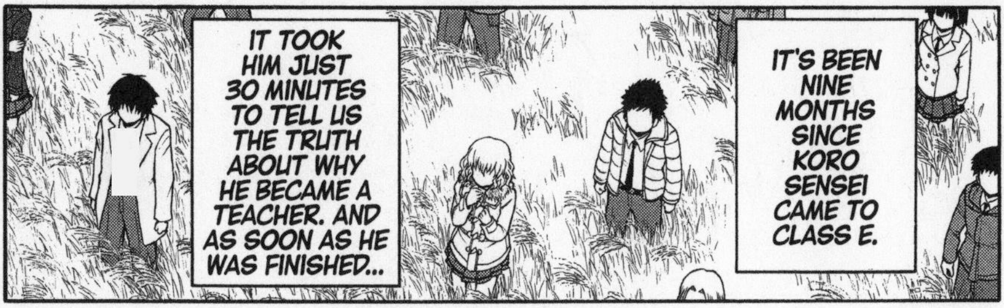
IT'S BEEN NINE MONTHS SINCE KORO SENSEI CAME TO CLASS E.
IT TOOK HIM JUST 30 MINUTES TO TELL US THE TRUTH ABOUT WHY HE BECAME A TEACHER. AND AS SOON AS HE WAS FINISHED...

SUDDENLY...

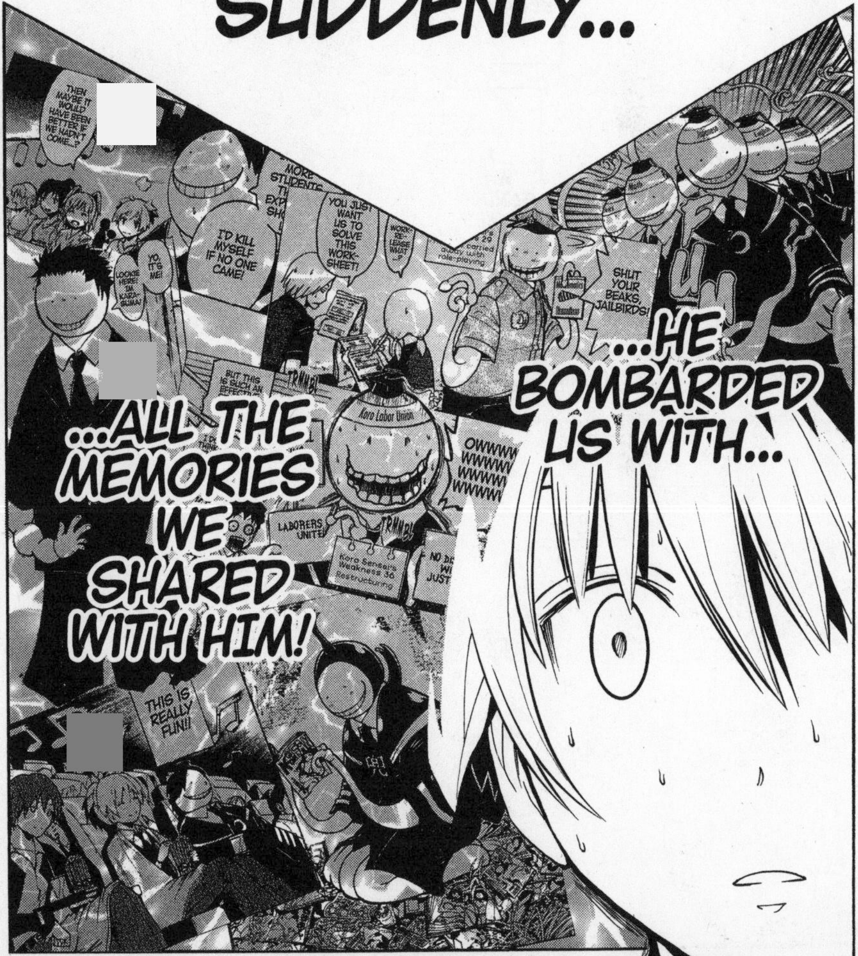
...HE BOMBARDED US WITH...
SHUT YOUR BEAKS, JAILBIRDS!
YOU JUST WANT US TO SOLVE THIS WORKSHEET!
I'D KILL MYSELF IF NO ONE CAME!
THEN MAYBE IT WOULD HAVE BEEN BETTER IF WE HADN'T COME...?
YO, IT'S ME!
LOOKIE HERE! I'M KARASUMA!
Koro Labor Union
LABORERS UNITE!
Koro Sensei's Weakness 36 Restructuring
THIS IS REALLY FUN!!
...ALL THE MEMORIES WE SHARED WITH HIM!

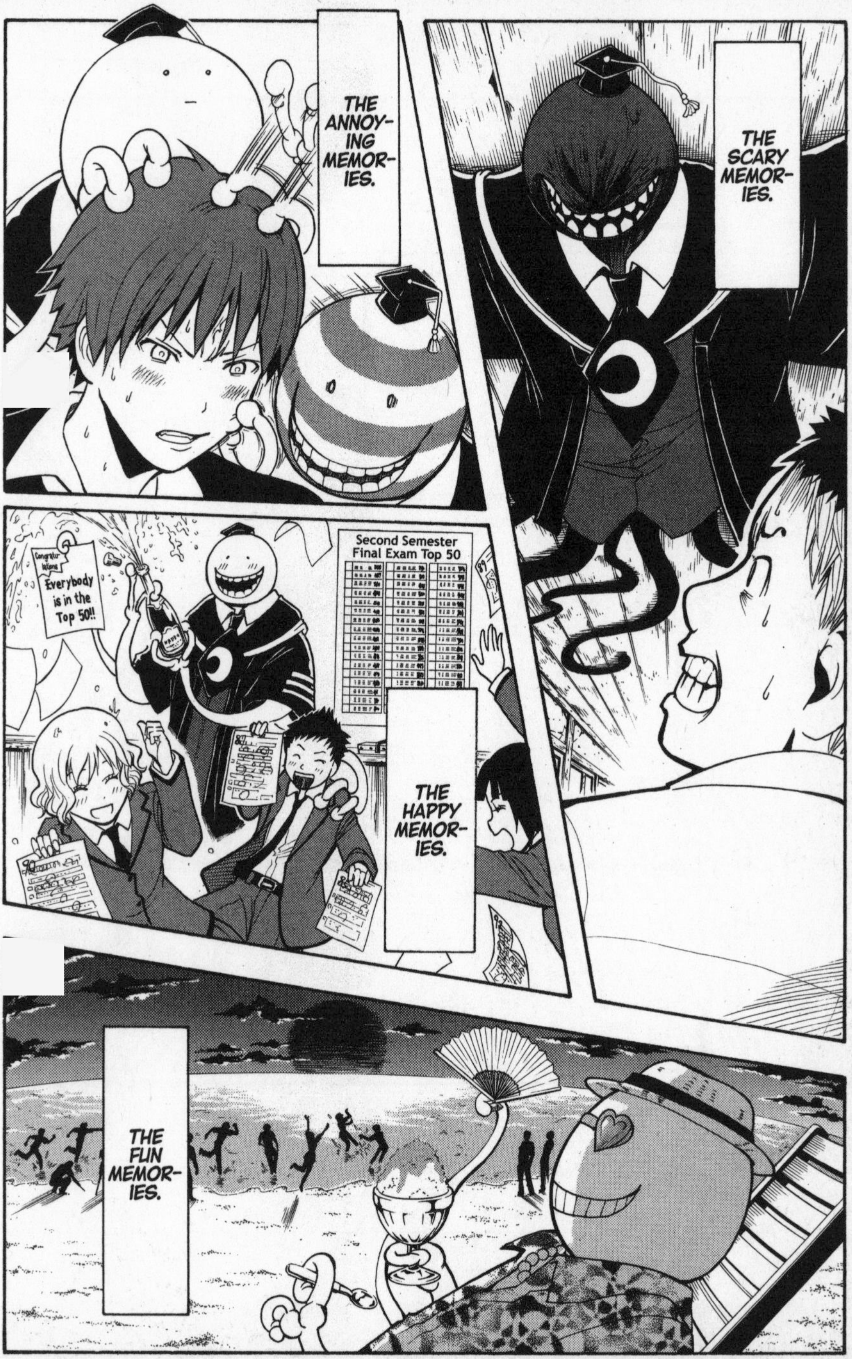
THE SCARY MEMORIES.
THE ANNOYING MEMORIES.
Second Semester Final Exam Top 50
Congratulations
Everybody is in the Top 50!!
THE HAPPY MEMORIES.
THE FUN MEMORIES.

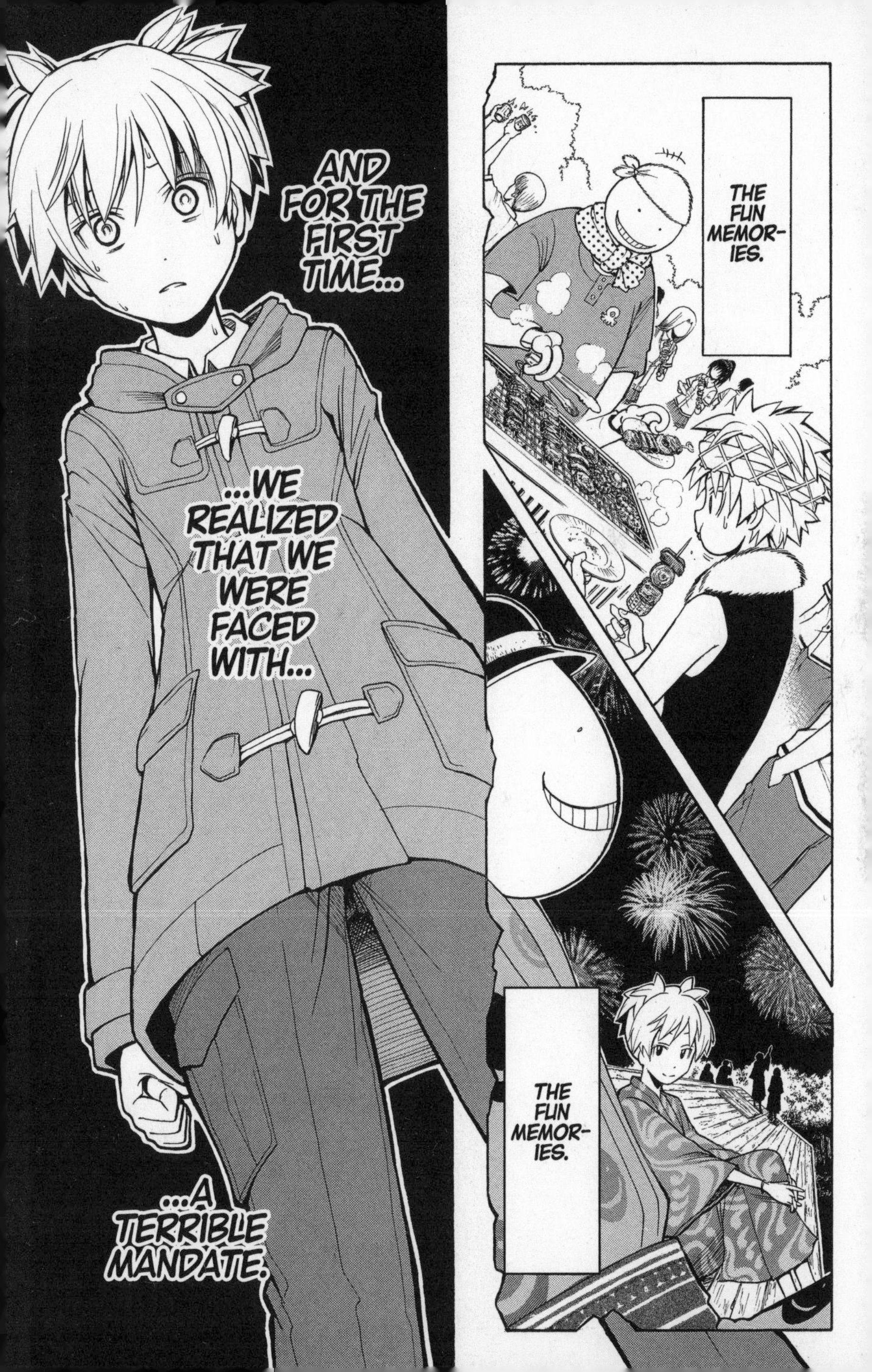
THE FUN MEMORIES.
THE FUN MEMORIES.
AND FOR THE FIRST TIME...
...WE REALIZED THAT WE WERE FACED WITH...
...A TERRIBLE MANDATE.

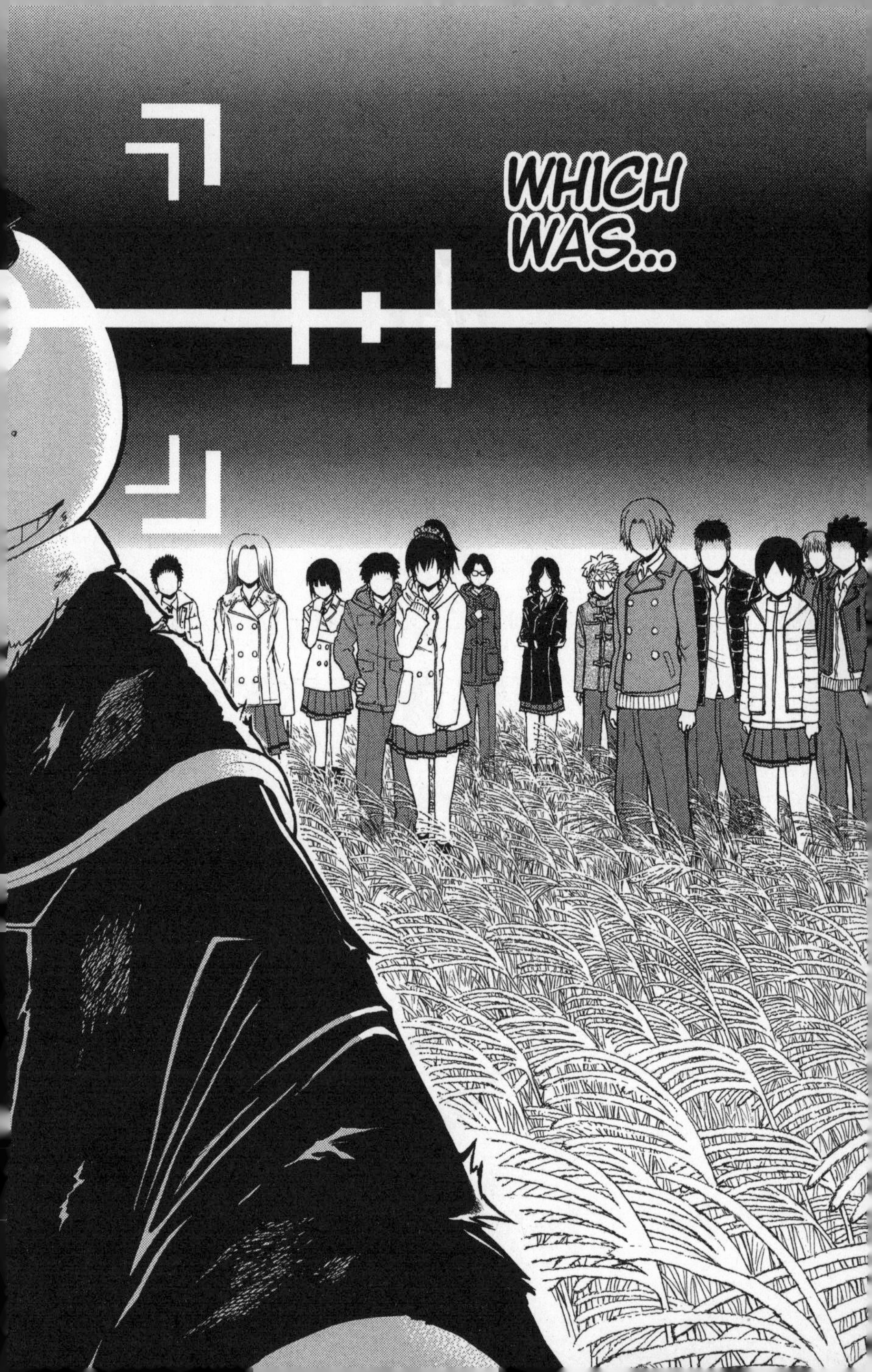
WHICH WAS...

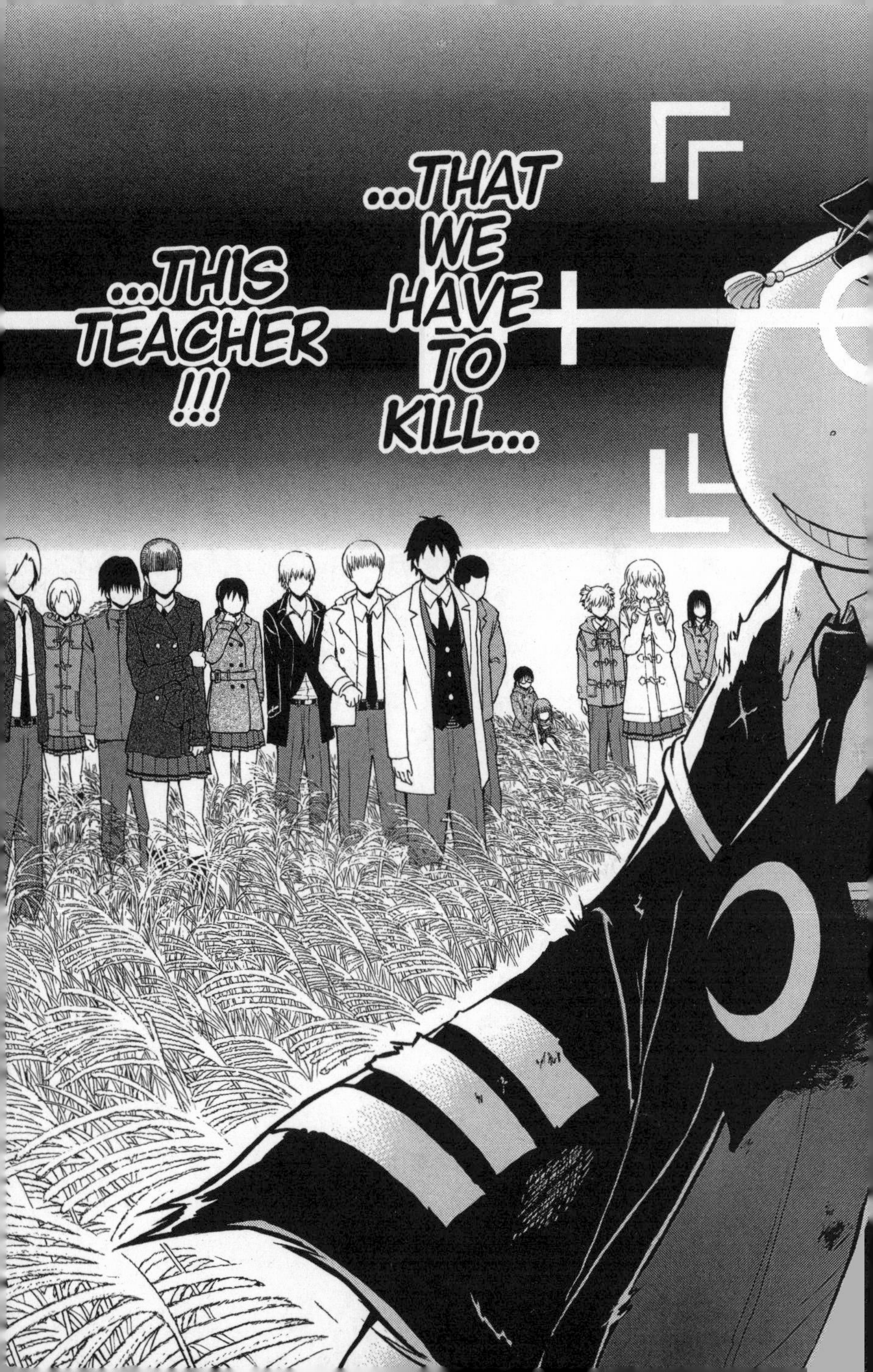
...THAT WE HAVE TO KILL...
...THIS TEACHER!!!

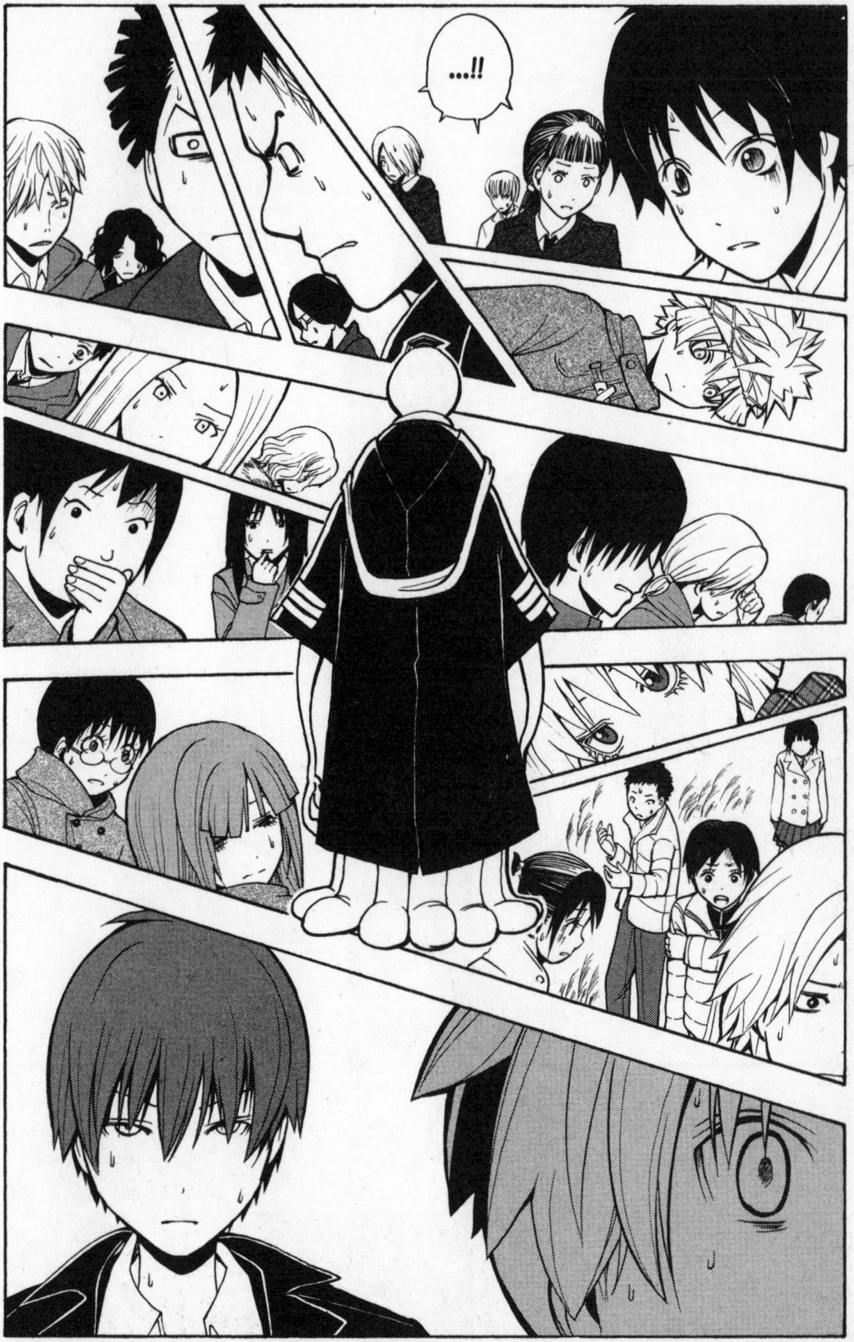
...!!

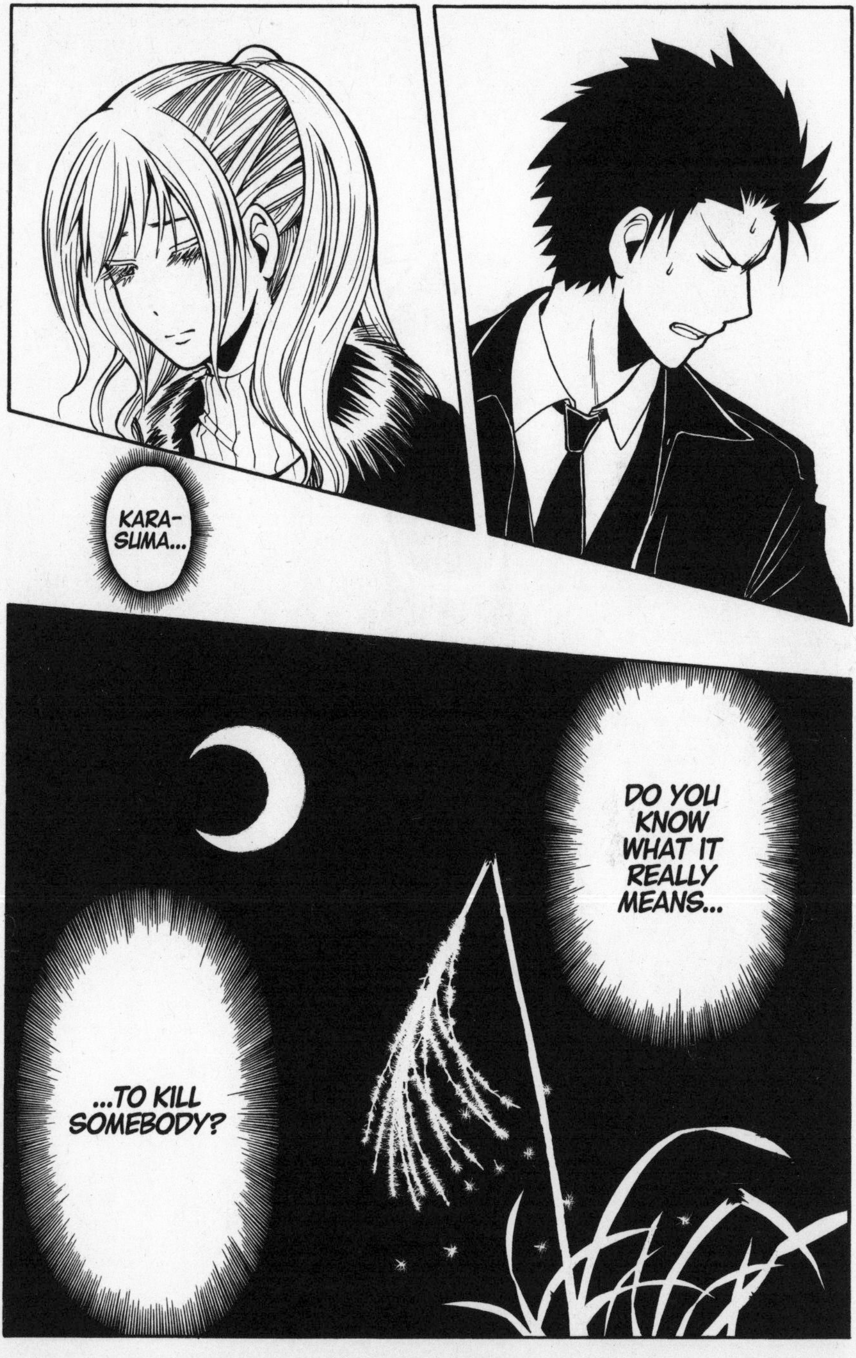
KARA-
SUMA...
DO YOU KNOW WHAT IT REALLY MEANS...
...TO KILL SOMEBODY?

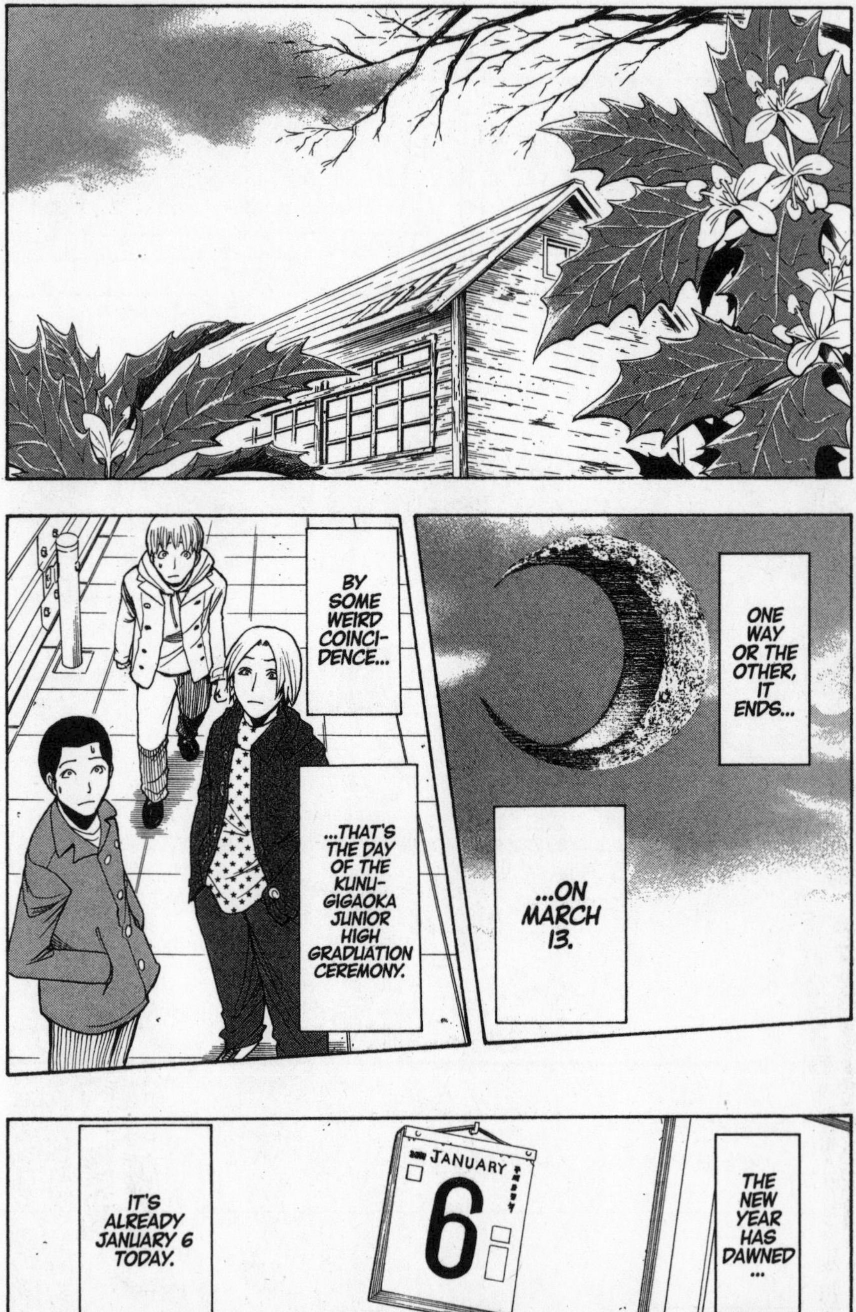
ONE WAY OR THE OTHER, IT ENDS...
...ON MARCH 13.
BY SOME WEIRD COINCIDENCE...
...THAT'S THE DAY OF THE KUNUGIGAOKA JUNIOR HIGH GRADUATION CEREMONY.
THE NEW YEAR HAS DAWNED...
JANUARY
6
IT'S ALREADY JANUARY 6 TODAY.

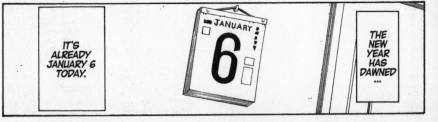

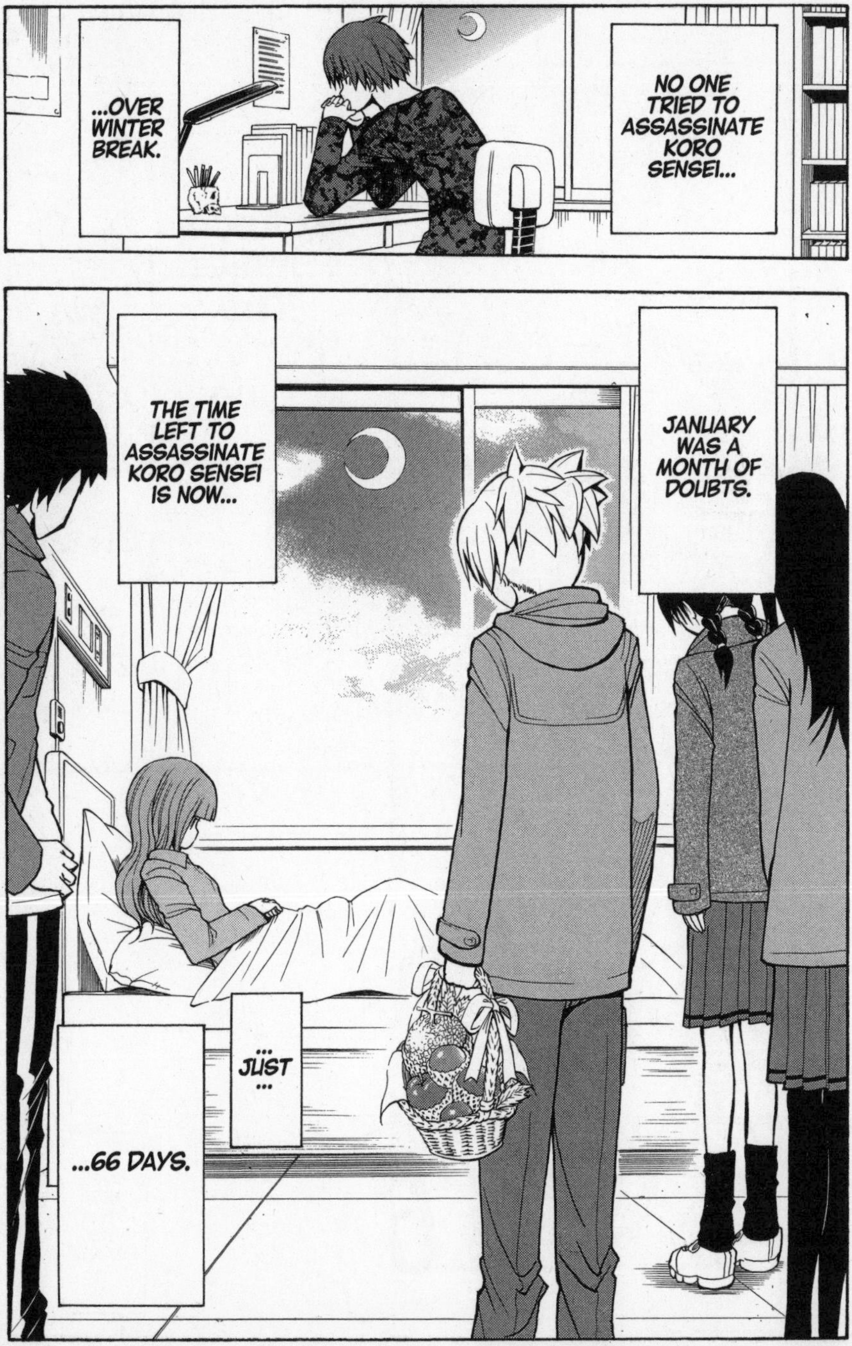
NO ONE TRIED TO ASSASSINATE KORO SENSEI...
...OVER WINTER BREAK.
JANUARY WAS A MONTH OF DOUBTS.
THE TIME LEFT TO ASSASSINATE KORO SENSEI IS NOW...
...JUST...
...66 DAYS.

Spasmodic Funnies: The Perfect Type

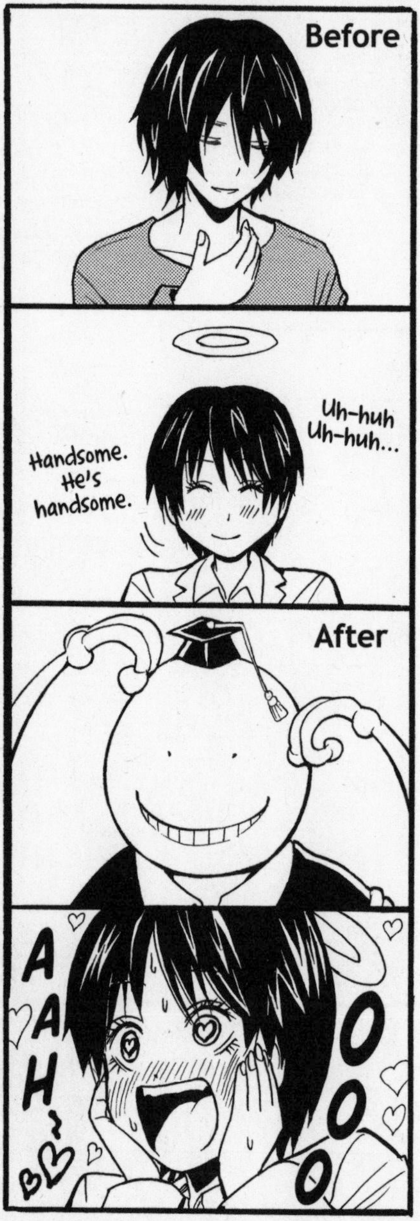
Before
Uh-huh
Uh-huh...
Handsome. He's handsome.
After
OOOO
AAH~
B♡

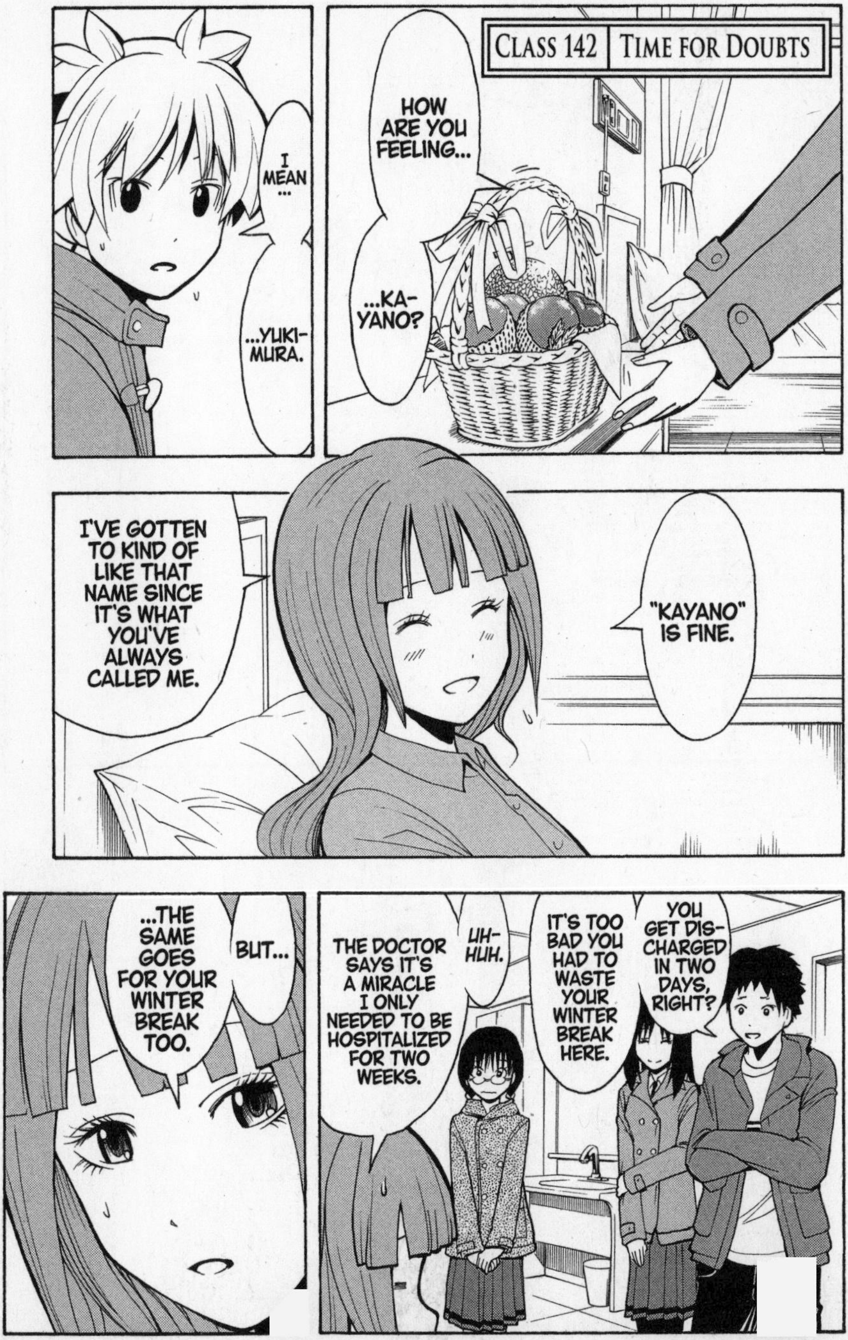
CLASS 142 TIME FOR DOUBTS
HOW ARE YOU FEELING...
...KA-YANO?
I MEAN ...
...YUKI-MURA.
"KAYANO" IS FINE.
I'VE GOTTEN TO KIND OF LIKE THAT NAME SINCE IT'S WHAT YOU'VE ALWAYS CALLED ME.
YOU GET DIS-CHARGED IN TWO DAYS, RIGHT?
IT'S TOO BAD YOU HAD TO WASTE YOUR WINTER BREAK HERE.
UH-HUH.
THE DOCTOR SAYS IT'S A MIRACLE I ONLY NEEDED TO BE HOSPITALIZED FOR TWO WEEKS.
BUT...
...THE SAME GOES FOR YOUR WINTER BREAK TOO.

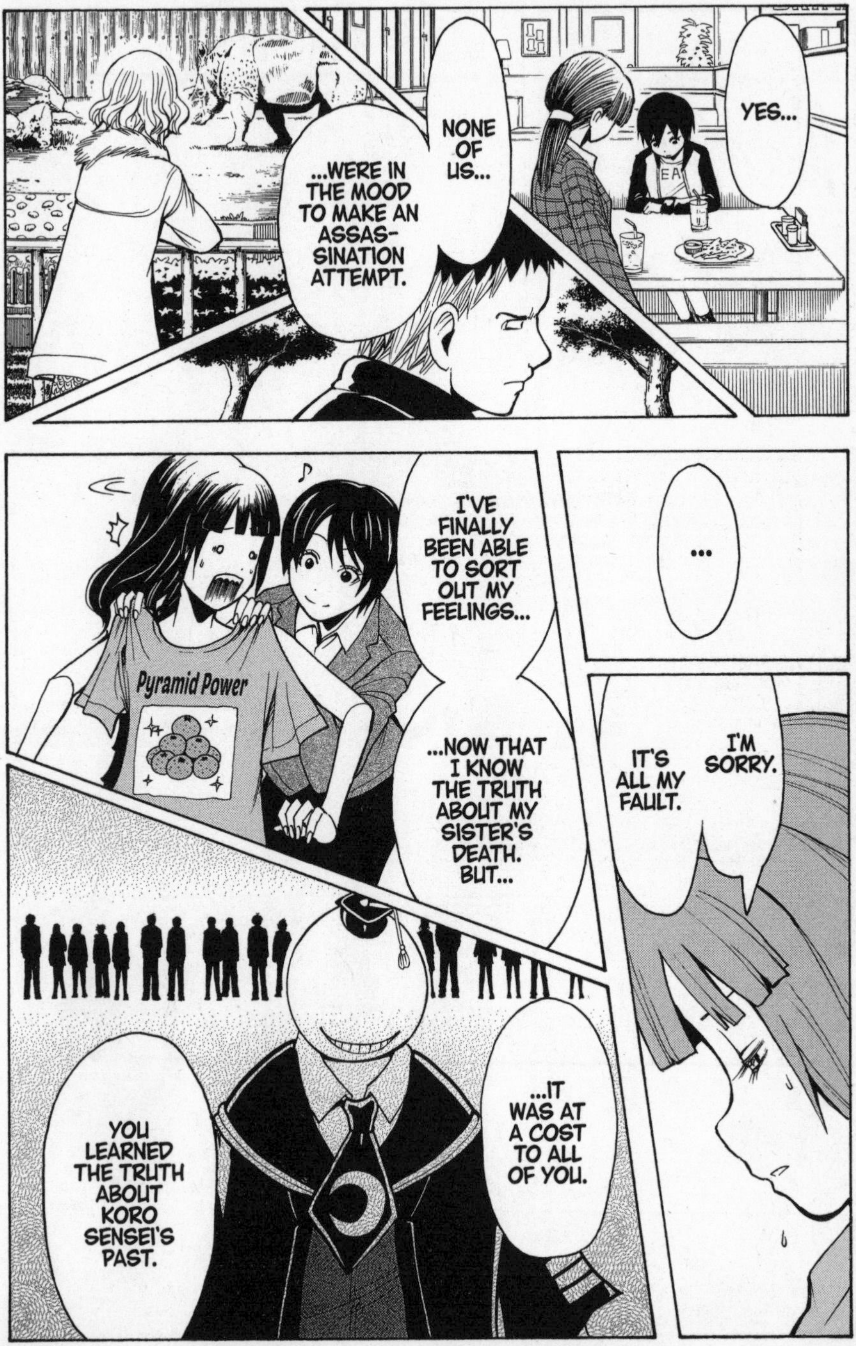
YES...
NONE OF US...
...WERE IN THE MOOD TO MAKE AN ASSAS-SINATION ATTEMPT.
...
I'M SORRY.
IT'S ALL MY FAULT.
I'VE FINALLY BEEN ABLE TO SORT OUT MY FEELINGS...
...NOW THAT I KNOW THE TRUTH ABOUT MY SISTER'S DEATH. BUT...
Pyramid Power
...IT WAS AT A COST TO ALL OF YOU.
YOU LEARNED THE TRUTH ABOUT KORO SENSEI'S PAST.

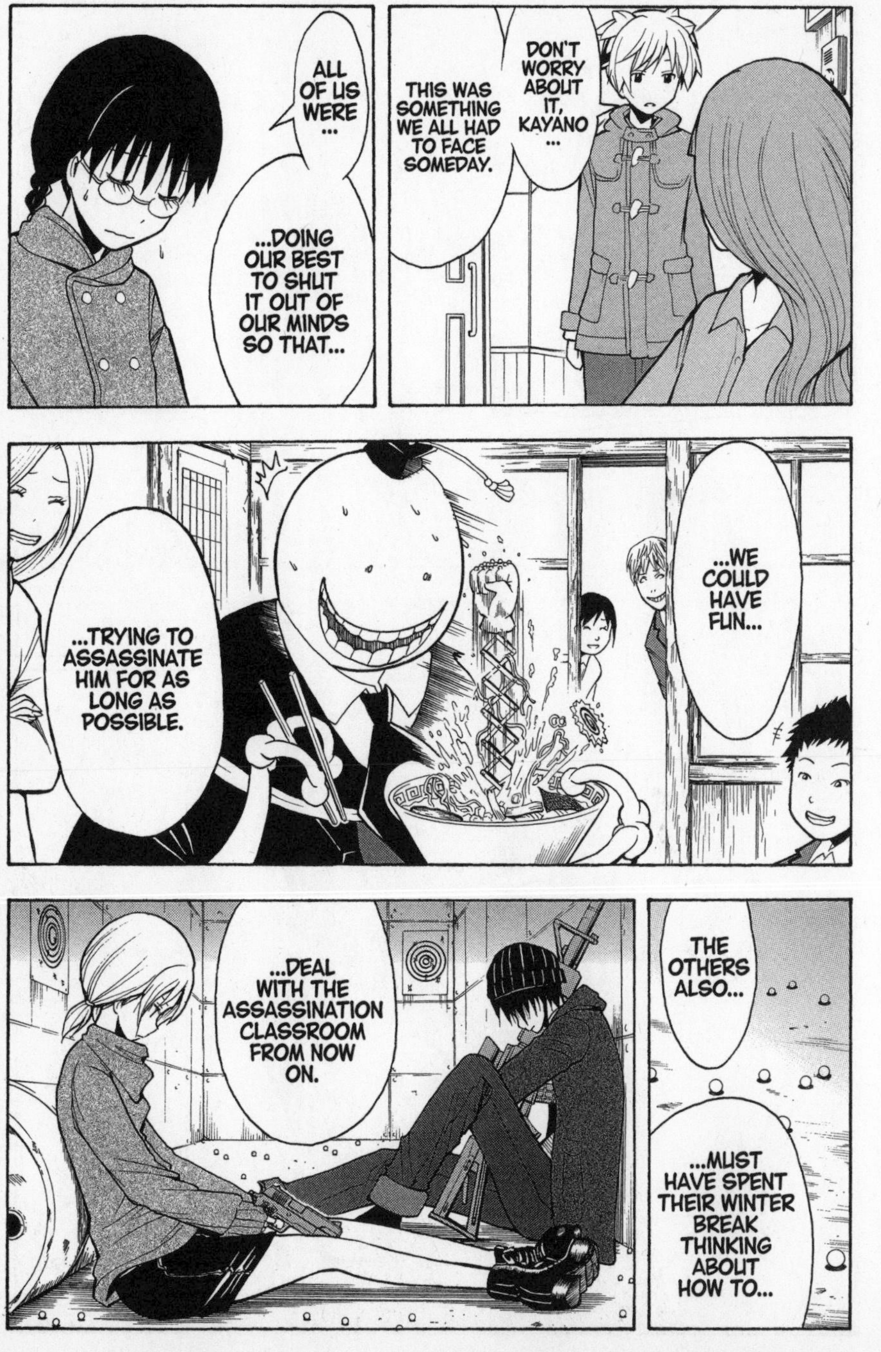
DON'T WORRY ABOUT IT, KAYANO...
THIS WAS SOMETHING WE ALL HAD TO FACE SOMEDAY.
ALL OF US WERE...
...DOING OUR BEST TO SHUT IT OUT OF OUR MINDS SO THAT...
...WE COULD HAVE FUN...
...TRYING TO ASSASSINATE HIM FOR AS LONG AS POSSIBLE.
THE OTHERS ALSO...
...MUST HAVE SPENT THEIR WINTER BREAK THINKING ABOUT HOW TO...
...DEAL WITH THE ASSASSINATION CLASSROOM FROM NOW ON.

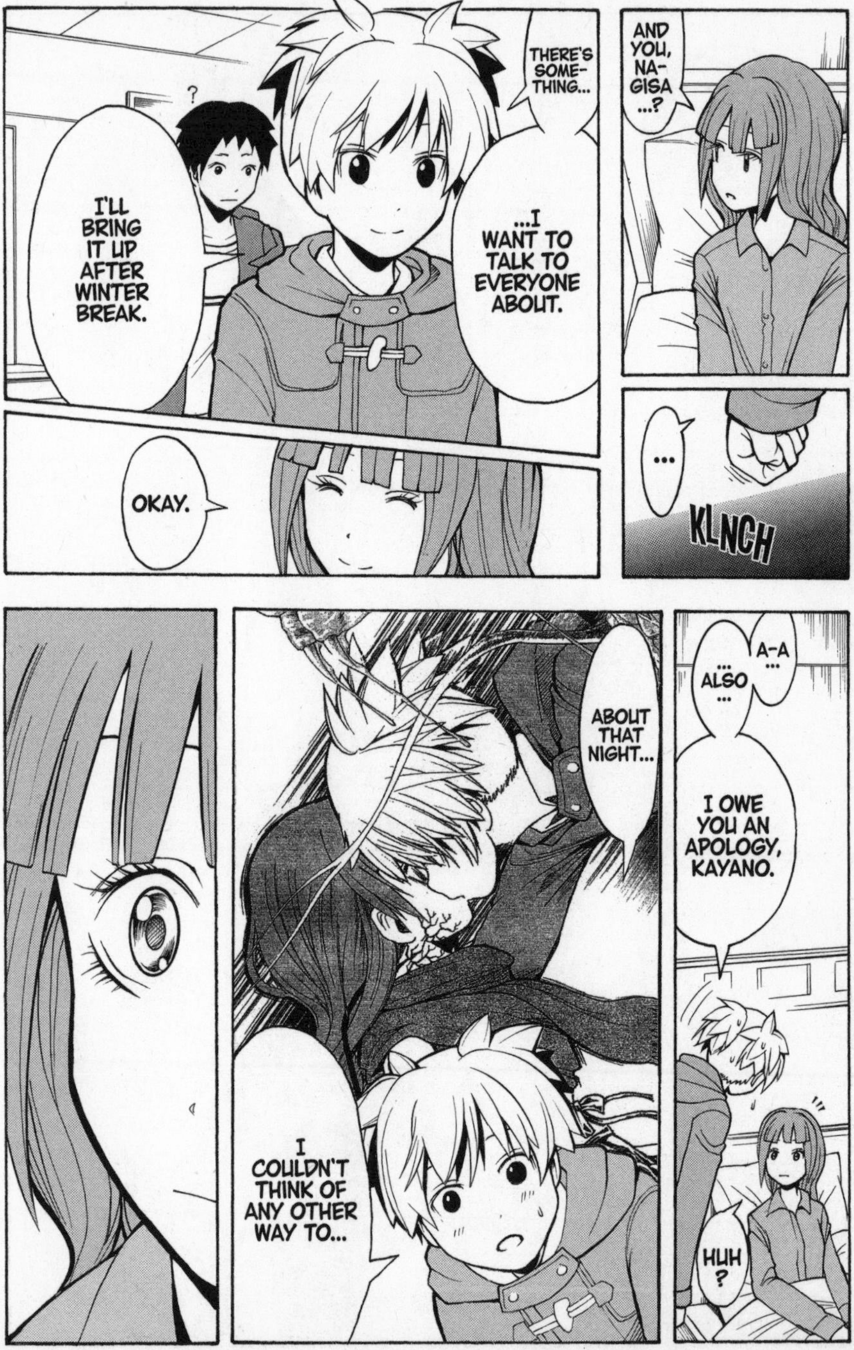
AND YOU, NA-GISA ...?
THERE'S SOME-THING...
...I WANT TO TALK TO EVERYONE ABOUT.
I'LL BRING IT UP AFTER WINTER BREAK.
...
KLNCH
OKAY.
A-A ...
... ALSO ...
I OWE YOU AN APOLOGY, KAYANO.
HUH ?
ABOUT THAT NIGHT...
I COULDN'T THINK OF ANY OTHER WAY TO...

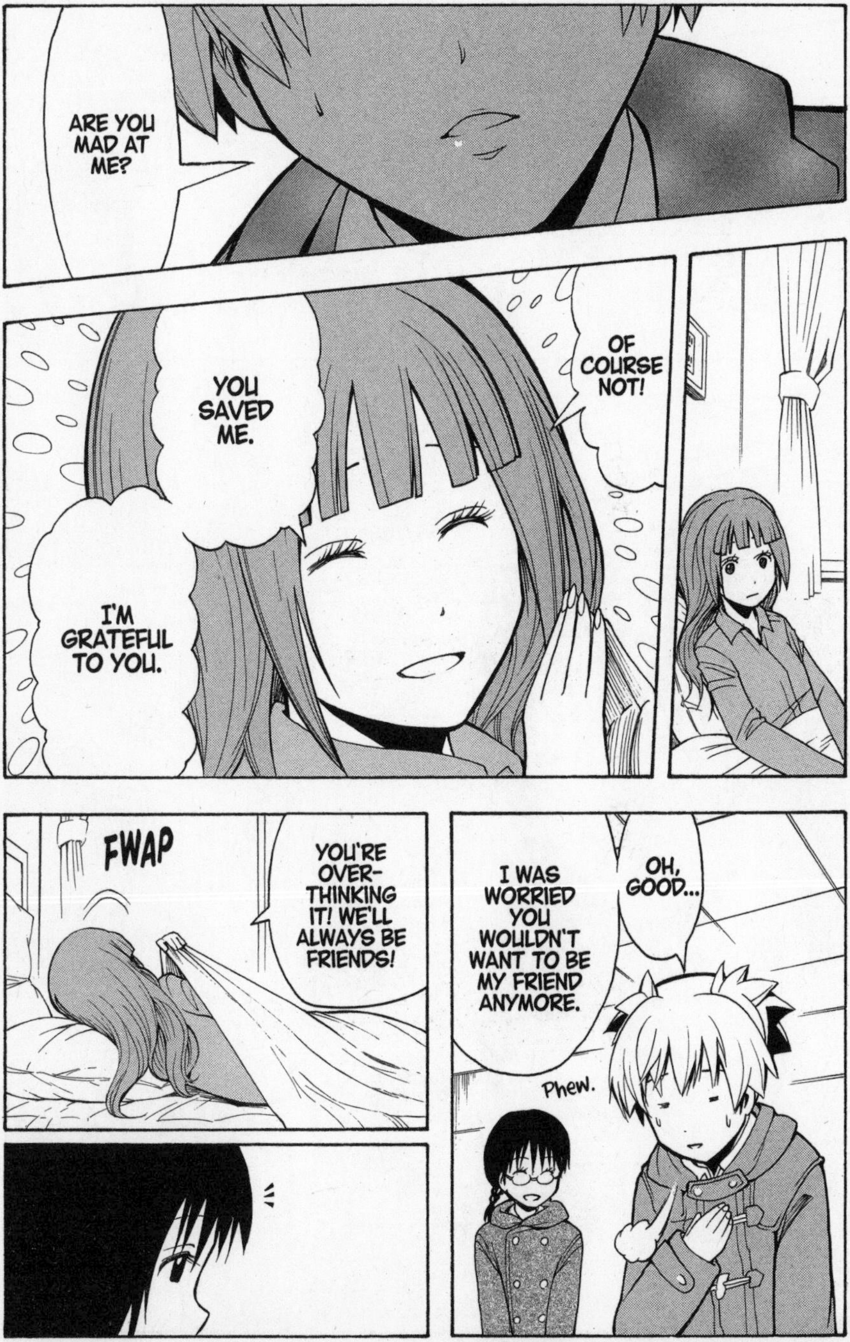
ARE YOU MAD AT ME?
OF COURSE NOT!
YOU SAVED ME.
I'M GRATEFUL TO YOU.
OH, GOOD...
I WAS WORRIED YOU WOULDN'T WANT TO BE MY FRIEND ANYMORE.
Phew.
FWAP
YOU'RE OVER-THINKING IT! WE'LL ALWAYS BE FRIENDS!

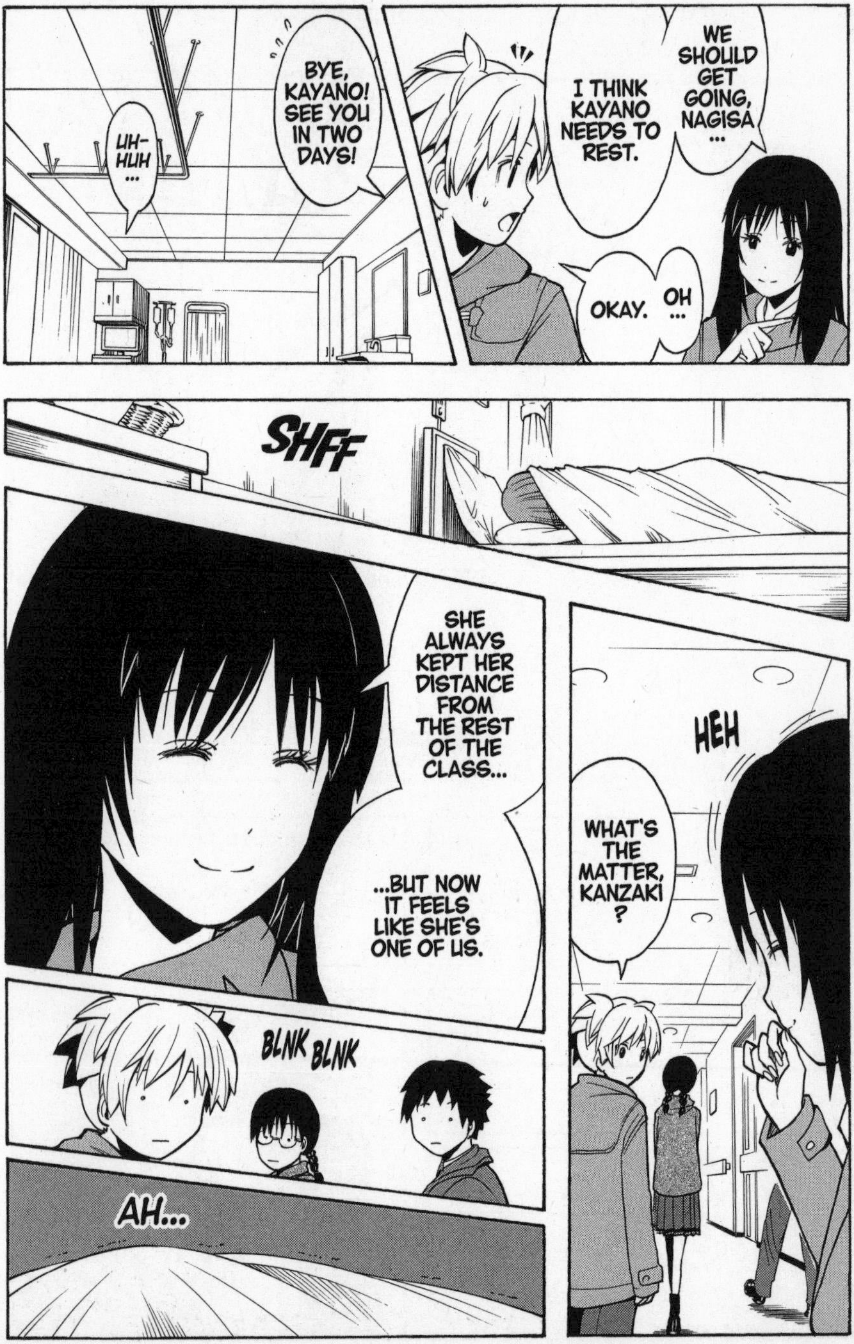
WE SHOULD GET GOING, NAGISA...
I THINK KAYANO NEEDS TO REST.
OH...
OKAY.
BYE, KAYANO! SEE YOU IN TWO DAYS!
UH-HUH...
SHFF
HEH
WHAT'S THE MATTER, KANZAKI?
SHE ALWAYS KEPT HER DISTANCE FROM THE REST OF THE CLASS...
...BUT NOW IT FEELS LIKE SHE'S ONE OF US.
BLNK BLNK
AH...

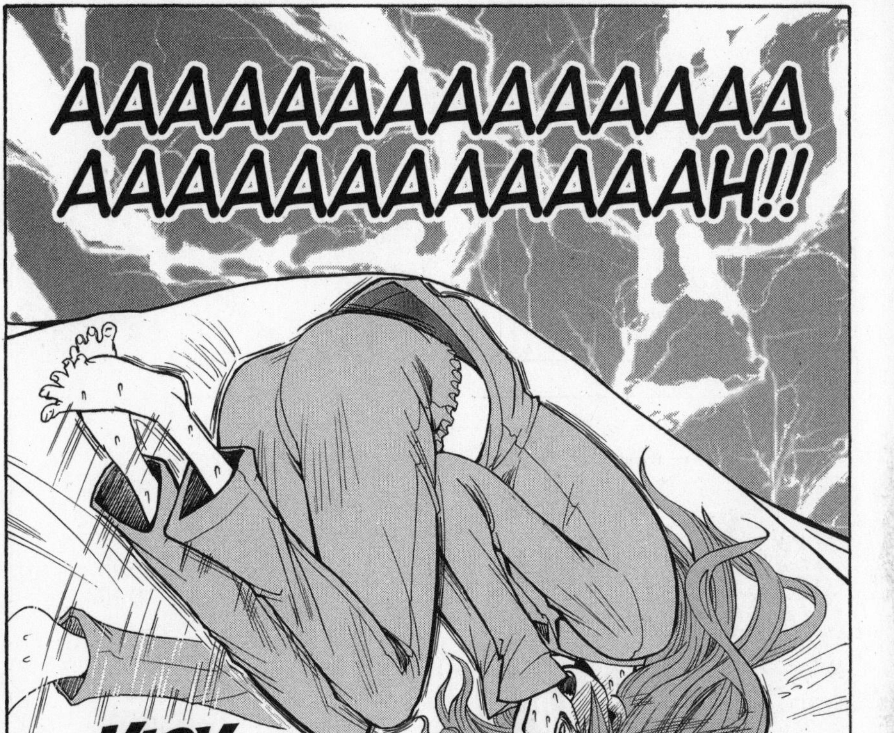
AAAAAAAAAAAAAA
AAAAAAAAAAAAAH!!
KICK
KICK
SHAKE
SHAKE
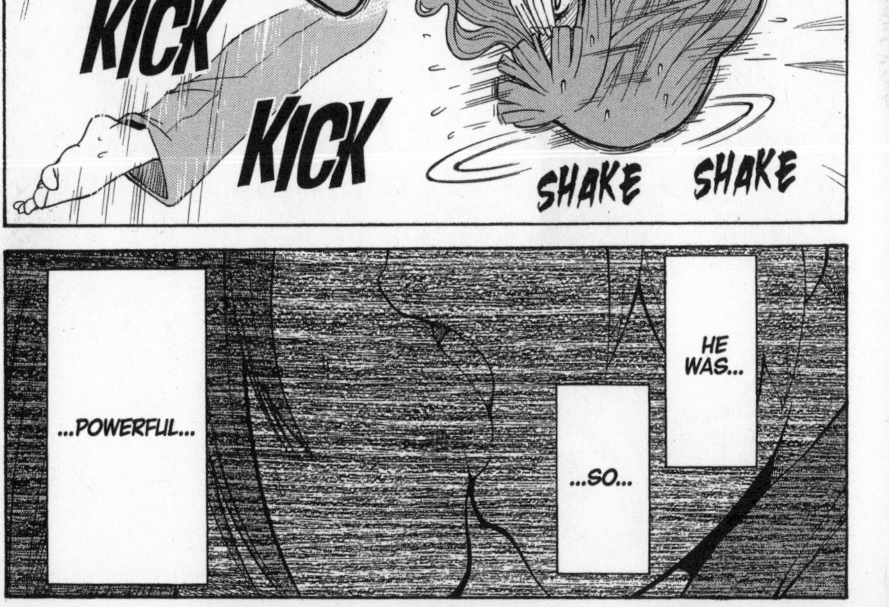
HE WAS...
...SO...
...POWERFUL...

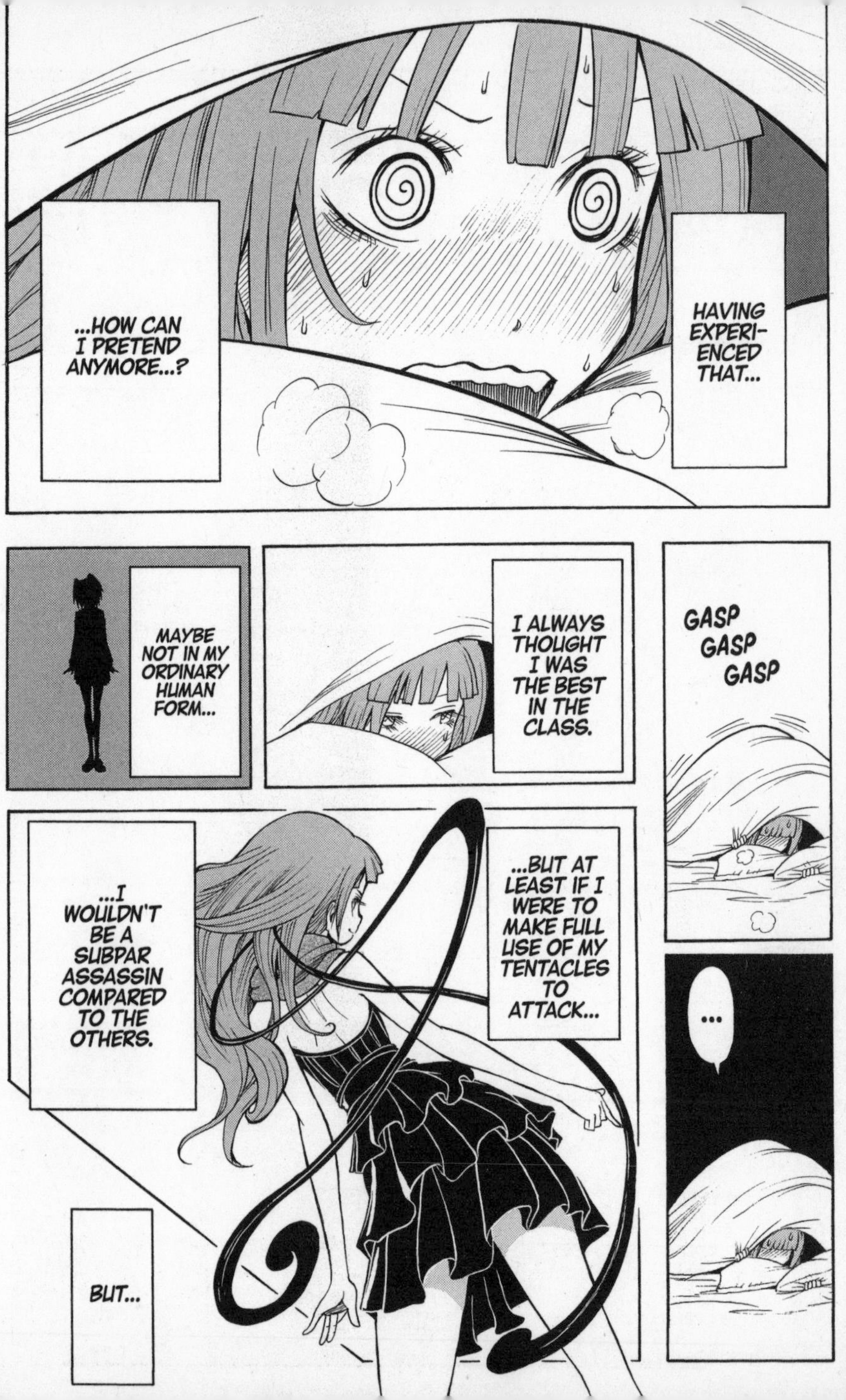
HAVING EXPERI-ENCED THAT...
...HOW CAN I PRETEND ANYMORE...?
GASP GASP GASP
I ALWAYS THOUGHT I WAS THE BEST IN THE CLASS.
MAYBE NOT IN MY ORDINARY HUMAN FORM...
...BUT AT LEAST IF I WERE TO MAKE FULL USE OF MY TENTACLES TO ATTACK...
...I WOULDN'T BE A SUBPAR ASSASSIN COMPARED TO THE OTHERS.
BUT...
...

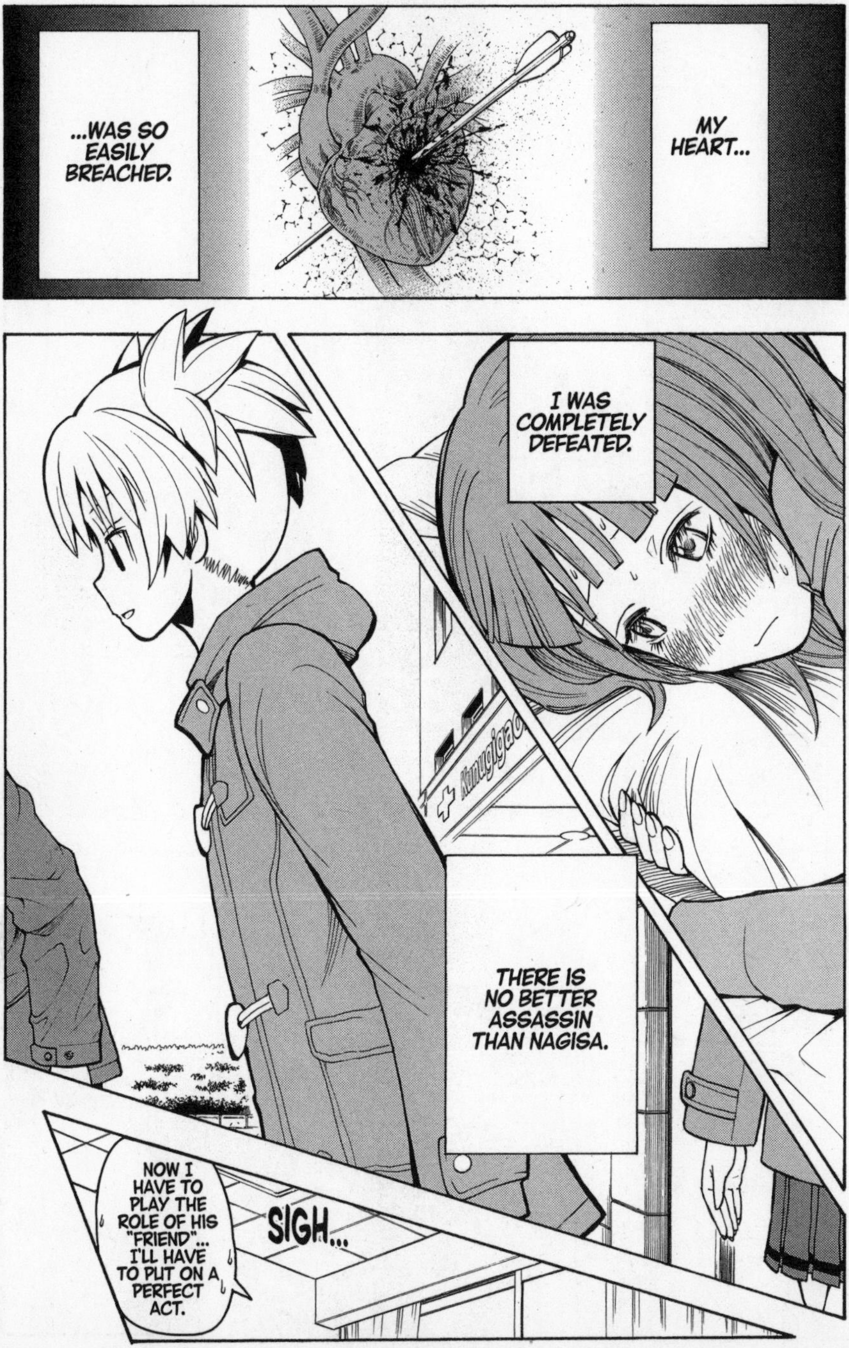
MY HEART...
...WAS SO EASILY BREACHED.
I WAS COMPLETELY DEFEATED.
THERE IS NO BETTER ASSASSIN THAN NAGISA.
SIGH...
NOW I HAVE TO PLAY THE ROLE OF HIS "FRIEND"... I'LL HAVE TO PUT ON A PERFECT ACT.

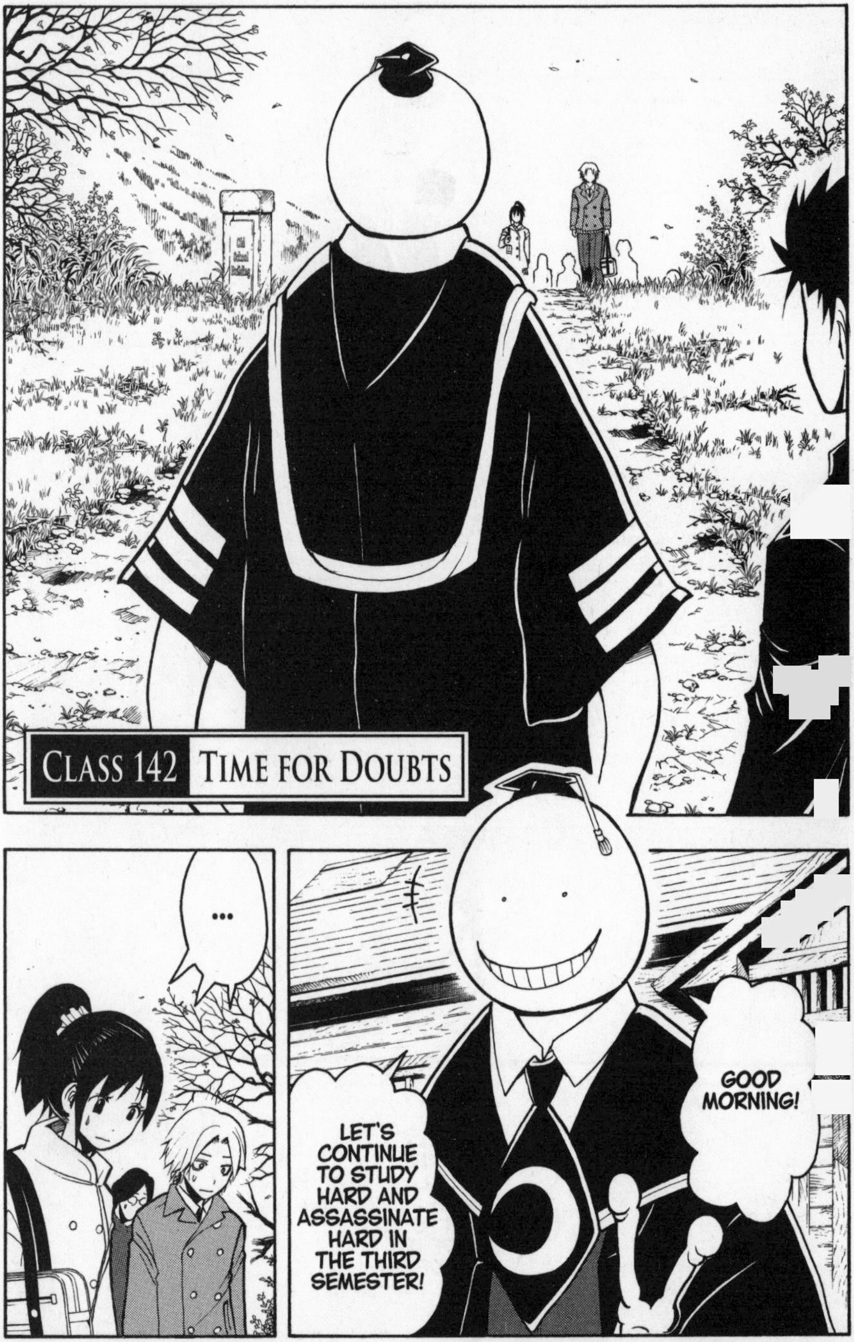
CLASS 142 TIME FOR DOUBTS
GOOD MORNING!
LET'S CONTINUE TO STUDY HARD AND ASSASSINATE HARD IN THE THIRD SEMESTER!
...

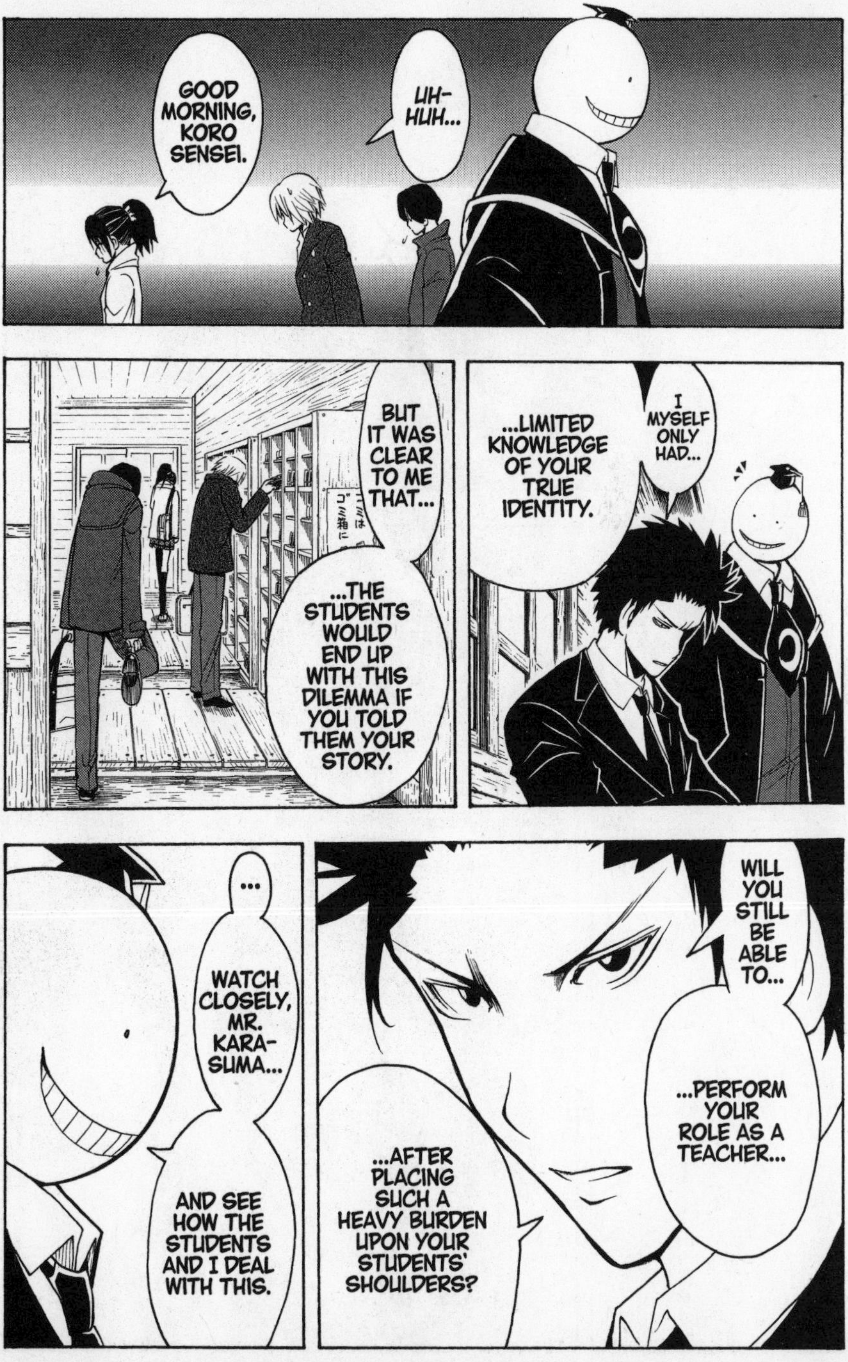
UH-HUH...
GOOD MORNING, KORO SENSEI.
I MYSELF ONLY HAD...
...LIMITED KNOWLEDGE OF YOUR TRUE IDENTITY.
BUT IT WAS CLEAR TO ME THAT...
...THE STUDENTS WOULD END UP WITH THIS DILEMMA IF YOU TOLD THEM YOUR STORY.
WILL YOU STILL BE ABLE TO...
...PERFORM YOUR ROLE AS A TEACHER...
...AFTER PLACING SUCH A HEAVY BURDEN UPON YOUR STUDENTS' SHOULDERS?
...
WATCH CLOSELY, MR. KARA-SUMA...
AND SEE HOW THE STUDENTS AND I DEAL WITH THIS.

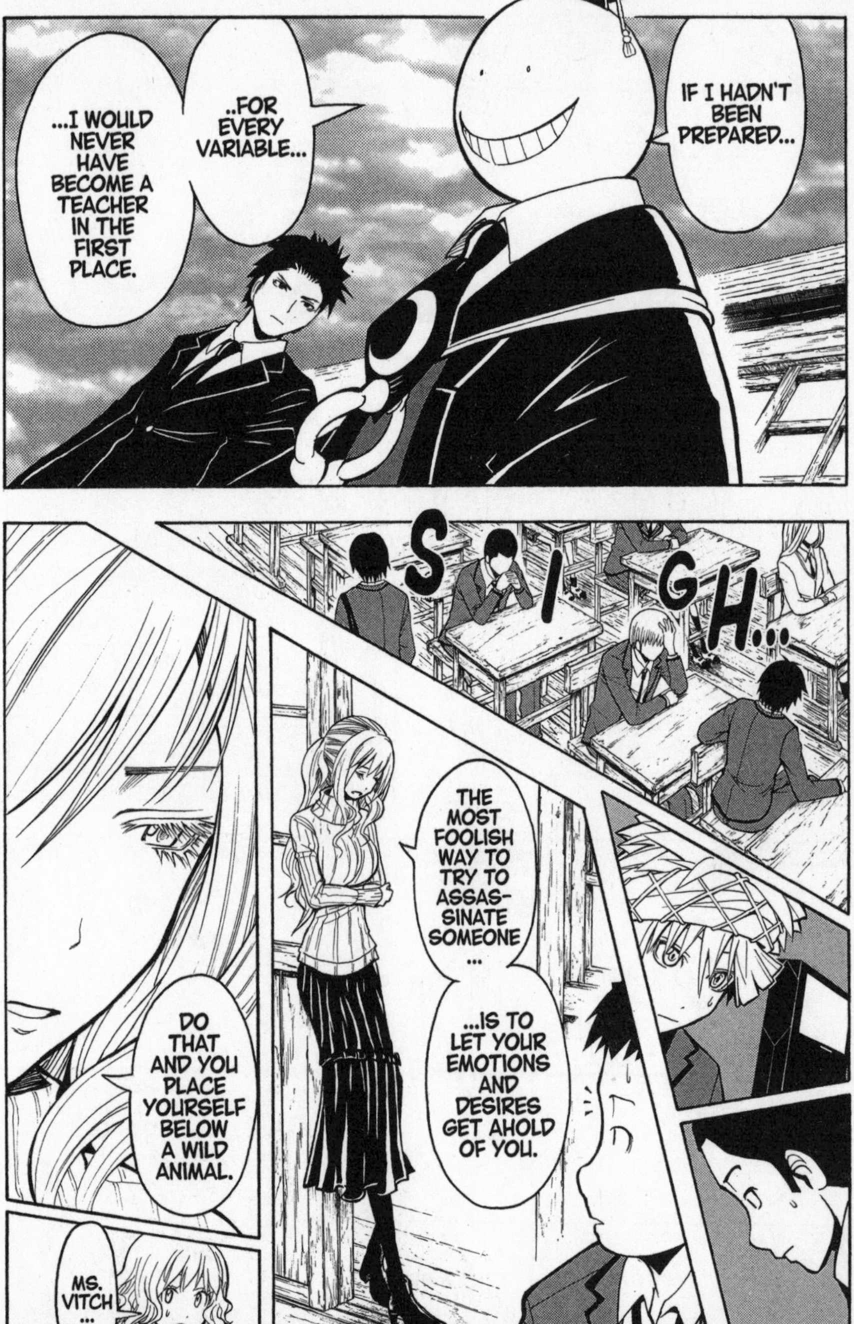
IF I HADN'T BEEN PREPARED...
..FOR EVERY VARIABLE...
...I WOULD NEVER HAVE BECOME A TEACHER IN THE FIRST PLACE.
SIGH...
THE MOST FOOLISH WAY TO TRY TO ASSAS-SINATE SOMEONE...
...IS TO LET YOUR EMOTIONS AND DESIRES GET AHOLD OF YOU.
DO THAT AND YOU PLACE YOURSELF BELOW A WILD ANIMAL.
MS. VITCH...

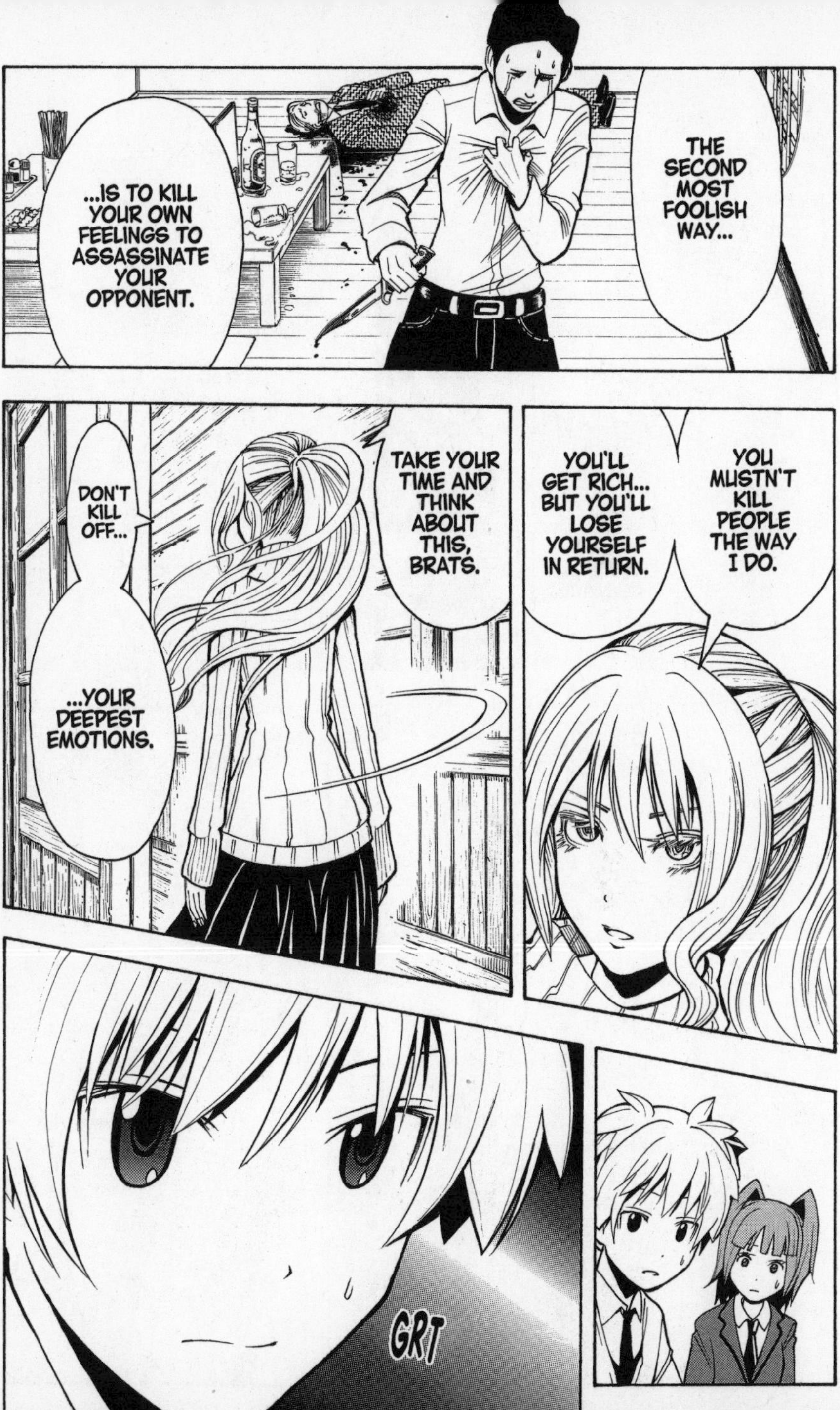
THE SECOND MOST FOOLISH WAY...
...IS TO KILL YOUR OWN FEELINGS TO ASSASSINATE YOUR OPPONENT.
YOU MUSTN'T KILL PEOPLE THE WAY I DO.
YOU'LL GET RICH... BUT YOU'LL LOSE YOURSELF IN RETURN.
TAKE YOUR TIME AND THINK ABOUT THIS, BRATS.
DON'T KILL OFF...
...YOUR DEEPEST EMOTIONS.
GRT

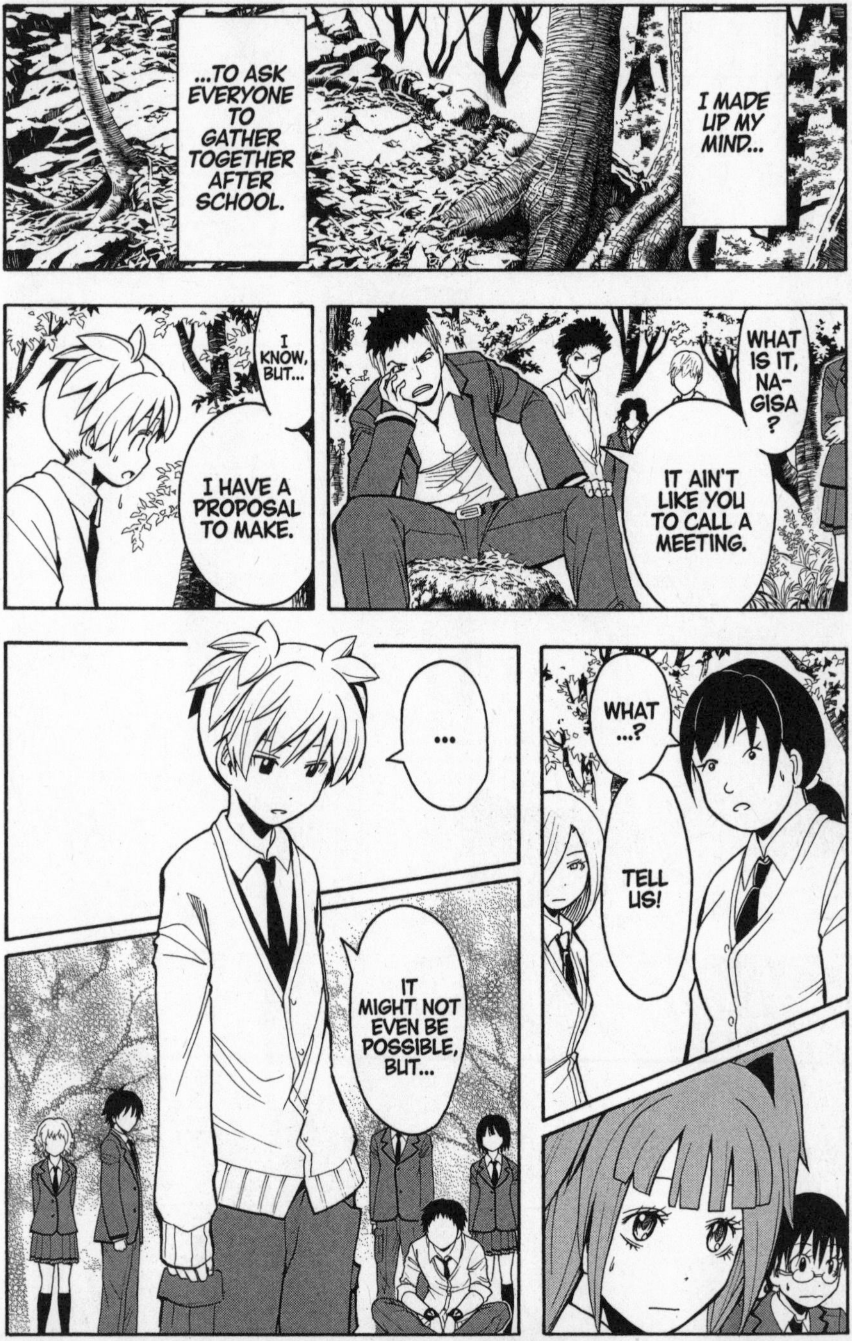
I MADE UP MY MIND...
...TO ASK EVERYONE TO GATHER TOGETHER AFTER SCHOOL.
WHAT IS IT, NA-GISA?
IT AIN'T LIKE YOU TO CALL A MEETING.
I KNOW, BUT...
I HAVE A PROPOSAL TO MAKE.
WHAT ...?
TELL US!
...
IT MIGHT NOT EVEN BE POSSIBLE, BUT...

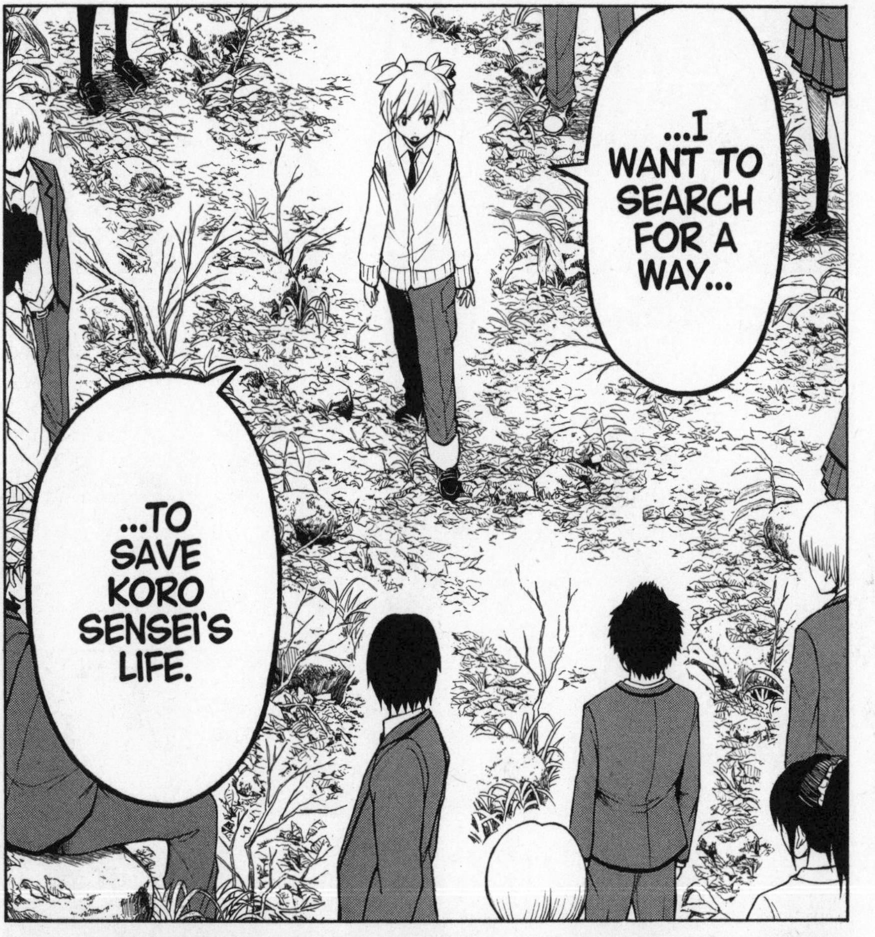
...I WANT TO SEARCH FOR A WAY...
...TO SAVE KORO SENSEI'S LIFE.
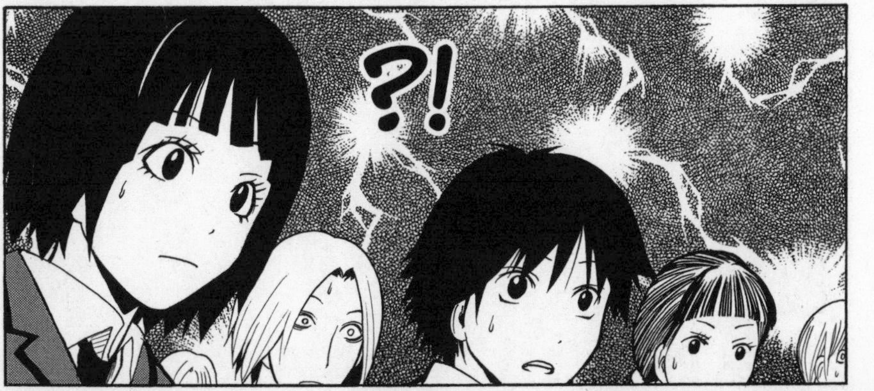
?!

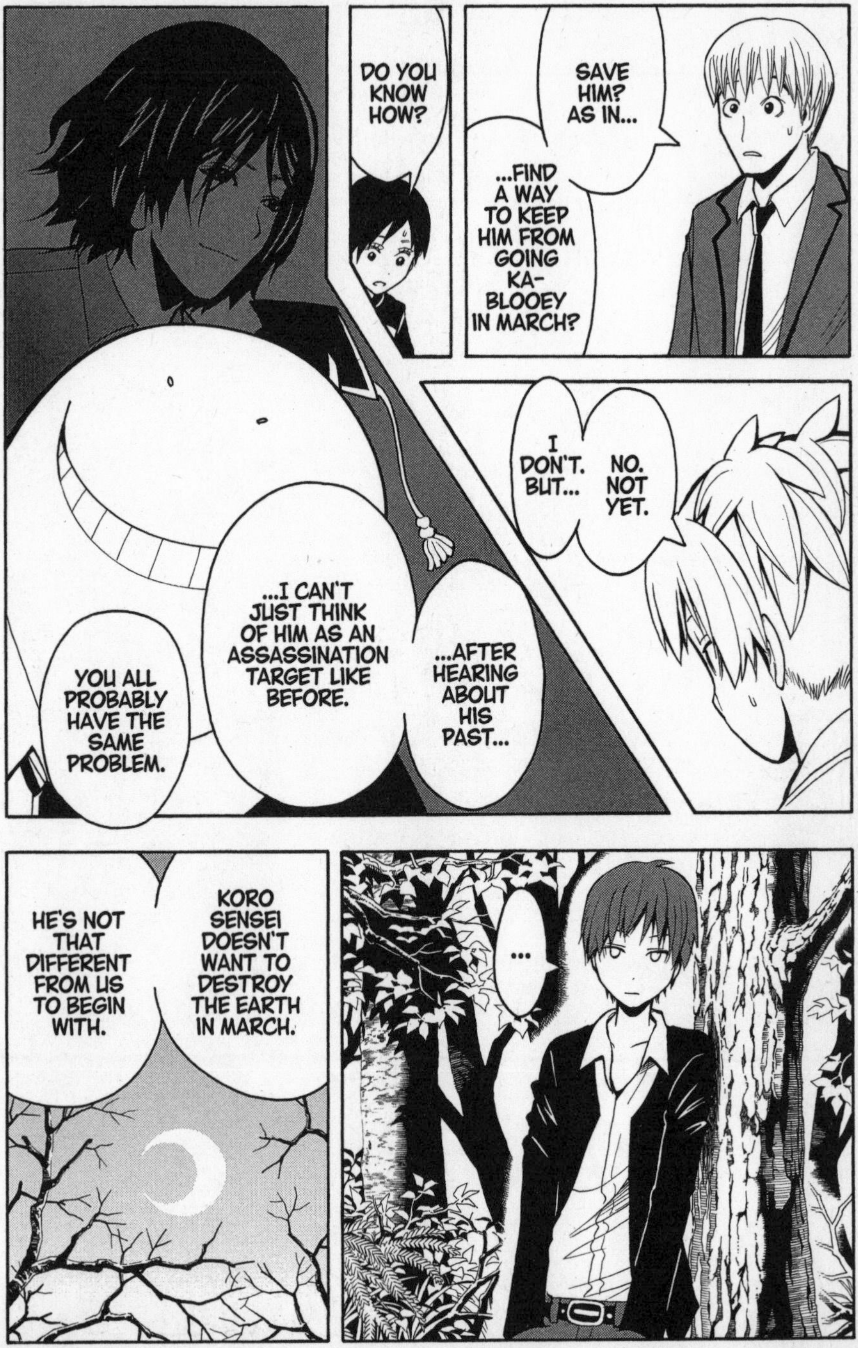
SAVE HIM? AS IN...
...FIND A WAY TO KEEP HIM FROM GOING KA-BLOOEY IN MARCH?
DO YOU KNOW HOW?
NO. NOT YET.
I DON'T. BUT...
...AFTER HEARING ABOUT HIS PAST...
...I CAN'T JUST THINK OF HIM AS AN ASSASSINATION TARGET LIKE BEFORE.
YOU ALL PROBABLY HAVE THE SAME PROBLEM.
...
KORO SENSEI DOESN'T WANT TO DESTROY THE EARTH IN MARCH.
HE'S NOT THAT DIFFERENT FROM US TO BEGIN WITH.

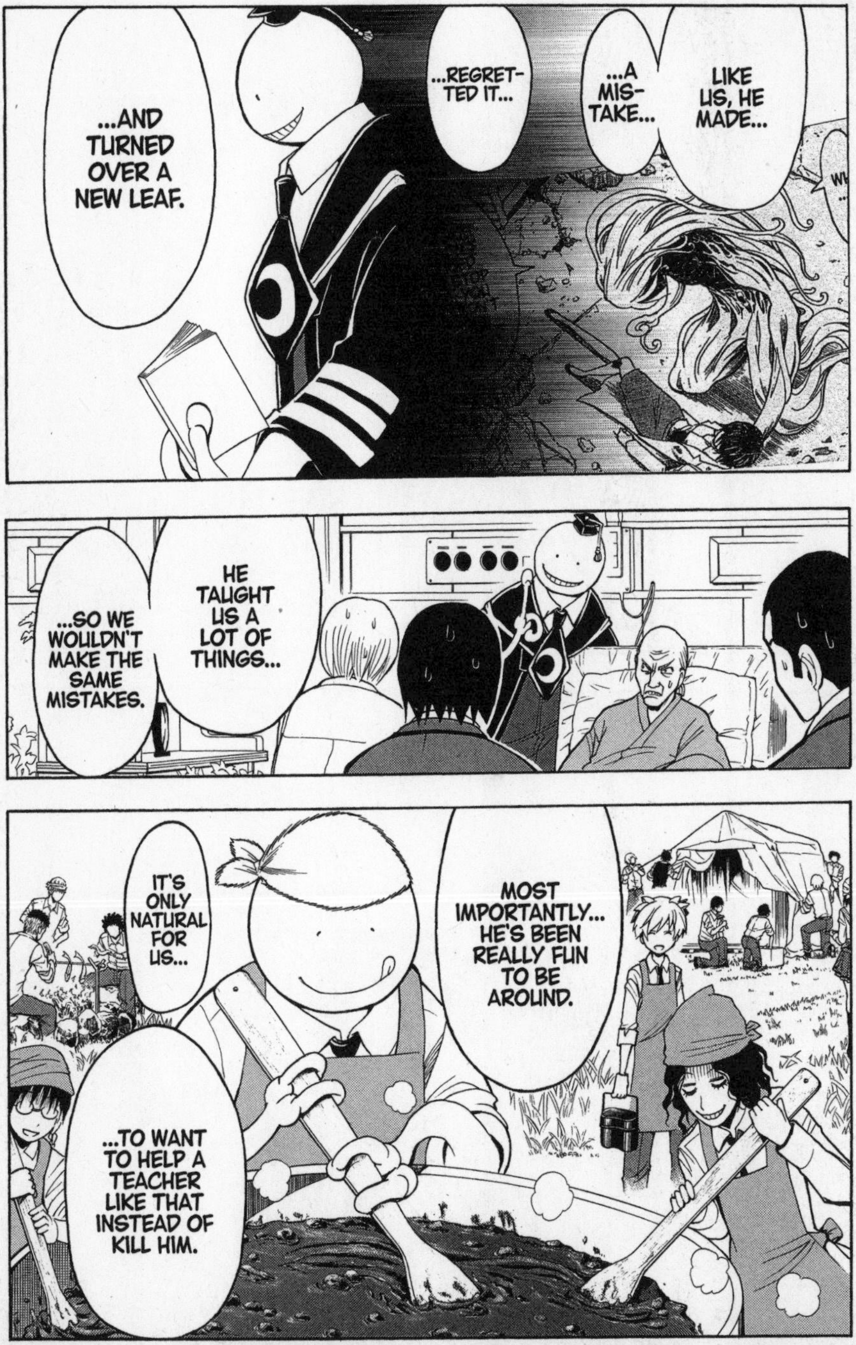
LIKE US, HE MADE...
...A MISTAKE...
...REGRETTED IT...
...AND TURNED OVER A NEW LEAF.
HE TAUGHT US A LOT OF THINGS...
...SO WE WOULDN'T MAKE THE SAME MISTAKES.
MOST IMPORTANTLY... HE'S BEEN REALLY FUN TO BE AROUND.
IT'S ONLY NATURAL FOR US...
...TO WANT TO HELP A TEACHER LIKE THAT INSTEAD OF KILL HIM.

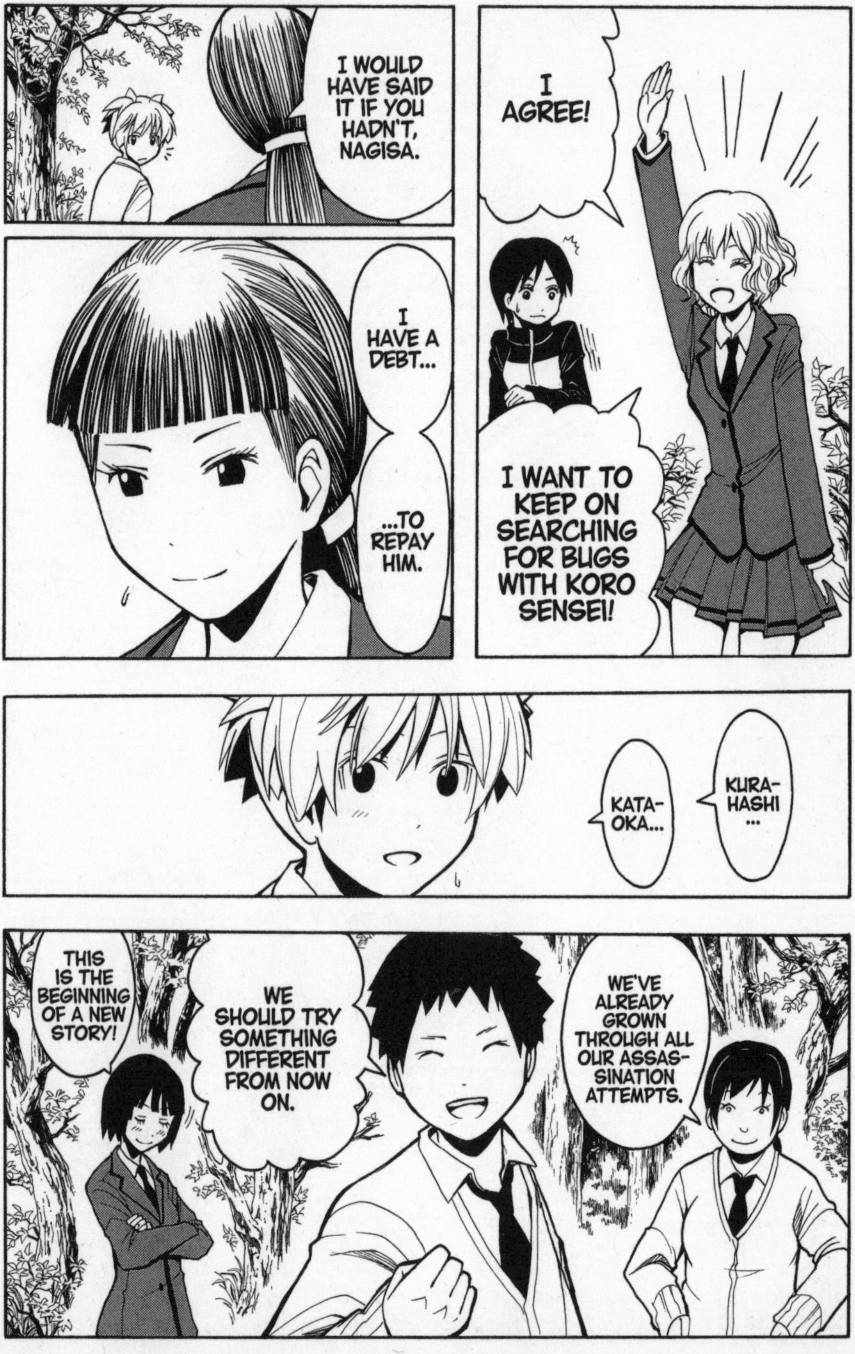
I AGREE!
I WANT TO KEEP ON SEARCHING FOR BUGS WITH KORO SENSEI!
I WOULD HAVE SAID IT IF YOU HADN'T, NAGISA.
I HAVE A DEBT...
...TO REPAY HIM.
KURA-HASHI...
KATA-OKA...
WE'VE ALREADY GROWN THROUGH ALL OUR ASSAS-SINATION ATTEMPTS.
WE SHOULD TRY SOMETHING DIFFERENT FROM NOW ON.
THIS IS THE BEGINNING OF A NEW STORY!

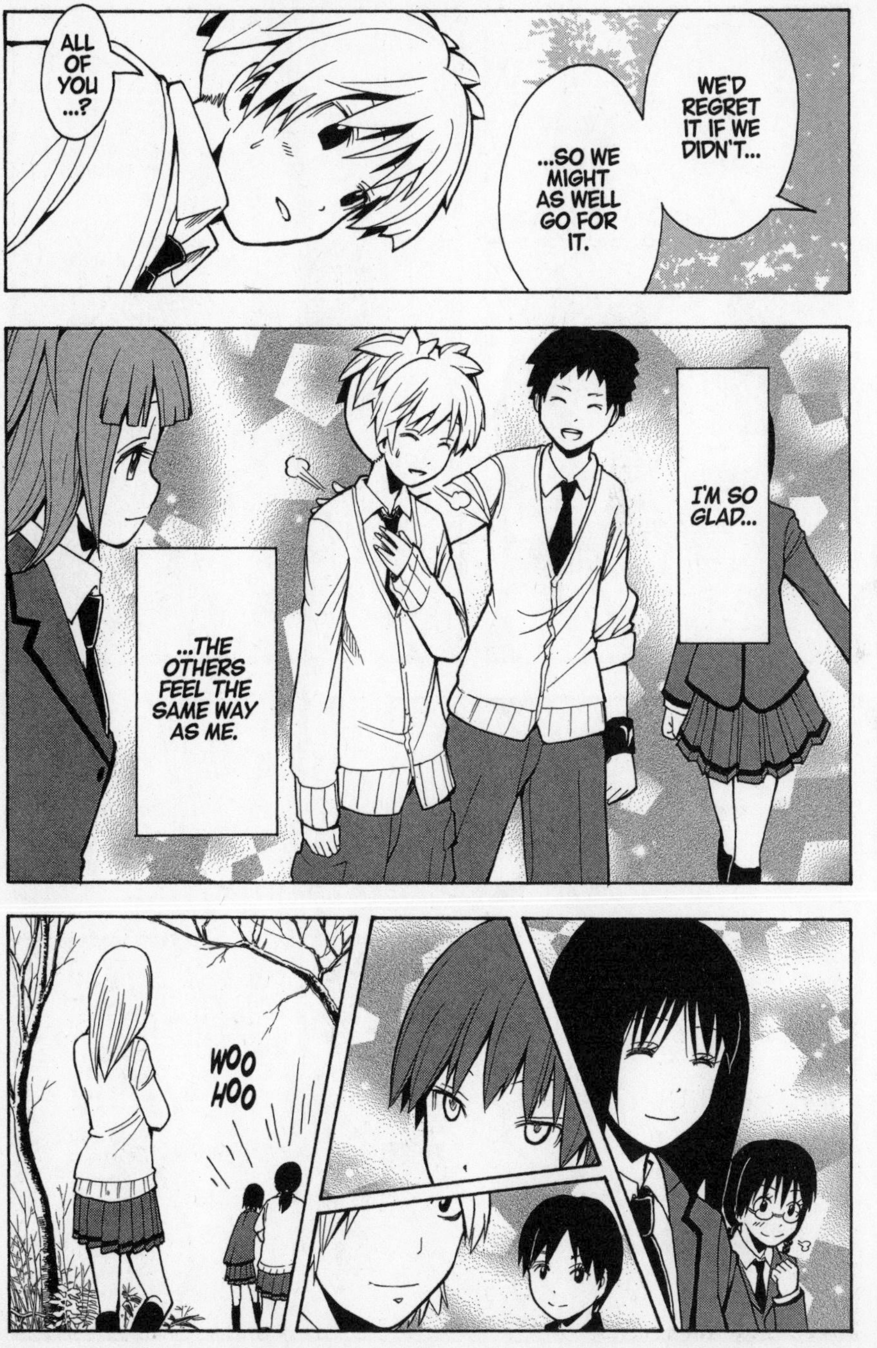
WE'D REGRET IT IF WE DIDN'T...
...SO WE MIGHT AS WELL GO FOR IT.
ALL OF YOU ...?
I'M SO GLAD...
...THE OTHERS FEEL THE SAME WAY AS ME.
WOO HOO

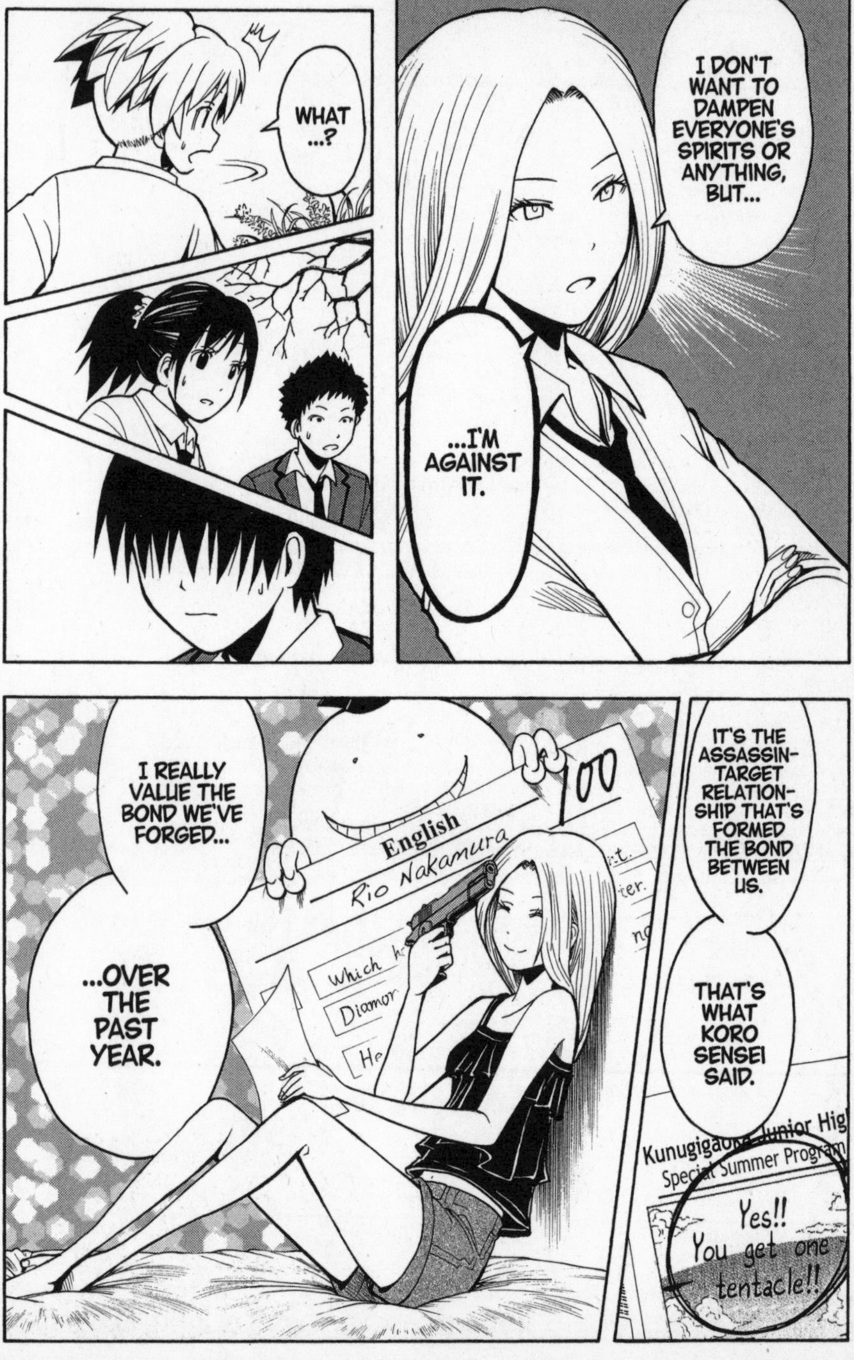
I DON'T WANT TO DAMPEN EVERYONE'S SPIRITS OR ANYTHING, BUT...
...I'M AGAINST IT.
WHAT ...?
IT'S THE ASSASSIN-TARGET RELATIONSHIP THAT'S FORMED THE BOND BETWEEN US.
THAT'S WHAT KORO SENSEI SAID.
Kunugigaoka Junior Hig
Special Summer Program
Yes!! You get one tentacle!!
I REALLY VALUE THE BOND WE'VE FORGED...
...OVER THE PAST YEAR.
100
English
Rio Nakamura

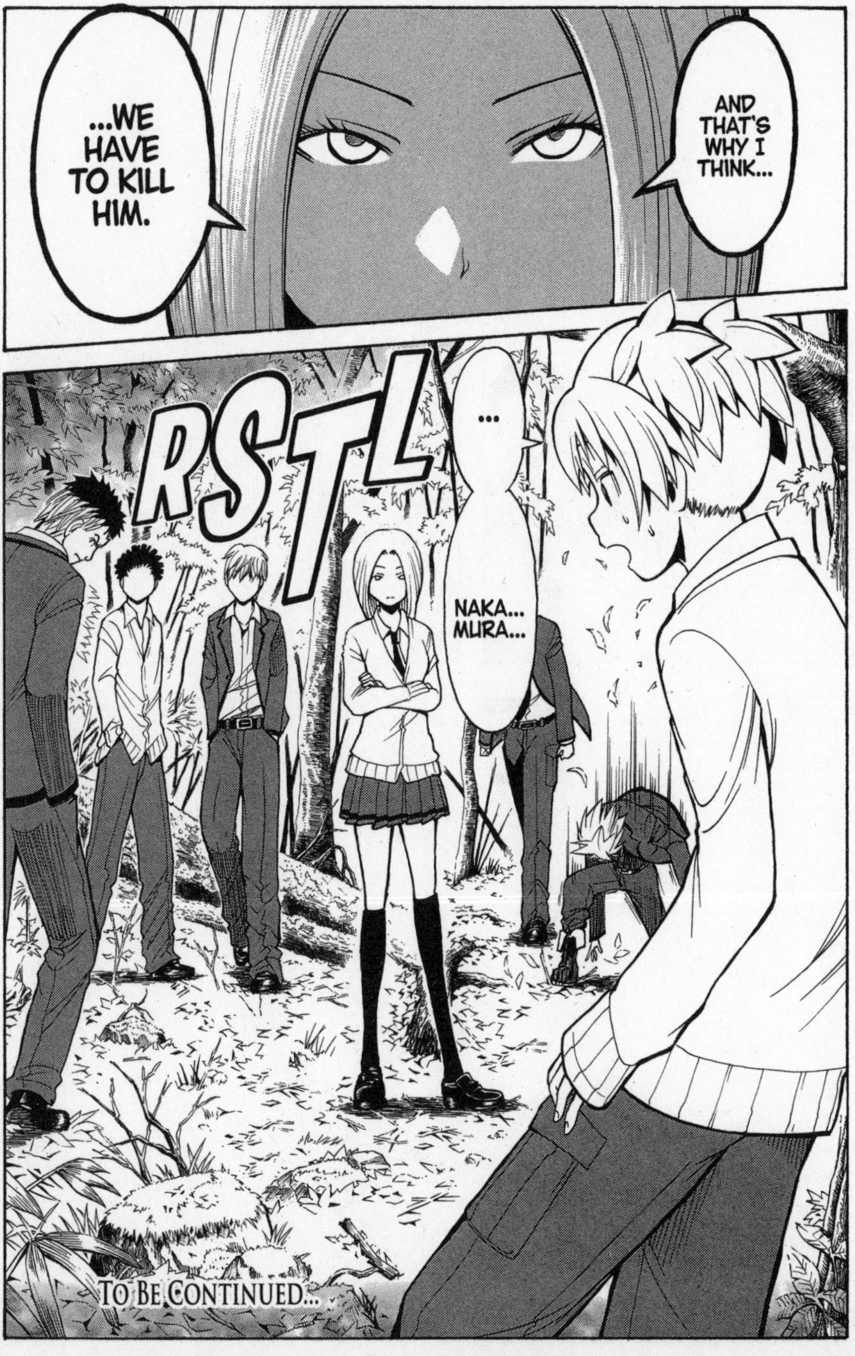
AND THAT'S WHY I THINK...
...WE HAVE TO KILL HIM.
...
NAKA... MURA...
RSTL
TO BE CONTINUED...

Eat
and
eat
and
eat.

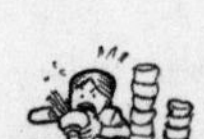

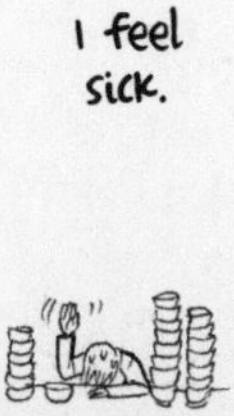
I feel sick.

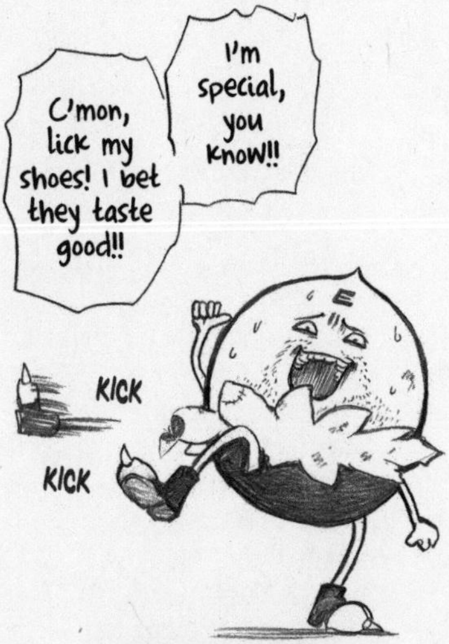
I'm special, you know!!
C'mon, lick my shoes! I bet they taste good!!
KICK
KICK

Kunugigaoka School Mascot
Kunudon

The story made a very sharp turn in the previous volume. It certainly was a long journey to get here...!

It feels like I made a long pass at the beginning of the series and I finally caught the ball. So I'm full of relief and intense emotions every time I complete one of these critical scenes.

This is the part where the story really takes off. I still have a lot of ups and downs planned though.

I hope you enjoy the story up through the very end!

—Yusei Matsui

Yusei Matsui was born on the last day of January in Saitama Prefecture, Japan. He has been drawing manga since elementary school. Some of his favorite manga series are *Bobobo-bo Bo-bobo*, *JoJo's Bizarre Adventure* and *Ultimate Muscle*. Matsui learned his trade working as an assistant to manga artist Yoshio Sawai, creator of *Bobobo-bo Bo-bobo*. In 2005, Matsui debuted his original manga *Neuro: Supernatural Detective* in *Weekly Shonen Jump*. In 2007, *Neuro* was adapted into an anime. In 2012, *Assassination Classroom* began serialization in *Weekly Shonen Jump*.

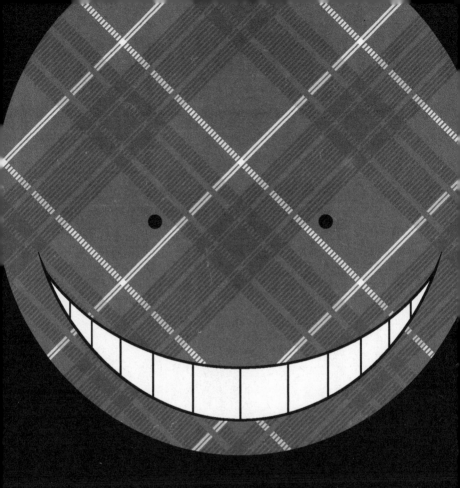

This proposal for a new pattern came from Koro Sensei himself. Paste a Koro Sensei face onto a classic tartan check pattern and you get "Koro Check." It could be a cute little design for a scarf or maybe on the skirt of a pop star. Look around and you'll see Koro Sensei everywhere!

ASSASSINATION CLASSROOM

YUSEI MATSUI

TIME FOR THE PAST

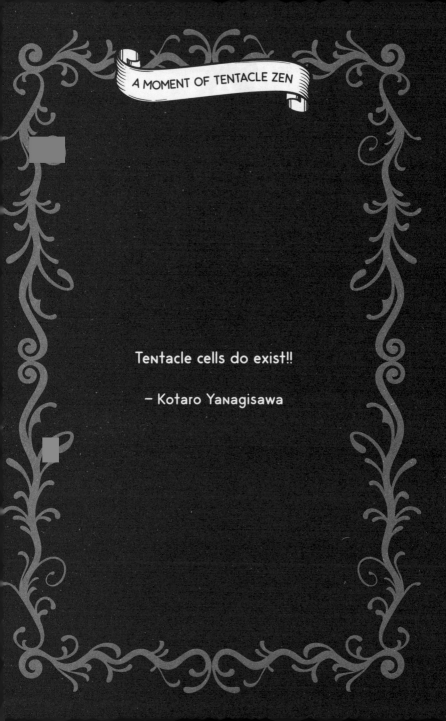

A MOMENT OF TENTACLE ZEN

Tentacle cells do exist!!

– Kotaro Yanagisawa

ASSASSINATION CLASSROOM

Volume 16
SHONEN JUMP ADVANCED Manga Edition

Story and Art by YUSEI MATSUI

Translation/Tetsuichiro Miyaki
English Adaptation/Bryant Turnage
Touch-up Art & Lettering/Stephen Dutro
Cover & Interior Design/Sam Elzway
Editor/Annette Roman

ANSATSU KYOSHITSU © 2012 by Yusei Matsui
All rights reserved.
First published in Japan in 2012 by SHUEISHA Inc., Tokyo.
English translation rights arranged by SHUEISHA Inc.

Printed in the U.S.A.

Published by VIZ Media, LLC
P.O. Box 77010
San Francisco, CA 94107

10 9 8 7 6 5 4 3 2 1
First printing, June 2017

www.viz.com

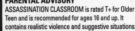

Syllabus for Assassination Classroom, Vol. 17

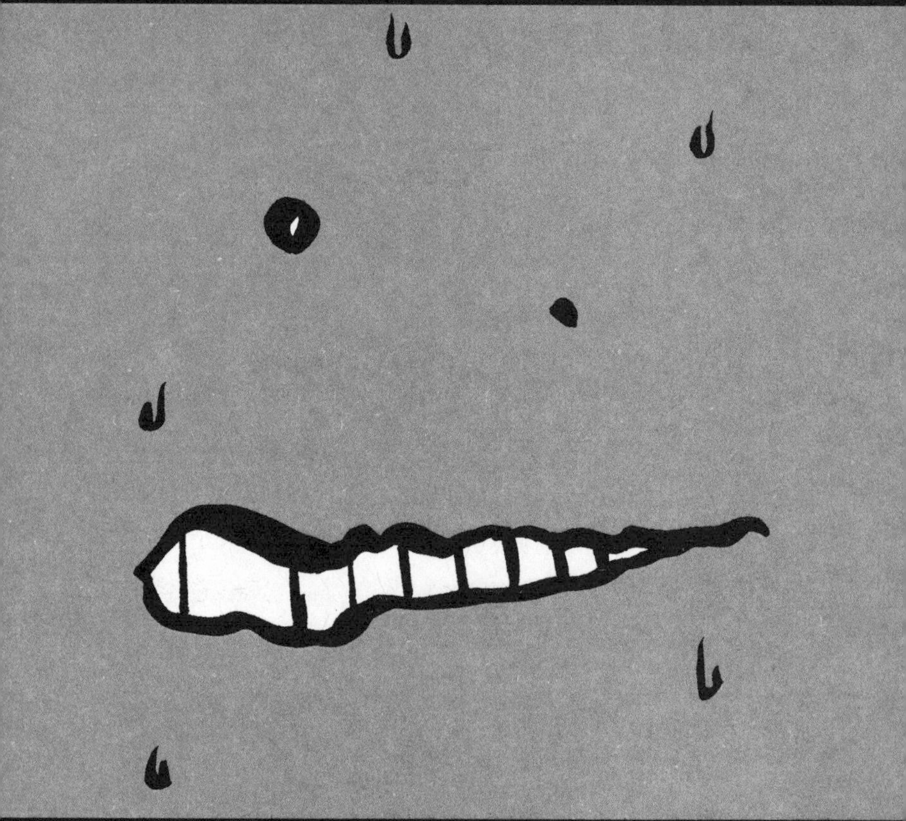

The class is divided: one half wants to carry on with the plan to assassinate Koro Sensei, while the other half wants to save him. So Koro Sensei splits them into two teams, led by Nagisa and Karma, and has them battle it out. The students of 3-E draw on everything they've learned so far to battle for or against Koro Sensei's life! Then, to uphold their now unified goal, they need to infiltrate the International Space Station...

Available August 2017!

STORY AND ART BY **Yoshiaki Sukeno**

The action-packed romantic comedy from the creator of *Good Luck Girl!*

Rokuro dreams of becoming *anything* but an exorcist!
Then mysterious Benio turns up. The pair are dubbed the
"Twin Star Exorcists" and learn they are fated to marry...

Can Rokuro escape both fates?

 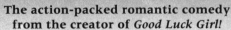

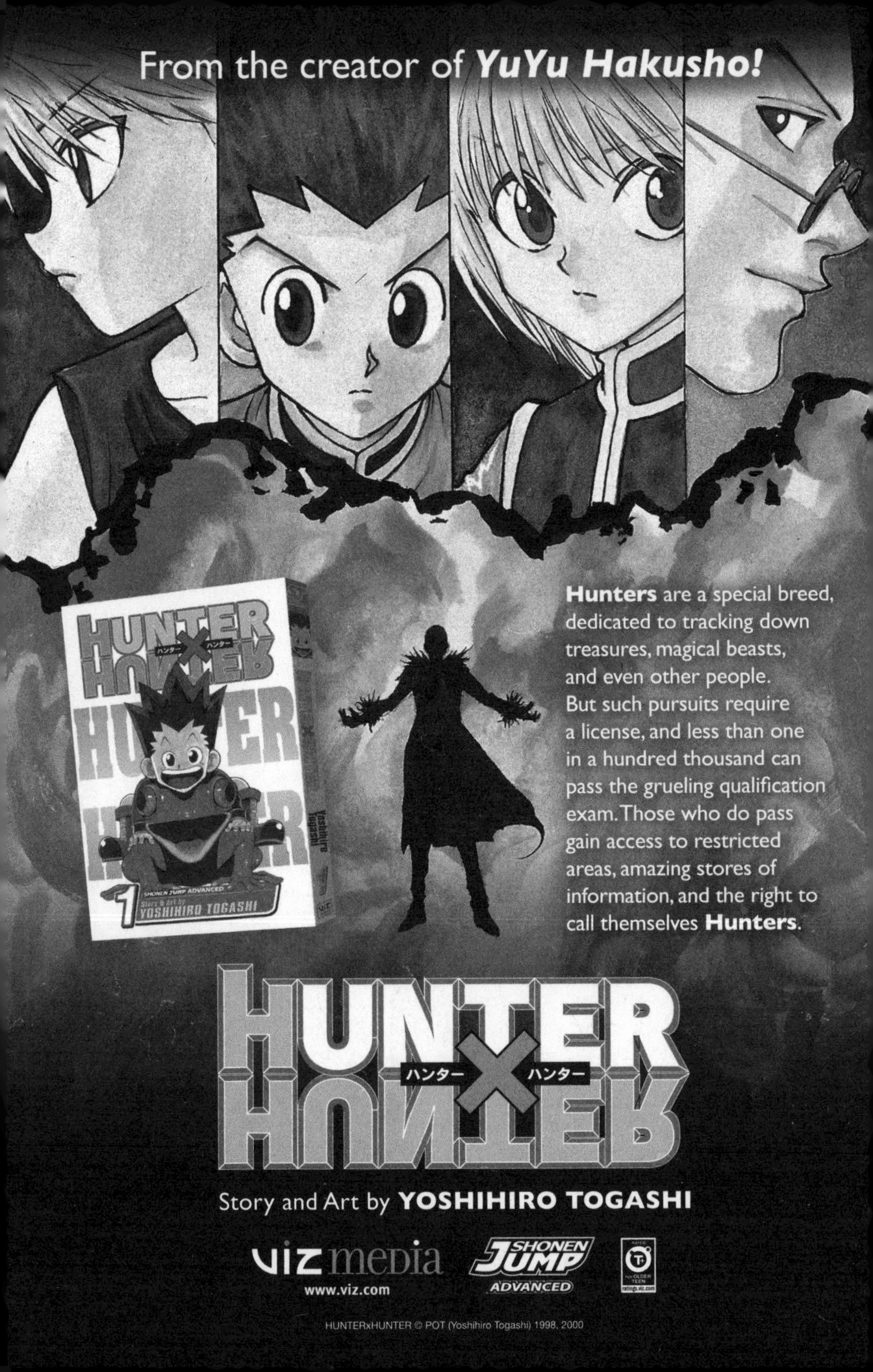
From the creator of YuYu Hakusho!
HUNTER × HUNTER
SHONEN JUMP ADVANCED
1
Story & Art by YOSHIHIRO TOGASHI
Hunters are a special breed, dedicated to tracking down treasures, magical beasts, and even other people. But such pursuits require a license, and less than one in a hundred thousand can pass the grueling qualification exam. Those who do pass gain access to restricted areas, amazing stores of information, and the right to call themselves Hunters.
HUNTER ハンター × ハンター HUNTER
Story and Art by YOSHIHIRO TOGASHI
viz media
www.viz.com
SHONEN JUMP ADVANCED
HUNTERxHUNTER © POT (Yoshihiro Togashi) 1998, 2000

You're Reading in the Wrong Direction!!

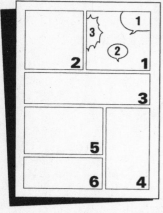

Whoops! Guess what? You're starting at the wrong end of the comic!

...It's true! In keeping with the original Japanese format, **Assassination Classroom** is meant to be read from right to left, starting in the upper-right corner.

Unlike English, which is read from left to right, Japanese is read from right to left, meaning that action, sound effects and word-balloon order are completely reversed... something which can make readers unfamiliar with Japanese feel pretty backwards themselves. For this reason, manga or Japanese comics published in the U.S. in English have sometimes been published "flopped"—that is, printed in exact reverse order, as though seen from the other side of a mirror.

By flopping pages, U.S. publishers can avoid confusing readers, but the compromise is not without its downside. For one thing, a character in a flopped manga series who once wore in the original Japanese version a T-shirt emblazoned with "M A Y" (as in "the merry month of") now wears one which reads "Y A M"! Additionally, many manga creators in Japan are themselves unhappy with the process, as some feel the mirror-imaging of their art skews their original intentions.

We are proud to bring you Yusei Matsui's **Assassination Classroom** in the original unflopped format.

For now, though, turn to the other side of the book and let the adventure begin...!

—Editor